The Best American
Sports Writing
2013

GUEST EDITORS OF
THE BEST AMERICAN SPORTS WRITING

1991 DAVID HALBERSTAM
1992 THOMAS MCGUANE
1993 FRANK DEFORD
1994 TOM BOSWELL
1995 DAN JENKINS
1996 JOHN FEINSTEIN
1997 GEORGE PLIMPTON
1998 BILL LITTLEFIELD
1999 RICHARD FORD
2000 DICK SCHAAP
2001 BUD COLLINS
2002 RICK REILLY
2003 BUZZ BISSINGER
2004 RICHARD BEN CRAMER
2005 MIKE LUPICA
2006 MICHAEL LEWIS
2007 DAVID MARANISS
2008 WILLIAM NACK
2009 LEIGH MONTVILLE
2010 PETER GAMMONS
2011 JANE LEAVY
2012 MICHAEL WILBON
2013 J. R. MOEHRINGER

The Best AMERICAN SPORTS WRITING™ 2013

Edited and with an Introduction
by J. R. Moehringer

Glenn Stout, *Series Editor*

A Mariner Original

HOUGHTON MIFFLIN HARCOURT
BOSTON • NEW YORK

ISSN 1056-8034
ISBN 978-0-547-88460-8

Printed in the United States of America
DOC 10 9 8 7 6 5 4 3 2

Contents

Foreword by Glenn Stout   xi

Introduction by J. R. Moehringer   xvii

KAREN RUSSELL. *The Blind Faith of the One-Eyed Matador*   1
from GQ

MICHAEL J. MOONEY. *The Most Amazing Bowling Story Ever*   19
from D Magazine

THOMAS LAKE. *The Legacy of Wes Leonard*   31
from Sports Illustrated

CHRIS BALLARD. *Mourning Glory*   48
from Sports Illustrated

BILL LITTLEFIELD. *The Gym at Third and Ross*   68
from Onlyagame.wbur.org

KENT BABB. *Arrowhead Anxiety*   76
from the Kansas City Star

JASON SCHWARTZ. *End Game*   87
from Boston Magazine

BILL GIFFORD. *It's Not About the Lab Rats*   101
from Outside

NICOLE PASULKA. *Eddie Is Gone*   118
from The Believer

JONATHAN SEGURA. *The Game of His Life* 129
  from GQ

ERIK MALINOWSKI. *The Making of "Homer at the Bat,"
  the Episode That Conquered Prime Time 20 Years Ago Tonight* 135
  from Deadspin.com

BRIDGET QUINN. *At Swim, Two Girls: A Memoir* 143
  from Narrativemagazine.com

ALLISON GLOCK. *At the Corner of Love and Basketball* 164
  from ESPN: The Magazine

RICK REILLY. *Special Team* 180
  from ESPN.com

BURKHARD BILGER. *The Strongest Man in the World* 183
  from The New Yorker

BARRY BEARAK. *Caballo Blanco's Last Run* 206
  from the New York Times

MARK SINGER. *Marathon Man* 224
  from The New Yorker

DAN KOEPPEL. *Redemption of the Running Man* 249
  from Runner's World

CINTHIA RITCHIE. *Running* 270
  from Sport Literate

CHARLES SIEBERT. *Goal to Go* 278
  from the New York Times Magazine

DAVID SIMON. *Fear the Bird* 301
  from Sports Illustrated

GARY SMITH. *Why Don't More Athletes Take a Stand?* 308
  from Sports Illustrated

PATRICK HRUBY. *Did Football Kill Austin Trenum?* 333
  from Washingtonian

WRIGHT THOMPSON. *Urban Meyer Will Be Home for Dinner* 351
  from ESPN: The Magazine

Contents ix

PAUL SOLOTAROFF. *The NFL's Secret Drug Problem* 370
  from Men's Journal

JEFF MACGREGOR. *Waiting for Goodell* 387
  from ESPN.com

Contributors' Notes 393

Notable Sports Writing of 2012 397

Foreword

I AM SITTING in a bar in Burlington, Vermont, drinking Guinness with a man whose work I have read but who I have never met before, hoping he'll say things I agree with about a subject I love, which may provide a way to write the foreword to a book a lot of people care deeply about. To distract myself from the barmaid who looks right through us and from the sun that shines too bright through the nearby window, I listen closely and file this away for future reference; another *Best American Sports Writing* foreword starts to write itself in my head.

This actually happened, and I was reminded as I sat in that bar how the best part of doing a book like this is not only the words, or the stories, but the short and intense friendships that sometimes develop while talking with another writer. Oh, I remember *BASW* stories, as I am certain the close reader has realized by now. (The above lede is an homage to the start of J. R. Moehringer's remarkable "Resurrecting the Champ" from *BASW 1998*.) Really, however, what I remember most are the people and the moments of recognition we discover in others when we realize our own ideas are not alone, but reside in stories shared, then recalled later and twisted and shaped to fit.

Sports is just a path for this, and notice that I just wrote "a" path, not "the" path. And it is certainly not "the only" path. For as the sportswriter above said to me, "Who really cares about sports? This is just a way for us to write about things we really care about." I thoroughly agree.

It struck me that this is the difference so often here in these pages. In this collection of writing about sports, there is hardly a single writer who, if pressed, would say he or she is "only" writing about sports. The kind of writing that was once "only" writing about sports filled thousands of newspapers every day. That doesn't happen much anymore, because now readers ask for more; outcomes and easy answers are often not enough, and that includes writing that is only about sports. That is, I think, one reason that readers have undeniably fled from the kind of writing that once first came to mind whenever anyone mentioned the word "sportswriting." But "sports writing," as we have always termed it in the title of this book? That is something else, and over the 23 years I have been doing the work of this series, if there is one thing I have noticed, it is that this book is more about people and what concerns us—love, death, desire, labor, and loss—than about the simple results of a game or competition. Wins and losses are the least important part of the equation—and the standings are often the worst measure of anything. It really is how you play the game . . . and how you think about it, and how you feel about that.

These are the subjects that draw writers to the keyboard, and readers to the page, and it has been that way since the beginning, whether the words have been crafted from ink or electronics, whether the page is made of papyrus or wood pulp or glass. The amazing thing is not how much the technology has changed over the years, but how much the relationship between the reader, the writer, and the word has *not* changed much at all. Increasingly there is a realization in this new era of reading on tablets and phones, with embedded links and GIFs and other technologies not yet imagined, that although the medium of communication has changed, little else has. For much of the last year I have served as an editor for a web page (SBNation.com/Longform), working closely with writers on the same kind of stories that appear in these pages, and the writer's work and responsibility is the same now as ever—something I have found gratifying beyond measure. Getting deep in the weeds of a story and breaking it down to sound? There is nothing better and nothing more important.

After a period of uncertainty and the misguided belief that the only writing that "worked" anymore was 140 characters or less, more recently readers have been returning to longer forms in droves, and the wise are beginning to realize that the web native was first a *word* native, and that the former is only a subset of the latter. Longer journalism—call it longform—has been enjoying something of a renaissance as the desire to read has proven unstoppable. While "the book" is still entering this new age of reading in fits and starts—for the adjustment period is a bit longer and the investment more costly—longform journalism and its readers have seamlessly embraced the future and filled that gap. Regardless of the format or medium, people are reading more than ever. In a world built around the notion of page views, this volume alone will probably collect eight or 10 million and occupy each reader for many, many hours—think about that for a moment. For all the worry over the future of writing and publishing, the need to read and to experience the things we really care about through the words of others is fundamental to our experience, as essential now as ever.

Each year I read every issue of hundreds of sports and general-interest magazines in search of writing that might merit inclusion in *The Best American Sports Writing*. I also write or email the editors of many hundreds of newspapers and magazines and request submissions, and I send email notices to hundreds of readers and writers whose addresses I have accumulated over the years. I search for writing all over the Internet and make regular stops at online sources like Sportsdesk.org, Gangrey.com, Byliner.com, Longreads.com, Longform.org, TheFeature.net, and other sites where notable sports writing is presented or discussed. What these sources turn up is still less than satisfactory, so each year I also encourage everyone—readers and writers, friends and family, enemies and editors—to send me stories they believe should appear in this volume. Writers, in particular, are encouraged to submit—do not shy away from sending me either your own work or the work of others for consideration.

All submissions to the upcoming edition must be made according to the following criteria. Each story

- must be column-length or longer.
- must have been published in 2013.
- must not be a reprint or book excerpt.
- must be published in the United States or Canada.
- must be received by February 1, 2014.

All submissions from either print or online publications *must be made in hard copy* and should include the name of the author, the date of publication, and the publication name and address. Photocopies, tear sheets, or clean copies are fine. Readable reductions to 8½-by-11 are preferred. Newspaper submissions should be a photocopy of the hard copy as originally published—not a printout. Since newsprint can suffer in transit, newspaper stories are best copied and made legible. If the story also appeared online, inclusion of the appropriate URL is often helpful. While there is no limit to the number of submissions either an individual or a publication may make, please use common sense. Because of the volume of material I receive, no submissions can be returned or acknowledged, and it is inappropriate for me to comment on or critique any submission. Publications that want to be absolutely certain their contributions are considered are advised to provide a complimentary subscription to the address listed below. Those that already do so should extend the subscription for another year.

All submissions must be made by U.S. mail—weather conditions in midwinter here at *BASW* headquarters mean I often cannot receive submissions sent by UPS or FedEx. Electronic submissions by any means—by email or Twitter—or URLs or PDFs or documents of any kind are not acceptable; please submit hard-copy printouts only. The February 1 deadline is real and work received after that date will not be considered.

Please submit either an original or a clear paper copy of each story, including publication name, author, and date the story appeared, to:

Glenn Stout
PO Box 549
Alburgh, VT 05440

Those with questions or comments may contact me at basweditor @yahoo.com. Copies of previous editions of this book can be ordered through most bookstores or online book dealers. An index of stories that have appeared in this series can be found at my website, glennstout.net, as can full instructions on how to submit a story. For updated information, readers and writers are also encouraged to join the *Best American Sports Writing* group on Facebook or to follow me on Twitter @GlennStout.

Thanks again go out to everyone at Houghton Mifflin Harcourt who supports this book, to guest editor J. R. Moehringer, and to Siobhan and Saorla, who remind me to keep everything neatly stacked. Each year I am gratified to learn how much this book means to the writers who have graced its pages. Serving you is an ongoing privilege.

GLENN STOUT
Alburgh, Vermont

Introduction

I WAS A FLEDGLING REPORTER in Denver, and the fledgling Colorado Rockies were just entering their first season. At the start of spring training the team looked over its talent-thin roster and sent out a desperate announcement, an unprecedented cry for help. Open tryouts. Come one, come all.

They came. From every corner of America, by every kind of vehicle (cars, buses, skateboards, motorcycles with sidecars), they descended just after dawn on a public park outside Tucson. Fat guys, skinny guys, old guys, drunk guys, guys limping like Fred Sanford—they were all so different, but they all had one thing in common. They'd always wanted to play in the majors, and they saw this as their last, best hope, their *American Idol* moment.

None had a shot. But a few at least had some justification (decent physique, expensive gear) for being there. I carved one out of this herd, a lanky young cowboy type. He told me that he'd driven all night from some small town in some sparsely populated state. I asked why. In a raw early-morning whisper he told me this was his dream, and he and his kid sister had been working hard for months to make it come true.

"You and your sister?"

Sis stepped forward. "Yes, sir. When he throws, I'm the batter. He hums it up there around 90 miles *per*."

She was a slip of a thing, thin as a paper straw. Late teens, tops. "He throws full speed?" I said. "With you in the batter's box?"

"Almost took my head clean off the other day," she said.

"Oh. The ball sailed on him?"

"No, sir. He threw it right at me."

"He threw at his own sister? In practice?"

She looked at me with teenage eye-rolling annoyance. Clearly I didn't get it. "I was *crowdin'* the *plate*," she said.

I looked at Big Bro. He was staring gravely at Sis. He turned and stared gravely at me. He may or may not have been gnawing a matchstick. I don't remember what he said then, but his wind-chiseled expression said: *This is damn serious business, Mister.*

Damn right it is. The more serious life gets, the more seriously we take sports.

Some take it too seriously, of course, which is the downside of sports writing. Fans these days seem more emotionally invested than ever before, to an unhealthy degree. They seem to derive more of their essential identity from the teams they follow, the jerseys they wear. Maybe it's the waning of other identity sources — family, society, religion, nature, jobs. But that still doesn't adequately explain the waves of outrage, the eruptions of anguish and toxic hubris triggered by the latest setback or defeat of the home team, or by the most recent disrespect in the media. I interviewed a popular athlete not long ago and wrote a profile in which I said some things that offended his fans. I also managed to rile up his detractors. Their online comments read like the lost haiku of Hannibal Lecter. Except that Dr. Lecter was educated. He knew how to spell *hate* and *murder.* As I shut off the computer — confused, alarmed — I asked myself, not for the first time, *Why do I do this?*

I don't know. Even on good days I have trouble answering that basic question. When it's posed by someone at a dinner or cocktail party, usually with dripping condescension ("So — why sports?"), I find myself groping for the right words, speaking in abstractions, mumbling about W. C. Heinz and Jimmy Cannon and other boyhood heroes who swung words as powerfully and gracefully as athletes swing bats and fists. Sometimes I explain that I'm not *technically* a sportswriter, I'm a writer who writes about sports now and then, which sounds irrelevant, and vaguely sketchy, like saying, "I'm not a doctor, but I play one on TV."

In fact it's a meaningful distinction. I tried to be a full-time sportswriter once, and didn't get the job. So I became a generalist, and as such I'd catch the occasional assignment to write a sports feature. For me, for my temperament, it turned out to be the best of all worlds. A baseball beat writer once warned me that cover-

ing baseball every single day will cure you of your love of baseball, quick. At the time I thought he was just being grumpy; now
I see the wisdom. Writing about sports occasionally, by chance, by
choice, has helped preserve my perspective, my wonder, my love.

I don't use that word casually. I *do* love sports, with a wide-eyed
openness I haven't quite outgrown. Maybe that's what I'll say the
next time someone asks. When everything falls into place, when
the interviews click, when the structure works, when the athlete or
coach says something real, the boorish fans don't matter, and the
job isn't a job, it's a labor of the purest love.

Also, at such in-the-zone moments, the piece isn't just about
sports. It's about loss.

Though every competition, from aikido to Xbox, is at surface
about winning, it's the losing that matters in the end, because
we're all going to lose more than we win. Our bedrock task as human beings is coping with loss, the knowledge of it, the memory
of it, the imminence of it, and sports have the power to show us,
starkly, bracingly, how. Sports are a theater of loss, of struggle and
despair, of real pain and real blood and primal disappointment,
which is why the best sports writing seems to reach back, back, like
a discus thrower, and touch the ancient myths. The Greeks were
perhaps the first people to fetishize both sports and stories. They
believed that sports and stories make us more human *and* more
divine. Sure, this isn't always true. Not every story can be mythic,
not every game is game seven. But on any given day, in the most
mundane newspaper feature, in the most meaningless midseason
game, there can be a moment of transcendence, a flash of genuine magic, which hints at all the possibilities. That's what keeps
you engaged, keeps you in your seat.

Okay, so maybe I'm one of those who take it all too seriously.

It's more fashionable these days to take nothing seriously. Irony
was declared dead some years ago, but like the stock market it
keeps roaring back. If some fans are too serious, some sportswriters are too cynical; they treat their subject with a strange amalgam
of avidity and mockery. Cover the games, analyze every atom and
particle of the games, but never miss an opportunity to assert their
unimportance, to rip all the money and the narcissism. While I
can't deny that some of the richest, most narcissistic people I've
ever met have been athletes (and their handlers), it's equally true
that some of the most beautiful moments I've ever witnessed have

been in arenas—and, my God, don't we need all the beauty we can get? The air is full of carbon dioxide, the water is full of chlorine and melted antidepressants, the body politic is in a deep, deep coma. So I can't give in to irony and cynicism, not all the way, and when asked to serve as editor of this marvelous anthology, I can't approach the task with anything but great seriousness.

Also, some dread. Though I'm pleased to have a chance to honor 25 excellent writers, I hate that I'll be leaving out many more. Like Kevin van Valkenburg. He wrote a gutsy, heartfelt essay about a semipro football player who died from a freak hit. And Ben Austen. He wrote a very funny ode to beleaguered fans of the Buffalo Bills. Both pieces were in the running until the last minute, and I want to assure both writers, and the reader, that they were omitted only because something had to be.

Before offering a few reasons and endorsements for several of the pieces I did pick, some housekeeping. It's become a tradition among editors of this anthology, right about here, to take stock of the precarious state of sports writing and issue some form of lamentation. I vowed I wasn't going to follow in that tradition . . . and then my mind kept going there. Ultimately I decided that it's not possible, and maybe not advisable, to introduce the year's best sports writing without at least acknowledging the adverse conditions under which it was produced, and to that end let me briefly mention the man in the sinkhole.

I think about the man in the sinkhole all the time. I'm haunted by him, actually, though he's already faded from the collective unconscious. (He was the Story Of The Year for days, until the next SOTY came along.) By most accounts he was home, fast asleep, when a 60-foot hole opened in the floor and swallowed him, along with his pillow and his blanket and his headboard and his bed and much of his bedroom. One minute the man was dreaming, snoring, and the next he was plunging down a chasm, luging toward the earth's core. His body will never be found. Too far down, rescuers said. Too risky. All they could do was knock over what remained of the house and fill in the hole and tell everyone to go on about their business.

Though he seems like a creation of Kafka, or Camus, or Vonnegut, or the Brothers Grimm, the man in the sinkhole strikes me as the paradigmatic figure of our time. Does it not feel many days as if the ground beneath us is opening, or is just about to? As if modern life is a patchwork of potential sinkholes on which we're forced to play hopscotch and Twister? And with sportswriters — writers of any kind, but our focus here is sports — does it not feel as if the Internet is the deepest, darkest sinkhole imaginable? It threatens to swallow everything we care about: newspapers, magazines, books, bookstores, theaters, publishing houses, films.

Optimists assure us that one day from this yawning sinkhole a wondrous beanstalk will go shooting into the sky, that if we can just grab a leaf or branch and hang on we'll all be dancing in the digitized, monetized clouds. But until then we must stand our ground, our terribly unstable ground. We must write and write, as best we can, knowing our readers and publications may be gone tomorrow. Hell, knowing *we* may be gone tomorrow.

And it's not just the Internet. More worrisome than technological changes in how we read is the continuing decline of reading in general, especially the reading of fiction, especially among males of the species. The last numbers I saw showed that 80 percent of fiction readers are now women. Of the many death knells tolling for this business, to my ears that's the loudest. You can't fully appreciate sports unless you have a sense of narrative, and of character, and of empathy, and you can't have a sense of narrative, or character, nor can you be fully empathetic, if you don't read fiction — just my opinion. If present trends continue, I don't see how sports writing, as I've always known it, and cherished it, can endure.

Here ends the lamentation, on this faintly upbeat note. All the uncertainty and gloom in the atmosphere added a dash of bravery, even gallantry, to every piece of sports writing I read, and gave an extra zing to the very best. I remember, while I was working with Andre Agassi on his memoir, the deadline was drawing near, the stress was running high, and I said something Andre liked, made a suggestion with which he wholly agreed. Suddenly he shouted: *I don't know whether to kiss you or knock you out!* I never understood exactly what he meant, but I think it had to do with that visceral reaction, that reflex of tenderness and vehemence we all experience when, just in time, the right words hit our inner target. At some point, while reading every piece in this book, that's what I felt. Bull's-eye.

For example, Jonathan Segura. As I read the first few lines of his piece it was late, I was dead tired, and then all at once I wasn't. I was out of my chair, pacing, laughing, clenching and unclenching my fists. In particular I want to single out Segura's lush and wanton profanity. I hope it shocks and mortifies every scold out there who's forever bitching about bad language. My philosophy: if you don't like bad language, don't use it. And if you can't rejoice in the life force pulsing through every lovely four-letter word in Segura's paean to his soccer-loving mate ("Whatever he did, he did the shit out of"), then you and I are probably not going to be able to hang out.

I'll admit, I dropped a few f-bombs while reading Wright Thompson's piece. Thompson is quietly becoming a one-man dynasty in the world of sports writing. He made last year's *BASW,* he's already reserved a spot in next year's, and he wrote several pieces that could have been selected for this year's. Faced with too many choices, I picked his epic portrait of Urban Meyer, a football coach driven, and nearly destroyed, by perfectionism. (Savor that incredible opening passage, in which the coach's daughter, and Thompson, bravely call out the coach.) Two other perennial All-Stars, Thomas Lake and Chris Ballard, weigh in with pieces that feel linked. Lake, employing just the right pathos-to-restraint ratio, tells the story of a high school basketball player who died shortly after making a game-winning shot. Ballard, with a novelist's sense of scene and pace, describes a high school baseball team that went on an impossible run after one of its players died in a car wreck. I will not soon forget the team bus wending its way home from the tournament, stopping at the cemetery, where the boys, hats off, observe a moment of silence.

I chose a few pieces more for their solid reporting, like Kent Babb's cold-blooded exposé of the gulag that was the 2012 Kansas City Chiefs. More than one NFL team is ruled by control freaks obsessed with secrecy, drunk with power, but my mouth hung open as I read about general manager Scott Pioli's brief reign of terror on Arrowhead Drive. The head coach running around thinking his office is bugged? The team president using a discarded candy wrapper as a "coaching moment"? Come on, guys. Get a grip.

In a year filled with downers, several pieces provided some badly needed levity, like Erik Malinowski's kooky analysis of one seminal sitcom episode, which cast real baseball players as themselves and thereby changed the way we think about both national pastimes—baseball and TV. Bill Littlefield might have scored the year's funniest line in his piece about a wayside boxing gym in Pittsburgh. (What the ring card girl asks the gym owner—I guffawed aloud.) And Jeff MacGregor slayed me with his *Godot*-esque goof on Roger Goodell. If some readers don't get it, wonderful. Here's hoping they'll be motivated to read some Beckett.

Pound for pound, the funniest piece to cross my desk might have been David Simon's tribute to last summer's valiant Orioles. The humor is wry, as one would expect from the creator of *The Wire*, and yet there's one joyfully silly exchange between Simon and his cousin, a Yankees fan, which ends with Simon texting: "Bite me, O pinstriped whore." Maybe it's the Mets fan in me, but I let out a soft, involuntary *yeeeah.*

Whenever possible, you want a love story in the mix, and I'm indebted to the incomparable Allison Glock for producing a fine one. Her anatomy of the doomed relationship between two basketball stars, Rosalind Ross and Malika Willoughby, was still on my mind days after I read it. Glock tells a difficult tale with compassion, insight, and her typical unblinking eye for detail. (What the father learns from the mortician—chilling.) A far less complicated love story is Rick Reilly's piece out of Queen Creek, Arizona. Bullies at the local high school were tormenting Chy Johnson, a mentally handicapped girl, until the football team stepped in. Reilly's reporting gives some richly deserved dap to Carson Jones, the quarterback, who first invited Chy to sit at his roundtable during lunch. If you've read anything in recent months that so sweetly and compactly restored your faith in people, please forward it to me.

Gary Smith's delicious piece about a hunger-striking football player hasn't yet gotten all the huzzahs it deserves, maybe because it's fearlessly, brazenly political, a no-no in sportswriting, as in sports, which is sort of Smith's point. A Hall of Famer several times over, Smith shows that he's not about to stop taking chances. This piece is a high-wire act, filled with risks that would trip up lesser writers, and though I held my breath in several places, Smith makes it safely to the other side.

Finally, two pieces stand apart for me. The first is Barry Bearak's. In the copies and printouts sent to me by *BASW*'s legendary curator, Glenn Stout, the name of every writer was redacted. But

I was three pages into the story of Micah True, the mythic runner who vanished in the New Mexico wilderness, when I looked up and thought: Bearak? His style is that Zorro-like, his voice that etched into my memory.

I had the good fortune of meeting Bearak once. We were both working at the *Los Angeles Times,* where he was a god, revered for his bravery and linguistic virtuosity. (Pull up his 1992 series on New York City crack addicts. Prepare to be stunned.) The boss invited Bearak to give a lunchtime talk to younger reporters, and I remember us all eagerly squeezing into the conference room, like batboys getting to meet Babe Ruth. I still find myself drawing on things Bearak said that day.

Many writers could have done something special with the story of True. Only Bearak could have written such a clean, tight yarn, while also finding room for such sparkling imagery. Marijuana "fluted" through True's head; cold air "scythed" through the forest. I read the piece while drinking coffee, sitting in the sun, but I was high, I was chilled—I was True.

Lastly, Karen Russell. I want to say it as plainly as I can: her piece about the one-eyed matador ranks with the finest sports writing I've ever read. Some will be surprised to discover that Russell isn't a sportswriter, nor even an occasional writer of sports. She's a novelist, a short story writer, a rising literary superstar. What I find hard to figure isn't *how* Russell writes so masterfully about sports, but *when.* This piece appeared just months before her acclaimed short story collection dropped, just months after her novel was a finalist for the Pulitzer. Does the woman sleep?

The one-eyed matador is Juan Jose Padilla, whose eye was pronged out by an 1,100-pound bull. Russell makes you feel the hideous wound, makes you want to reach up and touch your own eye to be sure it's still there, then follows Padilla through his healing and improbable comeback. Don't read the piece once. Read it twice, read it three times, and slow down each time you come to the scene where Padilla stands before a young cow, ready to *torear* an animal for the first time since his injury. The cow moves forward, Padilla steps aside, and there it is, one man's quiet triumph over—everything. But especially loss. The moment takes place at the end of December, Russell tells us, because Padilla is determined that the year will not end without him dressing again as a bullfighter. His need for the cape, she says, is like "the longing of a ghost recalling its body."

Oh, Russell. When I read that line I didn't know whether to kiss you or knock you out, so I just shook my head and gently placed your piece on top of the yes pile. You were born to be atop the yes pile.

But that's the problem. With so much talent, you'll always be in great demand, pulled in many directions at once. Please, continue to make time now and then for sports. This business needs writers like you, voices like yours, if we're going to avoid the next sinkhole. And each of us, individually, when we fall in? Masterpieces like the tale of the one-eyed matador can help us cope, and might even inspire us to climb our way out.

J. R. MOEHRINGER

The Best American
Sports Writing
2013

KAREN RUSSELL

The Blind Faith of the
One-Eyed Matador

FROM GQ

I. Zaragoza, Spain—October 7, 2011

WHAT DOES THE bull see as it charges the matador? What does
the bull feel? This is an ancient mystery, but it seems like a safe
bet that to *this* bull, Marques—ashy black, five years old, 1,100
pounds—the bullfighter is just a moving target, a shadow to catch
and penetrate and rip apart. Not a man with a history, not Juan
Jose Padilla, the Cyclone of Jerez, 38 years old, father of two, one
of Spain's top matadors, taking on his last bull of the afternoon
here at the Feria del Pilar, a hugely anticipated date on the bullfighting calendar.

When Marques comes galloping across the sand at Padilla, the
bullfighter also begins to run—not away from the animal but toward its horns. Padilla is luminously scaled in fuchsia and gold,
his "suit of lights." He lifts his arms high above his head, like a
viper preparing to strike. For fangs, he has two wooden sticks with
harpoonlike barbs, two banderillas, old technologies for turning a
bull's confusion into rage. Padilla and Marques are alone in the
sandy pit, but a carousel of faces swirls around them. A thousand
eyes beat down on Padilla, causing sweat to bead on his neck. Just
before Marques can gore him, he jumps up and jabs the sticks into
the bull's furry shoulder. He brings down both sticks at once, an
outrageous risk. Then he spins around so that he is *facing* Marques,
running backward on the sand, toe to heel.

A glancing blow from Marques unsteadies Padilla; his feet get
tangled. At the apex of his fall, he still has time to right himself,

escape the bull. His chin tilts up: there is the wheeling sky, all blue. His last-ever binocular view. This milestone whistles past him, the whole sky flooding through the bracket of the bull's horns, and now he's lost it. The sun flickers on and off. *My balance—*

Padilla has the bad luck, the terrible luck, of landing on his side. And now his luck gets worse.

Marques scoops his head toward Padilla's face on the sandy floor, a move that resembles canine tenderness, as if he's leaning down to lick him, but instead the bull drives his sharp left horn through the bullfighter's jaw. When Marques tusks up, the horn crunches through Padilla's skin and bone, exiting through his left eye socket. Cameras clock the instant that a glistening orb pops loose onto the matador's cheek. A frightening silence descends on the crowd. Nobody knows the depth of the wound.

Marques gallops on, and Padilla gets towed for a few feet, pulled by his cheek. He loses a shoe. Skin stretches away from his jawbone with the fragile elasticity of taffy.

Then Padilla's prone body is left in the bull's dust. He springs up like a jack-in-the-box and hops around. His face is completely red. As the blood gushes down his cheek, he holds his dislodged eye in place with his pinkie. He thinks he must be dying. *I can't breathe. I can't see.*

Marques, meanwhile, has trotted a little ways down the sand. He stands there panting softly. His four legs are perfectly still. What unfolds is a scene that Beckett and Hemingway and Stephen King might have collaborated to produce, because this is real horror, the blackest gallows humor: the contrast between the bullfighter crying out *"Oh, my eye! I can't see! I can't see!"* and the cud-chewing obliviousness of the animal.

In the bullring, other bullfighters spill onto the sand and rush to Padilla's aid. They lift him, hustle him toward the infirmary. Meanwhile, the bullfight must go on. Miguel Abellan, another matador on the bill, steps in for Padilla. He kills Marques in a trancelike state that he later swears he can't remember. Tears run down his cheeks. He's survived 27 gorings himself, but what he sees in Zaragoza makes him consider quitting the profession.

Cornadas—gorings—are so common that every plaza is legally required to have a surgeon on site. Bullfighters now routinely survive injuries that would have killed their fathers and grandfathers.

Good luck, now, excellent luck: Carlos Val-Carreres is the Zaragoza surgeon, one of the best in Spain.

"I'm asphyxiating," Padilla gasps as they bring him in. Many hands guide him into the shadowy infirmary. Someone scissors off his clothing. Someone inserts a breathing tube into his windpipe. Val-Carreres understands instantly that this is a potentially fatal *cornada*, one of the worst he's seen in 30 years, and one they are ill equipped to handle in the infirmary. Padilla, now tracheally intubated, is loaded into an ambulance.

Pronóstico muy grave, Val-Carreres tells reporters.

At 7:52 P.M., half an hour after the goring, Padilla arrives at the emergency room. He presents with multiple fractures to the left side of his face, a detached ear, a protruding eyeball, and hemorrhage at the base of his skull. A five-hour operation saves his life. The surgeons rebuild his cheekbone and eyelid and nose, with mesh and titanium plates. But they are unable to repair his split facial nerve, which has been divided by the bull's horn, because they cannot locate the base of the nerve. Padilla wakes up from the anesthesia to discover that he can no longer move the left side of his face. It is paralyzed.

When he comes to, his first words to his manager, Diego Robles, are: "Don't cancel any of my contracts in South America." Padilla has November bullfights in Venezuela, Peru, and Ecuador.

His first words to his youngest brother, Jaime, who is also a bullfighter, a *banderillero,* and scheduled to perform in two days' time: "Don't cancel your fight. You have to do it for us. You can't let this get the best of you."

His first words to his wife, Lidia: "Where is my eye?"

The eye is back in its proper place, but sightless—the optic nerve has been elongated and lesioned by the horn. He's also deaf in his left ear, and the entire left side of his face is purple and bloated, like something viewed underwater. His eyelid is sealed shut. His mouth curls inward like a wilted leaf.

"I was there when he saw himself for the first time after the accident," recalls Diego. "He saw the reality in front of him. He said, *'Es que no soy yo—'*"

No. That's not me. Here is a vertigo a thousand times more destabilizing than his slip in the plaza: he does not recognize himself.

There is the physical pain, which the doctors reduce with morphine, and then there is the terror. They're telling him he might never again wear his "suit of lights." Never stand before another bull. If he can't return to a plaza, he'll be exiled from his life. Evicted from his own skin.

In his hospital room, as soon as he can move again, he begins to rehearse bullfighting moves with the sheets. And on October 19, less than two weeks after the accident, he gives a press conference in a wheelchair with his face uncovered.

"I have no rancor toward this bull or toward my profession," he slurs into the mike. He makes the following pledge: "I will return to dress as a *torero*."

II. The Wild Feast and the Matador's Famine

A millennium and a half after Moorish cavaliers rode into Spain and began to cultivate the bullfighting tradition, a few hundred years after trendy nobles staged bullfights to celebrate weddings and Catholic festivals, nearly a century since the golden age of the matador, when Juan Belmonte and Joselito "the Little Rooster" pioneered the mad modern style of "artistic" caping (working within inches of the enraged animal), bullfighting remains the national fiesta or the *fiesta brava*—"the wild feast."

In a standard *corrida de toros,* the common term for the spectacle, there are three matadors on the bill and six matches total. The fame and fees of 21st-century matadors range wildly, depending on official ranking and also "cachet"—a torero's reputation. Group A matadors such as Padilla must perform in at least 43 corridas per season. These guys are the *seguras,* and the industry can support only a dozen or so of them. To maintain their status, Group As need to be frequent fliers and serial killers, traveling fiendishly from February to October, sometimes performing in plazas on opposite coasts in the same week. For Group B matadors, the minimum is 13 corridas. Group C? No minimums. It's the ladder rung where rookies get classed with semiretired stars. Padilla spent years in Group C before finally breaking through.

Today it's harder than it's ever been to earn a living in the bullring. Unemployment in Spain is nearing 25 percent, and the country's flailing economy is taking its toll on the *mundo taurino.* ("We will *torear la crisis,*" said Prime Minister Mariano Rajoy in a press conference, invoking the figure of the bullfighter to salve

Eurozone panic.) Nearly a hundred corridas have been cut from the season, and still plazas are often only half full.

Is bullfighting an art, a sport, torture? Dying out, or more popular than ever? You can find evidence in every direction. Spanish newspapers cover bullfighting in the culture pages, alongside theater reviews. In 2010, Catalonia outlawed *corridas de toros*; in Madrid they are legally protected as a "cultural good" and publicly subsidized, like the National Ballet. Telemadrid's latest reality show is *Quiero Ser Torero*— "I Want to Be a Bullfighter."

"We Spaniards don't understand ourselves, the majority of Spaniards, we don't understand our country without our fiesta," says Juan Jose Padilla. "The fiesta unites the nation."

Bullshit, say Spain's anti-*taurinos*. "The majority of Spaniards are against the bullfight," says Silvia Barquero, spokeswoman for Spain's animal-rights party, PACMA, who believes the Catalonian ban augurs a new and enlightened era in Spain. "We should not cause suffering to an animal that has the same right to life as our species." (You certainly don't have to be a member of PACMA or PETA to find a corrida alienating, cruel, and atavistic.)

Then there is the controversy over televised corridas. In 2006, when the socialist party was in charge, Spain's national TV network, TVE, stopped showing them. Now, with Rajoy and his conservative Popular Party back in power, the bulls have returned to the public airwaves. On August 24, TVE said that it would again air live bullfights after the six-year hiatus. Previously the network had pulled them from its schedule to protect minors from violence, but superfans could still get the afternoon corridas on premium cable channels. This is how Pepe and Ana Padilla were able to watch their son's goring in the instant it occurred.

Not only could they watch it—thanks to a freakish coincidence, you can now watch them watching it: on October 7, a Canal Sur production crew happened to be taping in the home of Ana and Pepe, filming them seated in front of their son's televised image for a newsmagazine segment titled "The Courage of a Bullfighter." When Marques gored Juan Jose, the glass eye of the camera was trained on Ana Padilla's face.

Should I stop taping? asked the cameraman.

"Siga! Siga!" said Pepe. Keep rolling. If these were Juan's *pasos ultimos,* his final moments, he wanted a record of them.

The cameraman obliged, and the result is an uncanny hall of

mirrors. The nested footage of Ana and Pepe reacting in real time
to the goring makes the scene exponentially more horrifying. Suddenly the tiny bullfighter is no remote cartoon of pain but a fully
dimensioned human: their son. After Marques spears Padilla, his
mother's face erupts in sobs. Pepe doesn't think he will ever recover from his son's accident.

"I thought that I had killed him," he says in a raw voice. "I
thought that I had murdered my son. I was the one who encouraged him in this profession . . ."

Pepe Padilla has raised three toreros. (Oscar, the middle son,
retired as a banderillero the day after Juan Jose's goring and now
runs a chain of pet-supply stores.) Pepe coached his sons after
school, caping cows with them in the green hills around Jerez. He
once dreamed of being a matador himself. As a teenager, he was a
novillero, a matador in training. "But I was a coward," he says, smiling. "Not like my Juan."

Today, Pepe is a charmer in his sixties with uncorrected teeth,
gold jewelry wreathed by silver chest hair, and one droopy eyelid.
For decades he worked as a baker in Jerez, sleeping three or four
hours, heading back out before dawn to support his seven children. (Seven children! Franco years, he grins, shaking his head.
Everything scarce and hard-won, including condoms.) Juan Jose
appeared on May 23, 1973; Pepe says he was born to *torear.* When
he was eight, he was written up in a bullfighting journal for having
"the courage of a 30-year-old matador." When he was 12, he killed
his first bull. At 21, he became the first and only man in his family
to achieve the rank of professional matador.

"All of my sons were good," Pepe says. "But Juan had something
special." He stares into space for a long time, as if seeking the precise descriptor for this ineffable quality.

"Huevos!" He grins. "Cojones!"

Later, as Juan Jose made his bones as a young matador, he
earned a reputation for fighting the world's most difficult and aggressive bulls: Victorinos, Pablo Romeros, and especially Miuras,
a strain of fighting bull notorious for maiming and killing many
toreros. Padilla's style was defined by his incredible—and lunatic—valor. He did moves nobody else would dare. He was one of
the few matadors to put in his own banderillas, to cape bulls on his
knees. One consequence of this bravura is that Padilla might well
be the record holder when it comes to bullring injuries: before the

Zaragoza goring, he had already been seriously wounded by the *toros* 38 times. He nearly died in Pamplona in 2001, when a Miura bull gored him in the neck.

Overnight, Padilla's story flies around the globe: he's a hero in Spain, elsewhere a grotesque footnote to the "real" daily news. A Twitter sensation: #Fuerzapadilla. His shattered face becomes the public face of bullfighting.

Once the media storm dies down and his condition is stabilized, Juan travels home to the seaside pueblo of Sanlucar, where he lives with Lidia and their two children, Paloma, eight, and Martin, six. At home, he is left to relearn kindergarten skills in private, miles from any bullring. How to chew and swallow. How to ride his bicycle and grocery shop, cycloptically. The ringing in his left ear never stops. It hurts to talk. Unable to train for a corrida, some days he can't stop crying. Prior to the accident, he was a joyful, open, easygoing guy. Which is not to say that he was necessarily an even-keeler. He has always had a strong character, just like the noble bulls he fights, Pepe explains, "because of his *raza*," his fiery lineage. Juan Jose can be tempestuous, irritable, "and then there's nothing to be done, you have to leave him alone!"

But the mood that sucks him under in October is something new. Like the eye he can't open, it's black and unchanging.

"I fell into a great depression," says Padilla.

"Estaba fatal," says Diego, his manager. *"Estaba hundido hundido hundido."*

He was sunk, sunk, sunk.

Lidia is not used to seeing her husband ashamed, in pain. "We were so afraid for him—the children too, it affected them . . ."

Lidia Padilla is a sedately beautiful woman, dark-haired, with a doll's porcelain face, and she's been Juan Jose's girl since *antes antes,* cradle-robbed when she was 14 and he was a high school senior, the handsome bread-delivery boy. Their first date was during Semana Santa, Easter week. Juan Jose believed it was his destiny to have a wife like Lidia, a woman both "passionate" and devoutly Catholic. "I found the balance I needed in her," he says.

Lidia has been with Juan his whole career, but she has never once watched her husband perform. Not in a plaza and not on TV, and during the 11-hour drive to Zaragoza, after the accident, she imagined begging him to retire. But when she saw him in the hospital, the speech she'd prepared dissolved. "I couldn't take that dream from him," she says. "To ask him not to be a torero. It would be like killing him while he was still alive."

Padilla realizes he needs to get back into the bullring as soon as humanly possible. So many people had suffered as a result of his accident, he says, that he wanted to give them "tranquillity, normalcy." He has a habit of describing his "return to normalcy" as something he has to do for other people, as if the Zaragoza fall upset some cosmic equilibrium, knocked the whole world (and not just his world) off its axis.

But what's the rush to resume a career that nearly killed him? Why the sprint back to such a chronically risky kind of normal?

"I couldn't conceive of my life without *el toreo*," he says. "If I couldn't have returned to my profession, it's clear that I would have been really affected. I could have dedicated myself to other things, business. I had some good offers, but none of that was going to fill me . . . Oh, it was affecting my head, I felt such a heaviness, at the beginning I was anguished, it was a tremendous anguish."

In the bullfighting world, there is this saying, *Torear la suerte:* an aphorism that contains an entire philosophy. Brutishly translated: "Bullfight your fate." Whatever bull God drums up for you, you face off against, you dance with, you dominate, and it's up to you to put on a splendid show, to use every bull as an opportunity to demonstrate all of your *arte.* Your valor and skill. *Torear la suerte,* in other words, combines religious fatalism with Nietzschean will.

Padilla's years as a torero, then, have prepared him to view his recovery as a special kind of corrida—a chance to use his faith and courage outside the bullring.

In late October, Padilla travels north to Oviedo to consult with an internationally renowned ophthalmic surgeon, who warns him that his comeback plan seems "unrealistic"—his optic nerve is still not responding to light. The next specialist to evaluate Padilla is Alberto Garcia-Perla, a maxillofacial surgeon. As Padilla recalls their first meeting, his voice grows rough with gratitude: "There was never a moment when Dr. Garcia-Perla responded negatively to my dream of returning to *torear.* He's always said that I would be the one to decide."

Garcia-Perla, the chief surgeon at Seville's Virgen del Rocio

Hospital, will direct a team of 18 doctors, including plastic surgeons, ear-nose-and-throat surgeons, and an anesthesiologist, in an attempt to repair Padilla's facial nerve. The plan is to reconnect the two ends of the nerve using an implant from the sural nerve in Padilla's leg. If the operation succeeds, Juan might regain the ability to blink and chew, lift both brows in surprise. Garcia-Perla is no stranger to this kind of high-stakes reconstructive surgery: his team successfully performed the second face-transplant surgery in Spain, the 11th in the world. But they've never had a case quite like Padilla's.

"We've seen facial trauma like Juan's before. What's unique here is the method: the horn of a bull. Ordinarily a goring of that depth to the face . . . it could have killed him." Think how narrowly he avoided brain damage, says Garcia-Perla. "It was a question of millimeters. He's lucky to be alive, and he's conscious of that."

The surgery gets under way at 9:00 A.M. on November 22. It lasts 14 hours. Moonrise, and Juan Padilla has a new face. And within weeks, the repaired facial nerve begins to "awaken." Little by little, Padilla regains limited motor control of his left eyebrow and lips. Over the next six months, Garcia-Perla believes, Padilla might recover as much as 80 percent of his facial mobility. But nerve regeneration is a slow process. One millimeter, more or less, per day.

On December 30, five weeks after his epic operation, Padilla stands in front of a *vaca brava,* a two-year-old cow, at Fuente Ymbro, a ranch in Cadiz that breeds fighting bulls. He's here to *torear* with a live animal for the first time since the accident. The day is cold and cloudless. Scallion green hills descend to an azure lake, and bulls that look camel-humped with muscle tissue percolate slowly around the low buildings. A dozen close friends and family members are standing around the miniature bullring, waiting to see what Juan Jose is capable of in his reconstructed body. It's a "closed-doors corrida"—a test and a performance.

With his eye patch in place, he shakes out the *muleta,* his red cape, and shouts: "*Toro!*" Everybody's eyes are full. Only the young cow, with her velvety, bumblebee-like ruff, seems distracted, unaware of the import of this moment. She charges Juan's blind side, and he expertly sidesteps her.

Padilla insisted on this date because he refused to let the year

end without "the sensation of dressing as a bullfighter" and standing before an animal. He describes his desire to "grab the cape" in
supple, tactile terms, with the longing of a ghost recalling its body.
"And above all I wanted to share it, to offer it as a gift to my family
and those close to me who suffered through this, to the doctors.
Afterward I realized that I hadn't been wrong, to have this hope of
returning."

In January the surgeon in Oviedo, the skeptic, examines Padilla
and is so impressed by the adaptation of his right eye that he re-
vises his initial prognosis: Padilla is able to measure distances and
spaces with only one eye, and so it's "perfectly fine" for him to
return to the bullring. Garcia-Perla, who attended the private corrida on the 30th, agrees.

So on March 4, in the southwestern town of Olivenza, the Cyclone reappeared, looking like a glittering apparition of his former self, haunting the afternoon, wearing a black eye patch and
a laurel green suit of lights. Olivenza is not a major venue on the
calendar *taurino,* but Juan Jose's one-eyed return magnetized the
world's gaze. In the moments before his first bull came rampaging
onto the sand, nobody knew what to expect: Were they about to
watch a man's suicide, a second goring? How much could he really see? Wasn't it just yesterday, practically, that his face was torn
apart in Zaragoza? Journalists flinched preemptively, prepared
for a literal collision between the man's blind ambition and the
sprinting animal. But Padilla swept his cape over the bulls' horns
a dozen times, as if he were intent on violently, defiantly erasing
every doubt.

III. Homecoming

At 8:30 every weekday morning, Juan Jose Padilla drives from his
home in Sanlucar to meet with a physical therapist. For 30 minutes, he endures an electroshock treatment that causes his face
to convulse and contort. This is exercise for his paralyzed facial
muscles, a daily attempt to coax that nerve to regenerate. He also
meets with his speech therapist and his ear doctor. Mornings are
for doctors' visits, afternoons for the bulls.

At noon, Padilla drives his white Mercedes to the Sanlucar Plaza
de Toros, a small, intimate bullring. "My office," he jokes. Walking
through the archway feels like entering a seashell, scrubbed clean

by years of sand and salt and light. Today, a Thursday in early May, the audience is me, my translator, and Diego's strawberry-blond dog, Geto.

What does training look like for a bullfighter?

Padilla strides into the ring, skeletally gaunt in a T-shirt and black bike leggings. An athlete, no question, but with a mauled look. Wild and fragile at once. He's dropped 40 pounds since Zaragoza. He's average height, but his extreme weight loss makes him look like a gangly giant; his large hands dangle from his wrists, and his Adam's apple tents his long throat. If Goya were to paint a *taurino* trading card, it would look like Juan Jose.

"Toro!" Padilla screams at Diego, furiously wagging his red cape.

Diego lowers his head and runs at him.

Diego Robles is 60-plus and leather-skinned, so super-*marrón* he seems to be getting tan from within, as if at any moment he might hiccup a tiny sun. He's an ex-torero with startlingly blue eyes, and he'll grab his jerky-lean stomach muscles to show you he has no "Michelins"—nary a spare tire.

Diego adjusts his backward powder blue baseball cap, paws the sand with a sneaker toe, and charges again. He runs with his head down, holding a pair of real bull's horns that look like yellowed saber teeth. He circles Padilla, huffing in an unconvincing imitation of a deranged bull. Padilla holds his body erect, drawing the cape over Diego's head with animatronic evenness.

Next, Diego disappears from the plaza and returns with what appears to be a Tim Burton movie prop—a wheelbarrow with a bull's skull affixed to its front end. The skull's a little crooked, which makes its grin look somehow bashful. A hay bale is lashed to the cart behind it, frizzing golden straw.

"What do bullfighters call that wheelbarrow?" I ask, preparing for a whimsical yet terrifying new vocabulary word.

"The wheelbarrow," says Diego, looking flustered. Geto greets the skull in cosmopolitan fashion, licking first one bony cheek and then the other.

The skull-barrow rolls my way.

"Grip the horns," says Diego. They're a foot long at least, thicker around than my wrist. It's a sickening exercise to imagine this bovine stalagmite tunneling through Padilla's eye socket.

Now Padilla practices the *volapié*—a death blow delivered to the bull by an airborne matador. He runs at the wheelbarrow, leaps over the skull's horns, and sinks his *estoque,* the needlelike sword, into the center of the hay bale. *"Bien!"* claps Diego. The hay bale looks like a cheese cube at the end of a gigantic toothpick. The skull grins vacantly into the stands; Geto, bored, has wandered off to lick his own foot.

To a foreigner, it's an almost comically surreal scene. *"Toro!"* Padilla screams into the empty ring.

Every May for 19 years, Padilla has returned to his hometown of Jerez de la Frontera, a 30-minute drive from Sanlucar, to *torear* at Jerez's annual fair.

My 20th Feria.

In Spain, every locality from Madrid to the most rinky-dink *pueblecito* celebrates its annual fair: a big weeklong street party, usually tied to a religious holiday. Portable tents go up like luminous mushrooms; inside these temporary pavilions, everybody boozes and shimmies. Jerez de la Frontera, the fifth-largest city in Andalucía, is located in Cadiz province. Halfway between the sea and the blue burrs of the mountains, it's the true cradle of what Americans consider to be stereotypically *Español:* sherry, stallions, flamenco, fighting bulls. The Jerez Feria is one of the major events on the bullfighting calendar, this year even more than usual. Padilla's canted face is on posters everywhere in town; he's wearing the laurel green jacket, extending his *montera*. On the posters his snarl looks stagy and flirtatious, deliberate; in person, you can see that this grimace is frozen onto him, a half smile he can't straighten.

It's Saturday, May 12, and I've been invited to Padilla's house about an hour before he'll leave for the corrida in Jerez. The Padilla homestead turns out to be a Sanlucar monument. Kids on bikes don't know the street address, but when I say "Padilla" their eyes go wide—"Ah! The house of the torero." Sanlucar and Jerez are not wealthy towns—Sanlucar has one of the lowest per capita incomes in Spain—so bullfighting can be something analogous to Hoop Dreams for the poor kids of Andalucía.

The house is a modest mansion surrounded by an eight-foot magenta wall, with a massive backyard that hosts a lemon tree and a bluish tile of Christ's face. There's a play area for Paloma and Martin, and a sandy junior bullring where their dad trains. The interior of the two-story house is set up like a self-curated museum: every room contains displays of bullfighting memorabilia. Swords, hats, and so many sequined jackets that you wonder if there's not a naked army of Prince's backup dancers wandering around San-lucar.

The accident, in career terms, has been a remarkable boon. Padilla has contracts everywhere—this season, he is planning to perform in 60 to 70 corridas. Diego can negotiate for fees that are double or in some cases triple what he was making before. He's also getting better bulls: "The people have always associated me with Miuras," Padilla says. "Now there's been a complete change in my professional life. They're giving me new opportunities." For the first time, he's facing off against the best-bred bulls in Spain. Stylistically, he explains, a different choreography is possible with a *toro* that charges rhythmically and follows the cape.

Half a dozen close family friends, including Dr. Garcia-Perla, are gathered around the coffee table, waiting for their audience with the Cyclone. (The title of the Padillas' lone coffee-table book: *The Cyclone.*) A papal hush drapes the house. Somehow, thanks to the mysterious intervention of Diego, I am admitted to Juan Jose's dressing room. In the inner chamber, Padilla is putting on a short, rigid jacket, the matador's exoskeleton. It's snowflake white with gold embroidery. He's wearing the matador's *coleta,* a clip-on bun made of his own hair. He's already got on the cropped breeches, the flamingo pink socks. After his weight loss last fall, he needed a whole new wardrobe.

He says he has around 50 suits, but only eight in rotation for any given season. The sword boy cleans them after each corrida. Padilla's sword "boy" is a kind, bespectacled man in his fifties named Juan Muñoz. He dresses and undresses Juan Jose and hands him his sword at the "hour of truth" and is perhaps the most feudal-manservant-seeming member of Team Padilla. Muñoz doesn't use OxiClean or Shout—no, nothing like that. He says he gets the blood off his boss's sequins with soap and water.

Padilla adjusts his skinny tie in the mirror. He smiles nervously at Lidia, who smiles back. Strides out to greet his fan base.

"How do I look?"

Spotlit by the risk that he's about to undertake in the plaza, Juan looks frailer than he has all week. Mummy-like in white. His legs are matchsticks. His eye patch is a blindfold he can't lift. Suddenly I feel very scared, truly scared, for this corrida.

"Very handsome!" everyone responds. People hug Padilla one

by one and file out to their cars. We leave Lidia behind in the
foyer.

The next time Juan Jose Padilla appears, he is a completely different person.

The plaza is crammed solid with Jerezanos. It's 7:00 P.M., but
the enormous, cheerfully brutal *sol* of Andalucía is still shining
above the bullring. Every matador on today's lineup is a star—Cayetano, in fact, is the scion of the Ordoñez bullfighting dynasty,
and Morante de la Puebla is a legendary artist with the cape. But
Padilla is the major attraction, hero and homeboy to all.

"Jerez, it's his *tierra*," says Diego. "It's going to be an incredibly
emotional moment. You have to be strong so that so much emotion doesn't overwhelm you. It can make you tender, weak . . ."

Acute excitement pulses in the stands. Two nights ago, at the
Thursday corrida, this same plaza was nearly empty. Everybody
blamed the economy: even the cheap seats cost 28 euros. But tonight there is no evidence that money is weighing on anybody's
mind. FUERZAPADILLA! read banners unscrolling throughout the
stadium.

When Padilla, Cayetano, and Morante parade onto the sand, a
roar erupts from the open mouth of the stadium into the blue sky
of Jerez, loud enough to ripple a flock of low-flying birds. In the
foyer of his home, Padilla looked so thin, like something prema-
turely sprung from its cocoon. But now he is fast, strong; the eye
patch looks menacing. His hoarse cry of "Jerez!" brings down the
house.

Padilla's first bull comes charging out and silences the rowdy
crowd. In a *corrida de toros,* the matador will have roughly 20 minutes to dominate and kill the bull. This block of time is subdivided
into three *tercios:* "the act of the lances," "the act of the banderillas," and "the act of death." If the matador performs well, the
crowd will petition the president of the bullfight to award him
trophies: the dead bull's ears or, for an exceptional corrida, the
gristly gray ribbon of the bull's tail. Death is always the outcome
for the bull, except in rare cases when an unusually "valiant" animal is pardoned.

Many have pointed out that the bullfight is not really a fight at
all—a contest between equals—but "a tragedy in three acts." The
rite's brutality can make bullfighting feel incomprehensible to a

foreigner and indefensible to an animal lover; and yet every bull-fighter I spoke to professed to feel what struck me as a genuine love for the *toros*. What kind of love is this? How is it possible to publicly kill the animal to which you have dedicated all your waking hours? "I give the *toro* everything, and he gives me everything," Padilla told me. His profession, he says proudly, is "the most dignified in the world" because of "its truth, its reality"—its blood-red engagement with the fate shared by all species. Every corrida, the matador greets his future death cloaked in fur, and today is no exception.

Act I: Juan Jose and his banderilleros swing their pink capotes around wildly, each man caping the bull in turn. Out trot the picadors, looking like dapper Lego men on horseback in their wide-brimmed hats and squarish leg armor. Their horses are swaddled in *petos*, mattresslike cloaks to protect them from the bulls' horns. The picadors insert their lances into the hump of muscle tissue at the base of the neck, the *morillo*, to get the bull to lower its head; otherwise Padilla won't be able to get over its horns to make the final kill. There is something scarily perfunctory about the way the picadors jab the bull with their long lances—they're like a cavalry of gas jockeys, only instead of filling up the tank, they are draining the bull's life.

Act II: Padilla dismisses his assistants, signals to the crowd that he will put in his own banderillas. Goddamnit, Padilla, *qué fuerte*. Everyone is aware that this is exactly how he lost his eye. And now, one-eyed, Padilla is flying onto the wooden running boards behind the bull. How does he get so high? He takes a running leap as if the sand were a trampoline and sinks another wooden flag into the bull. He places the final pair of banderillas *al violín*, a one-handed maneuver that recalls the dramatic acrobatics that caused his fall in Zaragoza.

Act III: *Tercio de la muerte*. Now Padilla is stalking the bull, with an unexpected sultriness and mock haughtiness. Via a sort of feline strut across the sand toward the animal, he slinks up to the bull and goads it into charging. It lowers its horns, tosses its head in a dozen vain attempts to catch the cape. When it comes up on Padilla's blind left side, we recoil, but we don't have to worry; he seems to have no trouble gauging distance or responding to the unhinged shadows in the bullring.

Padilla's body language changes tone continually over the next seven minutes, as his *pasos* transmit contempt and urgency, comedy and reverence. Sometimes the bullfight looks a lot like a game of freeze tag, and his pranks get juvenile; he does everything short of blowing a raspberry at the bull. Sometimes it's more like an awkward cocktail party: the bull refusing to charge, Padilla doing the torero catcall that is like emphatic forced laughter: "Eh, *toro!* He-he-HEH!"

Soon everyone can tell from the bull's ragged breathing that the end is near. Padilla and the bull are staring into each other's faces with an opaque intimacy. Something visible to everyone in the stands, but as ultimately impenetrable as any couple's love-or-hate affair. It's almost sunset now; the planks of blood down the bull's back look violet. As if on the conductor's cue, two seagulls choose this moment to swoop through the invisible membrane between bull and man. Padilla's dark hair is sticking to his head. The matador, underweight, with his twisted face and his eye patch, appears unmistakably mortal. His face fossilizes his brush with death, the way that fire gets incarnated by cold, tender welts. His return to the ring, one could argue, gives the crowd a sense that death will come for all of us, sooner or later, that death is certainly imminent, but *it ain't here yet*.

Inside the plaza's walls, the concrete parentheses that enclose Padilla and the bull, everybody straightens; *erguirse* is the Spanish verb for this, electric shivers racing up spines. Juan Jose directs the creature's horns around his waist, as if he is carving his own hips out of black space. Drawing beautiful shapes with the cape and the bull. Drawing breaths.

Padilla squares his feet, positions himself for the kill. The bull is four feet away from him. Here it comes: the "hour of truth." It's a crazy, horrible, ugly, enraging, senseless, sublime, endless moment to witness—a moment that swallows every adjective you want to hurl at it.

In the balcony, the orchestra has stopped playing. The conductor is craning over his shoulder, watching Padilla for his cue. His baton trembles in midair at the exact angle as Padilla's sword.

Padilla draws the sword back at eye level, as if the *estoque* is an arrow in an invisible quiver.

He runs. He flies, just as he did during his training with the wheelbarrow. *Volapié*. He leaps and leans his torso over the bull's lowered horns and plunges the sword into the vulnerable *morillo*.

The crowd lets out one single, tidal exhalation.

Did he "win"? Bullfighting is less straightforward than American spectacles like pro football; in this regard, it's a little more like *American Idol.* But thanks to the thunderous petition of the crowd, tonight the president awards him two ears from his first bull and two ears from his second. Before he exits the arena, Padilla drops onto his knees and kisses the sand of Jerez. Then he is carried through the great doors of his home plaza, *de hombros,* twinkling like a living torch on his brother Jaime's shoulders. Escorted by the longest ovation you have ever heard.

Forty minutes after his triumphant exit through the Puerta Grande, Padilla is back home in Sanlucar, changing out of his work clothes. Outside, a few guys are loading up the shuttle bus; at 4:30 A.M. tomorrow, Padilla and his entourage will leave for their next fight in Talavera. Some freckly taurine roadie carries swords and a bleached skull to the trunk.

Where is the wild torero after-party? Lidia and the family friends are having a quiet dinner. Paloma is bouncing around, getting ready for bed. The Cyclone of Jerez emerges from his dressing room as Juan Jose, wearing a suit jacket and spiffy loafers.

"Four ears, Paloma!" he crows to his daughter, sinking into his armchair. ("The kids are always begging him, 'Papi, bring me two ears!'—you know the typical things," Lidia explains.) He smooches her to make her giggle.

How does he feel about tonight's corrida?

"This was one of the afternoons of maximum responsibility in my life," he says. "To be able to dress in my suit of lights in this new phase of my life, in front of my countrymen, my doctors, my family—" He smiles. For the past week, he explains, he's been terrified that it would be "an empty afternoon, a sad afternoon, that the bulls wouldn't help me . . ." That he would fail to achieve his dream of leaving *de hombros,* piggybacking on his brother's shoulders through the great gates.

"Well, I think it was a triumphant afternoon. I dedicate it to *toda mi tierra.*"

Is it uncomfortable to get sedimented into legend while you are still alive? Is it like another sort of paralysis?

"I feel supremely content, proud, for all that the bull has given me, all that it's added to my life, personal as well as professional.

I can't complain or feel victimized by my injury; this is the profession I chose. And this accident of mine, my recovery, I think it's touched the whole world . . ." He leans forward, his enormous hands cupping his bony knees, shaping his words carefully. "There was a time when I couldn't show my face, when my head was a little screwed up. But now I've entered a period of great pride, great happiness."

His working eye follows his daughter, who is babbling some song under the taxidermied heads of six Miura bulls that Padilla killed in a single afternoon in Bilbao.

"And there is always a new goal tomorrow." It's the *"amor por los toros,"* he says—his love of the bulls—that drives him.

If some of these phrases sound like Hallmark propaganda, you have to imagine them spoken by a man who is teaching himself to speak again. It's a legitimate medical miracle that Juan Jose Padilla can even vocalize his "love for the *toros*" today. Tomorrow he'll fight three horned beasts in Talavera; on Monday it's back to the ABCs in speech therapy. Somehow he's managed to surrender without bitterness to his new situation while simultaneously working without pause to reclaim his life. His feats in the bullring are as impressive as they've ever been, but for my money it's Padilla's daily diligence, his unglorious microsteps back from paralysis, that distinguish him as a true *figura*.

For all the talk of rewards and triumphs and miracles, the life of a bullfighter seems incredibly grueling, dangerous, uncertain.

Vale la pena? Is it worth it?

No, says Padilla's mother without a second's hesitation.

No, says Pepe Padilla, who during the Franco years used to ride trains and sleep under the stars to stand before a fighting bull. For the parents of a torero, "there is more *pena* than *gloria*."

Sí, says Lidia, *because you see his happiness!*

Sí, says Juan Jose Padilla, smiling as wide as his new face permits him, because God is giving me my *recompensa*. Now I see better with one eye than two.

MICHAEL J. MOONEY

The Most Amazing Bowling Story Ever

FROM D MAGAZINE

WHEN BILL FONG approaches the lane, 15-pound bowling ball in hand, he tries not to breathe. He tries not to think about not breathing. He wants his body to perform a series of complex movements that his muscles themselves have memorized. In short, he wants to become a robot.

Fong, 48 years old, six feet tall with broad shoulders, pulls the ball into his chest and does a quick shimmy with his hips. He swings the ball first backward, then forward, his arm a pendulum of kinetic energy, as he takes five measured steps toward the foul line. He releases the ball, and it glides across the oiled wooden planks like it's floating, hydroplaning, spinning counterclockwise along a trajectory that seems to be taking it straight for the right-hand gutter. But as the ball nears the edge of the lane, it veers back toward the center, as if guided by remote control. The hook carries the ball back just in time. In a heartbeat, what was a wide, sneering mouth of pins is now—nothing.

He comes back to the table where his teammates are seated — they always sit and bowl in the same order—and they congratulate him the same way they have thousands of times over the last decade. But Fong looks displeased. His strike wasn't good enough.

"I got pretty lucky that time," he says in his distinctly Chicago accent. "The seven was hanging there before it fell. I've got to make adjustments." With a pencil, he jots down notes on a folded piece of blue paper.

His teammates aren't interested in talking about what he can do to make his strikes more solid, though, or even tonight's mildly competitive league game. They're still discussing a night two years ago. They mention it every week, without fail. In fact, all you have to do is say the words "That Night" and everyone at the Plano Super Bowl knows what you're talking about. They also refer to it as "The Incident" or "That Incredible Series." It's the only time anyone can remember a local recreational bowler making the sports section of the *Dallas Morning News*. One man, an opponent of Fong's that evening, calls it "the most amazing thing I've ever seen in a bowling alley."

Bill Fong needs no reminders, of course. He thinks about that moment—those hours—every single day of his life.

Most people think perfection in bowling is a 300 game, but it isn't. Any reasonably good recreational bowler can get lucky one night and roll 12 consecutive strikes. If you count all the bowling alleys all over America, somebody somewhere bowls a 300 every night. But only a human robot can roll three 300s in a row—36 straight strikes—for what's called a "perfect series." More than 95 million Americans go bowling, but, according to the United States Bowling Congress, there have been only 21 certified 900s since anyone started keeping track.

Bill Fong's run at perfection started as most of his nights do, with practice at around 5:30 P.M. He bowls in four active leagues and he rolls at least 20 games a week, every week. That night, January 18, 2010, he wanted to focus on his timing.

Timing is everything. When your timing is right, when your arms, legs, and torso all move in rhythm toward the lane, you have better balance. When you're balanced, you're also more accurate. And when you're accurate, your decision-making also improves. By contrast, if your timing is off, your balance is off, and you don't hit your targets. There are too many variables to assess, too many elements to gauge, and you can't possibly make the best decisions. Fong knows a hot streak is all about timing. So in practice that night, he breathed, he tried to erase all thoughts, and he tried to make his approach with each body part functioning as programmed.

That night, he didn't roll many strikes in practice. There was nothing to make him think this night would be anything special.

Fong's team, the Crazy Eights (he picked the name because

eights are lucky in Chinese culture), was assigned lanes 27 and 28, one of Fong's favorite pairs. The left lane, 27, hooks more, he says. The right lane, 28, tends to be more direct.

Frame one was on the left lane. As always, he was last in the bowling order, the anchor position. He watched his teammates roll and noticed each one throw a ball that hooked early and missed the pocket, the sweet spot between the head pin and the 3 pin on the right, the place that gives you the best chance of getting a strike. So when it was Fong's turn, he opted to roll a deeper hook, to stay outside and ride the edge of the gutter a little longer.

The result was a loud, powerful strike. His ball slammed into the pocket with a vengeance, obliterating all 10 pins. His next roll, on 28, was another violent strike. All four of the first frames were robust strikes, actually. But his teammates barely took notice.

"To tell you the truth, that wasn't that unusual," says JoAnn Gibson, a sweet Southern woman who enjoys the company more than she does the actual bowling.

"Bowlers like Bill can roll off mini-streaks like that all the time," says Tom Dunn, a more serious bowler who sometimes flirts innocently with JoAnn.

Both Gibson and Dunn have bowled with or against Fong in this league since the Clinton administration. They've been teammates for nine years. James Race, who, with his perpetual smile and polite demeanor, reminds the other teammates of Mister Rogers, came a few years later. They don't really hang out much outside the bowling alley, but no matter what's going on in life, they go to Plano Super Bowl for a few hours on Monday nights.

Fong's fifth roll of the night wasn't so beautiful. His approach and release seemed the same—he was becoming the robot—and the ball hit the pocket, but the pins didn't go down quickly. The 10 pin was wobbling upright, teetering, when Fong got what is called a "messenger." From the left, one of the pins he'd just sent bouncing came back across the lane, clipping the 10 just enough to knock it off balance. When he got back to the table, his teammates congratulated him, but Fong called it what it was: a lucky strike.

In the sixth frame, he had another loud, devastating strike. Then another. Then another. With each throw, he could tell it was a strike from the moment it left his hand. He'd watch as the pins were there one second, then gone the next. "It felt like driving and catching a green light, then the next one, then the next, then turning, and still catching every green light everywhere you go," Fong says.

Before he knew it, it was the 10th frame. Back on the right lane, he again tried to swing the ball wide, let it run along the outside of the lane, next to the gutter. The first two rolls of the 10th frame both tucked into the pocket just as Fong hoped, and both were solid strikes.

On the last roll, though, something happened. He could tell from the sound of the pins. As the clutter at the end of the lane cleared, he could see the 9 pin (the second from the right on the last row) still standing. He watched the chaos of the flying pins, each rotating right past the upright 9. Fong craned his neck, watching, hoping. Until one of the pins popped up from its side and swiped the 9 down.

"The best way to describe the first 300 was just 'powerful,'" Race says.

One of the Super Bowl employees announced Fong's name and score over the loudspeaker, something Fong is a particular fan of. There was a round of applause.

"Sometimes, when you have a lot of 300s, or if you get more than one in a week, they won't announce it," he says.

The night was just beginning.

Aside from bowling, Bill Fong hasn't had a lot of success in life. His Chinese mother demanded perfection, but he was a C student. He never finished college, he divorced young, and he never made a lot of money. By his own account, his parents didn't like him much. As a bowler, his average in the high 230s means he's probably better than anyone you know. But he's still only tied as the 15th best bowler in Plano's most competitive league. Almost nothing in life has gone according to plan.

He likes to say he got his approach to bowling from the hard-hitting alleys in his native Chicago, where he went to high school with Michelle Obama. He was one of the few kids from Chinatown interested in bowling at the time. Despite his strict mother and the fact that his friends were all on the honor roll, little William preferred sports. He dreamed of being a professional athlete one day.

He wasn't big—too short for basketball, too slender for football—but he'd run up and down the block as a boy, racing imaginary friends.

When Fong was young, his parents divorced. He remembers the man who would become his stepdad taking his mom out on dates to a local bowling alley, where they could bring the kids. He noticed that when he was bowling, he wasn't thinking about whatever was going on behind him. His mind could focus on the ball, the lane, the pins—and the rest of the world would disappear. He had never been captivated by anything like that.

While still courting Fong's mother, his stepdad promised that if the boy ever got a score higher than 120 he'd buy him his own ball. "He never did," Fong says. "I bought it myself."

After his mother remarried and moved away, he still had his siblings, his quiet, hardworking father, and his bowling. He joined the high school team. He went to the public library and checked out stacks of books about bowling theory. After a stint in college, he found himself smoking a lot of pot and staying out all night bowling, trying to hustle people out of small bets. He'd leave the alley after the sun came up, go out to breakfast, sleep until 6:00 P.M., and then repeat the process.

At 22, he got married and his wife encouraged him to "grow up." He realized he wasn't ever going to become a professional bowler like the men he watched on TV every week, and he took a job cutting hair.

"It was just something I could always do for money," he says. "I like the artistic side, but it's not my passion."

Soon he gave up bowling and took up golf. It was a lot like bowling—timing, balance, accuracy—and he'd heard that with 10 years of practice, anyone could become a top-level golfer. He read books about golf, took a job at a pro shop, and learned to cut his own clubs. For 10 years, through career changes, through his divorce, through his move to Dallas (several family members had moved to Texas for various reasons and he'd always enjoyed visiting), Fong played golf. His younger sister was by then a standout on the Baylor University golf team. But after all those years of playing nearly every day, he still wasn't a scratch golfer. He couldn't take the frustration, and he swore off the game for good.

He remembered how much he'd enjoyed bowling. He didn't

miss the up-all-night-gambling lifestyle, but the game itself, shutting out the world and making himself robotic—those things he missed. He joined a few leagues and bowled in tournaments all over North Texas, but no alley felt to him quite like the Super Bowl in Plano. There was something about the friendly faces, the way a great strike sounded there. It felt right.

After 14 years, he knows all 48 lanes. He equates it to the way Tiger Woods knows the holes on his home golf course. Fong has rolled on each of these lanes dozens of times over the years, and he keeps detailed records.

"No two lanes are the same," he says.

He documents which lanes hook better and which seem to suck the ball into the gutter. He notes any tiny divot and nearly imperceptible slope, any imperfection he can find. Lane 5, for example, has a higher strike percentage when people throw straighter. On lane 16, the oil tends to swirl closer to the pins.

In the years she's known Fong, Gibson has had very few conversations with him that didn't involve ball movement and oil patterns, though she admits most of the technical bowling talk flies right over her head. But she smiles, not wanting to offend anyone. "This really is Bill's life," she says.

"Looking back," Fong says, "I guess bowling just always filled whatever emptiness I had."

That night, people were still coming over to congratulate Bill Fong on the 300, when he did something unimaginable: for his second game, he switched bowling balls.

He remembered, two weeks earlier, practicing on lanes 27 and 28. He remembered that after a few games, the oil pattern on the right lane shifted. So to start game two on the right lane, he switched to his more polished ball, the one that hooks less and rolls straighter.

Someone on another lane saw him making the change. "Is Bill Fong switching balls?" the man called out to his friends incredulously.

Fong heard him and turned around.

"Yep," he said.

The man called back to him: "You're crazy!"

Fong grinned and turned back toward the lane.

He stepped forward and unleashed a solid, thorough strike — his 13th of the night. Then he stood there, arms wide, shaking his head. His gutsy move had paid off.

Dunn remembers the feeling in the air. "Because he started out by switching balls, and that was so incredible, the second game was definitely more emotional," he says.

Throughout the second game, Fong continued using his more aggressive ball on the left lane, and the more polished, less aggressive ball on the right lane. And the strikes kept coming.

It seemed like even members of the other team were smiling when Fong was up to roll. Fong himself was laughing and smiling, pointing and calling out to friends at other lanes. He remembers shrugging a lot. "I felt loose as a goose," he says.

As he sent strike after strike down the lanes, he began to feel magical. Literally, the way he was commanding the balls to turn and burrow into the unsuspecting pins, it felt a little like he was moving heavy objects with only the power of his mind. In the fourth frame, both the 7 and the 10 pins stayed up just a bit longer than he wanted. As he gestured with both arms, they fell. Something similar happened in the eighth frame.

"It was like Moses parting the sea," he says. "I'd move my hands and everything would get out of the way."

Soon the other bowlers began stepping back when he was up, taking extra precaution not to get in his way. "Nobody wants to mess up a streak like that," Dunn says.

By the 10th frame, Fong found that most people around him wouldn't make eye contact for fear they would be the last thing he would see before rolling a dud. On the first roll of the last frame, he had what he calls a "happy accident." For the first time that night, one of his powerful throws missed its mark ever so slightly. But because the oil was now evaporating on the left lane too, the ball found the pocket for a perfect strike. Noticing what happened on the first roll, he adjusted his position and finished the game with two more powerful strikes, numbers 23 and 24 of the night.

Once again, Fong got to hear his name called from the speakers. And again he took a moment to shake hands with the line of people waiting to congratulate him. A few were embarrassed that they hadn't come over after the first 300. People were delightfully confused, shaking their heads as they patted Fong on the back.

"Never seen anything like it," they said. "Back-to-back 300s."
And Fong shook his own head. "Me neither," he said.

There's almost never a time when every decision you make is correct and every step is in the right direction. Life, like bowling,
is full of complicating factors, unpredictable variables, plenty of
times when there is no right answer. But Bill Fong had some experience with near-perfection prior to the night. He'd had another
amazing run two years before that. He'd bowled a 297, then a
300. Someone mentioned to him that with another great game he
could beat the Texas state series record, which was 890. Fong can
admit it now: he choked in that third game. He could feel himself
thinking too much, slipping out of the zone. Soon he was out of
rhythm and his balance was off. That night he shot a 169 in the last
game; he didn't even break 800 for the series. It was exactly what
he was trying to avoid after his two straight 300s.

So this time, before game three, he approached a friend who
was bowling a few lanes down. Fong mentioned that he was thinking about switching balls again, using the less aggressive ball on
both lanes in the final game. His friend, who had plenty of 300s
under his own belt, was surprised but gave him simple advice:
"Trust your instinct."

When that first roll of the third game produced another strike—
another risky decision rewarded—Fong felt like he was floating.
He wasn't drinking, but he felt a little drunk. Both his teammates
and his opponents bowled as fast as they could to get out of his
way. By the time he struck in the fifth frame, he realized he would
almost certainly break the coveted 800 mark. He was relieved.

By the sixth frame, a large crowd had formed behind Fong.
Dozens of people had stopped bowling to watch. Texts were sent
and statuses posted to Facebook, and the audience grew.

"We were more nervous than he was at the time," Gibson says.
"It was almost like he was putting on a show up there."

Each time he approached the lane, the entire bowling alley
went silent. Every time he let fly another roll, there were audi-
ble moans from strangers and shouts from the crowd: "That's it,
baby!" Each time he struck, the room erupted with applause. In all
his life, Bill Fong had never heard anyone cheering him like that.

He had 33 straight strikes entering the 10th frame of the third
game. Out came the cell-phone cameras. There were whispers, but

as soon as Fong picked up his ball, it was dead quiet. He turned to look at the crowd behind him, now well over 100 people, densely packed from the end of the snack bar to the vending machines 80 feet away.

That's when the magic left him. Fong began to feel nervous, like the world was watching him pee. He felt the buzz—whatever it had been—leave his body. As he stood in front of lane 28, he felt numb. He tried to push through it.

He lined up and threw a ball without much hook on it. As soon as it left his hand, Fong began waving at it, trying to will the ball left. It connected with the pocket but without the usual force. As the other pins dropped, the 9 pin stayed up for what seemed like ages. But just as the gasp of the crowd reached a crescendo, one of the pins rolling meekly across the lane bumped the 9 just enough to tip it. The room exploded with cheers and whistles. The sound was enough to shake one of the cameras now capturing the moment.

Fong looked dizzy as he walked back to the ball exchange. For the first time that night, he began sweating profusely. But he realized the mistake he'd made on his last throw, and the second roll was much cleaner. Again there were shouts from the audience as the ball blazed down the lane, zipping back in time to smash the pins apart in a powerful, driving strike. And there was even more cheering as all 10 pins fell. Thirty-five strikes down, one to go.

Before his final roll, Fong wiped his ball with his towel. He heard a woman's voice behind him, a stranger, saying, "We are having fun, aren't we?" He lifted the ball to his chest and stood calmly for a moment. Then he took five steps and released the ball toward perfection.

It looked good from his hand, arcing out the way so many of his great strikes that night had, cutting back to the pocket just in time. Several people started applauding before the ball even reached the end of the lane—that's how good it looked. But this time, as the pins scrambled, something unimaginable happened. The 10 pin, farthest to the right, wobbled. But it didn't fall.

Some of the people in the room couldn't process what they'd just witnessed. How could the last roll, like the 35 before it, not be a strike? Strangers fell to their knees. It was hard for anyone to breathe.

Fong turned and walked to his right. He was empty. Blank.

His friends, the ones who were prepared seconds ago to tackle him in celebration, grabbed him and held him still. As he stood there, Fong wanted to say something—anything—but he couldn't make a sound.

Sitting around the table two years after that night, Bill Fong and his teammates still argue. Fong truly believes that the last pin could have made his life perfect. "It would have made all the difference," he says. With a 900, he theorizes, he might have made *SportsCenter,* and he would surely have sponsors. He thinks he might have had a chance to join the pro tour. At least, he figures, he'd be the best of all time at something, with the name Bill Fong immortalized above even the legends of the game—and he wouldn't be just a regular guy.

"That pin makes me like the Rodney Dangerfield of bowling," he says. "I get no respect."

He goes over that last roll in his mind all the time. He watches the shaky cell-phone video.

"It looked so good as it left my hand," he says.

When that 15-pound sphere collides with the pins, so many things happen so fast that there's no way of knowing exactly what went wrong in those milliseconds.

That hasn't stopped Fong from searching for some reason. He wonders if he could have practiced more. He blames the 10 years he was away from bowling. Like that single pin represents the Bowling Fates punishing him for his insolence.

His teammates disagree. They don't think that pin would have made much of a difference in Bill Fong's life at all. What he did was amazing, something that will come up in conversation around the Plano Super Bowl for years.

"It was mind-boggling," Gibson says.

The fact that he missed perfection by the last pin on the last roll—that makes the whole thing more human, less robotic. And that, somehow, makes it seem almost beautiful. Besides, they argue, Fong still holds the Texas state record. And because there have been only 21 perfect 900s, he is technically tied for the 22nd greatest night in the annals of bowling history. (There have been only 11 899s.)

His life is also better now. Around the time of the 899, Fong got a part-time job at the pro shop at the Super Bowl. Recently, he opened his own place down the road, Bowling Medic Pro Shop. A lot of people from his four leagues come by to have him drill their balls. Sometimes he cuts their hair too.

There's also this: that night, after the 899, his friends bought him a few beers. He doesn't usually drink, but at the time, he felt like the best day of his life had just turned into the worst. After a beer or two—and at least an hour of excited congratulations from strangers—he felt dizzy. When he got home, he went into the bathroom and vomited in the toilet. The walls were spinning.

It turns out Bill Fong was having a stroke. With the stress, the tension of the night, his already high blood pressure had surpassed dangerous levels. Not long after, he had another stroke. When the doctor saw the scar tissue and heard about the night of dizziness, he explained to Fong that he had suffered what could very easily have been a fatal stroke. That night at the bowling alley, had things gone differently, he could have died.

It also means that with the sweating and dizziness he was feeling in the third game, it's likely that Fong bowled the last few frames through the beginning of that stroke—which makes the accomplishment that much more amazing.

When he had his heart surgery, he was in the hospital for a week. Not many family members visited him. Nobody came from his haircutting days. But he didn't lack for visitors. Plenty of people from the bowling alley took the time to see him, not just teammates but also some longtime opponents. They asked him how he felt and encouraged him to get well quickly. And, one by one, they each mentioned that incredible night in January, when Bill Fong fell just one pin short of perfect.

Rehab was hard at first. The strokes took a lot of his strength. But within a few months—earlier than doctors recommend—Fong was back to his usual form, back to rolling five days a week. More recently, he's been sharper than ever. Since that night, Fong has rolled 10 more 300s and four series of at least 800.

As they're talking about that night, one of his teammates poses the question: wouldn't Fong rather be alive with an 899 than dead with a 900? It's really a rhetorical question, but Fong takes a moment to consider it seriously. It takes him a while, but eventually Fong says he'd rather be alive.

"Well," says Race, the Mister Rogers of the group, "we're sure happy to have you still here and bowling with us."

Tonight, Fong struggles through the first few games. But in the final game of the night, he starts with three straight strikes. Then a fourth. Then a fifth. In the sixth frame, he throws it well but leaves the 10 pin standing, taunting him.

After picking up the spare, Fong comes back to the table, shaking his head and looking at his teammates.

"I've got to make adjustments," he says, and he begins making notes.

THOMAS LAKE

The Legacy of Wes Leonard

FROM SPORTS ILLUSTRATED

AFTER THE AUTOPSY, when the doctor found white blossoms of scar tissue on Wes Leonard's heart, he guessed they had been secretly building there for several months. That would mean Wes's heart was slowly breaking throughout the Fennville Blackhawks' 2010–2011 regular season, when he led them in scoring and the team won 20 games without a loss.

It would mean his heart was already moving toward electrical meltdown in December, when he scored 26 on Decatur with that big left shoulder clearing a path to the hoop. It would mean his heart swelled and weakened all through January (25 against Hopkins, 33 against Martin) even as it pumped enough blood to fill at least 10 swimming pools. This heart pounded two million times in February, probably more, heaving under its own weight, propelling Wes's six-foot-two, 230-pound frame along the glimmering hardwood with such precision and force that finally a kid from Hartford gave up on the rules and tackled him in the lane. By March 3, the night of Wes's last and most glorious game, his heart weighed 21½ ounces, double the weight of a normal heart, and it gave him all he needed from the opening tip to the final buzzer. Then the wiring failed, the current going as jagged as a thunderbolt, and Wes fell to the floor with his big heart quivering.

If all this seems implausible—that Wes could play so well for so long with such faulty equipment—consider a scientific phenomenon called *functional reserve*. The human heart has a reservoir of unused ability, like a powerful car that can go 150 miles per hour but never gets pushed above 75. A normal heart will pump about

60 percent of its blood volume with each beat. But one cardiologist tells the story of a bodybuilder who thrived for nearly a decade with a heart that could pump only about 10 percent per beat. Pistol Pete Maravich, arguably the greatest college basketball player of all time, was born with no left coronary artery. His right one worked twice as hard. It kept him alive for 40 years. The body finds a way to compensate, at least for a while. Functional reserve is not just for the heart. Every organ has this hidden power, this ability to outperform its perceived limits when the need is desperate.

Fennville is a blue-collar town in southwestern Michigan, six miles east of Lake Michigan, with a high school gym large enough to fit all of the 1,400 citizens. It nearly did so toward the end of Wes Leonard's junior season, as the Blackhawks won game after game behind his 19-point scoring average. It was the best show in town and, for some, a welcome escape.

Fennville High principal Amber Lugten guessed that in half of her students' families, at least one parent was looking for work. A man not at the game might be at Steven's on Main Street, a good dark place to drink canned domestic lager while pondering his career options now that the old fruit cannery was a shell of its former self and the Life Savers factory had gone to Canada and the welding company had laid him off months earlier. He could risk his last dollars on the Club Keno game playing on the monitor above the bar, watch the red sphere fall like a drop of blood on a grid of 72 numbers, pray for the jackpot. Otherwise he could collect scrap metal to sell by the pound, or ride his bike along the roadside with plastic bags dangling from the handlebars, filling them with 10-cent aluminum cans, and then ride out to the woods, scavenging deer camps for the relics of drunken hunters. After the summer he might find a job picking apples on the hills outside town, alongside the itinerant Mexicans whose children push Fennville's school enrollment up every March and back down in October, as regular as a heartbeat.

Yes, they've heard of functional reserve in Fennville. Whether by that name or some other.

1. The Two Rivals

The key to this story is a boy named Xavier Grigg, who could have been the finest three-sport athlete in Fennville. In 2005 he was not especially tall or strong for an 11-year-old, but he was quick and crafty, with a slingshot arm he'd been developing since his days as a toddler throwing imaginary baseballs. His best sport was baseball, and his third-best was basketball. In the middle was football, which put him on a clear path toward the most exalted position a teenage boy can reach in a small U.S. town: starting varsity quarterback.

Everything changed when Wes Leonard came to Fennville that fall. He was 27 days younger than Xavier but so physically advanced that his mother carried his birth certificate in a ziplock bag in her purse, just to prove he wasn't a ringer. Xavier tried to defend his territory, telling Wes, "I don't care how big you are, I'm gonna beat you," but he couldn't, except maybe in baseball, in which they took turns throwing no-hitters. In basketball and football there was no contest. Wes sharpened his jump shot all winter on a 10-foot goal in the converted garage that adjoined his bedroom. He and his father, Gary, a six-five hulk of a man who'd been recruited in football by several Division I universities, used to hurl a football back and forth at top speed, taking a step closer with each throw, to see who would drop it first. If Xavier had a slingshot, then Wes had a cannon. In their youth football leagues Xavier finally accepted the role of backup quarterback, taking snaps only when Wes got hurt and otherwise catching one touchdown after another as Wes's favorite receiver.

Through all this, Wes and Xavier became best friends. Xavier loved the spotlight but hated the pressure that came with it, so he didn't mind handing that pressure off to Wes. More than anything he hated losing, and with Wes on his team he didn't lose much. And Xavier proved his worth in social situations, in which Wes could be painfully insecure. Kids at school saw Wes as a paragon of self-confidence—he made friends with an autistic girl, for example, and sat with her at lunch every day—but he was timid compared with Xavier. When Wes's mother, Jocelyn, dispatched him to the grocery store for fruit juice, he was too shy to ask a clerk for help. When they went shopping at Hollister, Wes sifted through piles of jeans, looking for the pair that would fit comfortably over his muscular legs, and Jocelyn stood in the corner awaiting the hand signal that meant he needed her approval. Wes may have felt invincible on the field and the court, but elsewhere he lived with the irrational fear that someone might discover his incompetence.

"You need me, Wes," Xavier said.

"You need *me*," Wes said.

"You're just big, and you're good," Xavier said. "I'm good-*lookin'*."

So it went. Wes put up the big numbers, and Xavier got the phone numbers. They went tanning together to look good for the ladies. When Xavier's uncle took them to Hooters, the waitresses signed Wes's T-shirt with generic inspirational messages. But Xavier played it so smoothly that one waitress wrote to him, *I hope all your ups and downs in life are in bed.*

The two families had little in common, other than sons who played sports. Gary and Jocelyn Leonard were married, solidly Methodist, with a sprawling house in the woods outside Fennville. Xavier's mother, Maria Flores, had gone to her junior prom six months pregnant with Xavier and now lived in a small house in town with her longtime boyfriend, Jerry Lemmons, probably the nicest man ever to have his forearm tattooed with the devil's face. They all got along fine, though. Gary and Jerry sat together at basketball and football games, talking man talk, while Jocelyn and Maria watched their respective sons from another part of the bleachers, occasionally yelling in maternal fury at spectators whose color commentary cut too deep.

Maria and Xavier hurled mock insults that made everyone laugh. Maria convinced Wes that his mother's spaghetti was no good, and Wes told Maria her dogs were ugly, and if Xavier talked too much trash then Wes wrestled him to the floor and made him take it all back.

In the spring of 2010 Maria broke her neck in a car crash after a drunk driver ran a stop sign. As Jerry and Gary stood over her hospital bed, talking in worried tones, they looked down and saw a hopeful sign: in spite of the drugs and the brain injury Maria was giving them the finger. But she had barely avoided paralysis. Doctors rebuilt her upper spine with a titanium plate and a cadaver bone. She had been a full-time caregiver for the mentally handicapped, and now she needed full-time care herself. She spent most of her days in a four-poster bed, Vicodin no match for the pain in her neck and shoulders; she cried at everything on the Lifetime network, including the commercials. Worst of all, the Leonards took Xavier on a Jet Skiing and parasailing vacation at a cabin near Lake Huron a few weeks after Maria was discharged from the hospital, and Maria had to stay home.

"Xavier!" she called when she heard Wes's car in the driveway late that summer. "Your *girl*friend's here."

All three of them got in the little coupe. Wes had a new driver's license and an old burgundy two-door Mitsubishi Eclipse he'd bought with earnings from mowing lawns and digging ditches. And this is who the varsity quarterback invited to ride shotgun: a 33-year-old woman in a neck brace who called his Eclipse a "girl car." He was taking her on a date to the grocery store, with his favorite receiver in the backseat.

2. *The One-Armed Quarterback*

One hundred seventy-four days before he died, Wes led the Fennville Blackhawks to Decatur, a neighboring town where the field was packed hard from 55 consecutive years of football. The Decatur Raiders' game plan boiled down to one imperative: stop Wes Leonard. They did, eventually. On the first play he took the snap and sprinted left for nearly 20 yards, somersaulting in the air as he was tackled, bouncing right back up. He ran well and threw even better, and on any given play it was almost impossible to stop both. Fennville scored twice in the first quarter for a 12–8 lead and lined up for a two-point conversion. The setting sun cast thin blades of shadow. Wes ran around right tackle, one defender to beat, but the guy got him around the ankles and then a 270-pound defensive tackle came from the backside and crushed Wes to the stony ground. When he got up his left arm was hanging limp.

On the sideline, Xavier saw tears in Wes's eyes. Wes asked for something to relieve the pain. Jocelyn went searching for ibuprofen and politely declined when Maria offered her Vicodin. She heard the coach tell Xavier to go in at quarterback, and then she saw Wes push Xavier back.

"You're my receiver," Wes said.

No one knew the extent of the injury because Wes waved the trainer away and refused to take off his shoulder pads. Gary Leonard, an assistant coach, knew his stubborn son well enough to know he might have to tackle Wes to keep him out of the game. The coaches found a compromise: Wes would stay out of the game on defense, where he usually played linebacker, and as quarterback he would try to stay in the pocket.

Jocelyn was crying. *This is gonna be a freakin' disaster,* she thought.

Fennville's one-armed quarterback marched onto the field and fumbled his first snap. Decatur recovered.

Even then, Wes would not step aside for Xavier. Near the end of the second quarter, with Fennville trailing 24–18 and the sky that pale fire between day and night, Wes led his team to the line at the Decatur 43 in a four-receiver shotgun formation. Xavier stood in the slot to the right. The snap came in high, but Wes snared it with both hands, and the pain in his bad arm must have been excruciating as he rolled right and looked downfield. He was 10 yards deep when he hurled the ball, and it whistled nearly 60 yards through the air, arcing down near the goal line. Two defenders strained for it, but Xavier had beaten them both. He squeezed the ball to his chest and fell to the ground in the end zone.

After every possession Gary asked Wes, "Think you'd better get out of there?"

Wes always said, "No way."

Fennville lost 32–26, partly because Wes couldn't play defense or run the ball, but he threw for two touchdowns with one good arm. When he took off his pads the end of his clavicle was sticking up under the skin of his left shoulder.

At the hospital, doctors found severe damage to Wes's left acromioclavicular joint, the part of the shoulder that helps raise the arm. The shoulder hung three or four inches below his right one. Full repair would require surgery, a cadaver ligament, and a recovery of six to eight weeks. But a doctor told the Leonards that Wes could put it off until after basketball season if he strengthened the shoulder with physical therapy. He might even return to football before then.

Now, against Hartford, Xavier had his chance to start at quarterback. Wes cheered from the sideline as Xavier completed passes of 37 and 43 yards and kept the game close into the fourth quarter. Hartford led 21–13 when Xavier took the Blackhawks down the field with less than a minute left. Fennville was in Hartford territory when he threw over the middle, across his body, without looking off the defender. The interception sealed the game. Xavier was inconsolable. He hurried to the bus to be alone with his failure.

Xavier gladly stepped aside when Wes came back after the next game. Even with a separated left shoulder, Wes seemed better than ever. He threw five touchdown passes against Bangor. Five more against Gobles. Seven touchdowns and 448 yards against Bloomingdale. In the big rematch with Hartford in the playoffs, after the Hartford fans displayed a Blackhawks effigy in a coffin, Wes completed 17 of 23 passes for 328 yards and four touchdowns—half of the yards and two of the touchdowns were to Xavier—and the Blackhawks quieted the Hartford fans with a 52–34 victory.

Fennville's loss on a bitter night to Montague in the round of 16 only hardened Wes's resolve to win a state basketball championship. At the start of the season he and Xavier agreed: they would finish that spring at the Breslin Center in East Lansing, playing together for the Class C state title.

In retrospect it seems absurd. The Blackhawks had no one resembling a center. They had only one consistent long-range shooter, Pete Alfaro, an unimposing sophomore who might have blown away in a strong wind. Their sixth man, Xavier, was playing his third-best sport in between doing the dishes and loads of laundry for a mother who could hardly get out of bed. They had just one starter over six-one: their point guard, Wes, who carried them with a busted shoulder and a swollen heart.

They were a blue-collar team for a blue-collar town, and with every win they lured more factory workers and fruit pickers into the gym. On March 3, as they prepared to face the formidable Bridgman Bees, who were 17-2, the Blackhawks stood at 19-0, one win from a perfect regular season.

If anyone on the court could outmuscle Wes that night it was Bridgman's Michael Kamp, a buzz-cut sharpshooter who looked like a member of Delta Force. The game boiled down to a one-on-one contest between them. Kamp won the first half. He hit a three from the right corner and another from the left to give Bridgman a 6–2 lead. Wes came back with a spinning pull-up jumper in the lane to make it 6–4. Kamp hit another long jumper in the second quarter, making it 26–15, and then faked Wes into the air and slipped past him on the baseline for a layup that made it 30–18. He had outscored Wes 12–7, and Bridgman led 35–24 at the break.

Jerry Lemmons, sitting with Gary Leonard, heard Gary say something like, "Wes keeps screwing around, we're gonna lose this game."

Still, Wes looked cool as he walked toward the locker room. He had two quarters left to preserve the winning streak.

3. Three Glorious Minutes

Later, when Gary and Jocelyn searched their memories for some outward sign of their son's declining health, they could find none. He never missed a game or complained about shortness of breath. In at least two games that winter, he had flulike symptoms but still played well. Even toward the end of the season he came home after every game to lift weights and jump rope. If there was pain in his heart, he kept it to himself. He had a cough and a sore throat the first week of March. But on the day of the Bridgman game he felt well enough to take on his friend and teammate DeMarcus McGee in a dunk contest, during which he bounced the ball off the backboard and jammed it home.

If Wes's normal appearance was an illusion made possible by his supreme tolerance for pain, one might conclude he was too tough for his own good. Pain, after all, is the body's alarm system.

But it's also possible that he felt just fine. His illness could have remained asymptomatic until the moment it became catastrophic.

Here's how Jeffrey Towbin, chief of pediatric cardiology at Cincinnati Children's Hospital, explains it. Although the doctor who performed the autopsy thought a previous viral infection might have caused the scar tissue, Towbin and other prominent cardiologists reviewed the report and reached a different conclusion: Wes Leonard was probably born with a rare genetic mutation that slowly weakened the bonds among the muscle cells in his heart. The technical term is arrythmogenic right ventricular cardiomyopathy. It's unusual enough—affecting perhaps one person in every 5,000—that the average doctor probably wouldn't recognize it. Over the years this defective gene caused the thin walls of his right ventricle to get even thinner. It thinned the left ventricle too. In the final months fat and scar tissue replaced so much muscle that the heart's electrical forces were disrupted. It couldn't maintain a regular beat.

Under this theory, Wes Leonard's heart went from all to nothing like a collapsing bridge. The bridge holds up for years, slowly worn down by the weight of cars and the ravages of weather. Bolts quietly work loose. A billion vehicles cross without incident. And then, one rush hour, it all falls into the river.

Hearts, like bridges, can be inspected to prevent failure. But the issue is less simple than it sounds. Heart examinations come in several forms. The cheapest and most common, the electrocardiogram, can detect one set of problems and miss a second set and even falsely diagnose a third. If Wes Leonard had taken an electrocardiogram on the day of his last game, it might have found nothing wrong. Other tests exist—the echocardiogram, the cardiac MRI—but they're expensive and less practical to administer on a massive scale.

Although Wes's genetic disease was very rare, it culminated in a terribly common event called sudden cardiac arrest. About 900 Americans die from it every day. And many of those deaths could be prevented with a machine called an automatic external defibrillator. The defibrillator is a portable box of electricity that can shock a quivering heart back into rhythmic pumping. It costs about $1,200. In theory anyone can use it—even a person with no medical training—because it analyzes the patient's heartbeat, gives step-by-step instructions in a computerized voice, and refuses to deliver a shock unless it determines a shock is actually needed.

Victims of sudden cardiac arrest almost always stand a better chance of survival if they're defibrillated within 10 minutes.

When Wes Leonard collapsed at Fennville High School on the night of March 3, 2011, there was a defibrillator in the building, perhaps 50 feet from the gym.

Xavier watched the start of the second half from his usual place on the bench. The coach liked Xavier's frantic energy and his three-point stroke, but his shot was off that night. Other Blackhawks were cold too, which meant Wes had to lead the comeback. He cut the lead to seven with a lovely midrange jumper in Michael Kamp's face. Wes pumped his fist and looked at his coach, who was yelling something, and that momentary distraction gave Kamp a chance to blaze down the right sideline and beat Wes for a layup. Bridgman led 37–28. Game on.

The two rivals carried on a respectful conversation during their battle. "Nice box-out," Wes said. Kamp hit a three in Wes's face to make it 43–37. Wes rattled in a fadeaway: 43–39. Wes drilled one from the top of the key. At the end of the third quarter, Bridgman's 11-point lead had dwindled to three.

Kamp tightened up his defense in the fourth, putting a left hand on Wes's rib cage, swiping at the ball with his right. Other Fennville players stepped up, giving the Blackhawks a brief lead

before Kamp's twisting runner off the glass put Bridgman ahead
53–52 with about 2:30 left. Fennville hit a free throw to tie it, and
then Bridgman burned nearly two minutes on its final possession.
Bellowing sounds came from the Fennville crowd. A Bridgman
player missed a three at the buzzer. The game spilled into overtime.

Wes Leonard scored 19 points in regulation. Michael Kamp
scored 20.

In overtime both teams played with an air of exhaustion. They'd
put up just two points each by the time Fennville came down for its
final possession. Kamp followed Wes in lockstep. Fennville coach
Ryan Klingler called time-out with 56 seconds on the clock. The
fans raised a deafening chant.

"BLACK-hawk POW-er!" *Clap-clap, clap-clap-clap.*

"BLACK-hawk POW-er!" *Clap-clap, clap-clap-clap.*

There was little mystery in the play Coach Klingler would be
calling. Some variation on getting the ball to Wes and getting out
of the way.

In the other huddle Bridgman coach Mike Miller switched
from a man defense to a trapping 1-3-1 zone. He hoped it would
disrupt Fennville's rhythm, and maybe it did, but it had this side
effect: Michael Kamp would no longer be Wes Leonard's shadow.

Fennville ran 25 seconds off the clock before Wes caught a pass
on the left wing, well behind the three-point line, with about 30
seconds remaining. Then the Bridgman defenders made two crucial mistakes. One, they seemed to relax, believing that Fennville
would hold for a shot in the final five seconds. Two, they missed a
rotation on the back side of the zone, leaving an open lane to the
basket.

Wes leaned in and charged. By the time he executed a flaw-
less crossover from left to right, he was approaching the foul line.
The defenders swarmed in, too late. He already had the angle to
the front of the rim. On the bench Xavier saw Wes take off and
thought he would throw down a dunk. No need. Wes dropped in
a finger roll, net cords rippling, and Maria shrieked her approval
with the other Fennville women. The Blackhawks led 57–55 with
25 seconds left.

Kamp had one more chance to surpass his rival: a clean look at
a three from the right wing. It felt right leaving his hand, and it
looked good sailing past the clock, 1.5, 1.4, 1.3.

Later, looking back, he was glad he missed it.

The ball hit the front rim, bounced high above the white square on the backboard and then fell away, nicking the distant edge of the rim as the buzzer sounded. The regular season was over, and the Blackhawks stood at 20-0. Wes Leonard's moment had begun.

No: the moment belonged to the whole town. Roughly 1,300 people in that overheated room held a share of it. Jerry and Gary hugged each other and tried not to fall off the bleachers. A boy danced and flailed with a pair of pom-poms while girls jumped around in their fleecy boots. A middle-aged woman raised her cell phone toward the ceiling and shivered, her straw-colored hair bouncing off her cheek. Maria Flores temporarily forgot about the pain in her neck. An unemployed welder named Terry Collins forgot about his daily voyage through the Help Wanted ads, and the feeling he got when his two teenage daughters asked him for spending money he didn't have. Elsewhere in the stands, Mike George forgot about the brief period in which he lost his wife, his truck-driving job, and part of his leg, to cancer. His friend Jayson Hicks was too busy jumping and screaming to think about the rare nerve disease that prevented him from buttoning his own shirts, or the snow-tubing accident that had paralyzed his wife from the chest down.

The charged air in the room seemed to briefly interfere with the perception of time itself, so that one participant thought the moment lasted barely 30 seconds while another felt it unspooling for as long as 15 minutes. In truth Wes probably had about three minutes. He roared and clenched his fists when the buzzer sounded but did not run or jump like his teammates. Calmly, almost casually, he strolled to midcourt and joined his friends. A small boy jumped to touch his shoulder blades. An older man put a hand on the small of his back. He lined up to shake hands with the other team. The Blackhawks huddled for a brief word from their coach. Two teammates lifted Wes off the floor, and he smiled down at Xavier.

"Great game," Xavier said. He would later say he felt on top of the world right then, even though he'd made no real contribution to the victory. He was Wes Leonard's best friend and fellow Blackhawk, and that was enough.

No one knows why it happened then. One prominent doctor thinks the glorious surge of adrenaline could have pushed Wes's heart to the breaking point. Another insists the circumstances were merely coincidental. The precise timing of sudden cardiac arrest has always been a mystery. Just after Wes's teammates set him down and just before Xavier could wrap him in a hug, Wes's knees buckled. He crashed to the floor.

Xavier felt everything slowing down, his field of vision narrowing. He ran to the bleachers and found Gary and Jocelyn and told them their son was down. Someone got on the public-address system and ordered spectators out of the gym. Coach Klingler took Xavier and the other Blackhawks to the locker room to get them out of the way. One boy cried on the floor in a fetal position. In the visitors' locker room the Bridgman Bees, realizing that something had gone wrong in the gym, stood in a circle and prayed.

Maria saw her son running and hobbled over to join the crowd. The gym had gone quiet. Wes lay gasping for air on the floor, his feet twitching. Gary knelt next to Wes and Jocelyn stood over him. Unsure what else to do, they called out desperate encouragement: "Come on, Wes!" Some people from the crowd with basic medical training thought it was heat exhaustion, so they took off Wes's shoes and socks, opened the doors, cooled him with ice. An emergency-room nurse named Victoria Barnes was cleaning the concessions stand when her husband told her Wes had collapsed. She ran to the gym, checked his pulse, and called for the defibrillator. She thought there was still a chance it could shock his heart back into rhythm before it stopped forever.

Amber Lugten, the high school principal, ran out of the gym to an empty office and found the defibrillator in a pile of unused athletic supplies. It had once hung on the wall in a hallway but was put away and nearly forgotten after too many students tampered with the case. Lugten picked it up and ran to the gym, where Barnes applied the pads to Wes's chest and waited for the robotic voice to guide her. But the machine made no sound. The battery was dead.

4. The Substitute

There was silence at first when the coach asked his boys what he had to ask. They were gathered at his house to commiserate over pizza while hiding from the satellite trucks. Wes had been gone less than 48 hours, long enough to draw attention from media around the world, and now the boys had to decide whether or not they would play on without him.

No, Xavier finally said.

No: Wes was their season. It lived and died with him. They coexisted in perfection. They should be buried together, undisturbed, in a field west of town, by a wall of maples, under a heart-shaped headstone.

No? Let's ask his parents, someone said.

Gary and Jocelyn were mourning in their house with the television off when Coach Klingler came to call.

Yes, Jocelyn said, without hesitation.

Yes: Wes would have wanted them to play. No matter the sport, he always wanted one more game. If he could play football with a busted shoulder and basketball with a double-sized heart, his fellow Blackhawks could play through a few tears.

Xavier and some other players slept at the Leonards' house for the next week or so, up the dogleg hallway from the carpeted garage gym with the indoor hoop where he and Wes used to play in their socks. They spent time with Wes's 13-year-old brother, Mitchell, who played on the Fennville junior high basketball team. Xavier slept all he could, just to turn his mind off, because he knew his days as sixth man were over. It was a simple matter of subtraction. On Monday the boy who wanted to bury the season would replace his best friend in the starting lineup.

If Maria could wait three bone-aching hours in line for tickets at the Hope College field house, afraid of being trampled, begging people not to jostle her, conspiring with her younger son to hustle for a good seat, as if it were the Oklahoma land rush—

If Gary and Jocelyn could show their faces for the television cameras with their 16-year-old son not yet in the ground—

If the Trappist monks of New Melleray Abbey in rural Iowa could build a walnut casket from their own sustainable forest and send it free of charge 365 miles to Fennville in a minivan that drove through the night—

If the opposing Lawrence Tigers could look at Wes in that casket one day and still try to beat his team the next—

Then maybe Xavier could hold it together.

His stomach churned as he knelt before the scorer's table, waiting to check in as a ceremonial substitute. No matter: everyone knew he was starting at point guard, just as Wes would have done.

Nine boys stood at midcourt, wiping dust from the soles of their shoes.

The substitution buzzer sounded.

Now entering the game for the Fennville Blackhawks, number 33, Xavier—

Applause drowned out the announcer's voice. Xavier had never heard such a crowd: about 3,500 people, more than double the population of Fennville, most of them screaming for the Blackhawks.

Xavier looked shaky on the first possession, after Fennville won the tip. He nearly lost the dribble at the top of the key. But after an awkward series of passes he found Pete Alfaro open in the left corner for a three. Fennville 3–0. The crowd roared.

Then, after Lawrence responded with a basket, Xavier was called for carrying the ball. He kept picking up his dribble too soon. He threw a clumsy pass that a defender knocked away. He back-rimmed an open three. He threw another tipped pass. Even as his teammates—Alfaro, Adam Siegel, DeMarcus McGee, Reid Sexton—fought through the grief and played above themselves, Xavier fell apart. He threw a ridiculous one-handed pass from midcourt that was easily stolen by a Lawrence defender. He played lazy defense and let a Lawrence player hit a three in his face. Finally, after Xavier committed a two-shot foul, Coach Klingler mercifully pulled him out.

"I don't wanna play anymore," Xavier said, starting toward the locker room.

The coach grabbed his arm. "If Jocelyn and Gary can be strong for you," he said, "you can be strong for them and stay on the bench."

Xavier sat down and sobbed.

About 15 rows back, where he sat holding his wife, Gary Leonard thought, *This was a mistake.* Next fall he would work up the courage to attend a Blackhawks football game, in what would have been his son's senior season at quarterback, and make it partway through the national anthem before leaving in a panic to sit in his truck. And then he would come back the next week and find a way to sit through the whole song.

Down on the bench, as the basketball game went on, Coach Klingler put a brawny arm around Xavier. "If you don't wanna go back out there, you don't have to," he said. Xavier lowered his head. The court reflected a grid of searing white lights.

Next to Gary, Jocelyn looked down at Xavier and wished she could hold him in her arms. Letters from other bereaved parents were rolling in. Across America, a trail of enlarged and broken hearts: a football lineman in Nebraska, a wrestler in Oregon, a basketball player in Georgia, a swimmer right there in Michigan, and on and on. Illinois, Iowa, Kentucky, Ohio. A defibrillator might have saved them, just as it might have saved Wes. Jocelyn blamed herself. She thought she'd been too slow, too indecisive, too uninformed. Well, never again. By summer she would be running a foundation to give schools and sports teams brand-new defibrillators and the training for their proper use. It would be called the Wes Leonard Heart Team. She would carry a defibrillator in her car and stand before group after group of teachers and coaches, showing them how to save lives by showing them how Fennville lost Wes. *This is what I did wrong,* she would say, the scene playing again and again like a movie in her head.

Maria looked down at her weeping son. When he was three years old, still rubbing her hair between his thumb and forefinger for comfort, Xavier got sick and had to stay in the hospital for three days. He was kept in a crib that looked like a cage. "Please, Mommy," he kept saying, "take me home." Now, with great effort, Maria stood up. She was going to take him home.

Weeks later, still bedridden on most days, Maria would receive a text message from Jocelyn inviting her to join the Wes Leonard Heart Team. This invitation would be her own defibrillator, the shock to bring her back into rhythm. Still too disabled to hold a regular job, she would make the Heart Team her volunteer occupation. Every day it would give her the strength to get out of bed.

Now, as she prepared to go get Xavier, someone asked her to sit down and give him a few more minutes. She did. The first quarter ended, with Lawrence leading 16–13. The fans chanted about Blackhawk power. They were still in the game for one reason: Siegel and McGee, two of Wes's best friends on the team, were playing like wild beasts.

A young assistant coach named Mike Raak put his arm around Xavier and tried to think of uplifting words. "He's here with you," the coach said. Xavier thought about Wes. They used to play in three-on-three tournaments in which players had to call their own fouls, and Wes never called a foul. It was a matter of principle. "If I can't take the pain, I'll just get out of the game," he'd say. Once the opponents realized they could get away with anything, they would hang on his arms every time he went near the hoop. Still, no call. He desperately wanted to win, but in those games he seemed to want something else even more: proof that he was strong enough to fight through anything.

The second quarter started. Jayson Hicks watched Xavier from across the court. With his paralyzed wife and his nerve disease, Jayson knew a few things about pain. Five years earlier, when the doctor cut off his lower right leg, he declined the epidural so he could get home sooner and see his kids. Now Jayson looked at Xavier and willed him to stand up. It had nothing to do with the final score. Jayson imagined Xavier at age 30, looking back on the biggest moment in his life and wishing he'd fought a little harder.

Xavier sat there, cubical scoreboard flashing above him, 3,500 fans roaring around him, the sneakers of other boys singing like birds on the polished wood at his feet. The burden of perfection was too great.

The Blackhawks would ride an emotional roller coaster for 11 days. They would beat Lawrence and then Bangor and then Covert, reaching the regional semifinals before losing by 24 points to Schoolcraft, the eventual state champion. Xavier would blame himself for failing in a task he never wanted.

That fall, with Wes gone, Xavier would get his chance to be the finest three-sport athlete in Fennville. He would start at quarterback, go down with a shoulder injury, come back as a receiver, and finally quit with one game left in a dismal season. He would join the basketball team late after threatening to quit. Once in a while he would walk into the gym, the last place he saw Wes, and feel on his skin a mild charge of electricity.

But as he sat on the bench in the second quarter with his team trailing by four points to the Lawrence Tigers, Xavier knew none of that. Nor did he know he was about to play the finest game of the season, with 11 points in the fourth quarter and 18 altogether, or that he'd come back two nights later and pour in 25, or that his playoff scoring average would nearly match the regular-season average of the all-state point guard who at this moment was back in

Fennville, in a lonely chapel, surrounded by Trappist-cut walnut, wearing his warm-up jacket.

No, Xavier didn't know what was next. What he knew was this: six minutes remained in the second quarter, and the season was still perfect, and the Blackhawks needed someone to step in for the boy they would bury tomorrow.

Xavier stood up.

CHRIS BALLARD

Mourning Glory

FROM SPORTS ILLUSTRATED

WHY DID HE TURN onto Lappans Road?

That's what Zach Lucas wondered as he watched the silver Honda S-2000 driven by his best friend, Brendon Colliflower, veer to the right on the way back from the senior prom just before midnight on Saturday, May 5. Everyone knew the faster route was Downsville Pike, with its wide lanes and broad shoulder. *Oh, well,* Zach thought, *who knows with Brendon?*

After all, Brendon wasn't like most kids in Williamsport, a town of about 2,100 in the northwest corner of Maryland, just across the border from West Virginia. Hemmed in by interstates, it's a place young people dream of leaving, a town on the way to everywhere but seldom a destination. Here U.S. flags dot porches, families swim in the muddy green Potomac River by the power plant, and jobs have been scarce since the leather tannery shut down eight years back. It's a baseball-mad hamlet where adults sit in their pickup trucks beyond the left-field fence at Williamsport High and where the local newspaper streams Little League state tournament games on its website. A place where someone like Brendon, the 2011 all-county pitcher of the year, can become a hero.

Brendon was the rare high school ace who "pitched backward," relying on his precipitous curveball rather than his fastball to start off each hitter. But more than that set him apart. Tall and skinny, with fine, almost elfin features, he wore crisp Nike T-shirts and spotless Air Max shoes while his friends sported sleeveless camo and cutoff jeans. He went to all the parties but didn't drink, seeming both younger and older than 17. On Saturdays, when the other baseball players trolled for catfish, dips wedged into their lower lips, Brendon instead wandered the banks, hurling rocks over the hulking power plant. Life was too short to sit on a plastic bucket all day.

On May 5, though, he wanted to stretch out the night forever. So if Brendon took a longer route back from Shepherdstown, West Virginia, if he dallied for the sake of dallying, it was with good reason, for Sam sat next to him. With dark blond hair and large blue eyes, Samantha Kelly was homecoming queen and the star of the volleyball team. She mingled with adults as easily as with teenagers and took to Twitter not to gossip but to post maxims such as *Don't be afraid to stand up for what you believe in.* That she'd chosen Brendon—the kid who'd never had a serious girlfriend, who'd been shy and a bit of a goofball much of his life—came as a surprise to many. She attended all his games, and she was the only girl allowed when the players gathered at the Waffle House on Saturday mornings to eat syrup-drenched chocolate-chip waffles and fire spitballs. Brendon's teammates teased him—"She's too good for you," they'd joke, or "You better wife her up"—but they all saw how happy he was.

Now, driving home from the prom with Sam, she in a blue strapless dress and he in a white suit with a powder-blue tie, Brendon must have been exhilarated to rocket through the countryside, windows open to the warm spring air. From Lappans he turned left onto Sharpsburg Pike and then left again onto Rench Road, which wound through darkened farmland, with only grass and trees abutting the white lines. As they crossed the railroad tracks, Brendon accelerated. If he saw the yellow sign at the top of a small hill, the one that read 30 MPH with a left arrow, he didn't heed it.

Five hours later the cell phone of Williamsport High baseball coach David Warrenfeltz beeped, jolting him from an uneasy sleep. Upon grabbing the phone, he saw a backlog of text messages and missed calls and felt nauseated with fear. Please, not again, he thought, remembering a call he received at this time of the night three years earlier. That one was about Nick.

The two had met in 1994, on the baseball field, when David was seven years old. Though neither tall nor strong, David was the son of a coach, the kind of smart, unassuming player who would earn the tag of *gamer.* Nick Adenhart was the opposite, the boy the coaches talked about in low, admiring whispers. Whereas most kids threw in loops and arcs at that age, Nick reared back and cracked the mitt. Plenty of kids were afraid to catch him, but not David. Over the next half-dozen years the two would be a tandem, the cocky right-hander and the smaller kid known to many only as Nick's catcher. They spent summers long-tossing, Nick pushing to throw from farther each time. Later David would look back on this time and credit two men with instilling in him the love of baseball: his father and Nick.

By the time Nick and David reached Williamsport High, Nick a class ahead, they were two of the best players on the team. But even though David was good, a savvy defensive catcher with in-the-gap power, he was nothing like Nick. By the spring of Nick's junior year, in 2003, major league scouts were flocking to his starts. They weren't disappointed; Nick's fastball was clocked as high as 95 miles per hour. The *Washington Post* sent a feature writer to see him, the local cable channel carried two of Williamsport's games, and *Baseball America* dubbed Nick the top prospect in the country.

Then, in the final regular-season game of his senior year, Nick blew out his right elbow. Playing DH, he still led Williamsport to the state finals, nearly winning the school's first title since 1975. After the season, he needed Tommy John surgery; as a result he dropped from a top-five pick in the 2004 draft to the 14th round, where the Angels chose him.

It took five years, but Adenhart regained his velocity, and he entered the 2009 season as the Angels' third starter. On April 8, in his season debut, he threw six scoreless innings against the As. Back home in Maryland, an overflow crowd watched at the Buffalo Wild Wings in Hagerstown. Afterward, in the Anaheim clubhouse, Nick hugged his father, Jim, then headed out with three friends to celebrate. A couple of hours later, shortly after midnight in nearby Fullerton, a drunk driver in a minivan ran a red light and broad-sided the Mitsubishi Eclipse in which Adenhart was traveling. Two of his friends were killed instantly; the third survived with seri-ous injuries. Adenhart died two hours later at a local hospital. He was 22.

Warrenfeltz, by then a senior catcher at Maryland–Baltimore County, received the news when his cell phone woke him at 5:23 A.M. He'd stayed up late watching the game on TV and planned on calling Adenhart in the morning to congratulate him. Now

Warrenfeltz was devastated. For eight hours he sobbed, inconsolable.

In Williamsport hundreds of people gathered at the high school field that day. Later 1,500 people showed up at Adenhart's memorial. A shrine was fashioned at the field, a framed Adenhart Angels jersey was hung in the Buffalo Wild Wings, and the Little League diamond in nearby Halfway, Maryland—where Nick and David played growing up—was renamed Nicholas James Adenhart Memorial Field.

In the months that followed, Warrenfeltz was haunted by his friend's death. He wrestled with why this happened to Adenhart, not to him—why he was allowed to keep playing baseball when Nick couldn't. Even years later Warrenfeltz would be driving and suddenly have to pull over, tears blurring his vision. Maybe that helps explain why he returned home after finishing college, to make a life in the place his friends once dreamed of leaving. Why he became a coach.

When Warrenfeltz was hired to lead the Williamsport program in 2011, some of the locals grumbled—at 23, he wasn't much older than the players, and his only coaching experience was one season of jayvee. Heck, they said, Warrenfeltz even *looks* like one of the players: baby-faced, with short brown hair, freckles, and an unimposing build. He didn't act like a player, though; during his first season Warrenfeltz remade the program, stressing discipline and structure. He posted a daily practice schedule broken into 10-minute intervals and drilled the team on fundamentals, from pick-offs to bunt defense to footwork on outfield throws. "Do the small things, and it'll lead to bigger things," he told the boys, sounding an awful lot like his father, Dave, a math teacher and former baseball coach at North Hagerstown High who valued ethics over flash, hard work over talent. The Wildcats, a sub-.500 team before Warrenfeltz, caught fire. They finished the 2011 season 17-5 and, behind Brendon's pitching, advanced all the way to the state semifinals.

Warrenfeltz rarely talked about Adenhart, but he didn't need to. The boys had watched Adenhart pitch, and when he died, they'd grieved too, if in a different way. Warrenfeltz had lost a friend; they'd lost a hero. So if their coach seemed stricter than he needed to be, they understood. Like at the beginning of the 2012 season, when Warrenfeltz suspended five of the team's best

players, including Brendon, for being out late at a St. Patrick's
Day house party that was broken up by police. It didn't matter that
Brendon hadn't been drinking or that none of the players were
arrested. To Warrenfeltz, it was about making good decisions.

Some parents, including Brendon's father, Chad, didn't like the
suspensions. The boys would miss the games against Walkersville, a
powerhouse, and rival North Hagerstown. The Wildcats had been
moved up to Class 2A, making them the smallest school in the
West region; they could ill afford to start 0-2. Yet they did, getting
blown out in both games. From there it went downhill. Four key
players got injured. Zach Lucas, the team's first baseman and best
hitter, went into a slump. Even Brendon struggled, giving up six
runs in three innings against Brunswick the day before the prom.
Heading into the playoffs, the Wildcats were 9-9-1 and had lost
their final three games by a combined score of 31–3. All the promise of the previous season—the trip to the state semis, the magical
team chemistry—had dissipated. The players were frustrated and
the parents angry.

Warrenfeltz might have tried to sweet-talk the critics, but that
wasn't his style. Meticulous and stoic, he spent hours reflecting,
*Did I get the most out of practice today? Could I be reaching this player
more effectively? How am I preparing these young men for the rest of their
lives?* Which is why, on the Friday of prom week, he'd gathered the
boys in the locker room and urged them to be safe on Saturday
night. "Have fun, but be careful," he said, "and don't do anything
to jeopardize yourselves, the team, or anyone around you. See you
on Monday for the game."

But now here it was, 5:20 A.M. after prom night, and his phone
was lighting up. Warrenfeltz didn't want to listen to the messages,
wanted to freeze the moment before he heard the bad news. He
called back the first number he saw. "It's Brendon," catcher Ryan
Butts said when he picked up. "He's been in a car accident. I'm
sorry, Coach."

Within 24 hours the police would reveal that Brendon had taken
the curve too fast and lost control, sending the S-2000 careering
into a tree head-on. Later, toxicology reports would confirm what
Chad Colliflower had known from the start: neither Brendon nor
Sam had been drinking or under the influence of drugs.

None of that mattered at the moment, though. All that mattered was what Ryan was now telling Warrenfeltz: Brendon and Sam were dead. It had happened again.

Grief washed over Warrenfeltz. He thought of the families, the school, and the town. More than anything, though, he thought about his team. The players would be looking to him for guidance, to explain the unexplainable. At 5:45, Warrenfeltz began calling his assistants. Then, just before sunrise, he sent a text message to all the players. All it said was, "I love you guys. I'll be at the field if you need me."

One by one the players arrived on Sunday morning: Zach with his father, center fielder Tyler Nally with his dad, first baseman Tyler Byers with his parents. Some of the boys had known for hours; others were just finding out. Of all the players it was Zach, the sturdy, power-hitting senior, who had borne the greatest load during the night. He'd been the first player to arrive at the scene of the accident, the one who woke Chad Colliflower with a phone call and drove to tell Ryan the news.

As the sun rose on a clear spring day, more cars pulled up: parents, friends, other students and alumni, more than 150 people in all. They came to the field, as they had after Adenhart's death, because it seemed the right place to go. Some stood around the mound, others lingered in the dugout with Warrenfeltz and his wife, Stephanie. That the town came out wasn't surprising. Everyone knew Brendon and Sam, just as everybody had known Nick. Their successes were communal successes. That's why those men parked their pickups in the grass beyond left field, sometimes three trucks deep, drinking tallboys and honking when the Wildcats scored.

Warrenfeltz thought about this when he finally left the field on Sunday around 1:00 P.M. He was conflicted. Monday's game, the last of the regular season, would be canceled. Should the team even practice? Would it be wrong to play baseball now? Or wrong not to? Needing counsel, he headed where he'd always gone: his parents' house. Only when he arrived, he was shocked to see who was sitting in the living room.

It was by a fluke that Nick's mom, Janet Gigeous, was in town that day. It had been years since she and Nick's father had separated. She spent most of the year in Florida now, but she still had ties to Williamsport and had come up for the weekend with her husband, Duane. Which is how Janet, one of the only people on the planet who knew what Warrenfeltz was going through, came to be at his father's house that afternoon.

For an hour the six of them talked and grieved: Janet and Duane, David's parents, and David and Stephanie, a tall, lanky former lacrosse player who'd been with him the day Adenhart died, back when she was David's girlfriend.

By the time David left, he knew what he needed to do. He sent a text to the boys. There would be no practice on Monday, it said, but he and the other coaches would be at the field after school.

What Zach Lucas remembers most is how quiet it was at school on Monday. Most students didn't even go to class; they just huddled near the gym, where an impromptu shrine to Brendon and Sam grew on the cork bulletin board: photos of Sam in her familiar number 2 volleyball shirt, of Brendon in a goofy pose when he entered a Ping-Pong tournament, of the two of them at the prom. Everywhere Zach looked he saw flowers, many of them blue or white, the school colors.

At 3:15 P.M. Warrenfeltz made his way down to the field. To an outsider it wasn't much to look at: bumpy green grass bordered by chain-link fencing, two concrete dugouts with skinny benches and, off each foul line, a set of metal bleachers. The tiny pressroom behind home plate, up a set of vertiginous wood steps, was hot and dark. Regardless, Warrenfeltz loved it there. He went to the field two or three times a day in the summer and at 3:00 P.M. during the school year, after he finished his day job as a third-grade teacher at Fountaindale Elementary. He turned on the sprinklers and planted seeds, locking the fence during the summer so kids didn't tear up the surface. If it began to rain, he could make it from his house in seven minutes flat to lay out the tarps. And on the rare occasions that he traveled out of town, he left a list of tasks for his father to perform. As he sometimes joked, "Since I don't have any children yet, this is kind of like my child."

Fifteen minutes after Warrenfeltz arrived, the players began to trickle in. Some, like senior Tyler Byers, had shut down completely. Others, like Tyler's brother, Colby, a talented freshman backup catcher, kept asking why this had happened. Warrenfeltz gathered them in the dugout. "The most important thing I want to say to you guys is this: however you feel is however you feel," he said. "If you're devastated to the point where you just need to sit down by yourself, away from everybody, that's fine. There's no timetable here, no way you're supposed to be feeling on this day or that day."

For the next two hours and each of the following two after-noons, the boys just hung out at the field. Some, like Ryan Butts and Tyler Nally, followed their usual routine—dressing, hitting off the tee—because they needed the structure and the distraction. Others sat in silence. A few threw the ball around; others played home run derby. Just being together anchored them. All season long the players had been exceptionally close. They'd gone out to eat together, fished together on Saturdays, and walked the school hallways in clusters of six or seven. In the days after the accident, though, they became a family. On Sunday night Tyler Byers slept at outfielder Brandon Greene's house for comfort. Sunday morn-ing, at the field, the freshmen had cried on the shoulders of the seniors. Watching this, Warrenfeltz realized the question wasn't whether they should keep playing but for how long they could. Every day they were together was precious.

There was only one problem: the playoff schedule. Williamsport was slated to play on Friday afternoon, during Brendon's viewing.

Warrenfeltz called Williamsport's athletic director, Stan Stouffer, who called the state office and explained the situation. The Wild-cats were given a choice: they could play on Friday afternoon or at 2:00 P.M. on Saturday. That wasn't much better, though; Bren-don's funeral was at 11:00 that morning. *Can we push the game back to Monday?* Warrenfeltz asked. The state office balked. It couldn't hold up the whole tournament for one team.

Torn, Warrenfeltz called Brendon's grandparents. They had helped raise him while Chad, who lived with the boy after splitting with his mother, Amy, worked 11-hour days as an X-ray technolo-gist at an outpatient facility in Leesburg, an hour away. He asked them one question: *Should we play?*

Gail Colliflower answered immediately: *You have to.*

The line of cars heading to Brendon's funeral stretched for nearly a mile, so that the Williamsport police closed down one lane of traffic and turned it into a parking strip. By 12:30 on Saturday, hundreds of people had gathered at Greenlawn Memorial Park cemetery as Brendon was buried in his blue number 6 Wildcats jersey. The morning was warm but hazy, and midway through the ceremony somebody pointed to the sky. Soon enough everyone was looking up, for there, circling the sun, was a rainbow. To Chad, it looked like a halo.

At one, the Wildcats said their final good-byes, laying their hands on their friend's casket and chanting, "One-two-three, Brendon!" Then they drove the half-mile to the field. They had less than 45 minutes to warm up. They changed into their uniforms in their cars and jogged to the field. More than a few still had tearstained faces.

It had been more than a week since the Wildcats had practiced. They were without their best player and star pitcher. Many parents wondered if their boys could even play. But even though the opponent, ninth-seeded Wheaton High of Silver Spring, was winless—in Maryland every team makes the playoffs—there is no way to explain what happened next.

The Wildcats hit with a power that had been missing all season. Tyler Byers drove in two runs; so did Brandon Greene. Zach crushed a home run that soared to where Warrenfeltz's grandmother, who preferred to watch the game in her car, was parked, 410 feet from home plate. As she scooted out of the way, the shot shattered her windshield, a piece of glass piercing the ball. The final score was 22–0. More astonishing, four Williamsport pitchers had combined to throw a no-hitter.

Afterward no one wanted to leave the field. The parents brought sandwiches and sodas and chips. Unable to stomach food before or immediately after the funeral, the hungry players scarfed it down. All around were the trappings of the day: the white rose that was on the mound before the game, the remnants of the spray-painted 2 and 6 next to it, the signs and flowers on the fence, the string from the 80 blue-and-white helium balloons that parents sent into the sky during a pregame moment of silence. All afternoon people approached and hugged Chad Colliflower, including players, something he never expected from 16- and 17-year-old boys, who usually find it so hard to hug another man. He saw people he hadn't seen in 20 years and old, red-nosed guys he'd seen only down on the corner but who were suddenly wearing Williamsport blue. Chad later said, "I never felt so much love in my life."

Before the game many of the boys had worried that they

shouldn't be playing. Now something flipped inside them. Zach had a feeling of empowerment—he was now in control. As for Warrenfeltz, he called his father that night and said of his team, "I just want more time to be together, that's all."

He knew that was unlikely, though. The Wildcats were slated to play again in two days, and Warrenfeltz had seen the brackets.

On Monday it rained, granting Williamsport a one-day reprieve. Tuesday brought no such luck. At 1:30 P.M. the Wildcats piled onto the bus, bound for Liberty. The top seed in the West region, Liberty boasted the best pitcher in Class 2A, Andrew Massey, whose arsenal included an 88-mile-per-hour fastball and a devastating 83-mile-per-hour cutter. This should have been the big showdown: Colliflower versus Massey. Now the Wildcats would be hard-pressed to keep it close.

For two seasons Warrenfeltz had relied on his ace in big games. Now he had to make a choice. There was Tyler Byers, the headstrong, wiseass country boy who threw exclusively fastballs, which wasn't such a bad thing considering they arrived at 87 miles per hour. Unfortunately, Tyler had taken a line drive on the ankle while pitching two weeks earlier. Assistant coach Kyle Lewis suspected the ankle was fractured, but there was no way Tyler's father, Mick, a demanding but loving man who put baseball right after God and country, was taking him to the doctor and no way Tyler would have gone. In the meantime Warrenfeltz had moved Tyler from first base to DH to keep his bat in the lineup.

That left Warrenfeltz with one option: he needed Zach to take the mound. Zach was a hitter first, a pitcher by necessity. For the season he had a 4.68 ERA and 22 strikeouts in $33^{2}/_{3}$ innings. He possessed neither a great fastball nor much of a curve.

What Zach did have was desire. The oldest son of a nurse and a cable-company engineer, he had been shy and chubby as an underclassman, but the summer after his sophomore year he began lifting weights. Week by week he added muscle to his five-foot-nine, 180-pound frame, becoming more confident. As a junior he set the team single-season record for RBIs. He also began spending more time with Brendon. The two were in some ways opposites, Zach struggling with his weight while the rail-thin Brendon went to the Waffle House and ordered a sausage-and-egg cheese wrap with a waffle, a side of sausage, a side of bacon, and hash browns. Yet they were, as Lewis says, "the same kind of weird." Everything between them was an inside joke. But when Brendon took the mound, all that changed; out there he had a swagger, and the Wildcats fed off that confidence.

Now it fell to Zach to lead. So as he walked out to the mound against Liberty, he tried to act self-assured as Brendon always had, even if he knew he was overmatched. The afternoon before, Warrenfeltz had told the players what to expect emotionally. "All we are is a baseball team," he said. "We can't make this situation right. All we can do is make the best of what we can do."

That was going to be hard against Massey. He retired the side in order in the first, struck out the side in the second, and went 1-2-3 in the third. Meanwhile Liberty touched Zach for two runs. Usually a 2–0 lead didn't seem insurmountable, but with Massey on the mound, it did.

Then, in the top of the fourth inning, Tyler Nally got lucky. Or maybe Massey made a bad pitch. Either way the ball shot up the middle for a single. And, just like that, it began: a Liberty error; then Zach crushed a double to make it 2–1; an inning later Williamsport added three more runs, then another in the sixth to make it 5–3.

Heading into the bottom of the seventh and last inning, Williamsport clung to its two-run lead. Out to the mound walked Tyler Byers, bad ankle and all. Warrenfeltz had expected to use him for one inning at most. This would be his second. It showed. He hit one batter, gave up a double to another, and soon enough it was 5–4, with two outs and a runner on third. Tyler got ahead 0-and-2. The Liberty batter sent the next fastball screaming over the Williamsport dugout. Twice more Tyler threw heaters, and twice the batter fouled them off. If there were ever a time to call for a change-up, it was now. Warrenfeltz considered it, then gave the sign. Tyler reared back and unleashed an eye-high heater. The boy didn't stand a chance. He swung, and the umpire yelled, "Strike three!"

On the mound Tyler rejoiced, then looked up and raised one arm straight above his head, as if signaling a first down to the sky. All around him the Wildcats hugged and yelled. On the other side of the diamond Liberty coach Erik Barnes walked over to Warrenfeltz. "Great job," he said. "Now go on and win this thing."

*

Win it? Hell, Warrenfeltz was ecstatic just to have another day of practice. Yet two days later Williamsport won again, beating South Carroll 5–4 on a bases-loaded walk in the bottom of the seventh. The following afternoon, in the regional final, the Wildcats beat Century High of Sykesville 11–6. It was Williamsport's fourth game in six days, yet, improbably, the team was only getting better. During the regular season the boys had occasionally played selfishly, concentrating on putting up numbers and earning college scholarships. Now the chemistry was back. No one cared about anything except not being the guy who ended the season. In one game reserve Aaron Green came up with a huge pinch-hit RBI single. In another Nick Sauble pitched two much-needed innings. If there was a concern, it was over the team's bunting, in particular that of sophomore shortstop Brandon Toloso. Three times in the playoffs Warrenfeltz had asked Brandon to sacrifice, and three times he had failed.

With each win the buzz built. The NBC affiliate in Hagerstown, WHAG, featured Williamsport on the evening news. Players on eliminated teams told the Wildcats on Twitter: *Win this s—*. Williamsporters patted the boys on the back at the Waffle House, flew blue-and-white flags on their cars. The Wildcats were back in the state semis.

It was a bittersweet time for the Colliflowers. Chad, a youthful-looking 41, couldn't stop thinking that his son would have reveled in the moment. The two of them, occasionally mistaken for brothers, had gone to rock concerts together and played video games in Chad's two-bedroom apartment. "He really was my best friend," Chad says. Yet he was amazed by Brendon's patience and drive, unable to believe this was his son. "Don't be like me," he often told Brendon. "Be better than me."

So on Tuesday, May 22, when Williamsport traveled to College Park to face Loch Raven on Maryland's turf field, Chad was there. He stood and cheered when Zach took the mound, wearing Brendon's number stitched on his hat. Chad roared when, two innings later, Zach jacked a triple to right-center to give Williamsport a 2–0 lead. And he high-fived everyone when Tyler Byers closed out the 3–0 win.

That night the Wildcats headed to the Waffle House, as they always had. They sat in their favorite booths, near the counter, and antagonized the night waitress, Minnie, as they always did, dipping their napkins in their water glasses and firing wet fastballs at each other and the front windows, the gobs sticking on the glass for a moment before sliding down, the streaks looking from the outside like tears.

The same night, as the clock neared midnight, Warrenfeltz huddled in his living room with his assistants, eating from cartons of Chinese food and preparing for the title game. Earlier that day Warrenfeltz had sent two of them to scout the other semifinal, instructing them to track pitch location. Now the coaches broke down Williamsport's opponent, Patuxent, a southern Maryland powerhouse with a 19-4 record. Patuxent was the clear favorite, a deep, pitching-rich team that excelled at small ball. But as Lewis pointed out, "We're not good enough to be here in the first place, so let's not worry about that."

Two afternoons later, on May 26, the team boarded a charter bus—the first one the boys had been on—and headed two hours east to Ripken Stadium in Aberdeen, home to the Class A Iron-Birds, an Orioles affiliate. The Wildcats peered up at the ballpark's towering brick facade, then walked through the tunnel to the field, staring at the two decks of stands and the big video scoreboard. Later Lewis would compare the boys' reaction to "the awe of *Hoosiers* combined with the excitement of getting dropped off at Disneyland."

Presently Warrenfeltz gathered the team and talked again about bunt defense. For nearly an hour on the previous afternoon they'd practiced it: covering first, the wheel play, guarding the line. The players loved to complain about it, but Warrenfeltz didn't care. As his father always said, "You can't expect them to do something that they've never practiced." His dad said something else too: there's no way to defend against a well-executed squeeze play.

While the position players warmed up, Zach sat in the dugout, icing his left arm. He was the kid who didn't stretch, who needed only three warm-up pitches. Now, however, Zach's shoulder and elbow were rebelling. He'd loaded up on four ibuprofen, swabbed on Icy Hot, and taken herbal medicine. His arm still shook involuntarily, but he didn't care. Besides, his friend Tyler Byers was playing on an ankle that was so badly busted that Warrenfeltz had told him to not run out ground balls. Ryan Butts had recently shaken off the lingering effects of a concussion suffered during a home plate collision late in the season. And, somewhere up there, Brendon was watching him. Zach was damned if he was going to give up the ball.

Warrenfeltz saw a look of resolve on Zach's face that he'd never seen before. "How do you feel?" the coach asked.

"Horrible," Zach said, "but I'm not coming out until my five innings are up."

An hour later, when the boys took the field, Zach looked up at the stands and saw only blue and white. There was the Colliflower family and Ryan Butts's father and the regulars, all having driven two hours. But there were so many more: face-painted students wearing blue wigs, a line of girls with W-I-L-D-C-A-T-S on their bellies, a guy in a Nick Adenhart jersey, and old men he'd seen only down at Tony's Pizzeria in Williamsport. Then there were the signs: WILDCAT PRIDE and WIN FOR BRENDON #6. Zach had never played in a ballpark like this. He had one thought: Brendon would have loved this.

The first Patuxent batter stepped in, and Warrenfeltz held his breath. He had no idea whether Zach had anything left in the tank. When the first pitch rocketed in, dangerously high but as hard as he'd thrown all season, Warrenfeltz had a different thought: *Maybe he's too pumped up.* Then, on the next pitch, Zach floated a beautiful curveball. The Patuxent batter swung right through it, as if flailing at smoke. Warrenfeltz exhaled.

The game remained scoreless for two innings. Then, in the bottom of the third, Brandon Toloso ripped a sinking shot over the Patuxent first baseman's head for a double. A bunt moved Brandon to third, and then Tyler Nally, a skinny, determined senior whose father played on the Williamsport team that won the title in 1975, cracked one through the left side. One-zip, Wildcats.

Meanwhile Zach was throwing two to three miles per hour harder than he had all season. "It was," assistant Doug Stottlemyer later said, "like Brendon was living through him." Even so, Zach was running on fumes. The Wildcats needed a cushion.

In the bottom of the fourth Zach appeared to give it to them when he crushed a ball to deep center. In any other Class 2A park it would have been a home run. But in spacious Ripken Field the center fielder just kept backing up and finally caught the ball in front of the 404 sign. Then, in the fifth, the Wildcats failed to bring home a runner from third for the second time in the game. Two innings later, with Williamsport still holding a 1–0 lead, it came down to this: three outs and the Wildcats were state champions.

On the mound to close it out stood Tyler Byers, who'd come in for Zach in the sixth. As a power pitcher, he was well suited to closing. As a near cripple, he was not well suited to playing defense. The day before, Lewis had asked Warrenfeltz what he planned to do if teams saw they could bunt on Tyler. Said Warrenfeltz, "Let's hope they don't."

The first Patuxent batter singled, and everyone on the Williamsport bench knew what was coming next: small ball. Lewis again walked over to Warrenfeltz. "You want someone to start warming up in the pen?"

"If I wanted someone to warm up," Warrenfeltz said, "there would be someone down in the pen." After all the team had been through, there was no way the coach was walking out to the mound to remove Byers, and even if he did, there was no way Byers was giving up the ball.

The next batter bunted, and so did the next. There were now runners on first and third with one out. Warrenfeltz grimaced. He knew what was coming next, but it didn't matter: Patuxent laid down a perfect squeeze, the kind Warrenfeltz's dad always talked about. Tyler's only play was at first, and he made it. Now the game was tied. And still, Warrenfeltz left Tyler in. He struck out the next batter swinging.

In the bottom of the seventh the Wildcats went down in order. In the stands the Williamsport fans went silent. Stephanie Warrenfeltz felt so anxious that she thought she might throw up. Meanwhile, in the dugout, Warrenfeltz worried about Tyler. The kid was a gamer, but he hadn't pitched more than two innings in a row since hurting his ankle.

Somehow Tyler made it through the eighth and the top of the ninth, but with each pitch he looked more tired. Time was running out. Finally, in the bottom of the ninth, Byers poked one to left for a single. Immediately Warrenfeltz signaled down the bench to Tyler Martin, a junior whom everyone called Brett Gardner on account of his speed. Martin rarely hit or played the field, but he might have been the best pinch runner in Washington County. On the second pitch he took off—"like he had jets on his heels," remembers Stottlemyer—and swiped second. The next batter, Ryan Butts, sent a perfect bunt down the first-base line to get Martin to third with one out.

So here it was, the opportunity the Wildcats had waited for. An inning earlier Williamsport had stranded a runner at third, and Stottlemyer had told Warrenfeltz, "Next time that happens, we have to go out guns blazing." Now Warrenfeltz looked at Stottlemyer and nodded: time for the squeeze.

Nick Williams, a fine bunter, came to the plate, but Patuxent intentionally walked him. The next batter, Riley Arnone, was the only Wildcat who'd successfully laid down a squeeze that season. Patuxent walked him too, loading the bases with one out. Looking back, Warrenfeltz wonders if Patuxent had a scouting report because walking to the plate was Brandon Toloso, who was 0 for the playoffs on bunts, whom Warrenfeltz had put through an extra 10 minutes of bunting practice a day earlier, with decidedly mixed results.

There are moments that reveal a lot about a coach. How much does he believe in his philosophy? Does he have the guts to make the big call? Brandon stepped into the box and looked at Warrenfeltz, who was standing on the field as third-base coach. Warrenfeltz went to his arm. In the dugout, Lewis turned to Colby Byers. The two had the same reaction. "Oh, Jesus!" whispered Lewis.

Byers stared back at his coach, eyes wide. "The sign's on!" Byers said, disbelieving. "The sign's on!"

Across the diamond Patuxent prepared for the possibility. "Watch the squeeze!" the third baseman shouted. The first baseman crept in. The pitcher looked toward third, where Tyler Martin was inching down the line, and went into his motion.

With that, Tyler broke for home. Brandon needed to remember everything he'd been taught: square up early, get the bat high, and slap the ball down. On the bench Zach couldn't breathe. They needed this. The town needed this. *Just get down one freaking bunt, Brandon.*

The pitch, a curveball, was difficult to judge. By the time it got to the plate, Tyler was two-thirds of the way home. If Brandon popped it up, it would be a sure double play. Had he missed it, Martin would have been out by a good 10 feet.

None of that mattered, though, because Brandon plopped a beautiful blooping bunt in front of the plate. The Patuxent pitcher dived, trying to use his glove to flip the ball to the catcher, but by then Tyler was sliding into home face-first, the dust billowing up like stirred ash.

There is a grainy video of what followed, captured by a Williamsport parent on a cell phone. In a split second the ballpark is engulfed by a deafening roar. Boys in blue fly out of the dugout, leap past the still-prone Patuxent pitcher and dog-pile Brandon at first base, some yelling and crying at the same time.

Warrenfeltz tried to keep his emotions in check, to act like an authority figure. Then, seeing those boys streaming across the field, he thought, *Aw, screw it.* And thus on the video you see a taller, older figure fly into the picture and leap on top of the dog pile, grinning maniacally. In that moment Warrenfeltz didn't care how it looked: he just wanted to be with his team.

The next 15 minutes remain hazy. Warrenfeltz remembers Tyler Byers pointing to the sky. He remembers the fans screaming as if they were 5,000 strong. He remembers thinking about Nick and Brendon and how each would have savored this moment, Williamsport's first title in 37 years. He remembers the security guards, who'd gathered to prevent the fans from storming the field but allowed Brendon's grandfather John to pass through so that one by one the Williamsport players embraced him, none harder or longer than Zach, who cradled his head against the older man's shoulder, both of them crying.

Warrenfeltz will always treasure the hours that followed: How the team rode back to Williamsport celebrating the whole way and stopped just off the I-81 exit to climb aboard one of the town's three yellow fire trucks and parade through town, followed by police trucks and a caravan of honking cars. How they looped the long way, past the Waffle House with its sign that read, 2012 STATE CHAMPS!!! GO WILDCATS BASEBALL 4 YOU NO. 6. How the team stopped at the cemetery for a moment of silence with hats off. And how the bus ended up back at the school, where 166 white plastic cups had been jammed into the fence of the football field nearly three weeks earlier. The word they spelled was HOPE.

*

Life goes on, yet part of it remains behind.

By late July, Warrenfeltz wasn't seeing the seniors as often. Zach was getting ready to head to Salisbury College, where Brendon had been slated to be his roommate. Four other Wildcats would also play college ball. When Warrenfeltz did see the boys, they reveled in putting in a dip in front of their old coach, just because they could. They were young men now, asserting their independence. Zach Lucas and Tyler Byers had let their hair grow, so that it curled up and around their blue Williamsport hats like flames licking a log.

In most ways they remained the same kids they had been, fishing and making crude jokes, but in deeper ways they had changed. Most days they wore their championship shirts, just as they would wear the championship rings that were being made, the ones that would read IN MEMORY OF B6C on the side. Even now the seniors remain in awe of what happened—how it seemed meant to be. How else to explain all the eerie coincidences? Like the fact that Sam's number was 2 and Brendon's was 6 and the team won the state championship on May 26 on two runs and six hits. Or the fact that Brandon Toloso, who dropped down the winning bunt, was number 2, the charter bus that day was number 426, and the Wildcats won six straight games in the playoffs. Or that the rainbow around the sun at Brendon's funeral had reappeared that day against Wheaton, just before the first pitch. Nor did they know what to make of the eeriest coincidence—that the last time Williamsport won the state title, in 1975, one of the team's best players, Mick Myers, had died earlier that year. In an auto accident.

Talk to the boys, the parents, and the assistant coaches, and they would tell you that it was Warrenfeltz who made this happen. "He was the rock, the foundation," said Gary Nally, Tyler's father.

"He was more than a coach to them," Chad Colliflower said. "I don't think they would have won the championship if it hadn't been for the accident. There was something greater going on."

Lewis, Warrenfeltz's longtime friend, is a jokester, but not on this subject. "After Brendon's accident, these parents just wanted to hold their kids," he said. "To put their kids in the hands of a 25-year-old?" He paused. "If I were a parent, I would want my kid grieving through me. But these parents relinquished their kids to David."

As for Warrenfeltz, it remained hard for him to talk about, just as it was still hard to talk about Adenhart. On this afternoon he took a visitor for a drive. It was warm and muggy, and the AC was going full blast. He passed Byers Market, the LIVE BAIT signs in the window, and Smitty's Williamsport Creamery, where Zach still got free ice cream. Warrenfeltz reached the river, then turned around and headed back, past the cemetery. Only then, after 20 minutes, did he open up.

He said he sometimes went jogging and ended up at the cemetery, and one time he stopped to look at Nick's and Brendon's graves, just across the slope from each other. Noticing something unusual, he began to walk off the distance between the two. It was almost exactly 60 feet.

He talked about how there was no end point to his grief, about what he said to the team. "You don't need to feel like you need to ever get over it," he said, "because it's something that we have no answer for, a situation that is so tragic and so close to you, it changes the person that you are and the way that you view the world, not necessarily in a bad way. I got a lot of strength from watching Nick's family. At some point you have to go back to living your life and chasing your dreams and doing the things that are good for you."

That's what Warrenfeltz himself was trying to do. He was hoping to raise enough money to redo the press box and put in a proper set of bleachers. When he first took the coaching job at Williamsport, some of his friends were surprised. "Don't you want to be a college coach?" asked Lewis. "Don't you want to move up the ladder?" But Warrenfeltz didn't understand this thinking. In October 2010 he took Stephanie out to dinner in Baltimore, and the two walked from the Inner Harbor up to Federal Hill. Looking out across the city, he turned to her. "Are you all right being with someone who's going to be a high school coach for the next 30 years?" he asked.

She looked at him, surprised by the question. "Yes," she said. Moments later, when he produced a small diamond ring from the pocket of his Williamsport High baseball jacket, she said it again.

In the meantime he will be here, where he ended up after a half-hour drive, where he always ends up: at the Williamsport High diamond. There on the fence was the photo of Nick, and next to it a photo of Brendon and Sam in their prom outfits, and metal placards with Brendon's and Adenhart's numbers. And, over in the cage, even though it was summer, Colby Byers was hitting off a tee, crushing balls into the netting. Next to him, his father sat on a plastic bucket, sweating in the heat. After each of his son's swings, he picked up another ball and placed it on the tee. And this is how it continues: one disappears, another takes its place.

The Gym at Third and Ross

FROM ONLYAGAME.WBUR.ORG

JIMMY CVETIC RUNS the gym at Third and Ross. Most people don't even realize it's there.

"I gotta a Golden Gloves thing I'm puttin' on that weekend," he said. "You could see that."

We'd been looking for a third story to fill up a trip to Pittsburgh that I was going to take, and one of *Only a Game*'s producers, Karen Given, found Jimmy Cvetic. Now Jimmy was telling me he was our guy. Story one was the Duquesne men's basketball team, which was in the course of putting together an unexpectedly successful season after five players had been shot at the beginning of the year. Story two was the Pittsburgh Penguins, who were looking forward to a new arena, which the city might or might not be in any position to help fund, although a lot of other cities have not let that get in the way. Jimmy and his tournament were story three.

"And I got a Russian kid, a heavyweight, who'll be working out at my gym. You could see him," Jimmy said. "And this guy who's been in prison half his life. Chisholm. He's about 65, and he comes down here to hold the mitts for some of the fighters."

Jimmy himself is a retired police detective, which is why he said that what I'd see if I made it to Pittsburgh was "the ex-commie, the ex-con, and the ex-cop."

"And the mayor," he said. "The mayor comes in here a lot. And a card girl if you want."

This was beginning to sound like a long story, especially for the radio. I'd met several fighters, and also some mayors, but I'd never met any card girls, who are the girls who strut around the ring in high heels and not much else with a big card that tells everybody what round is coming up next, in case they have not been paying attention.

"I'll tell her to dress like she's going to work," Jimmy said.

So that was settled and he hung up the phone.

About midday on a Sunday a couple of weeks later I landed in Pittsburgh, and the idea was that I'd go see Jimmy first, because the Golden Gloves thing was that night. He'd told me to call him from the airport.

"Jimmy," I said when he answered the phone, "it's Bill Little-field."

"Who?" he said.

"Bill Littlefield," I said. "I'm the guy from public radio. We talked a couple of weeks ago. I'm here for that Golden Gloves thing tonight."

"Oh," he said. "Yeah, I had to cancel that. They were givin' me a hard time about the lights in the room there in the hotel where it was supposed to be, the chandeliers, that they were afraid it might get broken if somebody threw something, I don't know."

"So there's no fights tonight?"

"There might be," he said. "There's a lot of fights."

"But none that you're promoting?"

"Where are you?" he asked.

"I'm at the airport," I said. "You said I should call you when I got to the airport."

"Okay," he said. "Come on over to the gym."

"Where is it?"

"Third and Ross," he said.

"Third and Ross," said the cab driver. "What's at Third and Ross?"

"Jimmy Cvetic's gym," I said.

"Not that I know of," he said.

The intersection of Third and Ross was quiet on that Sunday afternoon. There was an office building that looked empty, and a couple of stores that looked just as empty, and nothing that looked like a gym. I know, because I got out of the cab and looked carefully at each corner of the intersection. I was about to get back in the cab and ask the driver to take me to the hotel where I'd be staying when a guy who looked like maybe he was a retired police detective came out of a building on the corner called the Third

Street Café, and he was waving his arm at me, which I knew because there was nobody else to wave at in the intersection of Third and Ross.

I walked toward him. "Jimmy Cvetic?" I asked.

"Come on in and get a sandwich," he said.

I got my bag out of the cab and paid the driver, who shrugged, perhaps because you learn something every day, and that day he learned that there was a gym at Third and Ross, or at least there was Jimmy Cvetic.

Jimmy led me up a concrete ramp, which meant you could get into the Third Street Café in a wheelchair, should anybody have to do that. Inside there was a young man painting the ceiling, and another young man was behind the counter.

"What kind of sandwich you want?" Jimmy asked.

"How about ham and cheese, sourdough bread, lettuce and tomato, mayo and mustard?"

Jimmy nodded at the young man behind the counter. While I was waiting for my sandwich, he showed me around the Third Street Café, which was one room with a few tables. The walls were covered with photographs, mostly of boxers, but one big frame had headshots of 30 Pittsburgh police officers who'd died on the job.

"I knew a lot of them," Jimmy said.

Lots of the photographs of boxers were signed. Jimmy had stories to tell about some of them. We stopped in front of the photo of Roberto Durán, who is infamous for saying "No más" in what would otherwise have been the middle of a fight with Ray Leonard, but instead it was the end. That wasn't the story Jimmy wanted to tell.

"This guy knocked out Pedro Mendoza's wife," he said.

I hadn't heard about that, and I must have looked it.

"1975," Jimmy said. "Durán knocked out Mendoza two minutes into the fight, which was in Nicaragua, where Mendoza was a hero. 'El Toro,' they called him, but not that night. After he went down, his wife come over the ropes screaming, 'Durán!' and he turns around and he coldcocks her. So then everybody starts screaming and throwing stuff, and Durán leaves the ring with his hands over his head, and I think he flew out of there the same night, to Costa Rica or some place. Neutral territory. Didn't even go back to his hotel. Or that's the way I heard it."

A couple of photos down the wall there was a picture of Charles Bukowski.

"This guy isn't a fighter," I said. "He's a poet."

Jimmy's face lit up. "You know Bukowski?" he asked.

"I know his poems."

This would matter, but not right then, because the kid who'd been making my sandwich was finished. It was a good sandwich too, though I learned later from Jimmy that the kid who made it was no more a sandwich maker than the kid who was painting the ceiling of the Third Street Café was a ceiling painter. They were both young guys who'd come to Jimmy at some point and said they wanted to learn to fight, and he'd taken them on. The one who was painting the ceiling had been married briefly to a woman who took off with somebody else and left him with a baby, whom he was presently supporting by painting Jimmy's ceiling.

"He's a good kid," Jimmy told me later. "He's trying to do it right."

We made it the rest of the way around the room, and Jimmy said if I was finished with my sandwich, we could go down to the gym, which we got to by going outside and then down some steps beside the café. If you didn't know it was there, you would walk right by it, which I say on behalf of the cab driver, who should not feel bad.

The gym was full of old equipment and a Russian fighter who certainly looked like a heavyweight to me, but who could not have told me so himself unless I knew the Russian word for "heavyweight." Jimmy and I watched the Russian bounce around in the ring for a while, and after a time the ex-con, Chisholm, showed up with two guys, one to hold his coat while he climbed into the ring with the Russian, and the other guy in case something else might come up. The ex-con, who told me that he had in fact spent about half his life in jail, put on the mitts trainers use to catch their fighters' punches, and the Russian guy whaled away at him for a time.

While we were watching, Jimmy pointed to the ex-con and said, "He could have been a cop, and I could have been a crook. He's not so dumb, and I'm not so smart, but it worked out the other way."

"How did you get into the boxing business?" I asked.

"One day when I was just starting out, way before I got to be a detective, I caught a little kid stealing the radios out of cars,"

Jimmy said. "He was about 12, 13. And I brought him in, and he went to juvenile court, and I guess he went away somewhere that wasn't any good for anybody, and I was thinking, even then, I wish there was somewhere else I could take him. But there wasn't, because I didn't have the gym, and a couple years later he was dead of a drug overdose. So after a while, I thought, no kid ever picked up a crack pipe with boxing gloves. I started this place, and anybody who wants to come in and learn to box, they can do it."

Other people came into the gym too, just as Jimmy Cvetic had promised they would. The card girl was among them, and you could not mistake her for anything other than a card girl, unless maybe you thought she was on her way to the beach where there was no boardwalk where she might catch a heel. Jimmy took a picture of me with the ex-con and the ex-commie, but I told him I'd pass on one with the card girl, which is why you can look all you like on the Internet and you won't find one.

Eventually I told Jimmy I ought to get over to my hotel, and he said he'd give me a ride. As I was getting out of the car, he asked if I had plans for dinner, which I didn't.

"I'll pick you up at 6:30," he said. "We'll get some Chinese food, and I got nobody here to talk about poetry with, so we can talk about poetry."

Over dinner, which Jimmy ate with chopsticks and I didn't, we did talk some about poetry, and not just Charles Bukowski, because Jimmy writes poetry of his own. "Thousands of poems," he told me. In a poem about a fellow officer who became addicted to the drugs he was supposed to be getting off the street and who died in jail, Jimmy wrote: "Youth is usually chained to ambition / And we strutted the chains cool like immortality," which seemed to me a pretty good line at the time, and also after we had finished dinner.

Jimmy talked about the theater pieces he produces from time to time, productions in which he sometimes uses the boxers from his gym.

"And the card girls," Jimmy said. "Because the people enjoy looking at them, even if they are not saying anything much, or anything at all."

Sometimes the smartest thing to do when you are talking with somebody like Jimmy Cvetic is not to say anything, because then he will realize that what he has just finished saying isn't finished after all, and he will say the rest of it.

"One of the card girls, her name was Stacy or Tracy or something, and she was excellent at standing there, and also at being a card girl. And then one night after she'd been working at the fights—and this is after I'd been employing her for quite a while— she said, 'Jimmy, what are those numbers on the cards for?'"

Besides running the little gym under the Third Street Café and keeping various boxers and card girls off the streets, Jimmy Cvetic is a trainer of sorts, and he is not without a claim to championship credentials in that respect, although the claim is a little tarnished.

His champion is a not-so-young-anymore fellow named Paul Spadafora, who was known as "The Pittsburgh Kid," I suppose because that sounded better than "The McKees Rocks Kid," which is where he was born. Although a guy I know named Carlo who is smarter about boxing than I am told me Paul Spadafora lacked a knockout punch, that didn't stop him from claiming the World Lightweight Championship, at least according to one of the many competing federations and authorities and gangsters who hand out such distinctions. Jimmy Cvetic worked with Paul Spadafora for a time, and stood up for him when he was arrested for urinating on a public thoroughfare, which is not something they put you in jail for if you are the World Lightweight Champion, although they do put you in jail for shooting your girlfriend, and that's what they did to Paul Spadafora after he did that.

"I convinced him to turn himself in," Jimmy told me. He also told me that the girlfriend recovered, and she visited Paul Spadafora in prison, where there was a thick plastic wall between them.

"And that was a good thing," Jimmy said. "Because she had to tell him that the pit bull he'd left with her had torn up the other pit bull he'd left with her, which was stuffed."

"A stuffed pit bull?" I asked.

Jimmy shrugged.

That evening Jimmy took me on a tour of Pittsburgh. He drove up to a point where we could look down on where the three rivers come together, which lots of people have seen, and then we drove back downtown and into a neighborhood called Hazlewood, which not so many people have seen, at least on purpose. Jimmy pointed out an old shack with some outside steps that led to an upper story and said that a cop had been shot there by a man who felt the police should let domestic disputes play out without interference.

"Guy come out the door of the apartment and banged away with an assault rifle," Jimmy said. "Got my guy in the chest. He was halfway up those stairs. Coleman McDonough was my guy's name. It was the last call on his shift, and he could have said he was off duty already, but he went on the call. Last thing he said was, 'Son, put the rifle down.' McDonough, his picture's on my wall, there."

We pulled away from the building, and Jimmy said, "Guy shot himself too."

Jimmy is not one for email, although he says his girlfriend, Gloria, takes care of that for him, and maybe she does, but not so as I would notice. So if I want to know how he's doing, I call Jimmy. A couple of years ago when I did that, he told me he'd had some problems with his heart, and I wondered if maybe it was too big, but that wasn't it. Then more recently I called to tell him my students had enjoyed some of his poems. He was glad to hear that, and he said things were pretty good with him.

"I had a hip replacement, and I was on one of those walkers for a while, but now I'm okay. I just have to stop and rest sometimes."

I did not ask Jimmy about Paul Spadafora, because I'd read that he'd been arrested recently for driving drunk, which is not as bad as shooting your girlfriend, but which is also not so good if you are a boxer in your midthirties who is still trying to convince somebody that you can be a contender.

I did ask Jimmy about Chisholm, the ex-con, and also about the ex-commie, and the news was not so good there either.

"The ex-con has got hepatitis A, B, C, and D," Jimmy said. "I haven't seen him in a while."

"What about the heavyweight?"

"He got deported," Jimmy said.

"What for?" I asked.

"I don't know," Jimmy said. "It's easy to get deported. But now I got a Czech guy in the gym, and his name's Attila."

"Good name for a fighter," I said.

"Absolutely," Jimmy said. "And we got a new ring in there too."

"How'd you manage that?" I asked him.

"Well," Jimmy said, "they were filming this movie, part of it anyway, here in Pittsburgh, called *The Warrior*. You seen it?"

"No," I said.

"Nick Nolte's in it, and he and I got to know each other. He's a good guy, and we're talkin' one day and he says, 'You should be in the movie.' The next thing I know the director says so too. And I told him, 'I don't want to be in your movie,' but then Nolte says it's gonna be easy, and they'd pay me. I told him I don't need you to do that, but for about five thousand dollars you can put a new ring in my gym for Attila and these other guys. So they did that, and now, you go see *The Warrior,* you can see me in it."

So the ex-cop who is a community organizer and a trainer of sorts is also in the movies now, which is something he did for other people, pretty much as he has done everything else, including getting the ceiling painted in the Third Street Café. And of course he is still a poet, and in one of his poems, "Porkchop Didn't Shoot Everybody," he tells the story of a guy who one night shot everybody he could see in a bar and also some people he couldn't see, but not everybody. The shooter is called Porkchop for reasons that are not explained, and during cross-examination of the state's star witnesses, one Silas Jones, Porkchop's attorney, attempts to clarify the situation by asking if his client was "just shooting at random."

> Silas said, "No, he wasn't shootin' at Random.
> Random wasn't even there."
> The judge hit the gavel:
> "With that last statement, we'll take a ten-minute break."

You could see it coming, but it makes me smile every time anyway, so when it was time to get off the phone, I said, "Well, keep writing poems."

"I will," Jimmy Cvetic said. "I got thousands of 'em. You keep readin' 'em."

And I suppose I will.

KENT BABB

Arrowhead Anxiety

FROM THE KANSAS CITY STAR

TODD HALEY WALKED into the public relations office at Chiefs headquarters on a Thursday in early December. Four days before he was fired as the team's coach, he wanted to talk about what life was like inside this organization. But he didn't know who else might be listening.

Looking up toward the ceiling, he darted into a back hallway before hesitating. Then he turned around, going back through a door and stopping again. Haley suspected that many rooms at the team facility were bugged so that team administrators could monitor employees' conversations. Stopping finally in a conference room, Haley said he believed his personal cell phone, a line he used before being hired by the Chiefs in 2009, had been tampered with.

Paranoid? The Chiefs have adamantly denied that they tap phones or listen in on conversations. But as the team enters another period of transition after elevating defensive coordinator Romeo Crennel last week to head coach, interviews with more than two dozen current and former employees suggest that intimidation and secrecy are among the Chiefs' principal management styles—and that Haley wasn't the only one with paranoid thoughts.

"When you're mentally abused, you eventually lose it too," one former longtime Chiefs executive said.

Since Scott Pioli was hired as general manager in January 2009, life for many inside the Chiefs' front office has been marked by massive staff turnover, fear, and insecurity about how closely they are watched. Numerous current and former staffers paint a picture of constant worry—and, in a few cases, of alleged age discrimination. Three former department heads sued the Chiefs in 2011, though the team has denied wrongdoing.

Clark Hunt, the team's chairman and CEO, rejected the notion that Arrowhead is a difficult place to work, but he said there has been an emphasis placed on responsibility. Change, he said, is often uncomfortable.

"We needed a culture that pursued excellence," he said. "One that valued honesty and integrity, one where the employees would be held accountable."

Stability has been another matter. In the last three years, more than half the workforce has turned over, and the vast majority of senior staff members are no longer with the team. As dozens have left the organization, with some of the holdovers and new hires trying to adapt to what many described as a restrictive working environment, dread has permeated the franchise.

"The level of paranoia was probably the highest that I had ever seen it anywhere," another former high-ranking staffer said. ". . . If you make the wrong step, you might not be able to pay your mortgage."

Three years ago, Pioli began ushering in a new culture on Arrowhead Drive. It centered on secrecy, extreme attention to detail, and putting an end to the way things had been under longtime general manager Carl Peterson.

"Part of it is not only changing the culture of your football team and your locker room," Pioli told *USA Today* in August 2009. "It's changing the culture of all the things that touch your football team and your locker room."

Some of the first changes involved shutting off access and protecting information. Non-football employees, including those who had worked for the Chiefs for decades, were told that they weren't allowed on certain floors, or in certain areas of the team facility. Business-side staffers with an office window facing the practice fields were made to keep their shades drawn during practices. The team president was no exception. A security guard made the rounds during practices, sometimes interrupting phone calls and meetings to lower shades.

Chiefs president Mark Donovan said his shade is drawn for the sake of consistency, to give the impression that no business-side employee is trusted more or less than another.

"This is making sure that everybody feels the same," he said.

Pioli's background was with the New England Patriots, a team known for its devotion to privacy and bending the rules. As he promised, the environment changed. Some said it changed too much.

"It's not Lamar Hunt's organization anymore," said Steve Schneider, the former stadium operations director who spent 14 years with the Chiefs before being fired in 2010, he said, for being disorganized.

Pioli, who was not made available by the team for this story, has said in the past that the changes were about ending a period of entitlement and emphasizing accountability. Those were the things, he repeated often, that lead a team to victories and championships.

During his first year, Pioli noticed a candy wrapper in a back stairwell and waited to see how long it took to be picked up. About a week passed, and it remained in the stairwell. He placed the wrapper in an envelope, and during a meeting of department heads, Donovan, then the team's chief operating officer, brandished the wrapper as evidence of the attention to detail that Chiefs employees had grown to ignore.

"A great coaching moment," Donovan said.

Some thought the example was overblown. Pioli frequently came down hard on minutiae. Some emphases made sense, some staffers said; others, though, seemed over the top. One executive, who's no longer with the team, was sent to human resources for casually referring to Pioli by his last name; the executive said, however, that first names were acceptable. Pioli also sent a memo with detailed instructions, including which stairway to use and which doorway to enter, when using the facility's gym.

After a while, a saying was adopted by top administrators for behavior that didn't fit the new standards: "That's so two-and-fourteen," they would say, referring to the Chiefs' win-loss record in 2008. This pertained to matters large and small: Stephanie Melton, who worked 11 years on the team's operations staff, recalled Pioli's reaction after she and a coworker, after working past midnight on a weekend, had parked a courier van in the unmarked space usually occupied by Pioli's car. The women had forgotten to move it, and Pioli was livid the next morning. Melton said she was made to feel for several days that she'd be fired.

"There was an incredible fear of saying and doing the wrong thing," said a former business-side executive, who was among a group of sources who requested anonymity—in some cases because they still worked for the Chiefs, and in others because they believed their comments might hinder their chances of getting another job in sports.

Some, though, paid little attention to the changes. Mike Davidson, who left the team last year after 22 years as equipment manager, said the new policies never seemed overbearing to him.

"Everybody has a style," he said, "and it's your job to figure out that style. I didn't have any problems."

A few former employees, though they don't deny that the working environment was tense, said they believed Pioli and Donovan simply carried out changes that Clark Hunt, a graduate of the results-oriented Goldman Sachs training program, had authorized.

"It's professional football, and I do think that it can be a bit of a pressure cooker," said Tammy Fruits, who resigned in October as the team's vice president of sales and marketing. "To attribute that to Scott Pioli is unfair."

Donovan said Hunt's instructions were clear—and necessary.

"Really focus on integrity and accountability," Donovan recalled Hunt suggesting. "He felt like we needed to take this place and focus on those two areas."

But many saw Pioli as the face of the new way—and of overreaction. Melton said she frequently took the brunt of Pioli's outbursts on such matters as the temperature in his office, the radio signal in the weight room, and how much the organization spent annually on coffee.

Ray Farmer, the Chiefs' pro personnel director, said his boss is thorough—sometimes surprisingly so. He said that's a good thing.

"In some instances," Farmer said, "you could say that he's a micromanager to a degree. I think he likes to know what information is and what you're doing . . . Scott wants to know, like as a math teacher, 'How did you get to your problem; how did you get to the answer of the problem?'"

Hunt agreed.

"I believe that good leaders do bring an attention to detail to their leadership roles," he said. "And something that I think we struggled with before both Mark and Scott got here was attention to detail. If you set an example with attention to detail, I think it spreads through the organization."

Melton had a different opinion, saying Pioli's fixation on trivial matters seemed misguided.

"He was so focused on what seemed like unimportant details for the general manager of a football team," she said. "We all had to step to the beat of his drum, but we all kept questioning: 'How is this building a better football team?'"

Nothing was emphasized like the commitment to secrecy. Pioli was with the Patriots in 2007, when that organization and its head coach, Bill Belichick, were disciplined for the "Spygate" controversy, in which one of the team's video assistants secretly filmed signals by the New York Jets' coaches. Belichick, Pioli's mentor and a longtime friend, was fined $500,000—the maximum-allowed fine by the NFL—for his role in the scandal.

When Pioli took over the Chiefs, he seemed determined to eliminate the chance of a competitor spying on his team. This past November, a security guard noticed a sedan stopped on Lancer Lane, a public road that runs adjacent to the Chiefs' practice fields, as the team's morning session was beginning. The driver took a photograph on his cell phone, and the guard ran toward him, standing there until the man deleted the picture. As the guard returned to his post, he told a *Star* reporter that, if the man hadn't erased the photo, the guard would've confiscated the phone.

Donovan said the efforts to control team information have a purpose.

"You may think it's harmless," he said when asked about some of the measures, such as lowering window shades. "Other people may think it's very harmful to our competitive advantage."

Then he continued.

"It's about winning."

This past year, Haley stopped talking on the phone and repeatedly checked his office for listening devices. After being fired, Haley didn't respond to interview requests; many former staffers said they signed confidentiality agreements upon being let go.

The Chiefs said there's nothing to substantiate Haley's fears, but some believed that anything was possible.

"I don't think that anything would surprise anyone, really," said a former employee who worked for the Chiefs for more than two decades. "That's how Scott wants it."

A common notion is that employees are constantly being watched. When they arrive and leave, where they're going within the building, and who they're talking to. Indeed, the technology exists at the Chiefs' offices, as it does in many corporate settings, to monitor phone calls and emails. But here, some staffers even hesitated before using their cell phones or speaking inside the building, because, like Haley, they suspected that conversations were monitored.

"The capability was definitely there for Big Brother to be watching," said Schneider, whose job was to oversee maintenance at team facilities.

Added Pete Penland, who worked in operations before retiring: "I just know that some of our bosses had always told us: be careful what we did, what we said, and where we were at in certain parts of the building."

Donovan denied that conversations are monitored or that the building is bugged. He said that in cases of suspected policy breaches or criminal activity, phone logs have been requested.

"I'm not going to say that we've never done it, but it's not something we do," Donovan said. "It's not how we operate this business."

The capability was installed during Peterson's tenure, one source said, for the Chiefs to monitor emails, web traffic, and call logs. Willie Davis, a current Chiefs scout hired by Peterson, said a former colleague was reprimanded during the previous regime for emails sent to another team's scout. But a former Chiefs executive, who was familiar with the team's policies under Peterson, said calls and emails weren't routinely monitored. The technology was used more for flagging inappropriate material, such as pornographic websites.

But in the last three years, another former staffer said, printouts of emails, some of them months old, were occasionally requested. The former employee said the belief was that the Chiefs were trying to discover who could be trusted and who couldn't, who was loyal to the cause and who was a liability. Pioli pored over former president Denny Thum's call log, a former high-ranking employee said, before Thum was asked to resign in September 2010 after 36 years with the team.

Thum declined comment when reached by telephone.

Kirsten Krug, the team's human resources director, said that no current or former employee has shared uneasiness that conversations were monitored. Hunt said no employee, past or present, has broached this concern with him—including Haley.

But the suspicion was prevalent enough that, when some staffers wanted to speak candidly, they set appointments with coworkers to meet outside the building so they could talk face-to-face. Others, trying to skirt an impression that employees shouldn't fraternize with those from different departments, occasionally left the facility at different times, in different cars, so that team administrators wouldn't know they were having lunch together.

"I don't think that's ever been an issue for me. I know that people have done it," Farmer said. "They don't want to be seen going with this person or that person. I understand—I hate to say this—I understand the process that some people felt they needed to take, but again, I never kind of adhered to that behavior."

Donovan said the widespread suspicions were unfounded.

"I can't control their beliefs," he said.

Hunt was more direct.

"It's not true at all," he said.

Still, other staffers were nervous that someone might report to administrators that they were at a place with people they weren't supposed to associate with.

"Every day," a former longtime staffer said, "you walked into the building like you were going to be put on the witness stand and be cross-examined, and you didn't know who it was going to be coming from."

For some, the pressure was more difficult to deal with than others.

"Whether it's a licensed professional or somebody else," the employee said, "hell yeah, you'd better talk to somebody. Because you'll go crazy."

In January 2010, the worry was amplified and legitimized by a series of staff cuts. When Pioli took over, there were 19 employees in director or vice president positions. Many of them had been with the Chiefs for decades. Three years later, only three—Farmer, video operations director Pat Brazil, and special-events director Gary Spani, a former Chiefs player—are still in executive positions.

"As they term it out there," Schneider said, "I was the class of '10."

A year later, the "class of '11" was let go. More senior staffers were shown the door, in the form of layoffs, firings, and resignations. When the 2008 season began, before Pioli arrived, the staff roster in the team's media guide listed 155 employees, not including coaches and players, working for the Chiefs. More than three years later, 82 of those staffers are gone, though most positions have been filled, in some cases with modified titles.

"Scott did give me a chance to kind of earn my job and do what I'm doing," Farmer said. "He could've parted ways with me. Why he didn't, I think that's probably a better question for him. But I would like to think that it's more based on my work product and what I'm able to accomplish."

Donovan said the changes were aimed at improving the organization from top to bottom.

"Trying to be the best in the National Football League at what we do," he said. "So that's going to come with people who get on board and thrive, and it's going to come with people who feel like it's not something they want to participate in, or maybe can't."

Sure, the cuts have come during a down economy, and turnover is typical during an organizational change. Donovan said such change, even at the top, is common in sports. But when the *Star* examined the staff rosters of the Tampa Bay Buccaneers, Seattle Seahawks, and Denver Broncos, teams that also overhauled their franchises in 2009, it found that those organizations left senior staff mostly untouched. Even the Atlanta Falcons, another team influenced by a former executive from the Patriots' lineage, have made only a few changes to senior staff in the four years since Thomas Dimitroff became GM. The Broncos and Falcons reached the playoffs this season.

Any Chiefs employee who had once worked for Peterson was on alert.

"I just saw everybody else kind of disappearing," said a former executive who had been hired by Peterson. ". . . When you're on the outside, it's pretty obvious you're on the outside."

The team has had a different public relations chief, the franchise's conduit to media and fans, in each of Pioli's three years.

Three of the Chiefs' former high-ranking staffers—former community-relations director Brenda Sniezek, former controller Larry Clemmons, and former maintenance manager Steve Cox— have sued the organization for age discrimination. In Sniezek's suit, filed in December, she alleged that she overheard Pioli telling a coworker that he planned to "get rid of everyone who was with Carl Peterson, especially anyone over the age of 40."

Sniezek, 52, alleged that she asked the team's PR staff to remove all references to her age on her biography. Reached by the *Star* late last month, Sniezek said that because of the suit, which sought damages of at least $25,000, she wouldn't discuss her nearly 29-year tenure with the Chiefs, and how it changed after Hunt put Pioli in charge.

"There will be a time, and all of this will come out," said Sniezek, who was let go last January.

Clemmons's petition, filed in November, alleged that he was informed upon being asked to retire that "You're the last."

Because of legal restrictions, Donovan said he couldn't discuss the suits, other than referring to a statement in which he said the claims "are both baseless and ridiculous."

"The plaintiff's claims are completely false," the statement read, "and we intend to vigorously defend ourselves."

In the Chiefs' answer to Cox's petition, the team denied his allegations. Cox's attorney, Lewis Galloway, said depositions will begin this week.

Before Christmas, a group of about 20 gathered at a café in Independence. They were mostly former Chiefs staffers, although some current employees also attended, and they came together to reminisce. They called it a reunion.

"It didn't matter which department you were in," said Cox, who is Melton's father, "everybody would pull together. It was amazing."

Now, Schneider said, most employees simply keep to themselves. He said staffers used to volunteer to help coworkers out of a jam. If there was snow in the stadium, colleagues from other departments ran down to help shovel it out. Those days, he said, are gone.

"It got to a point where people just kept their heads down, didn't want to go outside the box and jeopardize getting in trouble," Schneider said.

He went on.

"I still get calls from people who are still there," he said. "All I can say is, 'I feel for you.'"

Several former staffers admitted that it's difficult being without a job, particularly one in sports. But some said leaving the new Chiefs was more about relief than regret.

"I sleep a hell of a lot better at night," a former employee said.

The Chiefs said they're happy now with the team's direction. But there hasn't been a significant improvement in the one area that Donovan said the changes were intended to support—the team's win-loss record. The Chiefs finished 7-9 in Pioli's third season, the team's second losing season since the changes began. Still, Donovan said the organization is in better shape compared to three years ago.

"There are a lot of people who have been here longer than I've been here," he said, "who will sit there and tell you that it's a much better place to work today."

In addition to the more than two dozen independent interviews conducted by the *Star,* the Chiefs arranged phone interviews with eight current employees. Farmer and Davis were among those, and their interviews were the only two conducted without a Chiefs PR staffer present. Each of the employees spoke favorably about the working environment and the team's direction. The team emphasized that the employees were not coached on what to say.

One of those was Allen Wright, the team's equipment manager, who was with the Chiefs when Peterson took over in 1988. Back then, the Chiefs also overhauled the staff: three years later, 62 percent of the staff had been retained, but seven of 10 department heads had been replaced. The organization was smaller then, but Wright recalled a similar reaction to the changes.

"I remember the same feelings and people saying the same things," he said. "I was a young kid working in the equipment department, and everybody was talking about how everybody was worried about getting fired . . . Any time there's change, that's just the feeling that people have."

On that Thursday in December, when Haley's suspicions peaked, the former Chiefs coach said he would be in touch to discuss the working environment—but that it would be from a number you didn't recognize. Haley's call never came, but in the time since, others have questioned how productive he could have been if he was so preoccupied with who might be watching him.

"No one could be successful in that environment," a former director-level employee said.

Melton left the Chiefs in 2010 after arriving at a similar conclusion. More than a year later, she was asked if she could see any benefit from the changes. After a long pause, she answered.

"I'm sure there's some good that has come out of it," she said. "I would be hard-pressed to be able to identify that right now, without really thinking about it. I don't think our football team is any better; I don't think our fans are being any more well-served."

She paused again.

"I couldn't tell you," she said. "I'm sorry. I'm not very helpful in that regard."

Melton was at the reunion last month. She said they talked about how much they missed working together. She said they tried not to dwell on stressful times, but there were plenty of things that former staffers said they wouldn't miss about working for the Chiefs.

"I don't miss being scared to go in every day," one former staffer said. "Thinking, *Who's going to yell at me now?* It's so sad, because it was a great job. There was a time that it was a great place."

JASON SCHWARTZ

End Game

FROM BOSTON MAGAZINE

THE SUN IS BEATING DOWN hard on the Dracut High School softball field, where Curt Schilling sits atop a bucket of balls beside the dugout.

He's helping coach his daughter's team, the Drifters, in a tournament, and they're on the verge of their second win of the day. Schilling could use the uplift: it's been a month since the extraordinary implosion of 38 Studios, the video-game company he founded and lost $50 million investing in. And though his face is not quite the ghastly shade of white it was at the height of his company's crisis, he doesn't exactly look good. Dressed in shorts and a standard-issue blue and orange coach's polo, his facial hair is scraggly and he's got heavy bags beneath his eyes.

"Come on! Let's close it out!" shouts the former Red Sox star, noted during his career for his precision arm and considerably wilder mouth. Moments later, there's a game-ending grounder to second. Drifters win, 9–0.

Despite keeping an uncharacteristically low media profile of late, Schilling has agreed to meet with me. So while the players wait for their next game of the tournament, the former pitcher takes a seat in a lawn chair and performs what winds up being an emotional, two-hour-long autopsy of 38 Studios. The company's death was grisly: before going under, it defaulted on the $75 million guaranteed loan that the state of Rhode Island had used in 2010 to lure it to Providence. As the money ran out, the company encouraged its 379 employees to continue coming into work, even though it knew it could not pay them. Staffers realized they'd been stiffed only when they noticed the money missing from their bank accounts. A pregnant woman had to find out from her doctor that her health care benefits had been cut off.

Add it all up, including interest, and already-cash-strapped Rhode Island could be out as much as $110 million on the loans. As Schilling sits beside the softball diamond, his company, with nearly $151 million in debt and just $22 million in assets, is being liquidated through Chapter 7 bankruptcy.

Asked about 38 Studios' failure, Schilling says his management team suffered from "significant dysfunction" and that his video-game developers worked too slowly. Those problems, he allows, are his fault. "As the chairman and founder," he says, "who's above me?"

But he also shovels much of the blame onto Rhode Island governor Lincoln Chafee, who he believes had a political agenda when it came to 38 Studios. The day before, Schilling alerted his former employees through a private Facebook message board that he planned to go on WEEI sports radio to talk about Chafee's role and "tell the untold side of this nightmare."

Many former 38 Studios employees, including the CEO, responded to that Facebook post with fierce attacks against Schilling himself. As the assaults mounted, Schilling's wife, Shonda, rose to her husband's defense. "50 million its [sic] not a fucking joke. It's gone," she wrote, adding that, "You have no idea what that last two weeks were like. Hope and hell. We hung on every telephone call. My husband couldn't function. My kids saw their father cry more in that month then [sic] any child should see."

Schilling's harshest critic in the online exchange was Bill Mrochek, the vice president of online services, whose wife required a bone marrow transplant at the time their health care disappeared. "Are you going to admit that your stupid hubris, pride, and arrogance would not allow you to accept that we failed—and help shut it down with dignity?" he asked Schilling.

Mrochek was talking only about 38 Studios' dramatic final weeks, but as interviews with Schilling, members of his former staff, and others associated with the company show, he might as well have been describing 38 Studios from the moment that Schilling—lacking any business experience, but full of the same confidence, bravado, and determination that made him a baseball legend—decided he could build a billion-dollar video-game company.

By 2006, Curt Schilling had earned more than $90 million playing baseball, not including endorsements. But what he really aspired to was being "Bill Gates rich." He admired the global impact the Microsoft founder had made through his philanthropy, and wanted to do the same. Schilling, who has an autistic son, imagined providing $200 million to open the Shonda Schilling Center for Autism Research.

Creating a video game would be what catapulted him to that wealth. More specifically, he would build a massively multiplayer online game (or, blessedly abbreviated, an MMO)—the type that allows people from across the world to play with and against one another. As a kid, Schilling had been obsessed with computers (his first was an Apple II), and during his baseball career, rather than go out carousing, he spent his time playing MMOs. A favorite of his was the industry leader, "World of Warcraft," a vast fantasy landscape filled with wizards, elves, and warriors that has more than 10 million paying subscribers.

Successful MMOs are incredibly lucrative, but they're also the hardest type of game to build. You're programming not just a game, explains Dan Scherlis, the first CEO of Turbine, a maker of MMOs, but a complex social system for thousands, if not millions, of users. A normal video game might require a couple of years to develop, but an MMO takes at least twice as long. Because of that, many gaming entrepreneurs start small, working their way up from something simple for a mobile device, or perhaps a single-player game for PlayStation or Xbox. But Schilling had grander ideas. He was going to challenge "World of Warcraft." His fantasy world would be similar (you want elves and wizards, you've got elves and wizards), but he envisioned deeper plot lines and more-striking visuals. He persuaded R. A. Salvatore, the best-selling novelist from Leominster, to dream up the fictional universe and the famed comic artist Todd McFarlane, a noted baseball fan, to conceive its artistic vision.

Industry experts often compare making video games to filming movies, given their similarly long production cycles and hit-or-miss nature. In movie terms, then, Schilling was attempting to start a studio from scratch, but instead of beginning with a low-budget indie flick, he was going straight for the summer blockbuster. His first time behind the camera, he was going to make *Avatar.*

"If it wasn't an MMO, I wouldn't have done it," Schilling tells me. "If you look at the game space now, if you want to build something that's a billion-dollar company, the only game to do that with is an MMO."

Schilling founded his company, originally called Green Monster Games, in August 2006, and set up shop in Maynard. (The name was changed a few months later on account of some other guys already owning the trademark on "Green Monster.") He code-named his game Project Copernicus, and set out to make it richer, more beautiful, and, in sum, more lovingly created than any before it. Copernicus's world would be deep enough to support a network of related products: toys, books, and other video games and media. Schilling calculated that it would cost $40 to $50 million to produce the MMO, of which he'd front about 10 percent. "I told my wife I was going to take $5 million and try it out," he says. The rest of the money would come from investors. He projected that Copernicus would debut by 2010, or in four years—an aggressive timeline for even an established video-game studio.

To industry observers, Schilling's quest seemed overwhelmingly difficult. To Schilling, it was just another opportunity to prove the naysayers wrong. "I had to beat the Yankees three times in nine days," he tells me, referring to when he led Arizona to the 2001 World Series title. "I never doubted I was going to do it. My whole life was spent doing things that people didn't believe were possible, because God blessed me with the ability to throw a baseball. And I carried that same mentality into everything I did here."

Schilling knew he'd been treated well during his baseball career, and wanted his staff at 38 Studios to feel the same. That meant gold-plated health care, for which employees had no paycheck deductions, and top-notch 401(k)s, with the company matching to the legal limit. As 38 Studios grew from 20 employees in 2006 to 42 in 2007 to 65 in 2008, there were plenty of other goodies along the way: free gym memberships, two homes the company rented to temporarily house new out-of-state hires (though that perk was short-lived), and, one year at Christmas, new laptop computers for every employee. Gifts like the computers came out of Schilling's pocket—he says he spent as much as $2.5 million on that sort of largesse over the years.

With midday Ultimate Frisbee games and a staff that got along remarkably well, the Maynard office appeared downright idyllic. Once, after an IT guy's rottweiler died, Schilling presented him with a brand-new pup during an all-staff meeting. There was much applause. Former employees say Schilling was an unparalleled cheerleader. He hadn't originally intended to be in the office full-time, but when he got hurt in 2008 and subsequently retired from baseball, he became a permanent fixture. Jesse Smith, a designer, says that at monthly meetings, Schilling would usually give his thoughts after employees presented their work. "There were a couple times that you could tell he was getting choked up," Smith says. "This was something that was just an idea and a dream to him, and now it's coming to reality . . . It was just powerful."

Everything at 38 Studios was not, however, perfect. It quickly became apparent that Schilling was new not just to video-game development, but to the basic concept of working in an office. In December 2009—months before Rhode Island signed on to the $75 million deal—Harvard Business School published a case study about the company titled "Curt Schilling's Next Pitch."

Brett Close, who joined 38 Studios as president in 2007 and soon after became its first CEO, put Schilling's inexperience into perspective for the study's authors, Noam Wasserman, Jeffrey Bussgang, and Rachel Gordon. "He really needed Company 101," Close told them. "For example, the whole concept of vacation was foreign to Curt. He actually said, 'People get weekends off, right?'" Schilling at one point suggested that people work 14 straight days and then take five days off. It jibed with his baseball experience.

That idea was never instituted, but other questionable ones were. Schilling put his wife, Shonda, on the board of directors. Shonda's father received a job in IT (by all accounts, he performed admirably), and her mother was given the title "philanthropy and charity manager." Meanwhile, Shonda's uncle, William Thomas, became COO. Though a seasoned businessman, Thomas had no experience with video games, much less MMOs. Schilling took to calling him "Uncle Bill" around the office, and even in meetings with outsiders. According to the case study, Thomas told Schilling it was making them look bad and to stop. The nickname caught on with the staff anyway.

Most troublesome of all was the unique profit-sharing plan Schilling devised for his first employees. Wasserman, Bussgang, and Gordon write that, since Schilling was bankrolling the company by himself, he was hesitant to give up equity in it. So instead of luring early prospective hires with stock options, he promised to share all profits 50-50 with them. Upon arriving as CEO, Close recognized that "investors' heads would explode" when they saw the model, since they'd be bearing all the risk but reaping only half the reward. Close eventually convinced Schilling to scrap the policy and replace it with stock options.

The CEO also tried to rein in Schilling's spending, doing away with ideas for company cars and cell phones. But Schilling was adamant about the rest of the perks. According to the case study, between fiscal years 2007 and 2008, the company spent more than $705,000 on "travel and entertainment," a sum Scherlis, the former Turbine CEO, calls "wildly high."

"It never had the culture of a start-up," says one former employee. "The message was being sent . . . that there was plenty of money."

As Schilling's personal investment shot past $5 million, he knew he would need outside financing. Since the Red Sox hero was able to get meetings with just about anyone within the broadcast range of NESN, he and his executives met with potential investors practically every week for the company's first three or four years.

Todd Dagres, a founder and general partner at Boston's Spark Capital, one of the top tech venture capital firms in the country, trekked out to Maynard for a meeting. He says he was looking to invest in games, but admits that he was also excited to meet the bloody-sock hero.

Schilling gave him an office tour, clicked through PowerPoint slides, and delivered a passionate pitch. But Dagres says Schilling came off as overconfident, as though he didn't understand what a huge bet he'd made with 38 Studios. Project Copernicus was going to require tons of cash, and if the game flopped, the company would go down with it. 38 Studios didn't have "the 'A' team that I thought you'd want to see developing such a difficult game," Dagres says. It lacked MMO development experience at the top. "Curt was not the CEO," Dagres says, "but you could see he was quite involved and had a lot of control. I was a little nervous." He also took note that the COO was Schilling's relative.

Then there was the issue of equity. Dagres says that Spark Capital likes to get 20 percent of a company it invests in, but that Schilling's offer was far too small. Schilling denies that he hoarded equity, but multiple sources say that, because he was funding the whole enterprise, he guarded it jealously.

"He was very forthcoming to tell you how much of his own money he put in," Dagres recalls. Schilling tells me that he considered that kind of disclosure a selling point: "I assumed that they would look at it as, 'If he's this far in, it's not going to fail. He's not going to let this thing fail.'" Instead, Dagres was shocked that Schilling was plunging so much into such a risky venture. The VC left with his checkbook firmly closed.

Time and again, though, Schilling emerged from meetings like this one thinking he'd hit a home run. "There was never a single one that he didn't walk out of saying he absolutely killed it," says a former employee who attended a number of investor meetings. But over and over, there was no investment. Still, Schilling remained optimistic. "Curt sincerely believed that Copernicus was the best thing since sliced bread," the former employee says. He "could not imagine a scenario where other people would not see the same potential he did. His attitude is always, This is gonna happen, the deal is going to close."

"Absolutely," Schilling tells me when I run that quote by him. "And that's the way I'm built. I think it's one of the reasons I was able to do what I did playing baseball. And it's not fake. I've been around situations where you can make people believe something they don't believe."

Perhaps, but no investors seemed to be believing—and as they continued to pass, sources say, Schilling and Close, the CEO, began clashing over the equity issue. Meanwhile, Jen MacLean, the VP of business development, was pushing 38 Studios to buy a Maryland video-game outfit called Big Huge Games, which was available for cheap. The deal closed in May 2009, giving 38 Studios 70 new employees. Three months later, Schilling fired Close and appointed MacLean CEO.

Hanging over everything, though, was the fact that there was no new money coming in. As the calendar raced toward 2010—Schilling's original deadline—Project Copernicus remained years away from completion. If Schilling wasn't able to track down money soon, the studio would be doomed. He needed a savior, and was convinced that if he worked hard enough, he'd find one.

On March 6, 2010, Schilling hosted a fund-raising event at his Medfield home. Then–Rhode Island governor Donald Carcieri attended, and the two men got to talking business. Schilling needed money. Carcieri was looking to beef up his state's high-tech sector.

The talks continued for months, with the outline of a deal to move 38 Studios to Rhode Island gradually taking shape. At one point, Schilling approached Governor Deval Patrick and asked for tax incentives to keep the company here, but Patrick politely passed. Given the warning signs flashing around 38 Studios, it remains difficult to understand why Rhode Island so freely handed over $75 million. But for Schilling, despite being a longtime proponent of small government, the guaranteed loan was a godsend. He'd get the cash without having to give up even the tiniest slice of ownership. And if everything went bust, it would be Rhode Island that was responsible for the money.

There were a few catches, though. The loan deal stipulated that 38 Studios had to hit certain hiring benchmarks to access some of the funds. The company would unlock $17.2 million for creating 80 new jobs in the state by spring 2011, another $4.2 million for adding 45 more by fall, and $3.1 million on top of that for 125 additional jobs by winter.

So as the company moved south in April 2011, it embarked on a hiring binge. In its midst, Schilling seemed to be handing out important titles to anybody who asked nicely for one. "It became a joke," one employee says. "Oh, you are a VP of lunch? Oh yeah, I'm a VP of doughnuts." Infighting inevitably resulted, with execs often giving conflicting directives to staffers. "They didn't work well together," Schilling says of his bloated management team. "I was amazed at the turf-building and protecting that went on."

The people working under Schilling had their own complaints about him. One says that he'd undermine managers by randomly dipping in to give direct orders to employees: "His requests added significant work, and were often contrary to the direction given by other people." Former staff members also charge that Schilling was stubborn and ignored people when he didn't like what they were saying. For instance, sources say Schilling froze out his vice president of business development by excluding her from meetings. "Once Curt turned on somebody," a former employee says, "you went from being a superstar to he doesn't want to talk to you, overnight."

Schilling disputes much of this, but 38 Studios churned through a litany of executives during its existence. One former employee says Schilling appreciated that there was a lot he didn't know about video-game development, and "tried to hire some of the best people in the industry to shore up those gaps. The problem is if you don't listen to those people."

Whatever the dysfunction at the executive level, most employees at 38 Studios were unaware of it, and remained happy at the beginning of 2012. There was great excitement in February when the company released "Kingdoms of Amalur: Reckoning," a single-player title produced by Big Huge Games. It did well, selling 1.3 million copies.

Schilling, meanwhile, kept up his free-spending ways. This past Christmas, he personally bought every staffer a computer tote bag with the 38 Studios logo. Add in the company's high staffing levels, frequent gratis lunches and dinners, and big travel budget, and it was easy to forget the whole thing was a start-up. "We never had that sense of urgency or panic," Schilling tells me. "I think there was a sense of invulnerability—I don't want to say invulnerability, but I think we were comfortable."

Deadlines were frequently missed, something for which staffers say Schilling rarely held anyone accountable. The ex-pitcher had a bigger concern. "The game wasn't fun," he says, unprompted, beside the softball field. "It was my biggest gripe for probably the past eight to 12 months." Visually, Copernicus was stunning, but the actual things you could do in the game weren't engaging enough. The combat aspects especially lagged. Schilling—who never wavered in his belief that the game *would be* great—says the MMO was improving, but after six years, it still wasn't there. When Schilling walked around during lunch hour, he says, nobody was playing Copernicus's internal demos. They were all on some other game.

By mid-March, a year and a half after moving to Rhode Island, 38 Studios had received $50 million from the state and had burned through nearly all of it. Because of the way the deal was structured, that would be all they ever got. So Schilling put up $5 million worth of gold coins as collateral for another loan, this one from Bank Rhode Island. Despite the money crunch, however, he brought in two new executives in March, one of whom moved from Texas. That same month, 38 Studios stopped paying vendors like Blue Cross Blue Shield. It had already been ignoring bills from Atlas Van Lines for some time.

Adding to March's chaos, CEO Jen MacLean, who'd been feuding with Schilling, suddenly went on leave. Her colleagues—and the press—were led to believe it was because of her pregnancy (she was roughly six months in), but according to a company source, MacLean's departure was not for medical reasons.

38 Studios was at its most desperate juncture yet. On May 1, a $1.125 million fee payment on the loan from Rhode Island was set to come due. And both the company and Schilling were all but tapped.

Hopeless as things seemed, Schilling remained confident that yet another lifesaving deal was imminent. He still owned 82.9 percent of the company, and says he was willing to part with a healthy chunk of it to save the studio. In April, 38 Studios sent eight employees to China to meet with a potential partner. Then there was a South Korean video-game concern called Nexon, whose executives had recently visited the Providence office and appeared interested in a deal. And finally, Schilling felt that 38 Studios was close to a pact with the company Take-Two Interactive to publish a sequel to "Kingdoms of Amalur: Reckoning."

But when May 1 arrived, 38 Studios was unable to make its loan payment. That put it into default and set off a series of private meetings with Governor Lincoln Chafee's office. Still, most staffers had no idea the company was in trouble until two weeks later, when, on May 14, Chafee told the Rhode Island media that he was working to keep 38 Studios solvent.

Schilling says the deal with Take-Two was ready for "final sign-off" the next day, May 15, but fell apart when the publisher got spooked by Chafee's comments. Take-Two seems to have had a different impression, however. "I am not aware that there were any negotiations," spokesman Alan Lewis says. "We do not comment on rumors and speculation." You'd need a microscope to read between the lines of that statement, but it seems clear that nothing was imminent. Both the Chinese investor and Nexon disappeared too. (Nexon declined comment.) Meanwhile, according to the Associated Press, 38 Studios' board of directors voted to authorize the company to go into bankruptcy, in case it became necessary.

May 15 brought more unwelcome news: 38 Studios missed payroll. Company officials assured employees that the salary issue would get resolved. Workers were told that they had the option to stay home, but that the office would remain open. Most everybody kept coming in.

MacLean, on leave since March, officially resigned as CEO on May 17. That same day, 38 Studios tried to make the $1.125 million payment to Rhode Island, but the company had insufficient funds to keep its check from bouncing. The day after that, Schilling tried again, sending the state a second check—a good one this time—to cover the missed payment. It was part of a complicated plan under which Schilling hoped that Chafee would deliver $6.5 million in additional tax credits—which 38 Studios would then sell to a broker for immediate cash. But Chafee declined. He told the press at a news conference that he didn't want to throw good money after bad. Barring another investor—the very type that 38 Studios had been unsuccessfully chasing for six years—those tax credits would have only kept the company going for a few more weeks anyway.

At the news conference, Chafee also revealed two pieces of information that to that point had been confidential: the anticipated release date of Copernicus—June 2013—and that 38 Studios was spending about $4 million a month. Schilling was outraged, believing that the info would help 38 Studios' competitors plan against the game. Schilling insists that Chafee, who opposed the 38 Studios loan guarantee when he ran for governor, was pursuing a vendetta against him. "There was a concerted effort to make this not succeed," Schilling tells me.

Meanwhile, as the media swarmed outside the 38 Studios office, employees inside began to realize that the company could be done for. Wanting the world to see their work, a few grabbed an old Copernicus trailer and began to brush it up. As they worked, colleagues crammed into a small set of cubicles, packing in 50 to 60 deep. When the video was ready, someone hit Play and "Project Copernicus" came up in gold lettering on the screen, followed by a shot of a foreign-looking world. With haunting music in the background, the camera zoomed in, whooshing through a series of distinct, beautifully rendered landscapes—a forest of trees decorated with ornate hanging lamps; a castle with a base of finely detailed sculptures; a palace topped with golden griffin statues. When the two-minute trailer ended, people lost it. "We're all leaning on each other," says Jesse Smith, the designer. "A lot of us were crying, a lot of us were happy. And after it happened, there was just an uproar of applause."

The trailer was played several times, with new groups of employees cramming in to watch. It was posted online and then played again for the full staff later in the day on a big projection screen. There was a standing ovation.

As the days marched on, most employees continued to come into work. Some figured it was their best chance at getting paid. Others did it out of loyalty. Thom Ang, the company's art director, says Schilling had always taken care of his employees, so he trusted that he would now. "Any time he was presented with options with how to set up the company, how to treat the employees, he always chose the best," Ang says.

On May 24, the entire 38 Studios staff was laid off via email. They hadn't been paid since the end of the previous month, but their problems were just beginning. In short order, their health care disappeared and their 401(k)s were frozen. Then, MoveTrek Mobility—a company 38 Studios hired during the relocation to Providence to buy and resell employees' Massachusetts homes—notified seven people that, because it had not yet sold their houses, they were potentially responsible for their old mortgages. And Atlas Van Lines alerted some individuals that they were on the hook for bills that management hadn't paid.

Thom Ang is one of those people suddenly stuck with his old mortgage. With two young kids, no salary, rent due on his Rhode Island home, and now a mortgage in Massachusetts to pay, he's afraid his credit is about to be ruined. "I wasn't even aware that this could or would happen," he says, "and then having it affect where I could possibly live and where I could possibly work?"

At the last minute, Schilling believed he'd found a white-knight investor to inject $15 million into the company. But that deal, too, was dependent on additional tax credits from the state, and fell apart. On June 7, 38 Studios filed for bankruptcy.

One of the company's final acts—between June 4 and June 6—was to pay COO William "Uncle Bill" Thomas just over $12,000 for his work shutting down 38 Studios, according to bankruptcy documents. Nearly every other employee had not been paid for more than a month. Many local industry veterans and tech investors tell me they're outraged by how Schilling failed to responsibly unwind the company and transparently communicate the dire situation to his employees long before May.

One former staff member vented his frustrations on Facebook, writing, "I'd like to honestly know why I was hired in the first place on January 16th, 2012 . . . when members of the company knew they were behind on bills and not doing well economically? I moved my pregnant wife, sold my house for a loss of 18k, relocated away from all my family and friends for a company I thought was honest and forthright to their employees. What did I get in return? An unpaid [$10,500] relocation package months after it should have been paid, a pregnant wife who found out our insurance had lapsed from our doctor, a ton of bounced checks and payments to bills when we found out our paychecks had not been paid through the media and a large debt to my unemployed father to help us survive."

Surprisingly, though, during and after the company's demise, many former employees continued to stand up for Schilling. When I attended a June 13 mini-reunion at a bar in Waltham, one ex-staffer told me, "I'd still take a bullet for him." On the phone, even Thom Ang—stuck with his old mortgage—said, "I love the man," adding that Schilling could not have been responsible for how he and his coworkers were misled and mistreated. "How the business was run? That's not Curt," Ang says.

But it was. Schilling acknowledges as much. In the private Facebook postings, executives like MacLean and Mrochek claim they tried to stop Schilling and he wouldn't listen. MacLean wrote that executives "brought their issues up many times and were largely ignored."

"You knew we had not been paying all the bills for months," Mrochek wrote to Schilling. "You bet our lives on the roulette wheel of Rhode Island state politics."

Schilling disputes that his lieutenants warned him. He says he pushed 38 Studios to the edge because, as ever, he was confident a deal would come through. "I believed with every ounce of my being that everything was going to work itself out," he says. "I'm $50 million in at this point, so I'm not going to walk away," he adds. "You could make an argument that that was blinding me, but there was the tenor and the velocity and the content of the conversations with the investors."

Back at the softball field in Dracut, Schilling is still having trouble fathoming what happened. "I'll find myself in the middle of the day, just aching," he says. He concedes that he'd promised his employees 60 days' warning if the money ever looked like it was going to run out, but argues that the situation was moving too fast for him to keep sending updates. "It wasn't that I didn't want to tell anyone," he says, "it's I didn't know what to say."

His company is now under federal and state investigation. Schilling denies any legal wrongdoing, and while Roger Williams Law School professor Michael Yelnosky says it's unlikely that Schilling will be held personally accountable for the unpaid salaries under Rhode Island law, there is federal precedent that could force him to pay the wages back, plus damages. Schilling says he would have paid his employees the roughly $1.5 million they're owed out of his pocket, but he doesn't have the money. That doesn't bode well for a lawsuit Citizens Bank filed against him, which seeks to recover $2.4 million in loans to 38 Studios that he'd personally guaranteed. Presumably, either the suit or having to repay lost wages could push him into personal bankruptcy.

As a baseball player, Schilling refused to ever consider the notion of defeat until the final out, even down three games to none to the Yankees. By his own admission, he carried that same attitude into business. One former employee describes it as "rampant and destructive optimism."

Asked if that's truly what undid him, Schilling says, "No," then stutters and pauses. "I don't know any other way to be," he says finally, his voice dropping to just above a whisper and his eyes welling up. "I don't know any other way to be."

BILL GIFFORD

It's Not About the Lab Rats

FROM OUTSIDE

IT'S A JOURNALISTIC AXIOM that when your phone rings early on a Monday, from a blocked number, it's generally not because somebody loves your work. I picked up to hear an angry Lance Armstrong on the line, along with Doug Ulman, the CEO of the Lance Armstrong Foundation—aka Livestrong. It was 8:00 A.M. in Austin. They were calling to berate me about what they considered my bias against Livestrong and Lance.

Which seemed strange, since I wasn't working on a Livestrong article. Not yet, anyway. Granted, I'd been sniffing around and had posted a tweet or two, but nothing more. One of those posts was written on April 17, 2011, the day *60 Minutes* aired its report on Greg Mortenson and the Central Asia Institute. According to allegations made by Steve Kroft and Jon Krakauer, Mortenson had used foundation money to fly himself around and promote his books, which were full of lies about his adventures in Pakistan and Afghanistan. Meanwhile, the charges went, the organization wasn't operating nearly as many schools as Mortenson liked to claim.

"*60 Minutes* takedown," I tweeted, "just goes to show that 'awareness' is the last refuge of a scoundrel." Admittedly, I had both Mortenson and Armstrong in mind when I wrote this: both were facing legal investigations, and both would end up using their philanthropic work as part of their PR defense. The "awareness" wording was a jab at Livestrong, since raising cancer awareness is a major part of the organization's mission.

A lame joke, perhaps, but that's all it was. Still, it made Armstrong livid. "You need to come down here and see what we do," he said sternly. "Ask us the hard questions." It was more a command than a request. "I know you're a hater and you're gonna write what you write, but I just want you to see it."

At the time, Armstrong was starting to take some serious flak of his own. The Jeff Novitzky–led federal investigation into his past was dragging former teammates and associates in front of a Los Angeles grand jury. In January, *Sports Illustrated* published an exposé that supported Floyd Landis's claims that Armstrong had doped to win his seven Tour de France titles. Now *60 Minutes* was said to be working on its own, more damaging story.

In the wake of the Mortenson report, bloggers and journalists (not just this one) were asking pointed questions about Livestrong, the disease-fighting charity that Armstrong founded in 1997, during his recovery from testicular cancer. Cynics wondered whether Armstrong was another Mortenson, living large on his foundation's dime. After all, Armstrong had recently spent $11 million on a personal jet. Was he really rich enough to pay for that out of his own pocket?

"The issue with Lance Armstrong isn't whether he has done good for cancer victims," accounting professor Mark Zimbelman wrote on his blog Fraudbytes, in a post comparing Mortenson to Armstrong, "but rather, whether he first cheated to beat his opponents, then used his fraudulent titles to help promote an organization that appears to do good but also enriches a fraudster."

Others noticed an annoying tendency: whenever questions about doping arose, Armstrong and his supporters changed the subject to his cancer work, a tactic that the bicycling website NY Velocity called "raising the cancer shield." After the *60 Minutes* segment on Armstrong aired in May—complete with damning claims from ex-teammate Tyler Hamilton that Armstrong had cheated— Armstrong's lawyers denied the allegations and quickly invoked Livestrong in his defense. In their one legal brief to date, they blasted the feds over alleged leaks to *60 Minutes* that, they said, were intended to legitimize "the government's investigation of a national hero, best known for his role in the fight against cancer."

But what did that fight amount to? Did Livestrong actually do much to eradicate cancer, or did it exist largely to promote Lance? If and when any indictments came down, would his good deeds help him escape conviction or jail time? It seemed likely that this

theme could come up. Barry Bonds's lawyers recently asked for
probation instead of prison time as punishment for the baseball
star's 2011 Balco conviction, citing his "significant history of charitable, civic, and prior good works."

Writers who've dealt with Lance and his associates are familiar
with their aggro style, but it seemed strange that they'd come on
so strong that morning. Still, Lance had a point: if I wanted to
write about Livestrong, I needed to go see things for myself.

For various reasons, I'm not Lance Armstrong's favorite journalist.
In 2006, I profiled Michele Ferrari, his longtime Italian trainer,
for *Bicycling*. Researching that story left me with serious doubts
about whether Armstrong had competed clean, as he continues to
insist. In 2009, I wrote a *Slate* story called "JerkStrong" that likened
his media-relations style to Sarah Palin's. But my skepticism about
Armstrong as an athlete did not extend to the cancer arena. More
than once, I have given his book *It's Not About the Bike* to friends
stricken with the disease. Not all of them survived, but I know that
none of them cared whether he doped to win the Tour.

Make no mistake, though: if Armstrong is indicted, the survival
of Livestrong will hang in the balance. It seems obvious that Novitzky, an aggressive former IRS agent, would be keenly interested
in the organization and how it operates. If so, he's not alone. At
least two other major publications have done serious reporting
on Livestrong—that is, they started to. In both cases, Livestrong
lawyers succeeded in shutting down the stories before they were
published. They applied the same pressures to *Outside*, blitzing my
editors with pissed-off emails, phone calls, and, eventually, a five-
page letter from general counsel Mona Patel complaining about
"Mr. Gifford's conduct, professionalism, and method of reporting." One of my crimes was a failed attempt to get a source to talk
off the record, an ordinary journalistic practice.

All of which now makes me wonder if I missed something. During an investigation that played out over several months—involving dozens of interviews and careful examination of Livestrong's
public financial records—I found no evidence that Armstrong has
done anything illegal in his role as the face of the organization. As
far as I can tell, he paid for the private jet himself—which is now
for sale, by the way, along with his ranch outside Austin—and he's

apparently been scrupulous about his expenditures as they relate to the nonprofit. When Armstrong travels on Livestrong business, the foundation insists, he picks up his own tabs.

"Since day one, Lance has never been reimbursed for an expense," says Greg Lee, Livestrong's CFO. "Period." Armstrong told me that Livestrong's board—which includes venture capitalist Jeff Garvey, CNN medical reporter Sanjay Gupta, and Harlem cancer fighter Harold Freeman—"would resign immediately if any of that shit happened."

The financial records appear to back up Armstrong's assertion, and if there's a more nefarious reality behind the curtain, it may take someone with subpoena power to bring it to light. In addition to Novitzky's investigation, the IRS examined the foundation's 2006 returns, although Livestrong officials say it was a routine review.

On the program side, I learned that Livestrong provides an innovative and expanding suite of direct services to help cancer survivors negotiate our Kafkaesque health care system. Beyond that, though, I found a curiously fuzzy mix of cancer-war goals like "survivorship" and "global awareness," labels that seem to entail plastering the yellow Livestrong logo on everything from T-shirts to medical conferences to soccer stadiums. Much of the foundation's work ends up buffing the image of one Lance Edward Armstrong, which seems fair—after all, Livestrong wouldn't exist without him. But Livestrong spends massively on advertising, PR, and "branding," all of which helps preserve Armstrong's marketability at a time when he's under fire. Meanwhile, Armstrong has used the goodwill of his foundation to cut business deals that have enriched him personally, an ethically questionable move.

"It's a win-win," says Daniel Borochoff, head of the American Institute of Philanthropy, a watchdog group. "He builds up the foundation, and they build up him."

Equally interesting is what the foundation doesn't do. Most people—including nearly everybody I surveyed while reporting this story—assume that Livestrong funnels large amounts of money into cancer research. Nope. The foundation gave out a total of $20 million in research grants between 1998 and 2005, the year it began phasing out its support of hard science. A note on the foundation's website informs visitors that, as of 2010, it no longer even accepts research proposals.

Nevertheless, the notion persists that Livestrong's main purpose is to help pay for lab research into cancer cures. In an online "*60 Minutes* Overtime" interview after the May broadcast, CBS anchor Scott Pelley said Armstrong's alleged misdeeds were mitigated because "he has raised hundreds of millions of dollars for cancer research."

Pelley isn't alone in getting that wrong: a search of the *New York Times* turns up dozens of hits for "Armstrong" and "cancer research." An Associated Press story from August 2010 described Livestrong as "one of the top 10 groups funding cancer research in the United States." The comments section of any article about Armstrong will inevitably include messages like this one from ESPN.com: "keep raising millions for cancer research lance, and ignore the haters." At one point, the foundation brought in a PR consultant to try and clarify the messaging, but Armstrong himself says there's only so much they can do. "We can't control what everybody says they're wearing the bracelets for," he told me.

At the same time, though, Armstrong and his supporters help perpetuate the notion that they are, in fact, helping battle cancer in the lab. "I am here to fight this disease," he angrily told journalist Paul Kimmage at a press conference held during his 2009 comeback. In 2010, the foundation agreed to let an Australian hospital call its new research facility the Livestrong Cancer Research Center. And when I recently visited my local RadioShack, a major Armstrong sponsor, the clerk asked, "Would you like to make a donation to the Livestrong foundation to help support cancer research?"

No wonder people get confused.

With its reclaimed-wood surfaces and industrial-chic design, Livestrong HQ resembles a cutting-edge Whole Foods—another signature Austin institution. Here in East Austin, the poorer side of town, there's no Whole Foods, just dusty *carnicerías* that sell fantastic tongue tacos. A renovated warehouse, the $9 million building opened in 2009.

In the lobby, I meet Livestrong spokeswoman Katherine McLane and Chris Dammert, head of what's known as navigation services. Our first stop is the building's walk-in navigation center, adjacent to the main entrance, where bilingual staffers offer cancer patients financial consultation, help with insurance issues, and counseling.

106 BILL GIFFORD

Since the center opened in late 2010, Dammert says, some 207 families have come in—lower traffic than he'd like. "We're hoping to build awareness over time," he says.

The walk-in center is a hands-on version of the online and telephone support services that Livestrong has offered since 2005. Dammert leads me upstairs to an area where two "navigators" are settling into their cubicles. This is where patients or loved ones can phone in to a hotline with questions. Depending on their needs, callers are either directed to one of two in-house social workers for emotional support or referred to outside agencies.

Livestrong sends about two-thirds of the callers to organizations like the Virginia-based Patient Advocate Foundation (PAF), which deals with insurance and billing issues. In 2010, Livestrong paid PAF $727,000 for helping its clients; the organization even has a staffer on-site in Austin. In addition, Livestrong helps connect people with clinical trials and offers assistance to patients who (like Lance did) need help learning about sperm banking or egg freezing. Last year, the foundation says, it saved its members more than $2 million on fertility services.

Lastly, Livestrong publishes a set of cancer guidebooks, which include a journal, a record keeper to help organize paperwork, and a manual walking readers through the many steps of treatment. These are available from the Livestrong website for free.

One unlikely "nav" beneficiary is cycling journalist Charles Pelkey, diagnosed last summer with male breast cancer. Pelkey has been a critic of Armstrong—"I don't particularly like the man," he says—but after he tweeted about his cancer, a Livestrong navigator contacted him to offer assistance. "There are really wonderful people who work there," Pelkey says. "I respect everything they do."

Dammert hands me off to McLane for the rest of the tour, and it's clear Armstrong didn't hire a milquetoast for the job. Tall and serious, she came to the foundation in 2007 from the Bush Department of Education. "My job was to defend the No Child Left Behind law," she says. "Every teacher in America hated it, including my parents."

Armstrong is a visitor, not a daily presence; when I was there in June, he had already decamped to Aspen for the summer. But his handprints are all over the place, from the framed yellow jerseys outside the staff gym to the enormous yellow chopper (a gift from the guys on *Orange County Choppers*) parked near the lobby. Every available surface is occupied by pieces from Armstrong's art collection—including the Shepard Fairey "Lance face" poster and a wooden carving of a female torso emerging from a globe.

We end up in a conference room with 34-year-old Doug Ulman, Livestrong's $320,000-a-year CEO. Earnest and intense, he looks like he could be Lance's younger brother. Ulman was a sophomore soccer player at Brown University when he was diagnosed with a rare tumor and two types of melanoma. After successful treatment, he started his own foundation for young adults with cancer; Armstrong read about him in the Brown alumni magazine and sent an admiring email. They hit it off, and Ulman came aboard in 2001. At the time, Livestrong had four staffers and a budget of about $7 million. Now it has a staff of 88, and it took in $48 million in 2010.

Like his boss, Ulman is energized by adversity. Tacked to the wall of his cube is a photocopied quote from Ken Berger, the head of Charity Navigator, an influential ratings and watchdog group. "It is just going to devastate them," he said in an Associated Press article.

"It" is the federal investigation against Armstrong, which Livestrong staffers have tried to compartmentalize. "We can't predict what's going to happen in the world of cycling," Ulman says. "We have to stay focused on fulfilling our mission."

That mission has evolved considerably. In the early years, Ulman says, the foundation awarded grants for research on both testicular cancer and cancer survivors. The grants were small, in the low six figures or less, and were aimed at scientists pursuing cutting-edge ideas.

"For a young researcher it was great," says Julien Sage, a Stanford professor who received a total of $150,000 from 2004 to 2005. "I had no data, just an idea." Small, speculative grants like his, he explains, are essential to young scientists who are developing the data they need to apply for more substantial government funding.

The main reason for the shift, Ulman says, was scale. The American Cancer Society raised $900 million last year. And the National Cancer Institute awards nearly $2 billion a year in research grants. Ulman says Livestrong was too small to make a difference in such a big pond. "We started to realize that there's literally billions of dollars in cancer research, and we asked, Is that the best use of the money we're raising?"

Point taken. It's worth noting, though, that the Michael J. Fox Foundation had about the same revenue as Livestrong in 2008— $40 million—and gave away $33 million of that in grants for Parkinson's research. The Susan G. Komen Foundation also does a huge amount of pink-ribbon "awareness" work, but it still dished out $145 million in breast-cancer research grants over the past two years. With Livestrong gone, there is no equivalent private funder for testicular-cancer research.

Sage says that the kind of contribution Livestrong was making is still needed. "It's a mistake to stop supporting basic research, because there are a lot of things we can learn," he says. "There are still people who die from testicular cancer, and we need to look for better ways to treat them."

Ulman doesn't see it that way. "We are all about people," he says. "Most organizations are about the disease. They're about trying to solve a disease, and we are about trying to improve the lives of people that are battling the disease . . . What can we do *today* to improve their lives? As opposed to saying we'll fund research that in 15 years might help somebody live a little longer."

McLane agrees. "If we applied the science we already have, we could cure almost everybody," she says. "The search for a cure could have already been successful. It's removing the barriers to the treatment that can cause that cure that is the real problem for many people all over the world."

After Armstrong retired from cycling, the only direction his foundation seemed to be moving was down. In 2005, the last year he won the Tour, revenues grew to $52 million, fueled largely by the famous $1 Nike Livestrong wristband. But when Armstrong left the spotlight, the wristband fad waned and foundation revenues sagged by $20 million the next year.

They stayed lower despite a notable success in 2007, perhaps Livestrong's greatest achievement. Armstrong spent much of that year campaigning for Proposition 15, a Texas ballot initiative to create a huge pool of public money for cancer research and prevention. He worked the Texas legislature and traveled the state by bus with then–state representative Patrick Rose, and the measure passed. "There is no chance that Prop 15 would have become a reality but for Lance's personal involvement," Rose says today.

But it took Comeback 2.0 to put Livestrong on people's radar again. Armstrong announced his plans in a September 2008 *Vanity Fair* interview, in which he said his return would be built around what he called a "global cancer summit." The comeback was portrayed as a completely charitable mission. "I am essentially racing for free," he told the magazine. "No salary. No bonus. This one's on the house."

His reboot was a smashing success: huge crowds and adoring headlines greeted Armstrong's return to racing at the Tour Down Under in Australia. In Sacramento, fans lined the prologue course of the Tour of California waving yellow signs with the Lance face and the slogan HOPE RIDES AGAIN. He ended up with a podium finish at the 2009 Tour de France, and Livestrong revenue surged back over the $40 million mark.

But the comeback also saw Livestrong's final evolution from a research nonprofit into something that looks more like a hip marketing agency. Rather than funding test-tube projects, it was deploying buzzwords like *leverage, partnering,* and *message.*

One way to spread the message is to slap Livestrong's name on just about everything, from Livestrong Survivorship Centers of Excellence (there are eight at major hospitals nationwide) to Oakley sunglasses to, at one point, a Livestrong Build-a-Bear (complete with yellow cycling outfit). The Livestrong label is so appealing that the owners of the Major League Soccer franchise Sporting KC decided to donate the naming rights for its new stadium, guaranteeing the foundation $7.5 million over six years. Normally, a corporation would pay to have its name put on such a venue, but team owners are betting that Livestrong Sporting Park will attract more business and goodwill than, say, AT&T Arena would. (Lance even has his own seat: Box 1, Seat 007.)

Did the doping allegations bother them? "We asked the foundation about that," says team co-owner Robb Heineman. "They said he's the most tested athlete in the history of sports, and he maintains he's never done it."

Livestrong prides itself on the fact that—on paper anyway— it spends 81 percent of every dollar on programs. This is a big improvement over 2005, when the American Institute of Philanthropy took Livestrong to task for spending 45 cents of every dollar on fund-raising. Now AIP gives Livestrong an A-minus, while Charity Navigator rates it three stars out of four.

But the foundation's financial reports from 2009 and 2010 show that Livestrong's resources pay for a very large amount of marketing and PR. During those years, the foundation raised $84 million and spent just over $60 million. (The rest went into a reserve of cash and assets that now tops $100 million.)

A surprising $4.2 million of that went straight to advertising, including large expenditures for banner ads and optimal search-engine placement. Outsourcing is the order of the day: $14 million of total spending, or more than 20 percent, went to outside consultants and professionals. That figure includes $2 million for construction, but much of the money went to independent organizations that actually run Livestrong programs. For example, Livestrong paid $1 million to a Boston-based public-health consulting firm to manage its campaigns in Mexico and South Africa against cancer stigma—the perception that cancer is contagious or invariably fatal.

Livestrong touts its stigma programs, but it spent more than triple that, $3.5 million in 2010 alone, for merchandise giveaways and order fulfillment. Curiously, on Livestrong's tax return most of those merchandise costs were categorized as "program" expenses. CFO Greg Lee says donating the wristbands counts as a program because "it raises awareness."

This kind of spending dwarfs Livestrong's outlays for its direct services and patient-focused programs like Livestrong at the YMCA, an exercise routine tailored to cancer survivors available at YMCAs nationwide ($424,000 in 2010). There's also a Livestrong at School program, offered in conjunction with *Scholastic* magazine ($630,000 in 2010). "Explain to students that Lance was very sick with cancer but that he was treated and got better," begins one sample lesson plan for grades three through six.

Livestrong spends as much on legal bills as on these two programs combined: $1.8 million in 2009–2010, mainly to protect its trademarks. In one memorable case, its lawyers shut down a man in Oklahoma who was selling Barkstrong dog collars. Meanwhile, "benefits to donors" (also merchandise, as well as travel expenses for Livestrong Challenge fund-raisers) accounted for another $1.4 million in spending in 2010.

There's still a research department, but now it focuses on things like quality-of-life surveys of cancer survivors. During my visit, I was plied with glossy reports and brochures, which are cranked out by the truckload. The foundation's 2010 copying-and-printing bill came to almost $1.5 million.

But Livestrong's largest single project in 2009—indeed, the main focus of Armstrong's comeback—was the Livestrong Global Cancer Summit, held in Dublin in August. The summit ate up close to 20 percent of the foundation's $30 million in program spending that year.

To kick things off, Livestrong hired Ogilvy, the famous advertising firm, to create a global cancer-awareness campaign leading up to the summit. Cost: $3.8 million. It spent another $1.2 million to hire a New York City production company to stage the three-day event. Then it paid more than $1 million to fly 600 cancer survivors and advocates to Dublin from all over the world—the United States, Russia, Bangladesh, and 60 other countries. The former president of Nigeria even showed up.

Often, the main output at gatherings like this is verbiage, and so it was at the summit. Participants declared cancer a "global health crisis." A report was produced titled "A World Without Cancer." And delegates called on every country to develop a national cancer plan to deal with the disease. At the end of the summit, 97 percent of participants answering a Livestrong survey said they had "developed a deeper level of understanding about the issues related to cancer."

"You wonder," AIP's Borochoff says. "If they just gave the money to cancer research, would it generate as much great publicity for Lance Armstrong?"

The foundation considers this money well spent, but if I were a Livestrong supporter I'd also ask: What's the product here? If not research, then what do I get for my $100 donation?

"I think the product is hope," says Mark McKinnon, the renowned GOP political consultant and a Livestrong board member. Armstrong's team approached McKinnon in 2001, seeking advice on positioning Lance for a post-cycling career. McKinnon, a media strategist for President George W. Bush, introduced Armstrong to another client, Bono. The two hit it off, and soon Armstrong seemed to be aiming toward a Bono-like role as a global cancer statesman.

"His goal was to change the way people look at cancer and the way people deal with cancer," says McKinnon. "In typical Lance fashion, he wanted to have a fundamental impact on the disease: how it's perceived, how it's dealt with."

Done. Thanks largely to Armstrong, we don't talk about cancer "victims" anymore; they're cancer *survivors*. And they don't "suffer" from the disease; they want to "Kick. Its. Ass"—as ESPN anchor and cancer patient Stuart Scott urged a crowd of high-level Livestrong fund-raisers and donors at a dinner before the Philadelphia Livestrong Challenge last August.

Sitting beside me at that event, a man named Scott Joy nodded fervently as he listened. In 2003, Joy was diagnosed with testicular cancer and found his way to Armstrong's book. "It told me I would get through this," he said. "I needed to hear that."

Joy is now a Livestrong Leader, part of an elite corps of fund-raisers and organizers. This year he raised more than $42,000 for Livestrong, but perhaps more important, he's been fiercely defending Lance and the foundation on Twitter and in the comments sections of online articles. Joy is one of many Livestrong Army members who remain passionate about their cause and their hero.

Nobody can doubt Armstrong's empathy for cancer patients or his power to inspire. In certain instances, though, he has leveraged this charitable appeal for personal gain. During his comeback, the lines between Cancer Lance and Business Lance became especially blurry.

Although Armstrong had told *Vanity Fair* he would be racing for free, he actually pocketed appearance fees in the high six figures from the organizers of both the Tour Down Under and the Giro d'Italia. An Australian government official told reporters that the money was a charitable donation, but Lance himself admitted to the *New York Times* that he was treating it as personal income.

It's a tricky thing. Armstrong is in demand not just as a cyclist but also as a cancer survivor and inspirational figure—in other words, because of the Livestrong Effect—yet he's never been shy about monetizing this appeal for personal gain. For example, when he spoke at the inaugural Pelotonia cancer ride in Columbus, Ohio, in August 2009, he charged the start-up charity his usual $200,000 speaking fee, including $100,000 worth of NetJets time, courtesy of Pelotonia sponsor and NetJets founder Rich Santulli. Pelotonia executive director Tom Lennox considers it worth the expense: the 2011 edition of the ride pulled in more than $11 million—all of which will be spent on cancer research, by the way.

In a sense, Livestrong and Lance are like conjoined twins, each depending on the other for survival. Separating them—or even figuring out where one ends and the other begins—is no small task. The foundation is a major reason why sponsors are attracted to Armstrong; as his agent Bill Stapleton put it in 2001, his survivor story "broadened and deepened the brand . . . and then everybody wanted him." But the reverse is also true: without Lance, Livestrong would be just another cancer charity scrapping for funds.

Nike is the best example of this symbiotic relationship: Armstrong's longtime sponsor produces a complete line of Livestrong apparel, from shorts and backpacks to running shoes and T-shirts, all of which it pays Armstrong to wear. Under a five-year deal negotiated in early 2010—before the Landis allegations broke—Nike agreed to pay Livestrong a minimum of $7.5 million per year from its merchandise profits.

Nike's commitment goes well beyond selling merchandise and sponsorship to producing ads that promote Livestrong, Armstrong, and the Nike brand all at once. In one particularly memorable spot from 2009, Armstrong verbally took on his critics. "They say I'm arrogant . . . a doper . . . washed up . . . a fraud," he said over scenes of himself on his bike intercut with shots of cancer patients getting chemo treatments, crawling out of bed, and unsteadily lifting weights. "I'm not back on my bike for *them*."

It was clear which side RadioShack wanted to be on. Not long after the Nike ad aired, during the 2009 Tour, the electronics retailer stepped up to sponsor a 2010 squad built around Armstrong, paying him a reported $10 million to be team leader. The deal was negotiated by L.A.-based superagent Casey Wasserman, who donated $1 million to Livestrong via his family foundation. The RadioShack deal was brilliant in its own way. Not only would the company support Lance and his team, but it also made a major commitment to support Livestrong. The cancer charity, in fact, was the key to the whole thing. "We wouldn't have done it without Livestrong," says Lee Applbaum, RadioShack's chief marketing officer.

But rather than simply donating money outright, RadioShack got its customers to pony up $1 or more at the checkout counter. So far, the Shack's customers have kicked in more than $10 million, according to company spokesman Eric Bruner. (Sometimes without knowing it: early on, a few customers complained that the $1 donation had been accidentally added to their bill.)

Not all the money goes where Livestrong says it goes, however. In January 2010, after the devastating earthquake in Haiti, Armstrong made a personal video statement: to help earthquake victims, Livestrong would give $125,000 each to the charitable organizations Doctors Without Borders and Partners in Health, which it subsequently did. RadioShack also hopped on board, soliciting $538,000 in customer donations for the Haitian cause. According to Livestrong, it gave $413,000 of the RadioShack money to Partners in Health. And the foundation's 2010 tax form shows a $458,000 donation to the group. But $333,000 of that had been previously allocated to a separate hospital project in Haiti that "had nothing to do with the earthquake," says a spokesperson for Partners in Health. That means Livestrong used the RadioShack earthquake donations to cover its prior hospital pledge.

In one case, Armstrong himself stood to profit from the sale of a major Livestrong asset: its name. Most people are unaware that there are two Livestrong websites. Livestrong.org is the site for the nonprofit Lance Armstrong Foundation, while Livestrong.com is a somewhat similar-looking page that features the same Livestrong logo and design but is actually a for-profit content farm owned by Demand Media.

In 2008, the foundation licensed the Livestrong brand name to Demand, the online media company behind eHow and Cracked .com, among other properties. Livestrong.com was positioned as a "health, fitness, and wellness community," offering an online calorie counter, exercise and yoga videos, and articles about such topics as "What Are the Signs and Symptoms of Rejecting Belly Button Rings?"

As compensation for the use of its name, the foundation received about 183,000 shares of stock, which it sold for $3.1 million when the company went public in January 2011. Armstrong also received 156,000 shares of his own as part of a spokesperson agreement. (His agents, Bill Stapleton and Bart Knaggs, also received shares.) After the deal was criticized in the media, Armstrong donated his initial sale proceeds—roughly $1.2 million—to the foundation and said he planned to donate the rest too.

Livestrong executives describe the deal as good for everyone, a way to spread their message of healthy lifestyles to a wider audience. Under the agreement, Armstrong provided blog entries, videos, and other content to Livestrong.com. "I actually have to do work for them," he told me in an interview.

Adds Ulman: "They guaranteed us certain levels of traffic. They said, 'We will build a site, and we will ultimately send people to the foundation.'" But traffic to the for-profit Demand Media site has surged, in part thanks to Lance's promotional work, while the foundation's traffic has remained essentially flat. And it was the foundation that paid to defend their joint trademark against the Barkstrong dog-collar salesman.

"It's definitely questionable," says Mark Zimbelman, the Brigham Young University professor behind Fraudbytes. "Imagine if the American Red Cross sold its name to Americanredcross .com, and you can go there and buy vitamins. You think you're donating or helping the American Red Cross, but you're really not. It's unheard of."

Armstrong benefits from his foundation in another, less tangible way: everything he does in connection with Livestrong gets him good press, diluting the flow of scandal stories. In September, he made a splash at a UN meeting on noncommunicable diseases, appearing at several forums to, as the foundation put it, "represent the 28 million people around the world living with cancer." New York City mayor Michael Bloomberg, himself a million-dollar donor, threw a lavish party that featured a Livestrong-produced documentary on young cancer patients in Rwanda and Jordan. Nike put up a three-story billboard near Madison Square Garden with Livestrong's latest slogan, FIGHT LIKE HELL.

That might as well be Lance's legal motto, since all signs point to a scorched-earth battle in his near future. At press time, Novitzky had been investigating Armstrong for more than 18 months, with still no indictments coming out of the Los Angeles grand jury.

Whether that's good news or bad news for Armstrong remains to be seen, but most observers think an indictment is coming.

The feds aren't his only worry. Waiting in the wings is the U.S. Anti-Doping Agency (USADA), which has been conducting its own investigation since it received Floyd Landis's accusatory emails in May 2010. And while it remains true that Armstrong has never tested positive, at least officially, nowadays you don't need to flunk a lab test to be sanctioned for performance-enhancing drugs.

For the past several years, USADA has been handing down non-analytical positives—sanctioning athletes based on evidence, including testimony from teammates, other than direct positive tests. In 2008, the agency banned the cyclist Kayle Leogrande for EPO use based almost entirely on the testimony of a soigneur and a team administrator. Armstrong now has at least two former teammates, Landis and Hamilton, who say they witnessed him using banned drugs—and there may be more if, as *60 Minutes* reported, George Hincapie and others told similar stories to the grand jury.

That means Armstrong could be looking at a doping sanction, possibly a lifetime ban, and the loss of at least two of his Tour titles. (The statute of limitations for doping offenses is eight years.)

And while the foundation takes care to distance itself from the doping drama—McLane calls it "issues in the cycling world"—the potential fallout is considerable. If Armstrong turns out to have used drugs, then *It's Not About the Bike*—Livestrong's creation myth—will ring just as false as *Three Cups of Tea*.

"It's going to have a huge impact," says Michael Birdsong, a former Livestrong supporter, now disillusioned, who estimates that he has given $50,000 to Livestrong over the years. "Who wants to support a foundation that was founded by a cheater? Not only a cheater, but a person who lied about it."

The foundation says that its 2011 donations are up, year over year. But more than a third of the foundation's support comes from corporate sources and cross-marketing deals with Armstrong's sponsors, starting with that $7.5 million from Nike. If he is sanctioned for doping, then that money, and revenue from his other sponsors, becomes vulnerable. While Nike and RadioShack say they are sticking by Armstrong, that can always change: when Marion Jones was busted for doping, Nike dropped her.

More tellingly, the Livestrong Challenge ride and run events— which depend on people asking friends and neighbors for donations—are bringing in much less money these days. The rides raised only $6.3 million in 2011, before expenses, versus more than $11 million the previous year, according to the foundation's 2010 annual report. "It was a lot more difficult to raise $250 for Livestrong this year," says one longtime foundation fund-raiser. "People asked a lot more questions."

For his part, Armstrong is staying the course: he's innocent, he says, and the public backing that he and Livestrong need will always be there. "I can only tell you what people come up and say with regard to that," he told me. "The support might even go to a place where they say, 'I don't fucking know, and I don't care. I know what Livestrong means to myself and my family. That's what I care about.'"

Still, in a 2006 deposition in another court case, even Armstrong sounded worried about how a scandal could affect his sponsors and followers. "If you have a doping offense or you test positive, it goes without saying that you're fired, from all of your contracts," he said. "It's not about money for me. It's all about the faith that people have put in me over the years. All of that would be erased. So I don't need it to say in a contract, You're fired if you test positive. That's not as important as losing the support of hundreds of millions of people."

NICOLE PASULKA

Eddie Is Gone

FROM THE BELIEVER

I. Occupy Frommer's

THE HAWAIIAN HISTORY that plays through headsets on the buses that shuttle tourists between the shops, hotels, restaurants, and beaches on Oahu is predictably bland, defanged, and heavy with half-truths. During the winter of 2011, I wrote such toothless audio tours for a popular tourism company. A typical paragraph might begin:

> Even hula has its heroes. Early missionaries to the Hawaiian Islands discouraged the dance for being too sexy, but, lucky for us, the fun-loving last king of Hawaii, King David Kalākaua, kept the hula alive in secret. In addition to preserving the hula, King Kalākaua took a trip around the world, and wrote "Hawai'i Pono'ī" ("Hawaii's Own"), which later became the state song. But Kalākaua's most visible achievement was the construction of the stunning 'Iolani Palace on our left—the only royal palace built on U.S. soil. Flanked by palm trees, this shining example of Hawaiian renaissance architecture was built at the astronomical (for 1882) cost of $300,000. Don't miss a stop at the regal coronation pavilion, located on the palace grounds. King Kalākaua ordered the palace's furniture from Boston, and Princess Lili'uokalani, King David's sister and heir, was the last Hawaiian monarch to live here.

There's more to Kalākaua and Princess Lili'uokalani's story than most tours imply. A group of white businessmen and descendants of missionaries deposed the monarch in 1893, leading to the United States' annexation of Hawaii. These businessmen later imprisoned the princess in the palace, claiming she was behind a counterrevolutionary plot that would have restored her to power.

"Too controversial," my project manager wrote in the comments. "Let's just say she *lived* here."

I soon learned that paying my rent by writing for Hawaii's tourists meant each story had to be carefully finessed to minimize any controversy or potentially depressing details. According to the history we produced, nothing bad had ever really happened in Hawaii—except possibly for Pearl Harbor, though we even tiptoed around that; after all, in 2010, 1.2 million Japanese tourists spent nearly $2 billion in Hawaii. The standard tourist narrative downplays or disregards disease epidemics, violence against native Hawaiians, and movements for native sovereignty. Because who wants to be reminded they're taking a holiday on illegally annexed land?

The whitewashed versions of local history celebrating the welcoming Hawaiian culture, ethnic diversity, and natural beauty don't simply dominate the tourism industry. They've been accepted chronicles of the islands in film and on TV, and were taught in local and mainland schools for much of the twentieth century. Today, a movie like *The Descendants* at least acknowledges the complicated history that left a few people in control of most of Hawaii's land, and many popular guidebooks describe the collapse of indigenous rule as a result of certain monarchs' poor choices and American colonialism. Hawaiian schools and universities teach rich ethnic-studies curricula of local history, mythology, culture, politics, and art. However, the fact remains that of the seven million tourists who visit the islands each year, a huge number will experience Hawaii as a Polynesian Disneyland, a place staffed and populated by smiling hula girls ready with leis and hollowed-out pineapples filled with rum.

For around a thousand years, Hawaiian kings and chiefs— known as *ali'i*—controlled the land, and access was determined by social order. As the Hawaiian monarchy adopted a constitution and began to democratize in the 1830s and '40s, a series of landownership laws called "the Great Mahele" made it possible for private citizens to own property on the islands for the first time. The Great Mahele was intended to provide a substantial amount of land for Hawaiian commoners, but the concept of property ownership was alien to Hawaiians, and only about 1 percent of native Hawaiians ended up being able to take advantage of the

law. American entrepreneurs and industrialists managed to acquire land that would become hugely lucrative sugar, pineapple,
and coffee plantations, and 70 percent of native Hawaiians found
themselves landless by the end of the nineteenth century.

King Kalākaua, who began his reign in 1874, was a Hawaiian
nationalist as well as a reckless partier (they called him "the Mer-
rie Monarch"). He defended traditions such as the hula from
the attacks of American missionaries, who disapproved of and
suppressed whatever they felt was irreligious or amoral. Unfortunately, the king's heavy drinking and reckless spending were what
probably left him vulnerable to a power grab by a group of white
businessmen calling themselves "the Hawaiian League." The Mahele had made it possible for these men to make or inherit ob-
scene amounts of money from pineapple and sugar plantations.
In 1887, the league forced Kalākaua to sign away most of his
power, some say at gunpoint. A cadre of Americans with growing
financial interest in Hawaii held Kalākaua's sister and successor,
Lili'uokalani, in the palace under house arrest for eight months
after a counterrevolutionary group of native Hawaiians attempted
to restore her authority as sovereign. Among these American businessmen were James Dole, founder of the Dole pineapple planta-
tion (where tourists can now lose themselves in the world's largest garden maze), and his cousin Sanford Dole, who then became
interim president of the Republic of Hawaii. Activists for native
sovereignty held several 20th-century protests of the monarchy's
overthrow at 'Iolani Palace; in 2008, a group of native Hawaiians
managed to lock the gates to the palace. To these activists, Hawaii
never should have become part of the United States.

When I was working in Honolulu, a trolley ride down Ward Avenue between the Ala Moana Shopping Center and another nearby
shopping mall, Ward Centers, offered views of the ocean and a
sprawling tent city of homeless people (until they were evicted
later that year). To distract riders from the encampments, tourist
companies offered flowery narratives of Hawaiian royalty, folklore,
and legend, generously sprinkled with innuendo about sexy hula
girls and tropical beverages.

Winter is big-wave season on Oahu's North Shore—on the radio, on the bus, in bars and restaurants, everyone was talking about
"the Eddie," a surf competition named after big-wave surfing icon
Eddie Aikau, which only takes place when the waves at Waimea

Bay are consistently breaking at over 20 feet. After I'd spent a deadening series of days composing pro-imperialist schlock for tour buses, Aikau's story captured my imagination. His life seemed to epitomize the tension between Hawaii's often-violent struggle against cultural interlopers and the popular image of a lush paradise for Western recreation and consumption. Neither tour guide nor separatist, Eddie embodied the oppositional forces of tourism and resistance. Through his friendships, his surfing, and his ill-fated voyage across the ocean in a canoe, Eddie attempted to reconcile Hawaii's cultural heritage with the aftermath of colonial destruction on the islands.

II. Beach Consciousness

Eddie Aikau was born in 1946, and grew up with his five siblings in a Chinese graveyard in Pauoa Valley, on Oahu. Hawaiians of Chinese ancestry have lived in Hawaii for more than 200 years, though most showed up in the mid to late nineteenth century to work on booming sugar and pineapple plantations. Pops Aikau and his kids maintained the cemetery grounds, digging up old bones and placing them in a mausoleum. The close-knit Aikau family spent most of their free time in the ocean. Diving, fishing, and paddleboarding animated a day-to-day existence of near poverty. As they became more proficient in the waves, Eddie and his brother Clyde started surfing with the native Hawaiian beach boys who partied with tourists and flirted with divorcées on the pristine beaches of Waikiki.

Hawaiians have been surfing for more than 1,000 years. There are legends and prayers dedicated to surfing, and the practice deeply influenced and reflected Hawaiians' social status. In *Waves of Resistance,* a groundbreaking study of the relationship between surfing, Hawaiian identity, and the movement for native sovereignty, historian Isaiah Helekunihi Walker identifies a "culture of respect and exchange" on the beaches of Hawaii. For hundreds of years, how one behaved in the surf defined one's place in society. Surfing brought prestige and generated community. A poor kid living in a graveyard could make a name for himself by holding his own in ocean breaks. Pops Aikau knew this, and convinced a local teacher and activist named John Kelly to take Eddie surfing on the winter swells at Waimea Bay.

Though the ocean is placid and family-friendly during the summer months, winter swells on the island's North Shore are about
as welcoming as a New England blizzard. Originating from storms
in the north Pacific Ocean, the waves at Waimea Bay, one of the 51
beaches covering the North Shore's 11 miles of shoreline, may not
be the world's biggest, but, measuring from the face of the wave,
they reach heights of more than 25 feet. From behind, they're
taller than four-story buildings. These were the waves that would
come to define Eddie as a surfer.

A Hawaiian-born *haole* (a common but difficult-to-translate
word that essentially means "foreigner," and effectively means
"white person"), John Kelly was a fierce visionary activist for environmental justice in Hawaii. He and a coalition of young surfers
led Save Our Surf (SOS), an organization that epitomized the connection between environmentalism and surfing. The group waged
high-profile battles against land developments that threatened to
destroy local surfing and fishing. In particular, it opposed extensive coastal land grabs by Dillingham, a corporation founded by
descendants of missionaries who drained the buggy Waikiki wet-
lands that had once held fish ponds and rice paddies, beginning
the process of transforming Waikiki into the tropical shopping
mall that it resembles today. In 1971, SOS occupied the state capi-
tol building to protest these developments. It also defended native
Hawaiian families against the threat of eviction. In its 30 years of
activism, the group managed to win 34 major environmental victories against corporate powers in Hawaii, at one point thwarting
a $56 million Dillingham project to dredge and fill reefs around
eastern Oahu for a highway.

Driving through pineapple fields on the way to the North
Shore, Kelly gave informal history lessons to Eddie and another
young Hawaiian surfer, Sammy Lee. He told them how a few rich
white landowners had exploited the Great Mahele, creating plantations and building resorts for tourists. The beach had been a
refuge for Eddie, but, like many Hawaiians during the 1960s, he
was becoming aware of the impact that annexation and statehood
had had on native traditions. It's impossible to know for sure how
many Native Hawaiians lived on the islands at the time of first contact with British explorers, in 1778, but historians estimate that
before Cook arrived there were around 500,000. By 1890, disease,
wars between islands, and poverty had reduced the number to a

mere 40,000. The history Kelly taught the younger surfers contradicted the story of a conflict-free annexation and statehood they'd learned in school. The reality was grim. The U.S. military was testing weapons on the island of Kaho'olawe; sugarcane and pineapple plantations had replaced diverse, sustainable agriculture that preserved the scarce freshwater supply; Hawaiians were subject to the rule of a government based nearly 5,000 miles away. As Kelly drove Eddie and his friends past Hawaiian valleys and mountains toward its beaches, they began to comprehend how Hawaii had been transformed into America.

III. Rip, Tear, and Lacerate

Eddie couldn't have been further from the mainland surfer stereotype of a bleach-blond show-off with a stoner drawl. In *Eddie Would Go,* a lovingly reported and extensive account of Eddie's life (and a source for much of the biographical history in this essay), the writer Stuart Holmes Coleman draws an affecting portrait of Eddie as a deep, shy, and quiet person. He was short, with shaggy dark hair—a kid in a red swimsuit with matching Hobie board. In pictures, Eddie often seems to be staring past the camera. He was already hooked on the surf at Waimea Bay when, at 22, he and another big-wave surfer, Butch Van Artsdalen, were hired to be the first lifeguards on the North Shore. Today, during the winter swells on Waimea, lifeguards on Jet Skis patrol just past the break, and yellow tape restricts dangerous sections of shoreline. Beachgoers respect the lifeguards' authority. In the '60s, however, swimmers regularly drowned at Waimea in the powerful current and unpredictable waves. Coleman writes that Eddie would let overconfident swimmers toss in the surf before rescuing them, so they'd leave the ocean with the necessary amount of fear and respect—what he called "the Aikau method of lifeguarding." But no one drowned on his watch.

Eddie continued to grow as a surfer, placing well year after year in the Duke Classic. Named after Hawaiian surf icon Duke Kahanamoku, it was one of the only invitational surfing competitions in Hawaii at the time. But Eddie's style of smooth, graceful turns and long, fluid rides began losing favor to a new approach. A group of Australians who had recently "discovered" the incredible surf in Hawaii pioneered a much more aggressive style of surfing, which they called "rip, tear, and lacerate." The Australians were closely affiliated with the International Professional Surfers (IPS) organization, which had formed in 1976, and together they hoped to monetize surfing and bring the sport worldwide recognition. For these surfers, legitimizing the practice meant engaging in cut-throat competition and domination of the waves.

In 1976, a lanky young Australian named Wayne "Rabbit" Bar-tholomew published an article in *Surfer* magazine called "Bustin' Down the Door," in which he praised the "spontaneous direction changes" and "radically carved faces" of this burgeoning style of surfing. Rabbit argued (in a largely unintelligible 1970s surfer dia-lect) that the surfing innovations of 1976—as opposed to the na-tive surfing tradition of the past thousand years—would be what finally brought respect to surfing as a sport. "The development of modern-day surfing is a bitchin' example of 'the extended limits principle,' and it is still a fairly young trip," Rabbit wrote. "When surfing became a popular pastime roughly twenty years ago, the objectives and directions were quite basic, as the pure novelty of riding waves was in itself a breakthrough and a stoker." To native Hawaiian surfers like Eddie, the notion that surfing in 1976 was "young" and "basic" was more than just laughable; it was insulting.

Rabbit and his compatriots' naive arrogance regarding surfing and its provenance enraged locals. During the winter of 1977, a group of Hawaiian surfers swam out to the break at Sunset Beach and assaulted Rabbit, holding him underwater. Back on the beach, they told him to leave the North Shore for good. Rabbit may have "busted down the door," but he clearly wouldn't be moving in anytime soon. Terrified, Rabbit and his friends hid out in a room at the Kuilima Resort, taking turns keeping watch with a tennis racket in hand for self-defense.

Rabbit and another Australian, Ian Cairns, spent several weeks this way, until Eddie decided to pay them a visit. Stuart Coleman describes a scene in which Eddie sat with Rabbit and Cairns in their hotel hideout and held forth on the history of Western ex-ploitation of Hawaiian land and culture. Surfing was the sport of Hawaiian kings. The Australian aggression and colonial attitude in local surf spots were unwelcome echoes of the violence that Hawaiians suffered during the nineteenth century. Rabbit, terri-fied of the angry locals and desperate to get back on the beach, repented.

Eddie scheduled a meeting between the Australian and local surfers. Tensions ran high, but the two parties managed to make amends. Eddie had become an educator, raising consciousness to forge a more equitable coexistence on the beach.

The same year surfers beat up Rabbit, a Hawaiian surf club called the *Hui o he'e nalu*—"Wave Slider Club"—began holding meetings in a house at Sunset Beach. Motivated by cultural pride and grievances against *haole*, the Hui wanted self-determination and tradition to prevail at popular surf breaks. The particulars of Eddie's relationship to the Hui are somewhat unclear—in *Eddie Would Go,* Coleman never links Eddie to the group explicitly. However, a 1987 *Honolulu Advertiser* article claims Eddie's father, Pops Aikau, founded the Hui. Isaiah Walker also suggests the Aikau family played an integral role in the group's formation. Whatever the case, conflicts between *haole* surfers and native Hawaiians continued to escalate throughout the late '70s.

International Professional Surfers was run by a notoriously mercenary *haole* surfer named Fred Hemmings, and the organization infuriated the Hui when it secured a permit from the city for an invitation-only contest and blocked access to the water. In 1977 and 1978, Hui members disrupted these competitions. Surfer Moot Ah Quin told Walker that IPS felt "the permits gave them the right to chase guys out of the water . . . when they started to do that, the braddahs would paddle out, brah. They would paddle out and sit in the lineup. And there is nothing you can do . . . but they not only going paddle out and sit down. Brah, they goin' start cracking guys if you tell [them] to move, you know. And they did."

In addition to leading these incidents of direct action, the Hui also got to work in the community, cleaning up beaches and hosting fund-raisers and events for locals and young surfers. Responding to pressure to share the proceeds from the contest with locals, IPS hired the Hui as security and lifeguards at surfing events. Like Eddie, they knew the water and kept people safe.

In 1987, Hemmings broke ties with the Hui. He was serving as a Republican in the Hawaiian House of Representatives, and had been elected on a criminal-justice platform. He claimed those security and lifeguarding jobs came about through extortion. Hemmings identified Pops Aikau as the organization's leader, and accused the group of "crime and corruption." That same year, the *Advertiser* ran stories on the *Hui o he'e nalu,* calling it a "North

Shore terrorist" group. The stigma's been hard to shake. In 2009, the *New York Times* described the Hui's "Mafia control of the surf," and reported regular "beat downs" that occurred on North Shore beaches.

Stories of native people's violent resistance are especially threatening to foreigners with a financial interest in controlling local land and earning profit from recreational events such as surfing competitions. The Hui were not docile; they'd been overlooked, and their fury felt justified. This anger threatened powerful locals, who labeled the Hui thugs, terrorists, enforcers, and criminals.

IV. Star of Gladness

When Eddie finally won the Duke, in 1977, it was the fulfillment of a lifelong dream. Duke was Eddie's hero. For both men, surfing was an expression of cultural identity, as well as a way to earn respect in Hawaii. "He was not trying to risk his life or defy death," Eddie's wife, Linda, told Stuart Coleman. Winning the Duke, she said, was "a way for him to feel worthy. He wanted to achieve something for the Hawaiian people."

There are clear similarities between Eddie and Duke, but while Duke branched out from surfing to act in Hollywood movies such as *Hula, The Pony Express,* and *Old Ironsides,* playing roles like "Indian Chief," "Hawaiian Boy," and "Pirate Captain," and later became the sheriff of Honolulu, Eddie's life outside surfing took a more anticolonial turn. As part of a thriving Hawaiian renaissance movement during the 1970s, Hawaiians protested militarization and war, celebrated indigenous art and traditions like hula, and demonstrated a surge of pride in their cultural identity. Eddie embraced it. In 1977, one of the most visible symbols of this cultural and political moment was *Hōkūlé'a* ("Star of Gladness" in Hawaiian). A 62-foot, eight-ton, double-hulled canoe built in the manner of ancient Polynesian vessels, *Hōkūlé'a* was the brainchild of Ben Finney, a *haole* anthropologist at the University of Hawaii; Herb Kane, a Hawaiian artist; and Tommy Holmes, a local beach boy. Anthropologists had claimed for decades that ancient voyagers from Polynesia—over 1,000 islands of genetically and culturally related people scattered across the south and central Pacific—arrived in Hawaii after their boats accidentally drifted there. This theory relied on the racist belief that ancient Polynesians weren't sophisticated enough to have made these voyages intentionally. The three men formed the Polynesian Voyaging Society in 1973 and began constructing a vessel that would prove that Polynesians, likely from Tahiti and the Marquesas, had intentionally navigated boats across 2,500 miles of ocean over 1,500 years ago.

The inaugural voyage to Tahiti, in 1976, was marred by power struggles, temper tantrums, and racial tensions. Despite these conflicts, *Hōkūlēʻa* became a rallying point for thousands of Hawaiians. Eddie wanted in. Because of his status as a waterman and lifeguard, he was selected to be part of the crew for the boat's second voyage to Tahiti, in 1978.

Captain Dave Lyman and navigator Nainoa Thompson had second thoughts about leaving when the forecast promised 35-mile-an-hour winds and eight- to 10-foot swells in the channel. But 10,000 well-wishers had gathered to celebrate the launch, and at sundown on March 16, 1978, *Hōkūlēʻa* left Magic Island and headed through the Kealaikahiki Channel toward Tahiti.

That night *Hōkūlēʻa* rode 15-foot swells. The boat began listing from water leakage, and eventually stopped dead in the water. The panicked crew huddled to one side of the craft in an effort to balance out the lilt of the boat with their weight. Around midnight, a rogue wave capsized the canoe, tossing the crew into the water and destroying their radio. The crew clung to the boat. Waiting to be spotted by a plane, they drifted farther from the flight patterns between the islands. Huge swells hammered the vessel. Less-seaworthy members of the crew were seasick and exhausted from exposure. Eddie eventually asked if he could paddle his surfboard nearly 20 miles to the island of Lānaʻi for help. Captain Lyman refused until, seeing no other option for rescue, he gave Eddie permission to go.

Nainoa Thompson remembers Eddie putting on a lifejacket, "and then he paddled off. And I swam out to him. I was so conflicted with this idea. We're tired, we're somewhat in shock, we're in denial. Emotionally, it was an extremely draining situation. But he was like a miracle man—he could do anything. So if he says he could go to Lānaʻi, he's gonna go."

Tours and guidebooks tend to present admirable historical figures as statues—static, immobile, their good deeds and bravery things of the past. Visitors sit on the bus, or the beach, admiring these surfers, but they often miss the real message—the messy, sometimes depressing story of conflict that defines the place they've gone for an exotic escape. Tourists don't need to adopt local customs to honor the history of their destination. But they do need to make an effort to learn about them.

Today, Eddie Aikau's legacy is commemorated in the Quiksilver in Memory of Eddie Aikau, the surfing contest I first learned about when I was working as a tour-guide writer. The competition takes place on Waimea Bay on a day when waves are consistently over 20 feet tall. When the Eddie is on, thousands head to the North Shore to watch surfers climb and descend these rushing walls of water. At the first Eddie competition, in 1985, the surf was especially forbidding. Surfer Mark Foo insisted on paddling out, telling contest organizers, "Eddie would go." Nearly 30 years later, this tribute to Eddie's fearlessness is emblazoned on T-shirts and bumper stickers across the island, universalizing Foo's sentiment: IF EDDIE WOULD GO, THEN SO WILL I. A visitor to the North Shore can find Eddie's legacy in the protest banners on lawns that decry "illegal statehood," and the sunburned foreigners wearing T-shirts with his name on them. Tourists eat it up, and locals wear the shirts and tell the story with pride. Everyone seems to love Eddie. But not everyone loves him for the same reason.

JONATHAN SEGURA

The Game of His Life

FROM GQ

MY WIFE GOT ME the best Valentine's Day gift ever last year. Surprise trip to London with a surprise-within-a-surprise double bonus of tickets to the Manchester United–Manchester City match. Bear with me here—this isn't about soccer, really, but you do need some grounding: I am a Manchester United supporter, and this was one of the premier matches of last season. You may remember it as the one where Wayne Rooney scored that amazing goal. A goal so incredible, so fantastic, so unreasonably and gloriously perfect, that it got covered here, in America, where nobody gives a fuck about the sport.

Three years ago, I couldn't have explained offsides or told you who that twat from Argentina was, or why. And yet. And yet shouting myself hoarse at that match is one of the very few highlights of my short life. Without question. My hit list goes something like: getting married to the woman who would later score tickets to the February 2011 Manchester derby, and then going to the February 2011 Manchester derby. That's all I got. Naturally the triumph is not without tragedy: my cruddy little heart broke in the East Stand before kickoff as "Glory, Glory Man United" played over the loudspeakers and I dumped an ounce or so of cremated human remains under my seat. Not quite an hour and a half later, it felt wrong to be jumping up and down on that small mound of ash, but holy shit, *that goal.*

Martin was a big guy, maybe 250. Scottish. Brilliant ad man. Drunk. Bipolar, occasionally unmedicated. Had gout, some plague-looking psoriasis. Lots of expensive dental work, taken care of by a previous wife, pro bono. Old enough to be my dad. Kind of guy you can't not love and are afraid of sometimes but just won't say no to about anything, not even another round at 3:00 A.M. on a Tuesday, which was the case about once a week. He lived down the hall, and surely we were the least favorite people on the ninth floor of our uptight building. That's how we met, actually, six years ago: at a meeting to shoot down a rule the building board wanted to implement, something about banning dogs from the lobby.

One of the good ones, Martin. Taught me important, basic stuff I'd somehow missed out on, like that it's okay—necessary, in fact—to say, "Fuck *them,* what do *you* want?" and to not believe that ridiculous bullshit about how you shouldn't take your single malt on the rocks. He'd actually put together and lived by a set of commandments. There were 12 of them, if I recall, and they boiled down to this: don't be an asshole, and do good work. For him, that was doing ad stuff and supporting Manchester United. Glasgow-born, Manchester-educated, Martin was a fearsome sup- porter of Manchester United. He *believed* in Manchester United. He also believed, much to the misfortune of his neighbors, that the louder he shouted at his TV, the more he could influence a match. He had framed newspapers on his wall from when United had won the league or the cup or whatever. He skipped work when it interfered with him watching his team.

As it turned out, Manchester United was the one thing I *could* say no to him about: his constant invites to join him—just once!— at some punishingly early hour at Nevada Smiths ("Where Foot- ball Is Religion") to watch Manchester United play those cunts from wherever. I never went. Not ever. I hated sports. I couldn't give a shit less about Liverpool or Chelsea.

He got me a Manchester United jersey anyway. An enticement, unrequited, to join him in support of his team. I wore it, once, to watch the 2008 Euro final when Spain beat Germany, 1–0. I didn't have anything else going on, so I threw on the jersey—why not?— and walked down the hall to watch the match at Martin's. He was patient in explaining things I would soon forget—the same things everyone new to the sport doesn't understand and soon forgets. (On injury time: "A few extra minutes to make up for the time they spent fucking about.") That was the only soccer game—sorry: *footie match*—I ever watched with Martin.

It was around Christmas 2008 when Martin and his wife separated. He'd been working in the U.K., and upon his return to New York City, Martin and his MacBook became a daily fixture in our household. I would wake up, miserably hungover from having been carousing with Martin, and there Martin would be, sitting at our table, chatting with my wife, using our Wi-Fi, happily pouring a dash of vodka into his coffee.

"Want some?" he'd ask, all sunshine. I'd decline, and then the day's soccer report would begin. I'd tune out and make coffee and nod along and politely decline his invites to watch whatever matches were on tap for that weekend. Martin was especially keen on someone named Rooney, whom, he said, I had to see and whose brilliance would convert me, instantly. *Surely!* But I nevertheless passed. My excuse: I was closing in on finishing a draft of my second novel and couldn't spare the time. (The novel is long since finished and remains unsold. Ha!)

Also, he was tough to be around all the time. This is a stupid thing to say, but it's true that whatever he did, he did the shit out of. As a bachelor, that consisted of herculean drinking. Some blow. Breaking our furniture. He'd show up with strange new bruises, but he didn't know how he got them, or why, or from whom. We would set out to walk our dogs, and it'd turn into a drink, and then another, and then—well, you get the idea. I took a silly pride in being able to hack, but then I couldn't anymore. I started avoiding him. I lied. I was busy. I had work to do. I had so much work to do I couldn't even walk down the hall to have a drink. He'd ring the bell and I wouldn't answer it. I loved Martin, but I could no longer do it. Self-preservation kicked in.

As March rolled around, Martin started getting his shit together. He was launching his own agency; his first potential account was a laundry detergent, and he was cooking up a campaign involving motocross racers. He began fostering shelter dogs and doing some work around his apartment that he'd been putting off. He got a better handle on his drinking and seemed to be getting on just fine. I saw him a couple of times, and it didn't end in a blackout. He seemed happier. Good stuff. One night, I ran into him in the hallway. He was coming back from walking one of his foster dogs and said that my wife and I were overdue for dinner at his place. I said yeah, sure, we'd figure something out, and that sounded good to him.

A week later, give or take, he jumped out of his window. I spent a few moments alone with Martin before the cops or EMTs or shrill neighbors showed up. I hope you never have this sort of opportunity, because it is fundamentally devastating. It changes you: your friend, dead, on some stranger's ruined patio in the rain, and what do you say? I said, inexplicably, "Oh, sugar pea. What'd you do?" Jesus, it's like the world's worst country song.

There was hardly any blood. He must've bounced, because he was faceup. His glasses were smashed and lying a few feet away. If it weren't for the split running down his forehead, he'd have looked like he was sleeping one off. The cops found his driver's license, passport, and a note, all of it wrapped in plastic and tucked in his inside jacket pocket, presumably so the rain and trauma wouldn't ruin the documents and slow down the identification process. The note itself wasn't Martin's best work.

Martin wanted to be cremated. His wife arranged it and left a bit of him with us, and my wife and I occasionally talked about finding him a more dignified home than a plastic bag in our liquor cabinet, but there he remained, near his quaich and my whiskey.

Six months later, I was at a friend's birthday party at a bar and saw a poster advertising the Premier League matches they'd be showing. *Why not?* I thought. I didn't have my would-be footie mentor around any longer, but I was going through a rather dark period and thought the experience might provide something in desperately short supply: fun. Plus, I missed Martin and thought, in a yucky bit of sentimentality, it'd be a nice tribute. The first match I watched was Manchester United's 2–0 victory over Blackburn on Halloween 2009. I didn't understand much of what went on, but I didn't have a horrible 90 minutes either. So the next weekend I went to a bar and watched the 1–0 defeat at Chelsea. I wish I could point to a pivotal match or a crucial goal and say that *that* was what converted me, but it wouldn't be true. Manchester United grew on me, quickly and mercilessly, like the Devil claiming your soul. I welcomed it, particularly the predawn bar crowds, whose passion and dedication were foreign and fascinating to a Midwestern-reared boy.

Soon I was fully in the sway, pounding pints before breakfast, and by Christmas—spent with my folks in Omaha—I was frantically calling around town to find somewhere to watch the match against Hull. I began to have an emotional investment in the team and the outcome of matches. I started referring to the Red Devils as "we." I developed superstitions about attire to wear, and in which fashion, to ensure victory. Alone at home, I cheered—raucously, at length—at goals. My blood pressure would shoot up if the opposition took the ball into the box late in a tight match. I started reading British sports sections online. I shopped in vain for a Manchester United scarf fitted for my bulldog. My wife—a lovely, patient, and understanding woman who deserves saint status—pretended to be interested when Paul Scholes knocked in that brilliant header in injury time to win the April 2010 Manchester derby and I kept rewinding the DVR and insisting she watch it *one more time* to fully appreciate the glory of it. Can you imagine, I asked her, what it must be like to be there?

Fast-forward to that Valentine's Day weekend. My wife had been planning a trip. All I officially knew was I had to take off a couple of days from work and pack a bag. She would take care of everything else. True, I had my suspicions she might be plotting a pilgrimage to the holy land—there'd been seemingly innocent questions about the stadium, and if the seating area was covered, and what happened if it rained—but I also knew there was no way in hell, ever, she'd be able to score tickets to one of the biggest matches of the season. *Just in case,* I scooped a bit of Martin into a film canister and tossed him in my suitcase. Worst case is I'd end up muling a bit of dead Martin to some quaint upstate B&B. Instead, we were soon marching up Sir Matt Busby Way alongside the other believers in red and white, weaving through a phalanx of police horses, and as the shouts of "Fuck off, City!" grew louder and more frequent, I felt at home and on fire with that white-hot zealotry reserved for converts, children, and suicide bombers.

We were tied 1–1 going into the 78th minute when Rooney misplayed a pass and then, seconds later, got the ball lobbed back to him and pulled off this unbelievable maneuver: with his back to the goal, he jumped a few feet off the ground, wheeled his leg up and over his head, nailed the ball, and sent it rocketing into the top-right corner of the net. The sound in the stadium was like a napalm strike, and yes, I did one of those frantic I'm-so-excited-I-don't-know-what-the-fuck-to-do jumping-hug things with the guy standing next to me. I like to think I ground a few grains of Martin into Old Trafford right then, and that he'll have those crazy-good seats forever.

Sir Alex Ferguson, United's manager, called it the best goal he'd ever seen at Old Trafford, a quote heavily featured in the near pornographic next-day coverage in the British papers. You have to understand that Rooney'd been having a fairly crappy game that was rather emblematic of his abysmal season—beset by injuries, a hooker scandal, and a silly tantrum about maybe leaving the club. That goal was his redemption, and I'll merely mention that a case could be made for a touch of divine Scottish intervention in it—that *that* goal happened in *that* match, right in front of us, on the day Martin came back after a long time away, and that Rooney, the limping front-man of Martin's beloved team, got the boost he needed to shut down those cunts from across town in such mythic fashion. Pretty cut-and-dried, I think, but you can do with that what you will.

ERIK MALINOWSKI

The Making of "Homer at the Bat," the Episode That Conquered Prime Time 20 Years Ago Tonight

FROM DEADSPIN.COM

ON FEBRUARY 20, 1992, more American homes tuned in to *The Simpsons* than they did *The Cosby Show* or the Winter Olympics from Albertville, France. A foul-mouthed cartoon on a fourth-place network bested the Huxtables and the world's best amateur athletes. Fox over NBC and CBS—its first-ever victory in prime time. New over old.

Why the shift? Well, the Olympic programming that night featured no marquee events, and *Cosby* was just two months away from ending its eight-season run. Meanwhile, *The Simpsons*, airing just its 52nd episode out of 500 (and counting), had put forth its most ambitious effort to date, an episode called "Homer at the Bat." Months of work went into corralling nine baseball players, a cross-section of young stars and established veterans, to guest-star as members of a rec-league softball team.

Sam Simon, the co-creator of *The Simpsons*, originally pitched the idea, and it was put into words by John Swartzwelder, a charter member of the show's writing staff, who would eventually pen 59 episodes, more than anyone else. On a staff full of fantasy baseball junkies, Swartzwelder was the über-geek, a fanatic who had rented out stadiums for hours at a time so he and his close friends could play ball. (Years after Swartzwelder's departure from the show, it's

136   ERIK MALINOWSKI

easy to see his influence endures. During the episode's roundtable
DVD commentary, the word "Swartzweldian" is used with a defer-
ence and awe usually reserved for long-dead Nobel laureates.)

If you're somehow unfamiliar with the episode, the premise
was relatively simple: Mr. Burns's company softball team, having
lost 28 of 30 games the previous season, goes on an incredible
run when Homer starts hitting, well, homers with his WonderBat,
carved from the fallen branch of a lightning-struck tree. (Sound
familiar?) As the season winds down, it becomes a two-team race
for the pennant: Springfield vs. Shelbyville. While dining at the
Millionaires' Club with the owner of the Shelbyville Power Plant, a
cocky Burns agrees to a handshake bet worth (you guessed it) $1
million.

To fix the game and secure his victory, Burns orders Smithers to
enlist ballplayers like Cap Anson, Honus Wagner, and Jim Creighton. (Swartzwelder's choice of Creighton was particularly inspired.
The ace pitcher for the Brooklyn Excelsiors in the 1850s and '60s,
Creighton supposedly didn't strike out once while batting during the 20 games of the 1860 season. Creighton died two years
later. He was 21.) Upon learning that his entire suggested lineup
is dead, Burns instructs Smithers to come back with real ballplayers. And so he sets off across the country: nabbing Jose Canseco
at a card convention, accosting a Graceland-touring Ozzie Smith,
nearly getting shot in the woods by Mike Scioscia, and stopping
by Don Mattingly's pink suburban house to interrupt his dish-
washing.

Before "Homer at the Bat," *The Simpsons* had used guest stars
only sporadically—and never more than four of them in a single
show, that I can remember. Recognizable voices popped up now
and then, but no athlete had appeared until Magic Johnson on
October 17, 1991, five episodes into the third season. (Exactly
three weeks later, Johnson held a press conference to announce
he was HIV-positive and would immediately retire from the NBA.)

Now it was using nine guests, some of whom were obvious baseball Hall of Famers. The end result was not only an iconic piece
of pop culture but a loving satire of baseball that looks downright
prescient today, here on the other side of the Mitchell Report.
Our heroes got drunk in bars, ingested odd substances because
they were told to, and mindlessly clucked like diseased poultry.

"Homer at the Bat" felt vaguely forbidden, like an animated addendum to *Ball Four*. This was the side of the sport we never saw.
We couldn't pull our eyes away then. We still can't.

Despite all the planning and prep, "Homer at the Bat" wasn't easy to put together. Of the players with guest-starring roles, only the Dodgers' Darryl Strawberry and Mike Scioscia were local. The script was pretty much locked down by summer 1991, but the writers and producers had to wait throughout the season for players to swing through Los Angeles to play the Dodgers or the California Angels so they could record their lines.

Aside from the Yankees' twofer of Don Mattingly and Steve Sax, each athlete coming to the Fox studios was booked for a single voice-over session, which often got cramped when friends and family tagged along. Ken Griffey Jr., then 21 and easing into his third season in the majors, showed up in early August with his father and Mariners teammate, who was a few months from retirement. (In the show's DVD commentary, show-runner Mike Reiss recalls Griffey Jr. laboring through his lines and getting increasingly upset. He "looked like he was going to beat the crap out of me," Reiss says.)

St. Louis Cardinals shortstop Ozzie Smith stopped by in early September with his Bart-impersonating son Nikko, who himself wound up on Fox television 14 years later as an *American Idol* finalist. "I knew he was a *Simpsons* fan and had the Bart thing down pretty good," Smith told me, "but I didn't know he could do *anything* like that." Smith also made sure to work through his script beforehand, unlike his peeved center fielder. "I worked on those lines, even though there wasn't really a whole lot of them," he says. "I just wanted to get the inflections in the right place."

Steve Sax, who retired three years after "Homer at the Bat" and did time as a financial adviser before becoming a life coach and motivational speaker, acknowledges a sizable debt to the show. (The writing staff's early preference for second base was Chicago's Ryne Sandberg.) "Sometimes, fans would yell, 'Hey, how's Homer?'" Sax told me. "I know they weren't talking about me hitting home runs, but it was a lot better than the stuff I used to hear."

Before *The Simpsons*, Sax was best known for a much-publicized case of the fielding yips that had dogged him throughout the '80s. His brief TV fame seemed to remove that period of his 14-year career from fans' minds. "Today, I still get people that ask me, 'What was it like to be on *The Simpsons?*' not, 'What was it like to face Nolan Ryan?'" (Actually, it's a legit question. Sax hit .265 lifetime against the Express. In their first matchup in April 1982, the rookie went 2-for-4 with an RBI triple. So, please, the next time you pass Steve Sax on the streets of Sacramento, ask him about Nolan Ryan.)

Sax's affability at the recording session also stuck with some members of the staff, with one later admitting (half-jokingly, maybe) that the "closest I ever came to falling in love with a man was Steve Sax. He was so handsome, so sweet."

Show-runner Al Jean has said the players who committed were more than happy to do the show. Well, *almost* all of them. "They were all really nice," Jean said on the DVD commentary, "except for one whose name rhymes with Manseco."

Aside from the logistics of recording nine separate guest roles, plot lines had to be rewritten on the fly. Jose Canseco's scene originally called for him and Mrs. Krabappel to engage in *Bull Durham*–inspired extramarital shenanigans. Canseco's wife rejected the scene, and the staff had to do a last-minute Saturday afternoon rewrite when Oakland came south on a mid-August road trip.

Instead of Lothario, Canseco got to play hero, rushing into a woman's burning house to rescue her baby, then cat, followed by a player piano, washer, dryer, couch and recliner combo, high chair, TV, rug, kitchen table and chairs, lamp, and grandfather clock. Requesting the new sequence turned out to be the wiser move. Canseco and his wife had nearly divorced earlier that year before reconciling, and a week before "Homer at the Bat" aired, Canseco was arrested by Miami police for chasing down and ramming his wife's BMW twice with his red Porsche at 4:30 A.M. After the chase ended, he allegedly got out of his car, came over to his wife's driver-side window, and spit on it.

The Don Mattingly of "Homer at the Bat" hit even closer to the mark. In August 1991, Yankees management ordered the team captain to cut his hair shorter. He refused, was benched by manager Stump Merrill, and fined $250, including $100 for every subsequent day that he didn't cut his hair. "I'm overwhelmed by the pettiness of it," Mattingly told reporters. "To me, long hair is down my back, touching my collar. I don't feel my hair is messy."

Six months later, when "Homer at the Bat" aired, Mattingly's story line centered around Mr. Burns's insane interpretation of his first baseman's "sideburns." Mattingly is booted from the team, muttering as he walks away, "I still like him better than Steinbrenner."

Most fans assumed that the show had cribbed from real-life events. In fact, Mr. Burns's sociopathic infatuation with sideburns was inspired by show-runner Al Jean's grandfather, who owned a hardware store in the '70s and would constantly berate his employees for their excessive follicular growth. Mattingly had recorded his dialogue a full month before his dustup with the Yankees.

Wade Boggs, who would labor through the worst year of his Hall of Fame career in 1992, was supposed to engage in a belching contest with Barney. As a player, Boggs was known for (among other pursuits) indulging in a bit o' drink from time to time; lore has it that he once drank dozens of beers during a team flight. Boggs tried to play down the story during a 2005 appearance on *Pardon the Interruption*—"It was a few Miller Lites," he claimed— but his occasional forays into boozy karaoke give the legend at least a little plausibility. For reasons now lost to history, the belching contest was scrapped in favor of a beer-fueled argument over who was England's greatest prime minister.

Still, rewriting plot lines was simple compared with getting the look of the players correct. The show's artists had never before had to tackle such a wide range of new faces on their animation cels. The show's biggest guest star to that point, Michael Jackson, posed no such challenge, as he voiced a morbidly obese white man. Matt Groening later said that "caricaturing real, living people" was the toughest challenge at the time, but they pulled it off, nailing features like Clemens's frat-boy spike, Strawberry's kiss-ass grin, and Canseco's chemistry-experiment-gone-wrong physique.

Beyond these aesthetic and creative challenges, *The Simpsons* was in the midst of fighting off a ginned-up national outrage over the show. A backlash was on. Retailers became saturated with growing piles of *Simpsons* merchandise, and some licensing deals were abruptly dropped. Elementary schools from Ohio to Orange County started banning Bart Simpson T-shirts that had been deemed offensive. The show even became a point of contention during the 1992 presidential election. George H. W. Bush, struggling to boost his bona fides with conservatives, took the stage at the annual convention of National Religious Broadcasters on January 27, three weeks before "Homer at the Bat" aired.

Bush ran through the usual Republican talking points, emphasizing "sanctity of life," working hard, sacrifice, and so forth. He then pivoted and started hammering nameless folks who would promote injustice and incivility.

"I speak of decency, the moral courage to say what is right and condemn what is wrong," Bush said. "And we need a nation closer to *The Waltons* than *The Simpsons*." The partisan crowd inside the Sheraton Washington Hotel roared with laughter, but it was priceless publicity that put the show square in the national conversation.

Bush, meanwhile, repeated the shot in August at the Republican National Convention. This time, it backfired. Though the next scheduled episode was a repeat, the *Simpsons* staff cobbled together a new show to open in just three days. In it, the family gathers around the TV to watch Bush's address, and Bart wryly observes how they're just like the Waltons: "We're praying for an end to the Depression too."

Bush really should've picked his battles more carefully. His wife was criticized in 1990 for calling the show "the dumbest thing I had ever seen." In return, "Marge Simpson" wrote her a letter in reply, explaining how she was deeply hurt by the comments. The situation was put to rest with the First Lady, amazingly, writing a letter back to the fictional TV mom, apologizing for her "loose tongue." It's hard to fathom now, two decades later, with the show ensconced in a family-hour time slot, but *The Simpsons* was once dangerous.

"Homer at the Bat" was not remotely close to what you might consider a typical *Simpsons* episode. You have Chief Wiggum (sounding more like an Edward G. Robinson rip-off than a fully formed character) acting responsibly, ordering his team to stop shooting in the air in post–home run celebration. Ralph, of all people, outwits Bart at picking players for sandlot baseball. Lisa, normally so moralistic and holier-than-thou, taunts Darryl Strawberry and brings him to tears. These weren't the conventional character patterns that had worked so well, and one could see why cast members Harry Shearer and Julie Kavner openly hated Swartzwelder's script.

Then there's the title of the episode, borrowed from "Casey at the Bat," the titular character being the ultimate symbol of baseball failure. In the end, Homer wins his team the pennant, albeit through inexplicable and unconventional means. But to see Homer excelling at *anything* flies in the face of the standard *Simpsons* script. In 22 minutes, he morphs from underdog to hero, and the contrast with the character we know from the rest of the series is more unnerving than welcome. The show was about inverting TV tropes. Homer's ineptitude was as vital to the show as Fred MacMurray's pipe was to *My Three Sons*. So when Homer smacks a bottom-of-the-ninth grand slam with his team down three runs, how the hell are we supposed to process that? Homer doesn't fail miserably; Bart doesn't quip his way out of trouble; Lisa doesn't roll her eyes in judgment. It was like watching some avant-garde, one-night-only experiment in ad hoc television.

Ratings might have had a little to do with that. Chasing *Cosby* was a priority for the Fox suits, and a splashy ensemble of ballplayers was likely to bring in big numbers. If the show had to tweak its own formula a little to do so, it was still young enough that it wouldn't look desperate; there were no sharks to jump, at that point. Die-hards might cringe a little, but in retrospect the episode looks a lot like a well-timed, what-the-hell swing for the fences.

And for all the "very special episode" feel of "Homer at the Bat," it certainly doesn't go easy on its targets. This wasn't Mel Allen doing bloopers on *This Week in Baseball*. Nor was this the game "designed to break your heart." This was a far more bemused look at the putative national pastime. Coaches' inspirational talk is often clichéd gibberish? You bet. Ballplayers sometimes drink too much and get into barroom trouble? Hell yeah, they do. Acute radiation poisoning, cranial gigantism, and pits of eternal darkness? Meet your 2011 Red Sox. And because there were actual, living ballplayers in the show, every manic twist carried the added fillip that we were looking in on something we weren't supposed to see, something funny and unauthorized. This was *Ball Four*'s demented stepson.

When the show aired in 1992, baseball was on the verge of a remarkable transformation. You could see hints of it in "Homer at the Bat." There is a meta-commentary on rising player salaries—

Canseco's $50,000 game check to play softball would've been a raise, not a pay cut, as he claimed. Two years earlier, remember, the last of owner collusion cases had been settled, setting the stage for the 1994 strike. Two of the Springfield Nine, Canseco and Clemens, would be closely associated with PED use in years to come.

And maybe there's even a whiff of the jock-nerd culture war that would overtake baseball a decade later. With the bases loaded and the score tied 43–43 in the bottom of the ninth, Mr. Burns benches Strawberry, who has hit nine home runs in the game to this point. Burns explains to his increasingly incredulous star— and viewers at home, by extension—that he's pulling him for a right-handed batter, since a left-handed pitcher is on the mound. (Never mind that the Shelbyville pitcher is clearly shown holding the ball in his right hand just seconds before.) "It's called playing the percentages," Burns explains. "It's what smart managers do to win ball games." The joke would come full circle in 2010, when the patron saint of sabermetrics, Bill James, appeared on a *Moneyball-*inspired episode and exuberantly took credit for making baseball "as much fun as doing your taxes."

"Homer at the Bat" was proof you could see baseball in all its silliness and still love the game. Even the stars who were both target and participant in the spoof remember the episode fondly. Ozzie Smith is generally regarded as the greatest defensive shortstop in baseball history. He has played in three World Series, and he's earned election to the Hall of Fame—and yet he still gets questions from fans about *The Simpsons* whenever he does a card show or some other event. He can't escape it, but with no hesitation, he reckons his tumble into the Springfield Mystery Spot to be one of the highlights of his career.

"It ranks right up there, and people are still talking about it today," Smith says. "*The Simpsons* are a part of Americana, so to be part of an episode that featured all of those ballplayers from a special time? I guess it'll go down in history."

At Swim, Two Girls: A Memoir

FROM NARRATIVEMAGAZINE.COM

SUMMERS IN THE EARLY SEVENTIES, we tumbled together with my mother's family, the Peitons, at Flathead Lake. Flathead was our inland sea, a chill green vastness ringed by snowy peaks, even in July. Dense stands of ponderosa and tamarack made the air ample as water, thick with pine and pitch. Behind that lurked smoke, from a distant forest fire out by Glacier or fresh-caught kokanee salmon grilling over nearby flames. Cherries, huckleberries, and blackcaps clotted the roads and lanes above the lake, and everything vibrated with the drone of yellow jackets, hummingbirds, and bees.

My mother brought most of her nine children to the lake—as did her sisters, who between them had 17 more. Only the first of the five Peiton girls was childless, and she did not come to the lake. Years ago she had become Sister Mary of the Incarnation, cloistered in a Carmelite convent in faraway Michigan. My own sister Padeen had Mary for her middle name, which I believed meant she was special. Smart and pretty, but also good. Chosen. I was ten years younger and could not fathom any burden in such notions. Mostly I worried Padeen might suck up every drop of greatness first, the way our six brothers sometimes finished off the milk before it made its way to the far end of the table.

I was five years old that summer, standing knee-high in cool water, squinting into the distance. Across the lake, my two sisters and girl cousins were sunning on inflatable rafts. They were like beautiful aquatic birds, bobbing up and down along the waves, swimsuits and hair and rafts of many hues disappearing and reappearing in view. In one hand, I held two or three smooth lake stones. With the other, I tried skipping each stone in the direction of their flotilla, like surface missiles seeking targets. When I finished with one handful, I'd reach beneath the surface and reload.

"Enough of that," my grandfather called from shore. "We don't throw rocks in the direction of other people. Family especially." I trudged back out of the water and plopped down beside him. He was my keeper that morning, though he couldn't swim any better than I, which is to say, not at all. I liked my grandfather, whom we called "Pops," but it was tiresome being stuck on shore with just him. My mother was up at the house with my little brother, a toddler, and with her sisters and the other youngest cousins, a baby girl and twin boys near my age. The twins might have been my playmates that day, but they'd eaten too many cherries the night before, pits included, and were now painfully ping-pinging the morning away on both toilets.

Across the lake I watched my sister Diane, tanned shoulders glossy with baby oil, dangle her long hair over the side and then flick it quickly back so that water sprayed in all directions, causing loud yelps and an outbreak of furious splashing. Diane was adopted, with dark hair, brown eyes, and warm skin that matched her warm heart. She liked to sweep me up and kiss me on the neck until I screamed, while Padeen and I circled each other, pale, cold-eyed, wary.

"What can I do?" I said.

"Do?" Pops said. He was bent over the water now, using tiny stones to shake clean a glass hummingbird feeder, and didn't look up. "There's a wide world out there of things to do."

I stepped into the lake. It was cold, enlivening, but my feet below the surface were sickly green, a dead Halloween color. More shrieks rang across the water. I stood knee-deep for a while, longing for those lively girls, and then waded in up to my chest, my neck, when the ground suddenly gave way. A chill opaque greenness surrounded me on all sides, a startling change from the senseless transparency of air, but I felt no panic as I sank. I watched the surface of the water as it rose away and noticed the strangeness of sunlight seen from below, bending and cracking as it sifted downward. Underwater plants twisted up from the lake bottom, a surprise. I'd never considered what might live below. A single fish darted above my head, a quick silhouette between me and the light, and then my feet touched sand and stone and I pushed off hard, suddenly frantic and afraid.

When my head broke the surface, I heard Pops and young voices shouting. I tried calling out—*Here I am!*—but water choked any sound. I was under again when Padeen's moonlike face appeared—soft and ethereal as a Hapsburg Madonna—hovering on the other side of water. Her slender fingers grabbed hard under one armpit and yanked me into the air. I sputtered and heaved, water mixing with snot that I couldn't manage to wipe away. My cheek was shoved up beneath Padeen's chin, and she swam us to shore like that, two heads along her own pale shoulders. One strong arm sliced the water, the other held me above it. Her blond hair tangled across my face, and for a short time I saw the world as she did.

Padeen hoisted me, cold and slippery, into Pops's arms. She bent her face near mine. She smelled like baby oil and cherry Lip Smackers. "You never listen," she said, pulling hair off her ashen face, her jaw tight. "Why don't you listen?"

"I wanted to be out there," I said, breathing hard and looking to where the older girls were now scattered, a few still on rafts, two standing waist-deep in the shallows, unsure what to do. "With you."

Our eyes locked, blue to blue. Padeen sighed, her breath hot on my cold forearm. "You got what you wanted," she said, not unkindly. She looked at Pops, holding me tight but starting to scold. "Somehow you always do." She turned and ducked back underwater, reappearing some yards away, swimming strong and sure back to the other girls.

I wanted to tell Padeen that, no, I didn't have what I wanted, not at all, but she was already gone.

Great Falls was five hours east from the lake by car, over the Continental Divide and down again, a smelting and air force town settled onto arid plains along the Missouri. The voluptuous cascade of our town's namesake and her four sister falls that once ran in successive torrents had long been dammed or flooded by the time Pops moved his girls to Great Falls in the thirties. By the time I was born, the waterfalls of the Missouri were a half-preserved plains legend, like the big stuffed buffalo at the park in Fort Benton.

That October after I nearly drowned I was six, and the only water that mattered was Bob McKinnon's backyard pool. Enclosed like a greenhouse, it was a chlorinated swamp even on the coldest Montana afternoon. Bob was once a competitive swimmer, and his father, Angus McKinnon, coached the local team—Gus's Guppies—a cringe-worthy name that only made their statewide strength more cruel. My middle brother, Pat, swam for Gus, and so did Padeen, before joining the high school team. I was brought to Gus's son to learn to swim.

Padeen pulled up outside Bob's in her jerking Volvo and yanked the emergency brake. I was seat belt–less in the bucket seat beside her and shot across the cracked plastic and onto the floor. "Hand me your clothes," she said.

"What?" I said from the seat well. "No." The floor of Padeen's car smelled of decomposing leaves, earthy and ripe. I considered burrowing like a small animal and resting safe and snug there.

"Don't you have your swimsuit on?" Padeen's voice rose, tense.

"Sort of," I said.

Padeen rolled her overly mascaraed eyes, a blond Liza Minnelli, and thrust a narrow hand out of her fitted ski jacket for my sweats. "Then go."

I sat up. To one side of the car was the long dog run where Bob kept half a dozen greyhounds he raced at venues across the state. To the other was the pool, a primordial soup behind fogged glass, like a worn diorama at some questionable natural history museum. "Aren't you coming?" I said, inching down my sweatpants, the seat cold and stiff beneath my goosefleshy thighs.

"I can't." She flipped her arm to see the watch face that spun freely on her thin wrist. "There's stuff I have to do. Hurry," she said, pulling the last bit of sweatshirt over my head. She reached across my chest and pushed open the door. "It's just an hour." She gave a little shove, and I raced toward the heat of the pool, hearing the Volvo grind down the driveway as soon as my feet hit gravel.

Two other girls were already there. One, dark-haired, was still dressed and holding her mother's hand; the other, skinny in a red bikini, shook her head and cried while a woman in a big wool coat stood over her.

"Quinn!" Bob shouted, and I jumped. I'd been around Bob enough to be wary. He was cool in his way, white T-shirt, rolled-up

jeans, handsome and moody and slightly failed, as if he'd meant
to be Brando or Kerouac but ended up racing greyhounds, not
motorcycles, teaching high school English instead of writing novels. Teaching little girls to swim. "Quinn," he said again wearily,
"you're not scared, are you?" The other girls watched, big-eyed. I
tried not to look at them. "Then get in," Bob said.

The pool was a strange, viscous green that hid the bottom.
Bob stood on the wet deck, an unlit cigarette behind one ear,
while a girl not much older than Padeen waited in the water. Bob
pointed toward her, and she waved cheerily for me to come in. I
stared at my feet, almost as gray as the concrete, toenails long and
ragged.

Bob looked toward the driveway beyond the glass. "Breaststroke's your sister's event, right?" He nodded, as if mulling things
over. "She's good. Think you could ever be that good, Quinn?" He
spat out my last name like a minor curse he enjoyed saying for the
hell of it.

"I don't know," I said, uncrossing the arms I'd been clenching
tight as a corset across my thin chest.

Bob pointed to the water with one hand and pushed between
my sharp shoulder blades with the other. I stumbled onto the top
step, and Bob's firm hand guided me down. The water was warm,
peelike. Bob wanted me to put my face in it. "C'mon," he said,
"you don't even have to leave the stairs." I felt the pressure of his
attention, firm and insistent as his palm had been. I took a deep
breath, then slapped my face at the water, cars still bone-dry. "Ha!"
Bob said, whacking one thigh. "See that?" he said to the pool in
general. "Quinn's not afraid."

I wanted Padeen, who would tell Bob how I could have died,
how I might just need a little time. I looked to see how soon an
hour was, but there was only a lap clock propped at one end of
the pool, its big red hand spinning freely. There was no room for
a regular clock on the pool's transparent walls, where branches of
barren trees pressed against them from outside. The only treeless
wall had a clear view down Bob's long, empty driveway to the road.

"What's the story, Quinn?" Bob said, fingering the cigarette
along his ear.

"No story," I said, giving in to fate. I let my body bump along the
stairs and slip under the water.

*

That night I sat with my brothers and sisters at our two matching kitchen tables, dark expanses of faux-wood Formica acquired
from a breakfast place at Holiday Village that went out of business.
A long bench upholstered with.blue vinyl flowers ran L-shaped
along the back wall. There was room for 11, though Mom rarely
sat down. Our father sat alone at the short end of the L, with a
tiny TV between him and us tuned loudly to the evening news.
This was not deemed rude, but sensible self-occupation. Reading
at meals was also encouraged, anything to keep conflict in check.
Dad still carried overlapping ellipses scars of fork tines tattooed
across the back of one hand, from mealtime skirmishes with his
own many siblings.

"I put my head underwater," I said, and no one seemed to hear.
"All the way under," I said, louder, as the bread basket moved
along the table.

"Duh," Pat said, "isn't that the point?" He adjusted heavy black
frames higher up his nose and grabbed three snail rolls, before
shoving the basket past me. He was the only one of us with glasses
and an easy tan, so that if people didn't know Bill, they might
think it was Pat who was Diane's biological brother.

"I was the only one who did it," I said, looking up and down the
table. "First day." I kicked my little brother, Brendhan, kitty-corner
under the table so at least he'd listen up.

Mom turned from where she hunched over the counter and
pointed a long knife my way. "Blushing is the color of virtue," she
said.

"Did you hear about Patty?" Diane said, sliding into her seat.
Her hair was so straight it looked ironed. Diane adored Cher and
Crystal Gayle, women with glossy dark hair so long they could sit
on it. "Did you tell them already?" she said to Padeen, sitting across
from me. "Patty" was what the older kids and their friends called
Padeen; I was not supposed to call her that. Everyone looked at
Padeen, who looked down, chewing.

"Dogcatcher let you go with just a warning?" Bill said, grinning
at his own joke. His teeth were white and straight. He and Diane
had nicer teeth than the rest of us, and Bill was extravagant, even
coercive, with his smiles.

John stared evenly at Padeen. "You put on 10 pounds," he said,
not smiling.

"I made cheerleader," she said flatly. Then John laughed. Padeen pushed two rolls off the end of her plate, and I snatched them up in one hand, sliding the butter dish near me with the other.

"What?" Bill said, mouth hanging open, but he already knew. It was no surprise to any of the oldest kids—Bill, Chris, John, Diane, and Padeen. They all went to the Catholic high school, Central, where girls trying out for cheerleader performed alone in the center of the gym while the rest of the school watched and then voted on the spot like Roman emperors, thumbs up or down.

Padeen shrugged. "I was the only girl with four siblings," she said, burnishing achievement with modesty. I stabbed the potato on my plate, annoyed.

"And three cousins," John said, "and those we bribed." He looked up and down the table. "Where's Chris?" he said. "Oh, shit, must've sold him into slavery."

"Don't say *shit*," Mom said, not turning around.

Bill reached over and yanked Padeen's plate from under her fork. "Better watch that," he said. "You're gettin' too fat to be a cheerleader." Padeen's slender forearm stayed poised above where her plate had been.

"Why do girls want to be cheerleaders?" Tom said, turning the page of an expensive art book he wasn't supposed to have at the table. He was red-haired and thoughtful, with skin translucent as any Flemish virgin in his book. In short, an easy target, and he'd had trouble ever since leaving Our Lady of Lourdes for the public junior high. "Don't they get how cheerleading objectifies women?"

Mom went on shoving the dull bread knife into the long French loaf she'd made that morning. She sometimes said that skirts were so short these days you could see girls' Maxi Pads. But Dad looked up from the TV, humming with news of Nixon, napalm, and Vietnam, his gaze rare and magnetic, pulling our eyeballs toward him. "Hell," he said, lifting his juice glass of Gallo toward Padeen, "good for you." He looked right at her, mouth overfull with big Irish teeth, and winked. "That's my girl."

I pushed most of the second roll into my mouth and chewed with some difficulty, lips clenched tight.

I learned to swim, of course. At my first swim meet I'd just turned seven, and since I competed in the Eight and Under division no one expected much, but I made the finals in four events and took second overall in breaststroke. I'd never felt such uncomplicated happiness. Even Pat looked up from his comic book and gave me a high five as I climbed onto the bus for the long drive over the mountains and back to Great Falls.

At home I tore through the smokehouse and made a hard left at the "Dad Pad," a name we used without smirk or innuendo; it was my father's room, and that was that. He was watching football cranked up in the old iron filigree and red leather barber chair he used as a recliner, so that sitting down he loomed above us standing. The Seahawks were playing, and I lingered near the door until I saw they were up by seven. When I stepped into the room, Dad's hand shot out, palm forward: *Don't talk.* I stood, trying not to scratch dry patches that smelled of chlorine, waiting for the Seahawks to at least make a first down.

His room was lined with the sort of books not allowed at meals, hardcovers on Herodotus, Plato, Aristotle, and Thomas Aquinas; leather-bound transcripts of the Salem witch trials, the Dred Scott decision, *Plessy v. Ferguson;* and a big set of illustrated biographies of great artists, Giotto to Van Gogh. On the wall across from the art books, above a hulking black-and-white television, was a framed reproduction of a dimpled and redheaded Renoir bather, nude from the waist up, whom I long believed to be my mother in younger days.

A Rainier commercial came on and Dad raised his own beer, gesturing me forward. I brought the ribbon from behind my back. I'd kept it pressed between the covers of a Hardy Boys book on the ride home, and it was crisp as if freshly made. "Look at that," Dad said, rubbing the strip of red between his big fingers. "Second place."

I brushed crispy chunks of hair out of my eyes and grinned up at him. "Pretty good," I said.

He smoothed the length of polyester across his broad, scarred palm and sucked in through his teeth. "Let me tell you something," he said, almost reluctantly. He did not look up. "Second place is like kissin' your sister."

Diane's and Padeen's rooms were above the rest of the house in a converted attic space accessed from the main floor by a yellow spiral staircase. Their bedrooms had peaked ceilings and views. Brendhan and I shared a corner bedroom in the basement, where we tried to guess by the tires whose car was outside when someone pulled into the driveway.

Diane's room looked south over alfalfa fields to the big trees and blue silos of the Ayshire Dairy. Padeen's pointed north, where the same fields ended in a looming crag known as "The Rocks," with its pair of white crosses bolted to the cliff edge. Padeen's brass bed was pushed underneath her window, our mother's hope chest at its foot. The chest was as big as a coffin, with the same high gloss to its curved lid. I could have played inside there but was sitting cross-legged on top, quiet as a ghost so as not to get kicked out.

Although I liked wearing boys' clothes, I couldn't get enough of Padeen and her cheerleading outfit. Watching her squeeze too-tight knee-highs along each muscular calf was like watching a female Achilles arming for battle. I held my breath as she wrestled the little sweater with the bucking mustang over her breasts and ribs, aligning the seams straight along each side. She tugged at her short skirt, with its alternating panels of blue and gold, until it hung low across her curving hips. She pulled both vinyl boots up to her knees, then turned toward the mirror and popped her eyes like a Kabuki master, layering on mascara. She slicked on red Lip Smackers, adding a dab high on both cheekbones until she was glowing and fierce. I breathed as quietly as I could through my open mouth. Something about Padeen's shining toughness reminded me of her closet, where, behind the minis and maxis, the wooden and brocade platforms, the leather boots, fitted jackets, and denim ankle dusters, there was a neat row of hunting rifles and a couple of compound bows.

Padeen took a small bottle off her dresser, clicked it open, and shook something into her palm.

"What's that?" I said, risking expulsion.

"A pill," she said, tipping back her head and taking it without water. We did not take pills, not even aspirin. Mom followed the doctrine of our family pediatrician, Dr. Urbanich, who held that children do not feel pain.

"What for?" I said.

Padeen started kicking at clumps of clothing on the floor. "Ulcers," she said finally.

"What's that?"

"Like a stomachache."

"Maybe you shouldn't go to the game—you might throw up."

"Not that kind of stomachache," Padeen said. "From other things."

"Milk?" I said. John had just found out he was allergic to milk, which struck Brendhan and me as hilarious, since we lived on a dairy.

"Not milk," Padeen said, lifting up a big down coat and finding her purse underneath. "Things like stress." She snapped open the purse and dropped in the pills.

I waited while she shrugged on the coat and checked herself in the mirror, then shook it onto the floor and went hunting for a different one. We weren't allowed to leave the house without "proper clothes" in winter, even if it was to go from overheated car to sweltering gym. We were regaled with stories of people dying after their car slid off the road, just because they couldn't stay warm enough until help arrived.

"Why are you stressed?" I said, this time risking the heart of things.

Padeen checked herself in the mirror again, turning this way and that. "Don't worry about it," she said.

"I'm not worried," I said.

Padeen turned from the mirror, hands on her hips. I watched her take in my short, matted hair and chapped lips, my dirty sweatshirt and jeans. "I know," she laughed. "You don't have anything to worry about."

"Yes, I do," I said. I worried about not being like other girls, and about not wanting to be. My greatest hope was to grow into a man, or short of that, into some kind of woman I couldn't imagine. Someone very different from the mothers and wives and nuns we knew.

"You should worry about being in my room," Padeen said. "Get out." She pulled me off the chest and pushed me toward the door. "And don't you dare come in while I'm gone." Over her shoulder, I caught sight of the Lip Smackers on the bedside table.

When Padeen was out of the house long enough, I stood at the landing vanity she shared with Diane and smeared on lip gloss. I looked at myself in the big pink mirror, tilting my head one way, then the other. I mostly looked the same, still pale, puffy, and un-combed, but with greasy lips. Nothing could transform me into Padeen, who would always be prettier, smarter, better, first.

But I followed Padeen the way a good defensive player does on the basketball court, eyes fixed at the heart of her, alert for signature moves and not letting her shake me.

One night that same winter, Chris took me along to a basketball game. We were supposedly going to see the Mustangs play, but I was there to watch Padeen, and Chris was there to meet up with Sue, the girl who would soon be his first wife. The roar in the gym was deafening, screaming fans stamping on wooden bleachers stacked from court to ceiling, the screech of refs' whistles and the bone-rattling buzz of shot clocks. At the epicenter of this delirious mayhem were cheerleaders, waving and smiling and egging it on. There was Padeen, thrusting pom-poms and raising her fist.

Chris tugged my hand to keep walking and leaned down to say something when I resisted. "What?" I shouted back.

He pointed to a section near the top, where Sue sat with some of her brothers and a group of other girls. Sue, straight hair, thin lips, and skinny body, made me nervous. I shook my head and pulled the other way, toward the court. Chris looked around, un-certain, then spotted a friend of Padeen's behind the Mustang bench, a blond boy who lived on Upper River Road, not far from us. Chris picked me up, babylike, and plunked me on the aisle next to Padeen's friend. Chris pointed to Padeen, then to me, and the boy smiled and gave Chris the thumbs-up.

"Don't move!" Chris shouted in my ear. "Dad's coming at half-time." I wasn't listening. I was watching the line of look-alike girls, long hair and longer legs, and all their parts swaying together. Soon I was moving too. I took a short step into the aisle and started cheering along, raising my hands in the air, looking over one shoulder, pretending to flip my cropped hair, and poking out first one hip, then the other. Teenagers on all sides clapped and laughed. I wiggled my butt up where Chris sat with Sue, then spun around and wiggled it at the other side of the gym. The kids around me roared for more.

At the halftime buzzer, people started pushing down the aisle. I stepped back to my seat, where Padeen was already leaning through the bench of players to reach me. I flew into her arms. She dropped me hard to the wood floor and marched across the slick court, pulling me behind. She hit the spring-loaded metal bar on the big gym door without breaking stride, and I flinched to see my father waiting on the other side. Padeen pushed me into him, where I was stung by the sudden shift from heated gym to chill parking lot.

"How was it?" Dad said, turning me around and holding on.

"Take her," Padeen said, shaking her blond, backlit hair so it shone like a halo around her face. Behind her was the silhouette of a bucking mustang above a sizable crucifix. "She's a brat."

I stared at the wall, not looking at either of them. My chest hurt.

"How's that?" Dad said, big hands heavy on my shoulders.

Padeen glanced back at the mass of people swarming across the stands. "How she acts," she said. "Just everything."

"They clapped," I said.

Padeen rolled her eyes. "They think you're a brat," she said, her face even with mine so I'd get it.

"I was being like you," I said.

She stood straight and took a cheerleader-like backward march into the gym. "You're not me," she said. "You're . . ."

I waited, hopeful. What was I?

"If you can't act like a big girl, you can't go places," Dad said, steering my shoulders away from the gym and toward the dark parking lot.

I pulled back, facing Padeen. "I was acting like a big girl," I said, "just like you."

"See what I mean?" Padeen said to Dad, then grabbed the door bar and yanked the door closed between us.

After her freshman year, Padeen left Central, where homework was placed in a little basket at each class door like donations tossed anonymously into a collection plate. When she did not tithe adequately in algebra, Dad said he'd be damned to pay for Cs from someone as smart as Padeen, and she was sent to public school.

Charles M. Russell High was all the way across town, a well-lit, modern building on a sprawling campus with an indoor pool, big theater, and manicured track. It opened just a few years before Padeen started there. Where Central had the fading head of Christ painted above the front doors (so like my brothers and their friends: gentle young features obscured by facial hair), CMR had a six-foot stone bison skull out front, with cowboy artist Charlie Russell's signature etched across it. Russell was our town's secular saint, a painter whose work captured the last days of the real frontier like an illustrated gospel of how God intended things to be.

CMR had nearly 1,500 students—a town by Montana standards—and a hard-driving reputation for excellence. A girl used to smaller and less might have struggled there, but not Padeen. She left cheerleading and made varsity swimming. She wrote for *The Stampede* and won awards for her columns and editorials across four states. She made editor, which got her the Silver Key of Journalism, given annually to a single Montana student. She was one of four CMR girls invited to the leadership conference at Girls' State. She was vice president of her class, Key Club Sweetheart, Thespian of the Year. One cold season, I sat in the CMR theater with my parents watching Padeen play Miep in *The Diary of Anne Frank*. Miep was the young woman who risked everything to do what her heart told her. She saved the diary but not the Franks, which didn't impress me much.

"I don't get it," I said when the lights went up.

My mother put her red hair next to mine and said quietly, "Anne died." She pulled a wadded Kleenex from under her cuff and wiped her nose. Dad was already gone. He'd fought in the war, lost two brothers in Europe, and once Padeen was offstage he'd cleared out.

"If I was Miep," I said, "I would've saved Anne."

"Sometimes that's just not possible," my mother said, taking my hand. I let her pull me past empty plush seats and up the wide center stairs, but I couldn't believe she was right.

Padeen was a snowball princess at the winter formal, where her prince was Rory Bosch. They were soon inseparable. Rory quarterbacked for the Rustlers in the fall and was on varsity track in the spring. His family had come from Croatia a generation or so back, and with his curly dark hair, a deep cleft in his strong chin, and an athlete's easy grace, Rory breathed a fragrant air of Mediterranean glamour onto our dry plains.

Padeen was taking me to swim practice one chill spring day

after school, and we swung by CMR first to get something from
her locker. She left me hunched in my mud-stained ski jacket by
the track, watching Rory practice the pole vault. Frost laced the
ground, but the sun was warm on my face. Nearby, a meadowlark
trilled endlessly for an answering mate.

Rory was all elbows and knees and shuddering horizontal pole
as he sprinted down the straightaway, like a warrior on an antique
vase. When he shoved the pole toward the track all forward mo-
mentum stopped, then he was floating upward, a graceful comma
interrupting endless blue before falling back to earth again. Rory
sprang from the mat, smiling, and waved my way. I grinned back
and started to raise my hand when I realized he was waving at Padeen, who'd come up behind me. I yanked it down, hoping they
hadn't noticed.

Rory leaped from the mat and bounded toward us. He grabbed
my jacket sleeve and pulled me against him, hugging hard, sweat
and chlorine puffing up between us, then tugged Padeen, cherry
and vanilla and herbal shampoo, into our huddle. "You are the
luckiest girls I know," he said.

"Because we have you?" Padeen laughed, but looked like she
might believe it.

"Naw," he said, hopping foot to foot in his shorts and singlet,
cleats crunching on the frosted grass. "Because you've got each
other."

Everyone knew about Rory's older brother, Kerry, who'd also
played football for CMR until he crashed in a Camaro at 18. The
other three boys in the car died on impact, but Kerry lingered in a
coma for nearly two years before his heartbroken parents removed
life support, 28 days before his 20th birthday. *Twenty-eight days before he turned 20.* I heard that so many times later, I just wanted
people to stop saying it.

"And you have us," Padeen said, touching Rory's shoulder
where his singlet met skin.

"Hey," Rory said, "hang out and I'll come with you." Rory lived
on the other side of us, farther down Route 2 South outside of
town.

"We can't," Padeen said, "she'll be late for swimming."

"Don't you want to wait for me?" Rory said, holding his hand
palm-up for me to slap.

"Yes," I said, giving it a hard whack.

Padeen hooked her hand under my armpit. "I'll be right back," she told Rory.

"I'll freeze by then."

"Put on a jacket."

"Don't have one," Rory said, hugging his shoulders for effect.

"Then run," my sister said.

Rory nodded seriously, then took off doing high knees across the grass. He glanced over his shoulder to see if we were looking, and we were. "You're coming back?" he shouted.

"Maybe," she yelled, smiling to herself even as we walked away.

Padeen had started teaching Brendhan and me Spanish when we were in the car. "Uno, dos, tres, cuatro, cinco," she began, as we pulled out of the high school parking lot.

She was fired up about Spanish because the previous month she'd gotten a bicycle trip for her birthday. Come summer, she was supposed to go with other Catholic kids to France, where they'd pick up bikes and ride a medieval pilgrimage road south, then over the Pyrenees and due west on to Santiago de Compostela in Spain. Padeen was actually on the waiting list, but the tour company said *Assume she's in,* since no one had ever missed going. She got her passport, bike shorts, and panniers before the letter came saying there wouldn't be room. Missing out on Spain would prove the opening blow, after so many charmed years.

Padeen rolled down her window and waved to Rory, who stood midtrack, watching us drive away. "Hasta pronto!" she trilled with Latin vigor, then rolled up the window against the cold.

"Are you going to marry Rory?" I said.

"Cuántos años tienes?" she said.

I counted in my head in Spanish. "Ocho?"

"Muy bien!"

"Are you?"

"Cómo?"

"Stop it."

"You can love someone," Padeen said slowly, "and not marry them right away." She raked her hair away from her face, and her broad forehead was clenched, serious. "You can wait."

"Chris and Sue didn't wait," I said. The previous summer I'd worn a purple halter dress and a shoulder-to-fingertip cast on

my right arm when Chris and Sue got married in our big backyard. Our neighbors who owned the dairy, the Mitchells, came to
the wedding, but that very morning my mother had stood at the
window watching the manure spreader inch along our perimeter
fence. "You'd think it could wait just this one day," she said, to no
one in particular. She sighed, not deeply, and went back to the
kitchen. None of us expected the world to adjust itself on our account.

"What are you waiting for?" I said, because I really didn't know.

"You sound like Rory," Padeen said, clicking on the radio and
turning it up.

Padeen's senior year, Rory waged a campaign to keep her in Great
Falls. He wrote letters, poems, songs for her, all variations on the
theme of her staying.

He knew what it meant to lose someone, and he didn't want
to lose her. He issued no ultimatums, no threats, but he hoped
she'd choose the good reality of him over a vague dream of college. Padeen compromised. With her grades and awards she might
have gone anywhere, but she chose the University of Montana,
just three hours—two and a half if you gunned it—from Great
Falls.

In late September 1975, John drove Padeen to Missoula with
her stuff rolling around the back of his pickup in a couple of black
garbage bags. At the corner of Arthur and Daly, he slammed to
a stop and cranked the emergency brake. He left the driver-side
door hanging open, engine running, and jumped out to haul her
bags onto the sidewalk. Padeen stepped into the street, zipped
up her jacket, and took a long look at the big buildings receding
toward the mountains. It was starting to snow. She walked slowly
around the back of the truck. "Where do I go?" she said.

"Hell if I know," John said, grinning. "It's your school." He
pointed toward the cluster of buildings across the street. "Over
there somewhere," he said, then jumped into his truck and took
off. Padeen hauled her own bags across the street and onto the big
gray paths of campus, pioneering two broad drag marks behind
her in the fresh snow.

In just days she'd made fast friends with the girls on her floor,
knew the secret back ways of campus, and was one of the first to

speak out in her classes, even the big ones. She took to all of it like a fish to water.

A few weeks after Padeen started school, I rode home with Mom and Brendhan from a swim meet in Helena. The plains were dark as lead but for pinpricks of stars above and the rare flash of headlights coming the other way. For once I wasn't annoyed with Brendhan, already asleep next to me, head propped on the seat divider and mouth open, snoring. His bad ears and tonsils kept him from swimming much, but he was often hauled to practices and meets.

My mother said the rosary softly from the front seat. *Holy Mary, mother of God, pray for us sinners now and at the hour of our death.* I closed my eyes, faking sleep, not wanting to do anything holy in that way. I fingered the ribbons in my lap, only one of them blue. My hero was Mark Spitz, the swimmer who never seemed to lose. Even at the Munich Olympics, where 11 other Jews died in a deluge of bullets, Spitz snatched fame from doom, taking gold seven times. I thought about luck and fate, and what part skill might play in salvation. I rubbed each ribbon between my fingertips, seeking a difference in the blue, but they felt alike.

I opened my eyes. My mother's voice grew louder when she caught sight of me in the rearview mirror. I joined in, but so quietly I could barely hear my voice above the tires. *Blessed art thou amongst women.* A strip of winking red lights appeared between the highway and the stars; the big smokestack was coming into view, meaning we were nearly home.

That same night Rory and three CMR buddies were at a bar on 10th Avenue owned by a former teacher turned barkeep. The drinking age in Montana was 18 then, and Rory, Ryan, Scott, and Tom had been going to bars together since high school. There was nothing delinquent about it, or wild. Rory had a few beers, so did his friends. Typical night.

But Rory missed Padeen; he could hardly shoot pool for talking about her blond hair, her wicked laugh, her Spanish and books and big ideas. By midnight the other guys had had enough. "Jesus, Rory, go see her already."

Scott's Camaro was parked out back and they all piled in. They headed west on 10th, crossed first the Missouri and then the Sun, outgunning the falls and smokestack and smelters as they headed out past Fort Shaw, past Square Butte and the ancient Ulm buffalo jump out there somewhere in the dark, before turning south and climbing the Continental Divide. Roger's Pass was in bad shape already in October—it had been snowing at that elevation for weeks—but they made it through just fine. The long drop into Lincoln should have been the easy part.

One by one they fell asleep in the warm hum of the Camaro, until even Scott at the wheel drifted off. Their car skidded sideways along the highway some 800 feet before it left the road, taking out a utility pole a hundred feet beyond that. The car flew on for another hundred feet before sticking fast in the Lander's Fork of the Blackfoot River. When the maintenance man from Montana Power showed up that morning, tragedy stretched the length of a football field from first skid marks to where they found Ryan's body, 135 feet downriver. Rory and Scott were thrown nearly as far. It's conceivable that Tom, the only one of them wearing a seat belt, might have survived the crash, but water filled the small car within minutes.

Clocks in Lincoln stopped at 3:50 A.M., October 4, 1975, 28 days before Rory would have turned 20. He died at the same age as his brother, from an accident in the same make of car, alongside the same number of friends.

John came back for Padeen just three weeks after he'd dropped her off. He took along a six-pack of Rainier, and they drove all the way to Great Falls that way, silent and drinking. When Padeen edged near the end of a bottle, John balanced a fresh one between his thighs and cracked it one-handed with the opener he kept on the dash. It was the best he knew of chivalry, and solace. He kept a slow beer going for himself as well. The boys in the Camaro were John's friends too, and a decade on he'd name his first child after Ryan.

Most of the town had turned out for the memorial service at the CMR theater. Long-haired girls staggered and wept, boys with shoulders so naturally broad that they looked suited up for the front line turned their chiseled faces to the ceiling so tears couldn't escape. White-faced adults held balled-up Kleenexes and whispered in little clumps on the landings and near doors. Padeen was cried out. She sat dry-eyed and hunched next to Rory's mom in the front row. Mrs. Bosch, a mother who offered comfort even from her own hell, kept Padeen's narrow hand in hers. She nodded to the stage, where a big photo of Rory in his football uniform was propped against a folding chair alongside his friends. "I believe you two are spiritually married," Mrs. Bosch said, squeezing hard on Padeen's hand to make sure she took it in. "You were destined for each other."

I sat alone with Brendhan while our older brothers served as ushers. Diane sat two rows behind Padeen with her girlfriends, their faces streaked with running mascara and concealer. Mom and Dad were taking condolences in the crowd, their exact position in things confusing for everyone. All around Brendhan and me the same conversation thrummed in slight variations around the same theme. *Marked for death . . . As if neither Bosch boy could live a day beyond that one . . . Same age, same make of car, same number of dead . . . Chosen by God, but why?*

I tried not to hear. It scared me that the world could hold such horrible symmetries, or that destiny could mean tragedy as much as fame. I concentrated on my sneakers—I'd refused to wear a dress or nice shoes, with no one in any mood to struggle—which were grabbing at something sticky on the floor. I turned to Brendhan, who hunched next to me, his blond eyebrows pinched to nearly touching. There were dark slashes under both his puffy eyes, making him seem even paler than usual. White as a ghost. I wondered if I looked like that.

"There's snot under my shoe," I said to him. Brendhan giggled. Heads whipped our way, and I heard someone hiss *Quinns*. A tall woman nearby shook her head, her thin lips pinched white against leathery skin. I turned my back to her, shielding both of us as best I could, and went on mashing my sneakers into the mess.

A few days after Rory's funeral, I was playing on the spiral staircase leading up to my sisters' rooms. I slid sidesaddle down the twisting banister and jumped where it ended, landing hard on both feet, then flinging my arms up like Olga Korbut. The floor shook, rattling the skeletal stairs, until Padeen came to the landing and asked what I was doing.

"Playing," I said.

Padeen started down. "Sometimes it really seems like you don't care," she said. I was mid-staircase, but she kept walking, her face partly covered by one hand, a small duffle bag in the other.

"What should I do?" I said, and it was a real question.

Padeen stopped a few steps above me. "Nothing," she said after a pause. "This, I guess."

"I can balance all the way from the top," I said as she edged past. She didn't answer. Her hair was loose and stringy around her face. Her jeans were worn to white threads in one knee, and she had on hiking boots that we called wafflestompers, like some backpacker heading into the wilderness. Padeen glanced up to where the staircase met the landing and sighed.

"What?" I said.

"I forgot my purse," she said.

"I'll get it," I said and took the stairs two at a time, not waiting to hear if I had permission to go into her room. The nylon sack she called her purse was alone in the middle of the made bed, but I stopped short before grabbing it. The many photos, ribbons, and awards, the half-used makeup and bits of clothing, were all gone. A few books still lined the low bookshelf in the wall—her Central and CMR yearbooks, two fat paperbacks of *Don Quixote* and *One Hundred Years of Solitude,* and a dog-eared copy of *Our Bodies, Ourselves*—but I didn't notice them until later.

I walked slowly back down the stairs and held out her bag. "Where are you going?" I said.

She undid the drawstring and looked inside. "Back to school," she said, without looking up. John was already gone, so she was getting a ride from a friend of the Mitchells, someone she'd never met. She closed the purse without touching anything inside, then turned the corner to the kitchen without saying good-bye. I could hear her talking to Mom, but I didn't try to listen. I'd overheard too much already, things I wanted to forget.

I tiptoed back up the staircase and into Padeen's room, where I found the books, then an old curling iron in the bedside table drawer with a cord so twisted the wires poked through in places. Tangled up with it was a green-and-gold graduation tassel with a plastic '75 attached to the topknot. The dresser drawers were empty but for two shiny plastic shells that once held pantyhose and a pair of bike shorts balled up in a dark corner of the bottom drawer. I didn't dare open the hope chest yet.

I crawled across the bed, then kneeled at the brass headboard as if it were a communion rail and pressed my cheek flat against the glass, waiting for a strange car to come down the driveway. I knelt there a long time, patient but expectant. I wanted to see Padeen do it, to bear witness to my sister, that strong swimmer, rescuing herself in the wake of fate. Striking out alone for a new destiny.

ALLISON GLOCK

At the Corner of Love and Basketball

FROM ESPN: THE MAGAZINE

Part 1

MALIKA WILLOUGHBY LOVED Rosalind Ross. She loved her from the moment she saw her, when Willoughby was only 14, playing summer league basketball, and Ross, 17, already a local star full of swagger, approached her and complimented her game. Ross told her she had potential, looked her right in the eye, and smiled. After that, Willoughby was seized with a sense of recognition so jarring that she could not stop thinking about Ross, about how Ross made her feel and what that might mean.

Rosalind Ross loved Malika Willoughby too, but she was cagier. Three years older, raised in Milwaukee's rough Harambee neighborhood, Ross had seen some things. She'd heard her father talk about "faggots." Seen what happened to those kids, the ones who were different, like her younger brother Spencer, who played with her dolls and knew how to double-Dutch jump.

When Ross and Willoughby met, Ross had a boyfriend, Kevin. He and Ross later attended the prom, where she'd wear the third dress of her entire life and pose for the camera, smiling, head tilted, demure, the way she knew she was supposed to be. Kevin was handsome and kind, but he was not Willoughby. He did not make her laugh or cry. He inspired no feeling at all, not like Willoughby, young and beautiful and hungry for Ross in a way neither of them fully understood.

"I'm not gay."

"I'm not either."

So they told each other, even as they courted, exchanging passionate letters, then kisses that Willoughby said made her "lose her mind for two days."

"I love you."

"I love you too."

So they told each other, and no one else, knowing what would happen if they did.

By all accounts, Rosalind Ross was a radiant baby. The family charmer who quickly became the family poster child, the hope. The eldest child of two high school dropouts, reared in a neighborhood where crime was wallpaper and dreams were for dummies, Ross dreamed anyway. Mostly, she dreamed of basketball.

Tall, strong, and attractive, with a wide, open face and cheekbones like switchblades, Ross stayed in school and out of trouble, devoting herself to making grades and mastering her court skills, which she told her parents would be "my ticket out."

A talented five-foot-nine guard, she played with monastic dedication, disregarding all temptation until the afternoon she spied Willoughby running down the court, all flop and fury, and broke into a grin so wide it hurt. Coyly, she suggested they play together, improve each other's game. "Okay," Willoughby agreed, mumbling, chin sunk to her chest.

From then on, the two teenagers spent every day and night together. "Best friends," they told everyone. "Sisters."

Ross taught Willoughby to drive. Told her she was beautiful. Gave her a ring. Before her senior season, Ross pulled her brother Spencer aside (also gay and then closeted to everyone but her), confiding that she "really liked Malika."

Spencer smiled.

"No," she repeated, her face flush. "I *really* like her."

These were the puppy love years: Ross and Willoughby alone in their bubble, planning their future in another, better world. Then one day, while going through her wallet, Ross's father, Willie, found a mash note from Willoughby. The bubble popped.

Willie was not reared to tolerate homosexuality. When Ross was a girl, Willie was the one who pinned her hair, ironed the creases in her slacks. The two had been tight as ticks, both larger than life, turning the attention in any room. "She was always the favorite,"

Spencer says with amicable resignation. "If we had a $100 budget for shoes, Rosalind's cost $80." Then Ross hit puberty, and with it, feelings unwelcome in Willie's home. The afternoon he discovered the letter, Willie confronted his daughter in a lather. The argument escalated, ending with Willie telling Ross she would have to leave home if she ever saw Willoughby again.

One month later, Willie found Willoughby sneaking away from the house. He demanded that Rosalind go with her.

"Growing up, my father was very hard on us," says Spencer. "He had so many expectations of Rosalind. After he kicked her out, she disassociated from him. They stopped speaking. He thought he was right."

Ross's mother, Pamela, did not share Willie's views but felt powerless to act. She could not choose between her husband and her daughter, and anyway, it was his house.

Ross, heading into her senior year, moved in with her grandmother, where she stayed until she left for college. She continued to see Willoughby. Rejected by members of their families, they became a family unto themselves. Us versus them, their bonds stronger for the adversity. "Like Thelma and Louise," Spencer recalls.

During this time, Ross persevered on the court, setting records and netting awards for Milwaukee Tech High School, her only weak games the ones against Willoughby's Washington High. "I didn't want to make her look bad," Ross would explain. Still, her father's rejection weighed on her. Spencer says he saw his sister "toughen up," felt "this wall she built." It was only with Willoughby that she softened. With her, Ross could relax, act giddy, let loose with what her teammates called her hyena laugh, a sound, says Spencer, "so crazy, all you could do was laugh too when you heard it." With Willoughby, Ross could be a girl.

Malika Willoughby did not have a contagious laugh. Born into Dickensian circumstances, Willoughby was reflexively serious, controlled. Her mother, Rebecca Harp, a bus driver, was erratic, unforgiving, often depressed. Willoughby's father, Craig, an admitted crack addict, "came and went," she says. As such, Willoughby was frequently left to raise her younger sisters, one of whom was severely disabled with cerebral palsy. She cooked, cleaned, changed feeding tubes and diapers, socializing little, except with Ross.

Willoughby's mother hated Ross, an abhorrence that only intensified when she discovered the true nature of her daughter's relationship.

"I didn't raise no dykes!" she screamed at Malika. Harp blamed Ross for corrupting her baby. For taking advantage of a 14-year-old girl with no previous sexual experience. For confusing her.

But Willoughby did not feel confused. She felt, for the first time, loved: she could listen to the sound of Ross's voice and see a dream unfolding in her head, a life together.

Though she was under five-foot-eight and rail-thin, Willoughby nonetheless excelled as a point guard at Washington High. She was scrappy, determined. According to Pam Kruse, Willoughby's coach, Willoughby understood that basketball would provide a college education, not a career. She knew, Kruse says, she was not pro material.

After graduation, Ross headed to a junior college, Northeastern A&M in Oklahoma, where she led the Lady Norse in scoring. Ross made promises to Willoughby, still in high school, told her not to worry. But college was college. Ross was studying, practicing, playing, her hours full. Willoughby consoled herself by hanging out with Spencer in Harambee. "She was always wondering what Roz was doing," Spencer remembers. "She wanted to be more important than her academics and athletics. It became too much for Rosalind."

In 2000, after being named a juco All-American, Ross transferred to Oklahoma. Before she left, she told Willoughby that after nearly three years of unremitting companionship, she needed a breather.

Willoughby handled the news poorly. Ross later told several family members and friends that Willoughby jumped on a bus to Oklahoma armed with a bowie knife. She sought Ross out at her apartment and confronted her, accusing her of cheating. Ross talked her down. Not long after, amid the unanimous dismay of their respective families, Ross and Willoughby resumed their relationship.

By 2001, Willoughby had earned a full scholarship to the University of Wisconsin–Milwaukee, but she seemed miserable. Hoping a change of scenery would help, she transferred to Kent State. During that time she met with therapist Anna Campbell, who subsequently diagnosed Willoughby with Avoidant Personality Disorder, a condition marked by feelings of persistent inadequacy and extreme sensitivity to rejection. In a letter to Willoughby's mother, Campbell warned that it would be "very difficult for [Willoughby] to develop friendships."

"When she came on at Kent, we were doing an open gym, and it was obvious she was talented but also very shy," recalls former teammate Jamie Rubis, 31. "But basketball was a common ground, and we became close."

Rubis, then a senior, mentored Willoughby. With her help, Willoughby was named captain in her second year and later tapped as one of five designated student-athletes to be featured on promotional posters hung throughout campus. In hers, she smiles sweetly, hair combed flat across her forehead, her eyebrows lifted high.

Rubis says she met Ross only once in those years, when Ross came to visit Willoughby on campus. "Malika did not tell anyone she was gay," Rubis says. "She told us they were close friends that grew up together." (Ross also remained closeted throughout college, believing the climate to be "unreceptive" to lesbian players, she told her mother.)

For a time, everything clicked. Willoughby was a Kent State role model with a promising future, and Ross had led Oklahoma to the 2002 national championship game, which helped make her a first-round pick of the L.A. Sparks. Later that year, Ross left for California, a few credits shy of her degree. There, she had dinner with Lisa Leslie. Fans kept approaching the table, which made Ross chuckle. It was improbable to her, so far removed from Harambee. Leslie told her new teammate: just you wait, this will happen to you too.

Ross imagined. She would be a professional basketball player. She would live in Los Angeles. She would be famous, free. Ross laughed her hyena laugh, let herself believe.

But Ross had white-knuckled through years of chronic knee pain (and an undiagnosed torn ACL and other knee ligaments). When she arrived at Sparks camp injured, the team sent her in for medical tests. She needed surgery. Then rehab. A year later, she got devastating news.

She would not be a professional basketball player. She would not live in Los Angeles. She would not play a single pro game. Instead, she was cut loose. Adrift, Ross rushed to the only anchor she knew.

In 2006, after Willoughby completed college, she and Ross, now in their midtwenties, moved back to Harambee. Ross took a job as a security guard for Briggs & Stratton. Willoughby looked for work, eventually finding it as a bank teller—and then a manager. They set up house in a tiny apartment. They tried not to focus on what could have been.

Though her pro career was over, Ross remained a neighborhood star. Locals would solicit her attention, succumb to her charms. "Roz was a trophy to Malika," says Spencer. She was also threatened by Ross's status.

Not long after Ross moved home, Spencer recalls, she said that Malika was doing "crazy things. Hiding Roz's keys. Deflating her tires so she couldn't leave."

Ross responded to her lover's insecurity by lying. Then cheating.

"Roz was always playing around," acknowledges her mother, Pamela. "She had trouble saying no when people came after her."

Willoughby swore to friends that she didn't care, as long as Ross came home to her. But the relationship deteriorated. Tempers flared. Suffocated, Ross would walk out. Inconsolable, Willoughby would lure her back. And so it went. Willoughby and Ross parting dramatically, then reuniting, the pattern recurring countless times over the decade and a half they stayed involved, the separations never true, the pull of the other constant as gravity.

"Your first love, sometimes you never get over it," surmises Spencer. "Malika had never been with anybody else. She still had the fairy tale in her head."

During the last effort at reconciliation, Ross, now 30, was broke. She had part-time work at an inner-city children's home and as a basketball referee, but it was a far cry from the future she'd envisioned. "One more shot," Ross told her brother about starting up again with Willoughby.

It was 2010. The strain was showing on them both. Willoughby, 27, had taken to drinking heavily, carrying a flask even at home. Already lean, she grew skeletal. Ross slept alone on the couch of their condo, numbing herself with pot and video games. They quit having sex. They argued loud enough for neighbors to hear. Ross told friends she felt dead inside, that she needed to get out. Willoughby promised Ross a Chevy Avalanche if she stayed. Ross hated herself for not leaving. Willoughby hated herself for trying to buy affection.

In February, Willoughby had purchased a weapon from Badger Guns; she wanted it "for protection," she said. She later upgraded to a more hand-friendly Beretta 84FS Cheetah .380 compact semi-automatic pistol, a light shot regarded for its easily accessible safety. Willoughby kept the pistol loaded under her and Ross's bed.

On the evening of September 12, 2010, Ross's mother awoke from a nightmare in a sweat. She'd had a vision of Rosalind in a casket, dressed in a mustard sport coat. She called Ross, told her about the dream.

Her daughter told her to relax, that she "had it under control."

"She said she was planning on leaving Malika—she just didn't know how," Pamela recalls.

Three days after her mother's vision, a little before 9:00 P.M., Ross's cell phone rang. It was, as ever, another woman.

"Who is that?" Willoughby asked, piqued.

They were in her used BMW, ordering dinner at the Popeyes drive-thru.

"None of your business," Ross snapped back.

"I pay your phone bills."

"Are you trying to front me off?"

Then the punching started. And yelling that could be heard by passersby on the street.

"I wish . . ." Willoughby spat out, stopping short.

"Wish what?" Ross taunted. "You hard? The gun is in the back."

And just like that, the dream Willoughby and Ross shared for 13 years collapsed on itself. In its place, a black hole of reality yawned open, a mirror held to the lie, and Willoughby, seized with despair, did the only thing she believed she could do to save herself. She killed the dream.

She killed it by taking the Beretta .380 compact semiautomatic pistol and firing a bullet into the left side of her lover Rosalind Ross's head.

Part 2

Pamela Collins, 51, still lives close to where she raised Rosalind and her brothers, Spencer, age 29, a Navy veteran and high school basketball coach, and Kenneth, 20, a tech-college student. The walls of the family home are covered with photos: Pamela vamping with her sister in '80s hair, wedding pictures of her and her husband, Willie, 53, older family portraits showing kin from generations back. The entire Collins and Ross clan is represented, but the bulk of the real estate belongs to Roz.

There are photographs of Ross as a schoolgirl in braids, snapshots with friends, and class portraits, but these evergreens have been largely eclipsed by newer pictures, collages and poster boards donated by friends and family, assembled as tributes after her death. There are so many memorials and donations that photos have found their way into potted plants and coffee mugs, albums stacked thick on the table, haunting collateral too heartbreaking to curate.

Beside the dining table sits a floor-to-ceiling china cabinet chockablock with trophies, plaques, and other evidence of Ross's high-achieving life. It is from this cabinet that Pamela retrieves the pack of Doublemint gum that her daughter was carrying the night she was shot. "You can see her blood on it," Willie says, wresting it from his wife's palm. He points at an indistinct splotch on the package, then delicately returns it to its place among the certificates and ribbons.

The family settles into the TV room. *America's Funniest Home Videos* plays at high volume. Spencer and Kenneth sit side by side, both dressed in snappy checked button-downs and well-fitted jeans, idly watching. Willie stands behind the couch, still wearing his leather jacket, restless.

Pamela points out Ross's rookie card with the Sparks. Then another photo album, this one from the funeral, which drew more than 1,000 attendees. "Roz was a cutup, a people person," Pamela says, her eyes glimmering. "Everybody loved her." Even the Harambee boys, who didn't seem to get the memo. "She would be at the barbershop getting a fade, and the guys there would try to pick her up," marvels Pamela, laughing.

"Rosalind had a fear of being alone," Spencer says, running his hands over his knees. "She would leave one relationship and go right into another. She was never just Rosalind. All her girlfriends knew about each other. One of them told me, 'We all knew our place.' But that doesn't make it right."

"You don't shoot someone for that," Willie interrupts, angrily. "If you shot everybody who played the field . . ." He begins to stutter.

"I'm not saying that, Dad." Spencer sighs.

"Roz was all about helping people," Willie begins again, his voice loud, deep. "She'd bring home kids when she was still a kid herself, make sure they were fed and clothed. She'd show love to people nobody else would."

He exhales, his mouth slack. Kenneth reaches over, strokes his father's sleeve at the cuff. Spencer drops his head. Beneath his shirt, his chest rises and falls.

Later, Spencer will explain how his father's homophobia alienated him and Ross from the family. How to be gay in Harambee is to be "doomed to be bashed, abused." How when he was outed, by a lover five years ago, it was Ross who forced him to go back to the neighborhood court and endure whatever it took to regain his standing, something he achieved, he believes, only because he was Roz's little brother. He will talk at length about living for years on the down-low and his refusal to do it anymore, because in his gut he feels that if his sister had been able to come up in a culture of acceptance and security, if she had not had to view the world as us versus them, if she hadn't so ardently needed to prove her father wrong about the consequences of loving women—Willoughby especially—then she would still be alive, and his family would not be crammed together in that room, broken with imaginings.

He will say all of this and more, but for now he remains quiet, ignoring everything but the blaring television, canned laughter echoing off the cluttered walls of his parents' house.

Often, facts and truth don't have much to do with each other. So it is in all crimes of the heart, especially those involving secrets. In this case, there is a particular flavor of truth for every surviving family member, friend, and former teammate leveled in the wake of ruin after Ross's death.

For Willoughby, the facts were simple: "She sold me a dream." So Willoughby wrote in a six-page, neatly lettered note to her mother nearly four months after she shot Rosalind Ross. The note starts, "Hey Mommie," and ends with palpable resignation, if not regret. "You has always been right when it came to Rosalind."

The envelope is sealed with a small penciled heart, "I love you" etched inside.

By all accounts, loving Willoughby's mother was no easy task, a volatile woman so divorced from reality that the day before her daughter's sentencing for the slaying she was making up Malika's room for her to come home. Willoughby chose not to correct her perception. There was, she told a friend, no point. (Willoughby declined to be interviewed. Harp could not be reached for comment.)

In her letter, Willoughby pleads with her mother for understanding and forgiveness, not for killing Ross but for loving her.

"I know you didn't want me to be gay and did not approve," she writes. "Mother, I loved her deeply. I wanted her to act like she loved me and most important I wanted to prove you wrong. I wanted you to see that Rosalind really did love me . . . that it was meant to be. I wanted to show you that being gay wasn't going to stop me becoming somebody in life."

The letter goes on, providing both a motive for the killing ("It was like I couldn't get her out of my system. When we wasn't together I thought about her all day. And I was sad that she was with somebody else and loved them more than she loved me") and, possibly, an explanation for it. "She tells me she didn't mean to hit me and I believed her, mother."

"It's called Intimate Partner Violence," explains Michael Hart, Willoughby's attorney. Hart's team told the judge hearing the *State of Wisconsin v. Willoughby* case that its client had been "belittled, threatened, humiliated, lied to, controlled and slapped around by Roz."

They hired an expert, Liz Marquardt of the Sojourner Family Peace Center, to interview Willoughby and vouch for her credibility as an abuse survivor and to explain the intricacies of same-sex domestic violence, how it is often overlooked, especially among women, whom society views as equals. Hart also gathered testimony from friends who said they had seen Willoughby with black eyes and bruises.

"We went to lunch one day at McDonald's, and she told me about the abuse," recalls Rubis. The meal happened in 2009, when

Willoughby was again living with Ross, by some accounts for the fifth time. Though Rubis "never observed anything" herself, she did hear from mutual acquaintances that Willoughby had reported to work with a "busted eardrum." Willoughby blamed basketball.

"I've played basketball my whole life," says Rubis. "I've never seen that happen."

In June 2010, Willoughby was treated for a bruised tailbone at Saint Joseph Hospital's ER. She would later attribute the injury to being battered by Ross. "She bruised her tailbone from playing basketball in the rec league," Spencer says flatly. "She went up for a rebound and she fell on her butt. I took her to the hospital after the game. To say Rosalind did that was a lie."

In court, the Milwaukee DA echoed the Ross family's rebuttals, detailing numerous instances of Willoughby's possessiveness and physical threats, almost all incited by Ross's talking to other women. Women like Ross's former lover, Belinda Huddleston.

Huddleston, 33, began dating Ross in February 2009. The IT tech and Ross saw each other privately for just over a year before deciding to stop. Huddleston had her first and only face-to-face encounter with Willoughby just after Christmas.

"It all started because Roz bought me a designer handbag, and I put it on my Facebook page," says Huddleston. After seeing the post on Ross's page, Willoughby went searching for Huddleston and Ross and found them visiting the Ross family home.

"I'll kill you," Willoughby said.

Huddleston didn't move.

"No you won't," Huddleston said calmly. "You're not stupid."

Ross saw what was happening, immediately ushered Huddleston into the house, and called the police. Willoughby pounded on the door, then fled the scene.

By April 2010, Ross had broken it off with Huddleston for Willoughby, but the two stayed in contact. "Roz told me she thought it was going to work out this time because they had known each other for so long," Huddleston says.

It didn't. Early that August, Ross confided to Huddleston that she wanted to leave the state, that it was the only way to be free. She wanted to move to Oklahoma and invited Huddleston to come with her. Ross planned to earn her degree, then use her old basketball connections to land a position as a recruiter. She believed basketball could save her again, like it had all those years before.

September 15, four days before she was due to leave Harambee, Ross departed Huddleston's house to break up with Willoughby for the last time. She assured Huddleston she'd be back for dinner.

Minutes before 9:00, a worried Huddleston called Ross. Ross answered from the Popeyes drive-thru.

"I could hear Malika in the background saying, 'Who is this? Who is this?' And Roz said, 'I'm going to have to call you back.' It was the last thing she ever said to me."

"The crime was intentional," she says, her voice thick with tears. "Malika knew exactly what she was doing."

She describes how Willoughby practiced shooting the gun on several occasions. How the weapon was no secret to Ross and Willoughby's circle. How both women spoke of it often, showed it around to friends and family like one would an engagement ring.

"It was never not loaded, as far as I knew," Huddleston recalls.

For all the haziness in the testimony and postmortem of the case, exhibit one—the West Silver Spring Popeyes exterior security surveillance tape—distinguishes itself in its clarity.

The video, recorded from a camera mounted on a high post at the edge of the parking lot, begins with the most crushingly ordinary of activities. Cars and trucks cruising through, placing orders for chicken and fries, then driving to the pickup window. It is 8:50 P.M.

After a few moments, Willoughby's BMW pulls up to the electronic-menu kiosk, Ross at the wheel. The women are already fighting.

For more than a minute, Willoughby can be seen windmill-punching Ross—an unhinged mania of fury almost comic in its expression, like something one would see in a *Three Stooges* skit. After a bit, she thrusts herself into the backseat and retrieves something from a book bag. Seconds later, Ross screeches the car forward, slamming the brakes to the right of the pickup window. It is 8:54 P.M.

Willoughby resolutely exits the passenger side, wearing a white shirt, straight-leg jeans, sneakers, a gun already in her hand. She is not frantic. She walks calmly to the back, where she pauses behind the right taillight and visibly adjusts the weapon.

She resumes walking to Ross's open window. Once there, she leans in and coldcocks her with the gun. Ross deflects the blow, and in less time than it takes to inhale, Willoughby forces the gun back through the window and fires a bullet into the left side of Ross's head, right behind her ear. It is 8:55.

Willoughby then draws back and begins bouncing around the parking lot like a boxer, her arms curved to her sides, flapping up and down. She jumps and paces, toes turned outward, stomping back and forth as if working a stage. Her face a rictus of confusion and horror, she returns to the car window. She flings open the driver's-side door and tugs at Ross's body. She pulls and heaves, finally jerking Ross onto the pavement, where she thuds with chilling finality.

Willoughby squats over Ross's motionless torso, cradles her head. She shakes her hard, harder, then jolts up again, resumes the frenetic circling, manic adrenal terror animating her limbs. She walks toward the pickup window, pivots, tramps back to Ross, every step a jackhammer. She shakes her once more. She then retreats to the edge of the parking lot, right beneath the security camera, tilts her head up, oblivious, consumed, and opens her arms wide, eyes closed, chin to God. It is 8:57.

Willoughby has yet to call for help. Instead, she doubles over as if wracked by cramps, her waist folding in on itself, heaving. The cops arrive, alerted by the interior Popeyes security alarm activated after the shot was fired. They swarm the scene. Willoughby does not run.

Amid the chaos lies Ross, in the drive-thru lane. Long and lean. Dressed in her favorite outfit, black polo, black jeans, limited-edition black-and-red Nike Air Force 1s. Improbably static, emanating dignity in its stillness, the only calm amid a flood of loss.

"I wanted to make her stop. I was angry. But I didn't want to kill her."

This is what Willoughby told police after her arrest. Before she became hysterical, confused. Before she was medicated and put on suicide watch. Before she hired Michael Hart.

She told officers she didn't even know for sure if Ross was dead. Then she saw a coffee mug with the word HOMICIDE printed across it in black letters.

That's when I knew she was gone," she told police.

A little more than a year after shooting the "only person I ever loved," as she told the court the final day of the hearing, Willoughby was sentenced to 13 years in prison, eight for first-degree reckless homicide and five for use of a dangerous weapon.

Her friend and teammate Jamie Rubis visited her the Saturday before she was sent away. To the end, Willoughby remained flummoxed.

"She was trying to understand how her life could change so quickly," Rubis says.

The Graceland Cemetery on North 43rd in Milwaukee is a vast, flat acreage with roads winding throughout the property. Willie drives, watching the headstones and monuments tick by. The windows are cracked, releasing the sounds of pop radio into the outside air.

"I do this every night," he says. "After my work shift at the foundry."

Willie brakes in front of a nondescript patch of grass, then gets out, walking cautiously between headstones until he reaches a flush bronze plaque with a single red carnation draped over the side.

"There she is," he says. He tries to smile, but his face trembles. "My baby girl."

He says hello, stares intently at the stone. In the center is a picture of Ross in a yellow tuxedo and boutonniere. Her hair is shaved tight. She looks comfortable, content.

"We were going to have her look more like a lady," Willie offers, "but this is the way she was. This is her."

He begins to cry, his voice rising, piercing the clear, empty space.

After a few minutes, he walks back to the car, his grief boiling to rage.

"I have to say good-night to my daughter in a graveyard," he sputters, his head shaking back and forth as if watching tennis.

Inside the car, he talks about how he and wife Pamela used to drive to see Roz most days. Sometimes they would scream and holler. Other days they would sit from noon to midnight, chatting with their child. More than a few times, they slept by their daughter's side. Some friends grew concerned.

So much hurt. How could they go there?

It was the wrong question. When your child is in the ground, the only real question is how do you ever leave?

Later that night, at Red Lobster, his daughter's favorite restaurant, Willie does not pretend to be doing well.

"I had a bad moment this weekend. I wrote on my Facebook page that there is no God."

He is dressed in his grieving uniform: a T-shirt with screen-printed photos of Rosalind all over the front and back, RIP scrolled along the bottom. Willie has more than a dozen shirts in the same vein. One features Willoughby's mug shot and the words: THE WOMAN WHO KILLED MY DAUGHTER. STONE COLD KILLER. In the winter, he switches to sweatshirts.

"All this hostility, it keeps coming up," he says. "I don't know what to do with it."

He refuses therapy or medication. "That isn't going to help me."

Instead, he screen-prints the shirts, attends stop-the-violence rallies, and tries to forget the years he let slip away while Ross was alive.

"She said to me once: 'You told me to be who I am. And you can't accept who I am. What am I supposed to do?'"

It would be a decade before Willie and his daughter had more than a cordial relationship as adults. The gap haunts Willie.

"If I had known," he says, "I would have set myself right."

In 2009, at Pamela's insistence, Ross and her father met for a talk.

"We got everything out in the open," Willie says. "I had to sit myself down and say my love for my kids was greater than my problems with homosexuality." For Ross, it would prove too little, too late.

Willie orders another bottle of beer, pushes his salad cucumbers to the side of his plate.

"Every day I put a mask on. There is this song, 'Champagne Life,' by Ne-Yo. She loved that track. I hear that and I break."

He talks about how when he saw his daughter's body at the morgue, he noticed some knots in her hair. He wanted them combed out, the way he had done when she was young. Neat and pretty.

"And the funeral director told me the knots were actually interior bumps from where the bullet ricocheted around her skull."

Willie takes a long gulp of beer.

"If they had a camera set up in Malika's jail cell, I would watch it 24 hours a day," he says, eyes dark. "It would be the only thing I did."

It is an unusually clear day in downtown Milwaukee, and the West Silver Spring Popeyes is doing a brisk business when the Ross family drives past.

The family does not make a habit of visiting the scene of the crime. At the same time, the restaurant sits right outside their neighborhood, on the corner of two main drags between other common stops. The landmark is unavoidable. They can't *not* see it.

A few blocks away, kids are shooting hoops on the same court where Ross honed her skills. The sun is glaring. A stiff breeze blows forgotten winter leaves across the park.

Pamela looks at the children, remembers her daughter. How she would play with the men. How when she grew older she gave pointers to the other kids. One time, she saw a boy shooting with a beach ball.

"She gave him her basketball," Pamela says with a slow nod.

Savoring the memory, she allows herself a small smile. It feels good, looking at the court, imagining her child there, alive and in flight, doing the thing she loved most, a crowd gathered to drink in her irrepressible blend of magic.

The people who know her say that once Malika Willoughby met Rosalind Ross, she never had another romantic relationship. They say that even now she has a photograph of the two of them in her cell.

Willie drives past the park, turns onto the highway that bisects their neighborhood.

"I told Malika once, 'Don't hurt my baby girl,'" he says quietly, inching into the flow of traffic.

"You know what she said? 'Mr. Collins, I love Roz.'"

Special Team

FROM ESPN.COM

HOW ABOUT A little good news?

In the scrub-brush desert town of Queen Creek, Arizona, high school bullies were throwing trash at sophomore Chy Johnson. Calling her "stupid." Pushing her in the halls.

Chy's brain works at only a third-grade level because of a genetic birth defect, but she knew enough to feel hate.

"She'd come home every night at the start of the school year crying and upset," says her mom, Liz Johnson. "That permanent smile she had, that gleam in her eye, that was all gone."

Her mom says she tried to talk to teachers and administrators and got nowhere. So she tried a whole new path—the starting quarterback of the undefeated football team. After all, senior Carson Jones had once escorted Chy to the Special Olympics.

"Just keep your ear to the ground," Liz wrote to Carson on his Facebook page. "Maybe get me some names?"

But Carson Jones did something better than that. Instead of ratting other kids out, he decided to take one in—Chy.

He started asking her to eat at the cool kids' lunch table with him and his teammates. "I just thought that if they saw her with us every day, maybe they'd start treating her better," Carson says. "Telling on kids would've just caused more problems."

It got better. Starting running back Tucker Workman made sure somebody was walking between classes with Chy. In classes, cornerback Colton Moore made sure she sat in the row right behind the team.

Just step back a second. In some schools, it's the football players doing the bullying. At Queen Creek, they're stopping it. And not with fists—with straight-up love for a kid most teenage football players wouldn't even notice, much less hang out with.

"I think about how sweet these boys are to her," says volleyball player Shelly Larson, "and I want to cry. I can't even talk about it."

It's working.

"I was parking my car yesterday, and I saw a couple of the guys talking to her and being nice," says offensive lineman Bryce Oakes. "I think it's making a difference around here."

And the best thing is? The football players didn't tell anybody.

"I didn't know about any of this until three weeks ago," says Carson's mom, Rondalee, who's raising four boys and a daughter by herself. "He finally showed me an article they wrote here locally. I said, 'Are you kidding me? Why didn't you tell me this?'"

All of a sudden, Chy started coming home as her bubbly self again. When her mom asked why she was so happy, she said, "I'm eating lunch with my boys!"

The boys take care of Chy, and she takes care of the boys. Carson, carrying a GPA of 4.4, got in a car accident last week; since then, Chy is always trying to carry his backpack. "I know his neck hurts," she says.

I get emailed stories like this a lot, but most of the time they don't pan out. They turn out to be half true, or true for the first week but not the second. But when I walked into the Queen Creek High School cafeteria Tuesday, unannounced, there was four-foot-high Chy with 11 senior football players, eating her lunch around the most packed lunch table you've ever seen, grinning like it was Christmas morning. It was Carson's birthday, and she'd made him a four-page card. On one page she wrote, in big crayon letters, "LUCKY GIRL."

I asked Chy to show me where she used to eat lunch. She pointed to a room in the back, away from the rest of the kids, the special-ed lunchroom. Much more fun out here, she said.

"I thank Carson every chance I see him," says Chy's mom. "He's an amazing young man. He's going to go far in life."

Nobody knows how far Chy Johnson will go in life. The life expectancy of those afflicted with her disease, microcephaly, is only 25–30 years. But her sophomore year, so far, has been unforgettable.

She'll be in the first row Friday night, cheering 10-0 QC as it plays its first playoff game, against Agua Fria. Some people think it will be QC's sixth shutout of the season. Sometime during the game, Carson probably will ask Chy to do their huddle-up "Bulldogs on 3" cheer, with everybody's helmet up in the air. You won't be able to see Chy, but she'll be in there.

"Why do I do these interviews?" Chy asked her mom the other night.

"Because you're so dang cute," her mom answered.

I've seen this before with athletes. Josh Hamilton used to look out every day for a Down's syndrome classmate at his Raleigh, North Carolina, high school. Joe Mauer ate lunch every day with a special-needs kid at his St. Paul, Minnesota, high school. In a great society, our most gifted take care of our least.

But what about next year, when Carson probably will be on his Mormon mission and all of Chy's boys will have graduated?

Not to worry. Carson has a little brother on the team, Curtis, who's in Chy's class.

"Mom," he announced at the dinner table the other night, "I got this."

Lucky girl.

BURKHARD BILGER

The Strongest Man in the World

FROM THE NEW YORKER

THE GIANT OF FORT LUPTON was born, like a cowbird's chick, to parents of ordinary size. His father, Jay Shaw, a lineman for a local power company, was six feet tall; his mother, Bonnie, was an inch or so shorter. At the age of three months, Brian weighed 17 pounds. At two years, he could grab his Sit 'n Spin and toss it nearly across the room. In photographs of his grade-school classes, he always looked out of place, his grinning, elephant-eared face floating like a parade balloon above the other kids in line. They used to pile on his back during recess, his mother told me—not because they didn't like him but because they wanted to see how many of them he could carry. "I just think Brian has been blessed," she said. "He has been blessed with size."

Fort Lupton is a city of 8,000 on the dry plains north of Denver. In a bigger place, Shaw might have been corralled into peewee football at eight or nine, and found his way among other oversized boys. But the local teams were lousy and, aside from a few Punt, Pass & Kick contests—which he won with discouraging ease— Shaw stuck to basketball. By seventh grade, he was six feet tall and weighed more than 200 pounds. When he went in for a dunk on his hoop at home, he snapped off the pole, leaving a jagged stump in the driveway. By his late teens, his bulk had become a menace. One player knocked himself out running into Shaw's chest; another met with his elbow coming down with a rebound, and was carried off with a broken nose and shattered facial bones. "It was bad," Shaw told me. "One guy, we dove for a ball together, and I literally broke his back. It wasn't that I was a dirty player. I wasn't even trying to do it hard."

Like other very large men, Shaw has a surprisingly sweet nature. His voice is higher and smaller than you'd expect, and he tends to inflect it with question marks. His face has the bulbous charm of a potato carving. "He's almost overly friendly," Terry Todd, a former champion weight lifter and an instructor at the University of Texas, told me. "It's like he thinks that if he's not you'll be frightened of him and run away." At six feet eight and 430 pounds, Shaw has such a massive build that most men don't bother trying to measure up. His torso is three feet wide at the shoulders; his biceps are nearly two feet around. His neck is thicker than other men's thighs. "I know I'm big," he told me. "I've been big my whole life. I've never had to prove how tough I am."

In the summer of 2005, when Shaw was 23, he went to Las Vegas for a strength-and-conditioning convention. He was feeling a little adrift. He had a degree in wellness management from Black Hills State University, in South Dakota, and was due to start a master's program at Arizona State that fall. But after moving to Tempe, a few weeks earlier, and working out with the football team, he was beginning to have second thoughts. "This was a big Division I, Pac-10 school, but I was a little surprised, to be honest," he told me. "I was so much stronger than all of them." One day at the convention, Shaw came upon a booth run by Sorinex, a company that has designed weight-lifting systems for the Denver Broncos and other football programs. The founder, Richard Sorin, liked to collect equipment used by old-time strongmen and had set out a few items for passersby to try. There were some kettle bells lying around, like cannonballs with handles attached, and a clumsy-looking thing called a Thomas Inch dumbbell.

Inch was an early-20th-century British strongman famous for his grip. His dumbbell, made of cast iron, weighed 172 pounds and had a handle as thick as a tin can, difficult to grasp. In his stage shows, Inch would offer a prize of more than $20,000 in today's currency to anyone who could lift the dumbbell off the floor with one hand. For more than 50 years, no one but Inch managed it, and only a few dozen have done so in the half century since. "A thousand people will try to lift it in a weekend, and a thousand won't lift it," Sorin told me. "A lot of strong people have left with their tails between their legs." It came as something of a shock, therefore, to see Shaw reach over and pick up the dumbbell as if it were a paperweight. "He was just standing there with a blank look on his face," Sorin said. "It was, like, *What's so very hard about this?*"

When Shaw set down the dumbbell and walked away, Sorin ran over to find him in the crowd. "His eyes were huge," Shaw recalls. "He said, 'Can you do that again?' And I said, 'Of course I can.' So he took a picture and sent it to me afterward." Sorin went on to tell Shaw about the modern strongman circuit—an extreme sport, based on the kinds of feats performed by men like Inch, which had a growing following worldwide. "He said that my kind of strength was unbelievable. It was a one in a million. If I didn't do something with my abilities, I was stupid. That was pretty cool."

Three months later, Shaw won his first strongman event. Within a year, he had turned pro. He has since deadlifted more than a thousand pounds and pressed a nearly quarter-ton log above his head. He has harnessed himself to fire engines, Mack trucks, and a Lockheed C-130 transport plane and dragged them hundreds of yards. In 2011, he became the only man ever to win the sport's two premier competitions in the same year. He has become, by some measures, the strongest man in history.

Shaw does his training in a storage facility in the town of Frederick, about 15 minutes from his hometown. His gym is behind the last garage door to the right, in a row of nearly identical bays. He leaves it open most of the year, framing a view of the snowcapped Front Range, to the west. Inside, the equipment has the same cartoonish scale as his body. One corner is given over to a set of giant concrete balls, known as Manhood Stones. Across the room, a flat steel frame leans against the wall, a pair of handles welded to one end. It's designed to have a vehicle parked on top of it and hoisted up like a wheelbarrow. (Shaw has lifted an SUV 11 times in 75 seconds.) Next to it sit piles of enormous tires, which will be threaded onto a pipe for the Hummer Tire Dead Lift.

Strongman events tend to be exaggerated versions of everyday tasks: heaving logs, carrying rocks, pushing carts. Awkwardness and unpredictability are part of the challenge. When I visited, Shaw was coaching his lifting buddies in the Super Yoke and the Duck Walk. The former harks back to the ancient strongman tradition of carrying a cow across your shoulders. (In the sixth century B.C., Milo of Croton, the greatest of Greek strongmen, is said to have lugged a four-year-old heifer the length of the Olympic arena.) The cow, in this case, was in the form of a steel frame loaded with weights, which the men took turns shouldering around the gym. The Duck Walk was something that a blacksmith might do. It involved lifting an anvil-like weight of around 300 pounds between your legs and waddling down a path with it as fast as possible.

Tyler Stickle, a 24-year-old strongman from nearby Lakewood, took the first walk. A bank manager by day, he had a line of Hebrew letters tattooed around his right calf: I CAN DO ALL THINGS THROUGH HIM WHO STRENGTHENS ME. It was a prayer from Philippians long beloved by followers of Muscular Christianity, a movement that sprang up in the mid-1800s with the notion that God deserves burlier believers. (As the Giants center fielder Brett Butler once put it, "If Jesus Christ was a baseball player, he'd go in hard to break up the double play and then pick up the guy and say, 'I love you.'") Muscular Christianity went on to give us the Fellowship of Christian Athletes, the Touchdown Jesus mural at Notre Dame's stadium, and a stained-glass window depicting wrestlers, boxers, and other athletes in the Cathedral of St. John the Divine, in New York. But Stickle just hoped that it might help him waddle a little faster. "I hate the Duck Walk," he said.

By the time he'd gone back and forth across the gym, his face had puffed up like a blowfish, and the tendons stood out from his neck. When he bent over to catch his breath, he saw that his inner thighs were chafed an angry red. "Wait till you see what it looks like a couple of days from now," one of the other lifters said. "It just chews up your legs."

"I hate the Duck Walk."

"You're mentally weak."

For a long time, strongmen didn't bother with specialized training. When CBS televised the first World's Strongest Man contest from Universal Studios, in 1977, the competitors all came from other sports. There were bodybuilders like Lou Ferrigno, football players like Robert Young, and weight lifters like Bruce Wilhelm, who won the contest. Even later, when the dilettantes had mostly dropped out of contention, there was no standardized equipment. Shaw had to cast his own Manhood Stones from a plastic mold, and he practiced the Keg Toss in his parents' backyard, in a large sandpit that they'd built for volleyball. "Even 10 or 12 years ago, you wouldn't have had a place like this," he told me at his gym.

"But a guy can't just come in off the street anymore and be amazing." These days, most of Shaw's equipment is custom-forged by a local company called Redd Iron; his diet and his workout clothes are subsidized by his sponsor, the supplement maker MHP—short for Maximum Human Performance.

"I see guys accomplish things that are just blowing my mind," Dennis Rogers, a grip master in the tradition of Thomas Inch, told me. Although the lifts vary from contest to contest, the most popular strongman events and records are now well established, and the latest feats circulate instantly on YouTube. "The weights they're moving, the dead lifts they're doing, the things they carry—it wasn't until 1953 that the first 500-pound bench press was done," Rogers said. "Today, you have guys who are doing a thousand pounds. How much can the human body take?"

The urge to perform feats of strength for no good reason seems to be deeply embedded in the male psyche. Shaw's Manhood Stones are just modern versions of the thousand-pound volcanic boulder unearthed on the Greek island of Santorini. It was etched with a boast from the sixth century B.C.: EUMASTAS, SON OF KRITOBOLOS, LIFTED ME FROM THE GROUND. Similar accounts crop up in countless early histories and anthropological studies. The Vikings tossed logs, the Scots threw sheaves of straw, the ancestors of the Inuit are rumored to have carried walruses around. Even a man as brilliant as Leonardo da Vinci felt the need to bend horseshoes and iron door knockers, just to show that he could.

By the 19th century, men like Thomas Topham, Louis Cyr, and a succession of German Goliaths had turned such feats into lucrative theater. Topham, an English fireplug who was five feet ten and weighed 200 pounds, could bend iron pokers with his bare hands, roll pewter dishes into cannoli, and win a tug-of-war with a horse. According to a playbill from 1736, cited in David Willoughby's classic history, *The Super-Athletes,* Topham's act included the following feats: "He lays the back Part of his Head on one Chair, and his Heels on another, and suffers four corpulent men to stand on his Body and heaves them up and down. At the same time, with Pleasure, he heaves up a large Table of Six Foot long by the Strength of his Teeth, with half a hundred Weight hanging at the farthest end; and dances two corpulent Men, one in each Arm, and snaps his fingers all the time."

The World's Strongest Man was a title of cheap coinage in those days: no circus ever made a shilling claiming to have the second strongest. Still, like other athletic skills, it eventually ceded to a stricter accounting. Equipment was standardized, rules established. The debatable merits of bouncing four fat men on your belly—because how fat were they, really, and how high did they bounce?—gave way to a pair of uniform and highly regulated lifts: the snatch and the clean and jerk. In the first, a barbell is gripped with both hands, thrown into the air, and held above the head in a single motion. In the second, the weight is swiftly lifted to the shoulders (the clean), then flipped up and caught overhead (the jerk). Carrying cows was left to amateurs.

Olympic weight lifting made its debut at the first modern Games, in Greece, in 1896. But it wasn't until 1920, when weight classes were created, and 1928, when one-hand lifts were abolished, that it settled into a predictable sport. Americans were soon the dominant power. Under the savvy sponsorship of Bob Hoffman, the founder of the York Barbell Company, in Pennsylvania, the national team produced a succession of gold medalists in the 1940s and 1950s, including Tommy Kono, John Davis, and Paul Anderson. Early on, to get around rules restricting Olympic participation to amateurs, Hoffman would hire the lifters at his factory for as little as $10 a week and let them train on-site. They would also promote York products in *Strength and Health*—the house organ, "edited in an atmosphere of perspiration and horseplay," as *Fortune* put it in 1946.

"Bob took a bunch of nobodies and turned them into the greatest team in the world," Arthur Drechsler, the chair of USA Weightlifting, told me recently. To Drechsler, a former junior national champion, Olympic weight lifting remains the finest test of strength ever devised. "This thing was created to cut through all the BS," he told me. "Are you the best or not? Let's see. Let's do two events and we'll see who's really good. Everyone lifts the bar from the same place; everyone is competing at the same level. We haven't discriminated by race, creed, or color since the 1920s. So we have a legitimate claim to having the strongest people in the world."

The awkward part, for Drechsler, is that this elite no longer includes Americans. Since 1960, the United States has suffered through an extended drought in the sport. Bulgarians, Hungarians, Cubans, Poles, Romanians, Koreans, an East German, and a Finn have all topped the podium, and Russians and Chinese have done so dozens of times. (Weight lifting, with its multiple weight classes, is an ideal means of amassing medals, they've found.) But aside from Tara Nott—a flyweight from Texas who won her division in 2000, when women's weight lifting was introduced at the Sydney Games—no American has won the gold. This year, the men's team didn't even qualify for the Olympics. (One American, Kendrick Farris, later qualified individually.)

It's this void that the strongmen have helped to fill. Like the rise of NASCAR over Formula One, professional wrestling over boxing, and *Jersey Shore* over *The Sopranos,* the return of men like Shaw seems to signal a shift in our appetites—a hunger for rougher, more outlandish thrills and ruder challenges. A modern strongman has to have explosive strength as well as raw power, Shaw told me, but most of all he has to be willing to lift almost anything, anywhere. "I'm a fan of functional strength," he said. "If you're the strongest man on the planet, you ought to be able to pick up a stone or flip a tire. Those Olympic lifters—how can you call someone the strongest man if he can't walk over to a car and pick it up?"

Early in March, I went to see Shaw defend his title at the Arnold Strongman Classic, the heaviest competition of its kind in the world. The Classic is held every year in Columbus, Ohio, as part of a sports festival that was founded by Arnold Schwarzenegger and a promoter named Jim Lorimer, in 1989. Like its namesake, the festival is a hybrid beast—part sporting event and part sideshow—that has ballooned to unprecedented size. It's now billed as the largest athletic festival in the world, with 18,000 competitors in 45 categories. (The London Olympics will have 10,500 athletes in 26 sports.) Lorimer calls it Strength Heaven.

At the Greater Columbus Convention Center, that Friday morning, the main hall felt like a circus tent. Black belts in judo tumbled next to archers, arm wrestlers, and Bulgarian hand-balancers. A thousand ballroom dancers mixed with more than 4,000 cheerleaders. In the atrium, a group of oil painters were dabbing furiously at canvases, vying to produce a gold-medal-winning sports portrait. The only unifying theme seemed to be competition, in any form; the only problem was telling the athletes from the audience. A hundred and seventy-five thousand visitors were expected at the festival that weekend, and half of them seemed to be bodybuilders. In the main hall, they made their way from booth to booth, chewing on protein bars and stocking up on free samples. YES, I CAN LIFT HEAVY THINGS, one T-shirt read. NO, I WON'T HELP YOU MOVE.

Up the street, at the hotel where most of the strongmen were staying, the breakfast buffet was provisioned like a bomb shelter. One side was lined with steel troughs filled with bacon, potatoes, scrambled eggs, and pancakes. The other side held specialty rations: boiled pasta and rubbery egg whites, white rice, brown rice, potatoes, and sweet potatoes. This was "clean food," as strength athletes call it—protein and carbohydrates unadulterated by fat or flavoring. The most competitive bodybuilders eliminate virtually all liquids and salt from their diet in the final days of the contest, to get rid of the water beneath their skin and give their muscles the maximum "cut." "What do you think I'm doing here, having fun?" I heard one man shout into his cell phone in the lobby. "This is work. This isn't playing around. My dad died, and I was lifting weights three days later. What am I supposed to do, go home and drop everything to take care of my girlfriend?"

If bodybuilders were the ascetics of the festival, the strongmen were its mead-swigging friars, lumbering by with plates piled high. "It's a March of the Elephants kind of thing," Terry Todd told me. "You expect that music to start playing in the background." Todd and his wife, Jan, have designed the lifts and overseen the judging at the Arnold since 2002. (Like Terry, Jan works at the University of Texas and had an illustrious athletic career: in 1977, she was profiled by *Sports Illustrated* as "the world's strongest woman.") They take unabashed delight in the strongmen and their feats, but as educators and advocates for their sport they have found themselves in an increasingly troubling position. The Arnold, like most strongmen contests, doesn't test for performance-enhancing drugs, and it's widely assumed that most of the top competitors take them. (In 2004, when Mariusz Pudzianowski, the dominant strongman at the time, was asked when he'd last taken anabolic steroids, he answered, "What time is it now?") The result has been an unending drive for more muscle and mass—an arms race unlimited by weight class.

"It's a little frightening," Todd told me. "The strength gains dictate that we make the weights higher, but at what point does the shoulder start to separate, or the wrist, or you get a compression fracture? We really don't know how strong people can be." Gaining weight has become an occupational necessity for strongmen. The things they lift are so inhumanly heavy that they have no choice but to turn their bodies into massive counterweights. "Centrifugal force is the killer," Mark Henry, a professional wrestler and one of the greatest of former Arnold champions, told me. "Once the weight starts to move, it's not going to stop." Fat is a strongman's shock absorber, like the bumper on a Volkswagen—his belly's buffer against the weights that continually slam into it. "I wouldn't want to be too lean," Shaw said. When I asked about steroids, he hesitated, then said that he preferred not to talk about them. "I really do wish that there was more drug testing," he added. "I would be the first one in line." The same is true for most of the strongmen, Todd told me, but they feel that they have little choice: "You don't want to take a knife to a gunfight."

In the past five years, Shaw has added more than 100 pounds to the svelte 300 that he weighed at his first contest. "It gets old, it really does," he said. "Sometimes you're not hungry, but you have to eat anyway. Training is easy compared to that." Pudzianowski once told an interviewer that his typical breakfast consisted of 10 eggs and two to three pounds of bacon. "Between meals, I eat lots of candy," he said. Shaw prefers to eat smaller portions every two hours or so, for maximum absorption, supplemented by "gainer shakes" of concentrated protein. ("His one shake is 1,200 calories," his girlfriend, a former model for Abercrombie & Fitch, told me. "That's my intake for the entire day.") Until he renewed his driver's license last year, Shaw often got hassled at airports: the guards couldn't recognize his 10-year-old picture because his face had fleshed out so much. "He's grown into his ears," one of his lifting partners, Andy Shaddeau, told me. "Those were not 300-pound ears."

On the night before the contest, the strongmen were summoned to the convention center for a private audience with Schwarzenegger. I could see them scanning the room for potential hazards as they filed in. The downside of being a giant is that nothing is built to your scale or structural requirements: ceilings loom, seams split, furniture collapses beneath you. "You only have to hit your head a few times before you start to watch out," Shaw told me. "Going into a restaurant, I have to look at the chairs and make sure that they don't have arms on them or I won't fit." When Shaw went shopping for a Hummer recently, he couldn't squeeze into the driver's seat, so he bought a Chevrolet Silverado pickup instead and had the central console ripped out and moved back. Even so, he has trouble reaching across his chest to get the seat belt.

Schwarzenegger had brought along two of his sons: Patrick, a slender, sandy-haired 18-year-old, and Christopher, a thickset 14-year-old. (It would prove to be a trying weekend for them. The following morning, in front of Veterans Memorial Auditorium, the city unveiled an eight-and-a-half-foot bronze statue of their father, while a heckler shouted from the crowd, "Hey, Arnold! How are your wife and kids? Been cheating on your wife today, Arnold?") Both boys were great fans of the strongmen—"They're my favorites by far!" Patrick told me. As they sat in the audience, their father talked about being a teenager in Vienna, watching the Russian Yury Vlasov clean-and-jerk nearly 500 pounds. "It was so impressive that I went home and started training," he said. "Instead of an hour a day, I did two hours a day, and then three hours a day." Years later, Schwarzenegger said, he was happy to be crowned the most muscular man in the world. But he was "at the same time very angry" because he knew that others could lift more. "So I am, of course, a big admirer of yours," he said. "You are the real strongest men in the world. I thank you for your training and I thank you for being so powerful."

The Arnold is an invitational event. Only the top 10 strongmen are asked to attend, so most were nearly as big as Shaw. Hafþór "Thor" Björnsson, an Icelandic behemoth, came in glowering like a Viking, his head honed smooth and his jawline edged by a beard. At 23, he was the youngest of the group but heir to a long line of champions from his island—a fact that he attributed to the spring-water. "We are meant to be strong," he told me. Žydrūnas Savickas, a six-time winner from Lithuania, credited his strength to another fluid. "My mother work in milk factory," he said. When Savickas was three years old, his grandmother found him in her backyard, building a fort out of cinder blocks. Now a baby-faced 36, he was the sport's elder statesman, voted the most popular athlete in Lithuania and a member of the Vilnius city council. "We have small country," he said. "Every athlete like diamond in Lithuania."

There were five Americans in the group, three of whom were serious contenders. Derek Poundstone, from Waterbury, Connecticut, had won the contest in 2009 and 2010, and was the runner-up in 2008. He was the only man here with the chiseled, armor-plated look of a bodybuilder, and he liked to play up that fact with a crowd. ("At some point in the competition, I predict, Derek will tear his shirt off," Jan Todd told me.) Mike Jenkins, an up-and-coming strongman from Hershey, Pennsylvania, had placed second to Shaw the year before. Six feet six and 390 pounds, he had a sharp wit buried in the rubbery form of a Stretch Armstrong doll. "Sometimes people talk to me like they think that I might be mildly retarded," he told me. "They hear that you lift rocks and pull trucks for a living, they don't think Nobel Prize. But a lot of us are educated." Jenkins had a master's degree from James Madison University, and many of the others had bachelor's degrees. Most of them had brought wives or girlfriends with them, as petite and straw-boned as their mates were gigantic.

This year's contest would stretch over two days and five events. Shaw was the odds-on favorite. He hadn't lost a competition in more than a year, and had been setting personal records in training all winter. But his best event—the Manhood Stones—had been replaced by a barbell lift called Apollon's Wheels. This played to Savickas's greatest strength: his immensely powerful arms. "I have a lot of things left to prove," Shaw told me later, in his hotel room. "Ideally, I'd like to walk away with the most championships ever. But Žydrūnas, he's tough, he's strong, and I'm sure he's hungry. He wants to prove that last year was a mistake. I want to prove the opposite."

Apollon's Wheels were named for one of the great strongmen of the 19th century, Louis "Apollon" Uni. A Frenchman from the southern city of Marsillargues, Uni was visiting a junkyard in Paris one day when he came across a pair of spoked railway wheels that were perfect for his stage show. Mounted on a thick steel axle, they formed a barbell that weighed 367 pounds. Apart from Uni, only four men had ever managed to clean-and-jerk the device: Charles Rigoulot, in 1930; John Davis, in 1949; Norbert Schemansky, in 1954; and Mark Henry, in 2002. Todd's version weighed almost 100 pounds more. The strongmen, rather than jerk it overhead (the easiest part of the lift), had to raise it to their chest, flip it up

to shoulder height, then drop it and repeat the lift as often as possible in 90 seconds.

The strongman stage was at one end of the convention center,
elevated above the crowd and flanked by enormous video screens.
It was covered with black rubber matting and reinforced with steel
beams—the contestants alone weighed close to 4,000 pounds. As
the strongmen trudged out one by one to attempt the lift, speed
metal blasted overhead, and several thousand people whooped
them on. But it was a discouraging start. On an ordinary barbell,
the grip spins freely, so the plates don't move as they're being
lifted. But these railway wheels were screwed tight to the axle. The
men had to rotate them around as they lifted—murder on the
arms and shoulders—then keep them from rolling out of their
hands. Dealing with this, while holding on to the two-inch-thick
axle, required an awkward grip: one hand over and the other hand
under. "Even now, most of the men in our contest can't clean it,"
Todd said.

Travis Ortmayer, a strongman from Texas, took a pass and
dropped to the bottom of the ranking. Two British strongmen,
Terry Hollands and Laurence Shahlaei, managed one lift each,
while Jenkins, Poundstone, and the Russian Mikhail Koklyaev did
two. The surprise of the contest was Mike Burke, one of Shaw's
protégés from Colorado, who lifted the wheels three times, his face
bulging like an overripe tomato. Then came Savickas. He'd put on
considerable weight in recent years, most of which had gone to his
gut—a sturdy protuberance on which he liked to rest the barbell
between lifts. When he'd raised it to his shoulders three times in
less than a minute, he took a little breather, like a traveler setting
down a suitcase, then casually lofted up a fourth.

Shaw had done as many or more in training, in the thin air of
his gym at 5,000 feet. But this time, when he brought the bar up
to his chest, something seemed to catch in his left arm. He re-
positioned his hands, dipped down at the knees, and flipped the
weight up beneath his chin. But it didn't look right. "I don't know
what happened," he told me later. "The warm-ups felt really good,
and the weight felt light off the ground. But when I went up . . .
it's a hard feeling to describe. Almost like electrical shocks—like
three different shocks in a row."

Afterward, Shaw reached over to touch his arm. By the time I
found him backstage, the situation was clear: he had "tweaked" his

left biceps. The strange shocks were from strands of tendon snapping loose, rolling up inside his arm like broken rubber bands.

Injuries, sometimes devastating, are almost intrinsic to strongman contests: the inevitable product of extreme weight and sudden motion. In 1977, at the first World's Strongest Man competition, one of the leaders in the early rounds was Franco Columbu, a former Mr. Olympia from Sardinia who weighed only 182 pounds— 100 less than his closest competitor. Columbu might have gone on to win, had the next event not been the Refrigerator Race. This involved strapping a 400-pound appliance, weighted with lead shot, onto your back and scuttling across a lot at Universal Studios. Within a few yards, Columbu's left leg crumpled beneath him. "It was at an L," he told me. "All the ligaments were torn, and the calf muscle and the hamstring, and the front patella went to the back." The injury required seven hours of surgery and threatened to cripple Columbu for life, but he came back to win the Mr. Olympia title again in 1981. (He later settled a lawsuit against the World's Strongest Man for $800,000.)

The Arnold has a somewhat better track record—"We've never had anyone hurt so bad that they had to be carried away," Todd told me—but its strongmen are a battle-scarred lot. "Man, you can almost go down the list," Shaw said. Ortmayer had ripped a pectoral muscle, and Poundstone had fractured his back. One man had damaged his shoulder while lifting the Hammer of Strength, and others had torn hamstrings and trapezius muscles. "In strongman, everybody injured," Savickas told me. "For us, stop just when it's broken totally—joints, bones, or muscles." In 2001, at a strongman contest on the Faeroe Islands, Savickas slipped on some sand while turning Conan's Wheel and tore the patella tendons off both knees. "I can't walk," he recalled. "I am laying down. Everybody says that I can't back. But I back—and won."

Shaw's injury was a small thing by comparison. But there were four events left, each of which would put a terrible strain on what remained of his left biceps. "It's wide open now," Mark Henry, the former Arnold champion and a judge at the contest, told me between rounds. "I think Brian's going to have to withdraw. It's like your daddy probably told you: if the stove's hot, don't touch it."

Ten minutes later, Shaw was back onstage. Using his right arm only, he proceeded to lift a 255-pound circus dumbbell above his head five times. "I was hoping to do eight or nine," he told me afterward. "My left arm is really stronger than my right." Even so, he took second place in the event—bested only by Jenkins, who did seven lifts—and was now within striking distance of the overall lead. But how long would his arm hold out?

Strength like Shaw's is hard to explain. Yes, he has big muscles, and strength tends to vary in proportion to muscle mass. But exceptions are easy to find. Pound for pound, the strongest girl in the world may be Naomi Kutin, a 10-year-old from Fair Lawn, New Jersey, who weighs only 99 pounds but can squat and dead-lift more than twice that much. John Brzenk, perhaps the greatest arm wrestler of all time, is famous for pinning opponents twice his size—his nickname is the Giant Crusher. And I remember, as a boy, being a little puzzled by the fact that the best weight lifter in the world—Vasily Alexeyev, a Russian, who broke 80 world records and won gold medals at the Munich and the Montreal Olympics—looked like the neighborhood plumber. Shaggy shoulders, flaccid arms, pendulous gut: what made him so strong?

"Power is strength divided by time," John Ivy, a physiologist at the University of Texas, told me. "The person that can generate the force the fastest will be the most powerful." This depends in part on what you were born with: the best weight lifters have muscles with far more fast-twitch fibers, which provide explosive strength, than slow-twitch fibers, which provide endurance. How and where those muscles are attached also matters: the longer the lever, the stronger the limb. But the biggest variable is what's known as "recruitment": how many fibers can you activate at once? A muscle is like a slave galley, with countless rowers pulling separately toward the same goal. Synchronizing that effort requires years of training and the right "neural hookup," Ivy said. Those who master it can lift far above their weight. Max Sick, a great early-19th-century German strongman, had such complete muscle control that he could make the various groups twitch in time to music. He was only five feet four and 145 pounds, yet he could take a man 40 pounds heavier, press him in the air 16 times with one hand, and hold a mug of beer in the other without spilling it.

The convention center was full of people searching for a short-cut to such strength, and vendors trying to convince them that they'd found it. There were 700 booths in all, staffed by muscle-bound men and balloon-breasted women, handing out samples with complicated ingredients but simple names: Monster Milk, Devil's Juice, Hemo Rage, Xtreme Shock. "That's the fastest-acting testosterone booster on the market," Ryan Keller, the marketing director for Mutant, a maker of "experimental muscle modifiers," told me, pointing to a product called Mutant Test. "Then there's Mutant Pump. It's for the hard-core guys." Mutant Pump contains a proprietary compound called Hyperox, which pushes the body's nitric-oxide production "past all previous limits," according to its marketing material. This allows the muscles to stay pumped full of blood long after a workout. "You can stop lifting, get in your car, and it's still working," Keller said. "Some guys say it almost hurts, it gets so hard." Shaw uses a similar supplement, called Dark Rage, designed to increase his red-blood-cell count. "When he drinks it, he gets excited and does this little dance," his girlfriend told me.

Here and there among the salespeople were a few who claimed to be doing damage control. I talked to an insurance agent who said that her firm had a strong "appetite" for extreme sports. When I asked if she would indemnify a strongman, she frowned. "Probably not," she said. "We do mixed martial arts, but if they have a 50 percent loss ratio we aren't going to do it." A few aisles over, I met Tom O'Connor, a physician from Hartford, who called himself the Metabolic Doc. A longtime weight lifter, O'Connor was in the business of treating muscle dysmorphia—a kind of reverse anorexia. The condition is often marked by obsessive bodybuilding, abetted by anabolic steroids. "It's an absolute epidemic!" O'Connor told me, leaning in so close that I could see his pupils dilate and sweat bead on his forehead. "The men come to me broken and hurt. They come to me with cardiac problems and libido problems and erectile dysfunction." His solution: low-dose hormone-replacement therapy. The sign above his booth read, GOT TESTOSTERONE?

It was tempting, to a flabby outsider like me, to dismiss all this as anomalous—an extreme subculture. But to athletes it was the new normal. "Are you kidding me?" O'Connor said. "Have you seen what's happening around here? It's never going to end." When I asked Jim Lorimer, the cofounder of the festival, what he thought about rising steroid use, he called it a "knotty problem." Then he told me a story. In 1970, when he brought the world weight-lifting championships to Columbus, the event was a bust at first. "We were at Ohio State University, at Mershon Auditorium, and the first three days—Monday, Tuesday, Wednesday—it was empty. Maybe a few family members." Then, on the third day, a scandal broke: eight of the nine top lifters tested positive for steroids. "Well, that Thursday evening Mershon filled up," Lorimer recalled. "Friday, Saturday, Sunday—it was filled every day. Now, what lesson do you think I learned from that?"

The bigger the body, the bigger the draw. When it comes to steroids, public censure and private acceptance have tended to rise in parallel. In 1998, after Mark McGwire admitted to doping while setting his home-run record, he was attacked in the press and later blackballed from the Hall of Fame. But sales of steroids skyrocketed. Eight years earlier, George H. W. Bush had both criminalized the use of steroids and appointed Arnold Schwarzenegger—the world's most famous steroid user—chairman of the President's Council on Physical Fitness and Sports. "It's like an oxymoron," a strongman said. "Arnold is the poster boy. But if you got into a private conversation, do you really think he'd say, 'I never should have done that'? Of course he would have done it! He's a movie star and a millionaire because of it. He was governor of California! He could never have done any of that without it."

Late one afternoon, when the thumping soundtrack in the main hall was giving me a headache, I ducked into one of the side rooms to watch the women's Olympic weight-lifting trials. The crowd here was a fraction of the size of the one outside, and the atmosphere was almost monastic by comparison. During the lifts, the room would go completely quiet—no whoops or catcalls, just the deep silence of absolute concentration. The athletes, too, seemed to be of a different species from the strongmen: flexible and surprisingly slender, with muscles that had the almost slack look I remembered in Alexeyev. There was a terrific fierceness about them—some would stamp their feet and let out a shriek before grasping the bar—but its focus was inward. The best female lifters can toss the equivalent of two very large men above their heads in a single motion. It's the closest that humans come to being superheroes, and these women acted accordingly.

"Weight lifting is 50 percent mental and 30 percent technique," Tommy Kono, among the greatest of all American lifters and a spectator in the crowd that day, told me during a break. "Power is only 20 percent, but everybody has it reversed." Kono was a prime example of the miraculous change that weight lifting can effect. A Japanese-American from Sacramento, he was a spindly 12-year-old in 1942, when his family was relocated to an internment camp at Tule Lake, in northern California. "The name is a misnomer, really," Kono said. "It was the bottom of a dried-up lake. When the wind blew, it really kicked up a sandstorm, but the dry air helped my asthmatic condition." It was there, in another boy's house, that Kono discovered weight lifting and began to train in secret. (His parents didn't think his body could handle it.) By the time his family was released, in 1945, he had put on 10 or 15 pounds of muscle. By 1952, he was the Olympic gold medalist as a lightweight. He went on to win another gold as a light heavyweight, and a silver as a middleweight.

Kono blamed the decline in American lifting on an influx of foreign coaches. "They brought in the European idea of training five or six days a week, twice a day," he said. "Instead of being athletes, they became like workers. Rather than improving, they started getting injuries and overtraining. Even the South American countries started passing us up." This women's team was an exception. Unlike the men, they'd qualified for two spots at the Olympics. The best athletes were in the middleweight classes: Amanda Sandoval and Rizelyx Rivera, at 58 kilos, and Natalie Burgener, at 69. But the competition at those weights was so stiff overseas that the heaviest lifters were more likely to get the spots. (At the trials, all that mattered was how your lifts compared with those of others in your weight class worldwide.) And so, once again, Lorimer's rule held true: the bigger the body, the bigger the draw. To judge by the cheering between lifts, most of the crowd was there to see Holley Mangold.

Mangold was something of a local celebrity. Born and reared in Dayton, she had played football in high school, on the offensive line, and come within a point of winning a state championship. (Her older brother, Nick, is an All-Pro center with the New York Jets.) Although she'd come late to lifting, Mangold had quickly climbed the ranks and was threatening to supplant the country's top super-heavyweight, Sarah Robles. "My little girl is all about pure power," her father, Vern, told me. Five feet eight and well over 300 pounds, Mangold was astonishingly quick and flexible for her size — she could drop into the full splits with ease. "I'm a huge girl," she said to me. "I've always been huge. At 350 pounds, I feel sluggish. But at 330 I feel like I can conquer the world."

In the end, Mangold and Robles both made the Olympic team—Mangold winning the clean and jerk, Robles the snatch. But their lifts were well short of medal contention. To Mangold's coach, Mark Cannella, the gap wasn't a matter of too much European-style training but of too little. "We need to be more like them," he said. "They're breaking it down, videotaping and analyzing every single lift." Like gymnastics and dance, Olympic lifting requires such balance, flexibility, and form that it greatly rewards early training—it's like "barbell ballet," Vern Mangold said. But most American schools have long since replaced their free weights with machines. "It's a national disgrace," Arthur Drechsler, of USA Weightlifting, told me. "If you want to fight childhood obesity or increase fitness, no sport can transform you as much as weight lifting—look at Tommy Kono. And it's one of the safest things you can do. We don't have spinal-cord injuries. We don't have head injuries. They just don't happen. But weight lifting is not part of the public schools."

Even with the right training, Americans might still not reach the podium. Unlike strongmen and bodybuilders, Olympic athletes are subject to stringent drug tests in this country, including unannounced visits to their homes. Oversight tends to be much spottier abroad. Since 1976, 12 lifters, all but one of them from Eastern Europe, have been stripped of Olympic medals owing to drug use. A weight lifter can expect about a 10 to 15 percent boost from performance-enhancing drugs, Terry Todd estimates—just about what separates Mangold from medal contention. It's a situation that reminds him of Mark Henry, another prodigy who came late to lifting, stayed clean, and fell short of Olympic gold: "If he had started early and didn't take drugs, he would have beaten them," Todd said. "If he had used the drugs and started later, he would have beaten them. But two hurdles was too much."

The strongmen didn't have that problem. Theirs, for better or for worse, was a sport without a rule book—an unregulated experiment. It set no limits and allowed no excuses. In the elevator at the hotel on the last night, I heard a groan and looked over to see Travis Ortmayer, the strongman from Texas, doubled over with his elbows on his knees. "You all right, Travis?" I asked. "I've been better," he said. "A thing like this puts the beat on you." The smallest man in the contest by 20 pounds, Ortmayer had been a late substitute for Benedikt Magnússon, an Icelandic strongman who tore one of his biceps in training. "I've never zeroed out of a competition like this before," he said. "Usually, I would have been getting ready since December. But after the World's I took three months off to give my body a rest." When I asked him what hurt, he said pretty much everything.

Earlier that day, Ortmayer and the others had completed two more rounds. First came an event called the Austrian Oak, in honor of Schwarzenegger's nickname as a bodybuilder. This involved lifting a 10-foot log from a stand at close to shoulder height, then pressing it overhead repeatedly. Banded with steel and coiled with thick rope at the ends, the Oak weighed 459 pounds—it took five large men to carry it onstage. Four of the strongmen declined to try to lift it at all, and four tried and failed. That left Savickas, who managed one lift, and Jenkins, who did two. Shaw, his left arm in obvious pain, was among those who had to settle for a lighter Oak, of 393 pounds. But in a display of incredible grit he lifted it seven times in a row—screaming himself hoarse on the sixth try—putting him in fourth place overall.

"Blood, sweat, and tears, broken bones and torn muscles," the commentator, a former World's Strongest Man named Bill Kazmaier, told the crowd. "This is strongman. It's the last man standing." On the speakers overhead, Alice in Chains sang "Check My Brain." The Hummer Tire Dead Lift was next: up to eight oversized tires hung on a bar with steel plates—the heaviest of all the lifts. Jenkins conceded the lead early, topping out at 928 pounds. Derek Poundstone, ranked third, outlifted him by over 100 pounds—more than enough, I thought, to beat Shaw with his biceps half gone. "Get behind an injured man who's shot in the arm," Kazmaier shouted. "C'mon, Brian! Everybody's behind you!"

Shaw's left hand had begun to lose its grip, but the rules allowed him to secure it to the bar with a nylon strap. As he bent down to take the weight—1,073 pounds, 11 pounds more than Poundstone's lift—he raised his face toward the crowd and bellowed. Then he blew out his cheeks once, twice, and lurched upward. The crowd was on its feet, as Kazmaier thundered into the microphone, "Power! Power! Power!" The barbell bent beneath its load, and Shaw's body began to oscillate like a tuning fork. By the time his back was straight, his eyes were burning and blood was streaming from his nose, into his mouth, and down his chin. But the lift was good.

He was now tied for second place with Jenkins and Poundstone, just two and a half points behind Savickas. The latter had set a new world record in the dead lift: 1,117 pounds. But the last event—the Timber Carry—was one of Savickas's worst, whereas Shaw had won it in record time the year before. If he could hang on one more time, the championship would be his.

On their way to Veterans Memorial Auditorium that night, for the final event of the contest, the men sat quietly in a private coach, submerged in their thoughts. They had the half-desperate look of soldiers in a convoy, advancing toward a beachhead. Strongman is a brotherhood, they said. There wasn't much trash talk or posturing at contests like this—the lifts were daunting enough on their own—but I'd often seen them cheer and comfort one another between lifts, and even offer advice. The year before, at the World's Strongest Man, they had to drag a 22,000-pound Titan truck more than 80 feet down a road. Shaw, who prided himself on fastidious preparation, had ordered a pair of custom truck-pulling shoes from England, with high-friction soles. He would have won the contest, had he not given his spare pair to Björnsson, who beat him by half a second.

Victory at the Arnold meant much more than bragging rights: it was a rare chance to earn a living at this sport. The purses for most strongman contests are paltry—$3,000 to $5,000—especially given the risks involved. But the winner of the Arnold would take home $55,000. Shaw and his girlfriend were living in a small two-bedroom apartment not far from his parents. And Jenkins had been laid off from a teaching job that fall, at a high school for troubled teenagers in Harrisburg. In November, he'd opened up a gym with money that he borrowed from his parents, but business was slow, and he was getting married that summer. "My gosh, $55,000 could change your life," he told me.

At the auditorium, the bodybuilding finals were just wrapping up. A line of women in high heels and glitter bikinis were posing for photographs backstage, their skin bronzed and lacquered, their implants all in a row. Theirs was the least bulky of the bodybuilding categories—which rose, in order of ascending mass, from Bikini to Figure to Fitness to Ms. International—but they looked as sinewy as velociraptors. When I asked the winner, a diminutive brunette named Sonia Gonzales, what set her apart, she flashed her teeth. "My sex," she said. Behind the curtain, the male bodybuilders were preparing for the final pose-down. They'd been dehydrating themselves for days, so every vein and striation showed, but their limbs were cramped, their minds depleted. They sat hunched on benches or stood flexing in front of mirrors, as hollow-eyed as statues in a sculpture garden.

The stage set had a classical theme—broken columns against a fiery sky—and a long, low ramp ran in front of it. When the strongman final began, a huge wooden frame, roughly bolted together out of barn timbers, was carried out and placed at one end. The object was to stand inside this frame, lift it by a pair of handles along the sides, and run up the ramp as fast as possible. The frame weighed nearly 900 pounds—more than most strongmen could deadlift—and, unlike the previous year, no wrist straps were allowed. This was a problem for Shaw, but no less so for Savickas. The great Lithuanian had lost some of his grip strength over the years, as the weight he'd gained had gone into his fingers. "It's like putting on a tight pair of gloves, then another pair, and another pair," Todd told me. "Each one makes it that much harder to grip—there's flesh where there used to be space."

The Timber Carry was the climax of the contest and extremely hard on the body. Four of the strongmen never made it up the ramp. The weight tore calluses from their hands, and the frame kept tipping and slipping as they ran. Savickas looked strong at first, then lost his grip, dropping the frame six times before leaving it for good—two yards from the finish line. Others fared better. Travis Ortmayer reached the top in just under nine and a half seconds—good enough for a touch of redemption—and Derek Poundstone was almost two seconds faster. Afterward, Poundstone tore off his shirt and flexed for the crowd, just as Jan Todd had predicted.

When Shaw came to the starting line, he looked loose and light on his feet. He shook the kinks from his arms and bounced on his toes like a boxer, then bent down to pick up the frame. It seemed, for a moment, as he charged up the slope, that he might just make it in time. "I could see the finish line," he told me the next morning. "But then you're trying to hold on, and your grip starts to lose it, and it's just opening, opening, opening. And it's just . . . pain. I feel the worst pain. I don't know anything else." He was less than two feet from the top when the last strands of his biceps tore free, and the frame came thudding down. He managed one last, agonizing push to the finish line, as blinded and enraged as Samson in the temple. Then he stumbled backstage and collapsed.

Victory, in the end, went to Mike Jenkins. He hurtled up the ramp in just under seven and a half seconds—14-100ths faster than Poundstone—and won the championship by a single point. Later that night, at the trophy presentation, Schwarzenegger asked him how he'd done it: "For schlepping up this weight up the ramp—I mean, how do you train for something like that?" Jenkins leveled his eyes at him, deadpan. "On Mondays, Wednesdays, and Fridays, I do yoga at 6:00 A.M.," he said. "Then Tuesdays, Thursdays, I have Zumba at 7:00 P.M." Schwarzenegger grinned and nodded. "That's very impressive," he said. "I can really visualize you in yoga positions. This is exciting. I think we can sell tickets to that one."

When I last saw Shaw, he was back home in Colorado, recuperating from surgery. The injury had been worse than he feared. The tendon had all but exploded—"It looked like the end of a mop," his surgeon, Peter J. Millett, told me—and the muscle had fully retracted inside his arm. To reattach it, they'd had to trim the tendon down, drill a hole through the radius bone, then pull it through and secure it with a titanium button. "He said my tendons were three times the size of normal," Shaw said. "They had to use a hip retractor." Still, if he was lucky, the repaired biceps would be even stronger than before and more sturdily attached. "I heard the sutures they used are like the strongest industrial space-age stuff they could find," Shaw said. I thought of a line that Terry Todd had quoted at the Arnold, from *A Farewell to Arms:* "The world breaks everyone and afterward many are strong at the broken places."

Shaw's left arm was in a removable cast, and he said that his skin felt rubbery and numb, but he insisted on driving me around anyway. "There's never a right time to get hurt," he said, as we circled past the old basketball courts at his high school, the fields where he used to bale hay for his uncle. "This was supposed to be the performance that people would talk about for years. That's probably what makes it harder to swallow." He shook his head.

"What's crazy is, if it had happened on the third rep of that first event, instead of the first, I still would have won." Even with the injury, Shaw had come within seven seconds of victory—perhaps his greatest feat, though it earned him only fourth place overall. In Fort Lupton, the city council had recently hung a banner across Main Street, declaring it HOME OF THE WORLD'S STRONGEST MAN. But the wind had blown the banner down, and it was nowhere to be seen.

Shaw hoped to be back in top form by late summer—time enough to get ready for the World's Strongest Man, in September. In the meantime, he had nothing to do but wait for his body to heal. Late in the afternoon, he pulled into a Toys "R" Us to buy a present for his nephew Caiden, who had just turned one. "This isn't exactly my specialty," he said. "When my niece had her birthday, I bought her a battery-powered Jeep. Turned out she couldn't even ride it." He spent the first few minutes in the electronics section, looking at toys marked for kids age four to nine—"I'd like to buy him a robot or something," he said—then finally settled on a car with a built-in cannon that shot rubber balls.

By the time we arrived at his parents' house, the party was in full swing. Relatives were circled in chairs around the living room, while toddlers romped across the carpet in the middle. Shaw sat on the couch, holding himself as still as possible as the kids crawled all over him. He looked happier than I'd seen him in a while. "When Caiden was born, Brian was too intimidated to hold him," his sister, Julie, told me. "He was six pounds 10 ounces and 19½ inches. Curled up in a ball, he was the same size as Brian's shoe." She sighed. "I pray my son won't take after him. Finding clothes is so hard. But I'm sure Caiden will want to bring Brian in for show-and-tell—holy cow! he's like a superhero!—and he'll want to rough around with him. I'll be, like, 'Brian, you just sit there. Don't give him a high five. You'll knock him out.'"

BARRY BEARAK

Caballo Blanco's Last Run

FROM THE NEW YORK TIMES

Gila Hot Springs, New Mexico

MICAH TRUE WENT off alone on a Tuesday morning to run through the rugged trails of the Gila Wilderness, and now it was already Saturday and he had not been seen again.

The search for him, once hopeful, was turning desperate. Weather stoked the fear. The missing man was wearing only shorts, a T-shirt, and running shoes. It was late March. Daytimes were warm, but the cold scythed through the spruce forest in the depth of night, the temperatures cutting into the 20s.

For three days, rescue teams had fanned out for 50 yards on each side of the marked trails. Riders on horseback ventured through the gnarly brush, pushing past the felled branches of pinyon-juniper and ponderosa pine. An airplane and a helicopter circled in the sky, their pilots squinting above the ridges, woodlands, river canyons, and meadows.

"We're in the middle of nowhere, and this guy could be anywhere," Tom Bemis, the rescue coordinator appointed by the state police, said gloomily. He was sitting in a command center, marking lines on a map that covered 200,000 acres. Some 150 trained volunteers were at his disposal, and dozens of others were there too, arrived from all over the country, eager and anxious, asking to enlist in the search.

"Coming out of the woodwork," Bemis said wryly.

Not only did Micah True have loyal friends, but he also had a devoted following. At age 58, he was a mythic figure, known by the nickname Caballo Blanco, or White Horse. He was a famous ultrarunner, competing in races two, three, or four times as long as marathons. The day he vanished, he said he was going on a 12-mile jaunt, for him as routine as a lap around a high school track.

But True's mythic renown owed less to his ability to run than to his capacity to inspire. He was a free spirit who survived on corn-meal, beans, and wild dreams, aloof to the allure of money and possessions. He lived in the remote Copper Canyons of northern Mexico to be near the reclusive Tarahumara Indians, reputed to be the greatest natural runners in the world.

His story was exuberantly molded into legend in the 2009 best-seller *Born to Run* by Christopher McDougall. Caballo Blanco, however private and self-effacing, was suddenly delivered to the world as a prophet, "the lone wanderer of the High Sierras." To many, he represented the road not taken, a purer path, away from career, away from capitalism, away from the clock.

McDougall, himself a runner, was one of the dozens who had hurried to southwestern New Mexico to join the search, as had the actor Peter Sarsgaard, who was about to direct a movie based on the book. In just a few days, the Gila Wilderness had become a lodestone to a who's who of ultramarathoners, athletes with loose limbs, lanky bodies, and now a shared sense of dread.

"We're thinking he could be lying out there hurt, unable to get help," said the ultrarunner Luis Escobar, who had driven all night from California.

Several of these athletes were impatient with the authorities' methodical search. The main footpaths had been scoured, but they wanted to venture onto the smaller elk trails and into the pockets and crannies of the cliffs.

Bemis, the rescue coordinator, was mildly annoyed: "This is a wilderness, not a walk in the park, and some of them might get lost. Then we'll be looking for them too."

Among the most restless was Ray Molina, who led mountain bike tours through the Copper Canyons and was one of True's closest friends.

Random Ray, some people called him. A nonstop talker, he was also a pack rat, collecting old bicycles, antique toys, manikins, and bleached bones. Skeletal remains jounced about in his car.

Molina, 44, had not learned of the disappearance until Friday. He rushed to the Gila in his beat-up 1979 Mercedes with two friends, Jessica Haines and Dean Bannon. They were agreeable to joining the organized search. But by 10:00 on Saturday morning, they were among a handful yet to be assigned to a team.

The hell with this, Molina concluded. He and his friends lightened their backpacks of unnecessary gear and went off on their own, simply walking a short distance down the access road, crossing the Gila River, and scurrying into the nearest arroyo.

This strategy, while not entirely random, was hardly well conceived. They were assisted only by a folded-up map and their own instincts and whims.

They rambled and they ran and they climbed. They called out, "Caballo!"

The name Micah True was a confection, the first part plucked from the Bible, the second an homage to True Dog, a beloved mutt. Michael Randall Hickman was his given name, and he was raised in northern California, the second of four children. His father was a Marine gunnery sergeant who later became a deputy sheriff and an insurance salesman.

The elder Hickmans were conservative Roman Catholics, but Mike's devotions were to the counterculture of the late '60s and early '70s. His blond hair hung past his shoulders. Marijuana fluted through his head. So did mysticism. His reading appetites ranged from Hemingway to French philosophy.

He wandered the country, "just to make things happen," he recalled later. His looks were fetching. One friend described him as "a lean Greek god in beachcomber garb." Hickman lived for 10 months in a cave in Hawaii, shaking papayas from trees on Maui and running along island trails. He fell in love with a rich girl, he said, "whose eyes sparkled blue like the sky." When she dumped him, it scuffed his heart.

To keep himself in pocket money, Hickman often chose unusual labor for a peaceable soul: prizefighting. A middleweight, he called himself the Gypsy Cowboy. His record in the ring, according to boxrec.com, was 9-11. He was knocked out nine times, although some of those defeats were dives taken for an easy payday, he said. Whoever the opponent, he tried to restrain his fists, inflicting "only the physical damage to get the job done, no more."

Neill Woelk, a former sportswriter, remembers seeing him—his name now Micah True—in 1982, winning a fight on an undercard in Denver's Rainbow Theater.

The boxer was nearing 30 at the time. "He didn't look anything like a fighter, but he might be one of the best pure athletes I ever saw," Woelk said, adding, "He didn't have arms; he had cables."

By then, True had moved to Boulder, Colorado, at the base of the eastern slope of the Rockies. The city listed hard to the left. Sometimes with sarcasm, sometimes with affection, it was referred to as the People's Republic of Boulder. At the same time, it was becoming the nation's high-altitude capital for high-endurance training.

To earn a living, the prizefighter was now a self-employed furniture mover, hauling people's belongings in a rattletrap pickup. He lived without electricity in a spare one-room cabin off Magnolia Road. He shared an outhouse.

Running had become his overwhelming passion, maybe even his addiction. He was a mountain runner, a different breed from folks who showed up by the thousands to run a breezy 10K. He preferred races with fewer people and wide-open terrain, less concerned with his times than the surrounding scenery.

He would get up early to run, then do a moving job, then run again. He was logging about 170 miles a week. Dan Bowers was a frequent companion. He recalled, "After we'd run, we'd eat a big meal, enough to bust a rib, and then Micah would look at me and say, 'You want to do another 10?'"

True's pattern was to remain in Boulder for six months, then, with winter coming, head south to the Guatemalan highlands, running the lush trails around Lake Atitlán. Villagers grew used to the sight of the loping gringo. He was a six-footer with a long mane and big teeth. Children surrounded him when he stopped to buy bananas and tortillas. They named him El Caballo Blanco.

The White Horse was winning ultraraces in those days, like the 50-miler between Cheyenne and Laramie on the back roads of Wyoming. He was serious about competition, interested in re-engineering his body to get more out of his lungs and legs, pushing the boundaries of stamina.

Injuries began to slow him as he closed in on 40, but he eventually viewed these annoyances as a liberation. He started to care less about piling on the megamileage and more about finding challenging trails. Running was an exploration, inside and out, endorphins feeding his cerebral bliss.

He did still run the occasional race. In 1993, he entered one of his favorites, the Leadville Trail 100, a punishing 100-mile push through the icy streams and boulder-clogged slopes of the Rockies. The very up-and-down of it was a killer, the altitude as high as 12,600 feet. Runners generally needed 18 to 30 hours to finish.

That year, a promoter brought along a handful of peasants from Chihuahua, Mexico. They were short. Some looked like grandfathers. They wore blousy shirts and loincloths to the starting line, and on their feet were sandals they themselves had just made from old tires fished from the Leadville dump.

When the race began, these odd interlopers immediately fell to the rear and stayed there for 40 miles. Then they started steadily moving up, passing others, barely winded by the arduous climbs. The first two of them finished about an hour ahead of anyone else. The winner was 55 years old.

These were the Tarahumara.

True's disappearance might have been something to shrug off at first. He sometimes liked to get lost in the wild, allowing only curiosity to steer his feet, bushwhacking his way through dense terrain. Geronimo, the Apache warrior, had used the Gila as a refuge, and he was one of True's boyhood heroes.

But the runner knew the geography here too well to get hopelessly turned around, and besides, he had left behind his beloved sidekick Guadajuko, a stray he had rescued from a Mexican river. At times, True retreated from humans, even from civilization itself. But he would never abandon his dog.

Ray Molina understood True's penchants and habits. "There's a good chance he's nowhere near a trail," Molina said. He and his two friends looked elsewhere, climbing a ridge toward the Gila high country. The ascent was time-consuming, very steep in parts, the footing unreliable.

Hours later, all they had for their efforts was frustration. They wanted to avoid the beaten path but kept finding the tracks of other searchers and even met up with a few, including two on horseback and another pair with dogs.

Studying his map, Molina was intrigued by a squiggly blue line

indicating a stream called Little Creek. He was in the sway of two
hunches. One was that an injured man might head for water. The
other was that this meandering creek emptied out of the canyon
only a mile or so from the lodge where True had been staying. His
friend might have used this stream as a shortcut.

"Has anyone been down that creek?" Molina kept asking.

The horsemen had ridden through the canyon a little ways but
stopped. They knew the area well and warned Molina that the passage got pretty rough.

"Go ahead, try it," one joked. "We'll come looking for you tomorrow."

It was already late afternoon, and Molina wondered if it was
wise to chance this hike so close to dark. But he, Jessica Haines,
and Dean Bannon enjoyed egging each other on. Molina had
known Bannon since the third grade. Unsettled between them
were decades of debate about who was gutsier.

The creek was ankle deep in some spots, knee high in others,
and about as wide as an automobile. They walked slowly because
it was hard to do otherwise. The banks were narrow. The three
would move over land on one side until they met an impassable
thicket or an overhang from the steep canyon wall. Then they
would look for the best spot to leap across the water.

They repeated this zigzag enough times to realize they may as
well slosh through the creek itself. The bed was gravel and sand,
but there were submerged rocks everywhere. It would have been
easy to turn an ankle.

Haines, 33, works in the engine room of a ferry in Alaska. However dour the purpose of this trek, she was pleased to be in a place
of such extraordinary beauty. The millenniums had intricately
sculptured the canyon, and the clear stream that ran through it
moved in a musical trickle. She could hear a gentle whoosh above
as breezes traipsed through the treetops.

Haines was the first to spot a footprint, its outline in the mud
beside the creek. They had been told True was wearing shoes with
a pattern of triangles on the tread. But this print was faint and
partly washed away.

They paused. They had already slogged through Little Creek
for 45 minutes, and the sun was getting low. If they went much
farther, they could be stuck for the night.

Still, they persisted, and 10 minutes later they found more foot-prints, and a few minutes after that, more again. These were better defined, and triangles were part of the design. They compared the length with their own shoes, measuring with a stick. True wore a size 11. These were about the right size.

Energized now, their hearts thumping, the three picked up the pace.

They were trotting, and each began finding more tracks.

They shouted back and forth. "Here's one, and here's another!"

Soon they were seeing so many they no longer bothered to call out.

Micah True had become obsessed with the Tarahumara. What did they know about running that others did not? Were they some sort of superhumans?

Tarahumara was the Spanish name. They called themselves the Rarámuri, loosely translated as the running people. They had re-treated into the massive canyons of the Sierra Madre centuries ago to escape the conquistadors.

Generation after generation, they traversed the mountains and ravines along tight footpaths. Freakish endurance was required to cover the immense distances. Some chasms in the land were deeper than the Grand Canyon.

To better understand these people, True readjusted the rhythms of his life in 1994, alternating between Boulder and the Copper Canyons, still a furniture mover for half the year but a student of the Rarámuri for the rest. He built a tiny home at the bottom of a canyon in the town of Batopilas, carrying rocks from the river valley to use as a foundation and erecting walls with cement and adobe.

"The man called horse," as he sometimes referred to himself in written musings, was rapturous with the adventure. He described getting lost in his new surroundings, scaling a rock-faced moun-tain, water bottle in his teeth, buzzards overhead, "crawling on his belly like a reptile" while "pulling himself upward by grasping at plants." The canyons were stupendous, with alpine forests in the high altitudes and subtropical jungle on the valley floor.

He was careful not to intrude on the Rarámuri. Relationships developed over time. The impoverished tribe believed in kórima, their word for sharing what they could spare. They sometimes left him tortillas and pinole, a porridge of crushed corn and water. He reciprocated in kind.

Like the Rarámuri, True now ran in sandals, delighting in the simple act of self-propulsion, bounding along the undulating trails like a Neolithic hunter. He called it "moving meditation." His motto was "run free," and he did.

Running was essential to the human experience, he had decided. Most people undervalued its importance. Running was not merely a sound cardiovascular choice in a fitness craze; it was an ancient art, part of mankind's genetic imprint. Humans had survived across geological time because they could chase animals until the prey dropped from exhaustion.

The Rarámuri, then, did not possess any locomotive secrets. They simply retained the "genetic cellular memory" most human beings had forgotten.

"Every one of us used to be a long-distance runner," True said.

But the Rarámuri were themselves unhinging from their ancestral past. Many of the running people no longer ran; they lived in towns and wore blue jeans and cowboy hats. Modernity now flooded into the canyons. Mining companies sent huge trucks down new roads. Marijuana thrived in the soil, and rival drug cartels were in a merciless war within the ravines.

True wanted to help the Rarámuri preserve their running heritage. In 2003, he organized a 29-mile race that was intended to be a festive celebration of local culture, a gathering of the Rarámuri from the caves and ranchos of the "mother mountains."

To advertise it, True ran from canyon to canyon, handing out fliers and spouting enthusiasm. He hoped for a large turnout, but come race day only seven runners showed up. True finished fifth, ahead of two thirsty Rarámuri who allowed themselves to be diverted by a spectator with beer.

The event wasn't all he had wanted, but it was a start. It became an annual ultramarathon race, and in 2006, True had an exciting brainstorm. He would entice American ultrarunners to the Rarámuri's home turf. Highest on his wish list was Scott Jurek, the greatest of them all.

Organizing such a thing was difficult for a man living without a phone or electricity. True journeyed to the town of Creel, where there was a computer to borrow and a dial-up connection. He reached out through cyberspace.

As it turned out, Jurek was a metaphysical soul mate, another man who considered running a cherished legacy from primitive times. To him, racing the legendary Rarámuri in their own canyons sounded awesome.

Getting there, on the other hand, was no simple matter. Once across the border, it involved a relay of bus rides—the vehicles hugging the road through narrow switchbacks—and True was not much help with logistical advice. Seven Americans showed up, uncertain what to expect, and although they found the landscape breathtaking, the course itself was a brutal and twisting 47 miles of forbidding climbs and frightening descents.

Caballo Blanco gave each of his visitors the nickname of a spirit-animal—the deer, the bear, the young wolf, the snow hawk—and the race was held on a glorious Sunday. Crowds congregated in the town of Urique, where the race started and ended. Avid spectators risked their pesos with wagers.

First to finish was Arnulfo Quimare, the swiftest of the Rarámuri, and then came Jurek, six minutes behind. Though unused to defeat, the American acknowledged the winner with a gracious bow. The race is vividly described in *Born to Run*. McDougall, the author, not only witnessed it but also ran in it. He had his own abiding interest in the Rarámuri—and he had previously met the curious American called Caballo Blanco who lived among them.

Earlier, McDougall had an idea to write a book about four ultra-runners. But his time in the Copper Canyons pushed him toward an entirely different project. Here was a hidden tribe of super-athletes who had "mastered the secret of happiness" and lived "as benignly as bodhisattvas." Here was an American dwelling among them, a "mysterious loner with a fake name."

This was the stuff of a mind-blowing book.

At one point, the canyon around Little Creek gets even narrower, and at the same time becomes straighter. Molina, Haines, and Bannon had been in the stream for 90 minutes when they saw something ahead that was blood red, a color out of harmony amid the shadings of greens and browns.

"Do you see that?" Molina asked.

He rushed ahead while Haines hesitated. She thought it could be a dead animal, and in Alaska she had been taught to be cautious when coming upon fresh kill.

Molina was not so heedful. He soon recognized that the patch of red was a shirt with limbs on either side. A surge of emotions pulsed through him. His first thought was that his old friend was alive if hurt.

But once nearer the body he knew instantly it was a corpse. True was lying face up, his eyes glossy, his jaw open. Flies were busy.

The others also forced themselves to look. True's body was reclining on an outcropping of small rocks and boulders. His legs were in 10 inches of water, and his arms were against his chest, the right one down, the left one up. One of his shoes was off, and nearby was a plastic water bottle, two-thirds empty.

It appeared that True had taken a bad tumble at some point. There were abrasions on his legs and the backs of his arms. The middle finger of his left hand was bent and purplish. It looked to be broken.

"Oh, man," Molina said softly, and he realized he was weeping.

The task now was to get the word out, but they had no radio. Nor did they know exactly where they were. They had no GPS device.

They discussed what to do. Perhaps someone should stay with the body while the others went back. But that seemed too spooky to contemplate further: out there, in the dark, alone with the body. Mountain lions were mentioned.

No, they decided, they would all go. Yet other images crept into their minds. Molina wondered if they should place rocks on the body to keep animals from dragging it off—either that or cover it up with reeds and branches.

But they decided this too was unwise. They shouldn't contaminate the scene. The medical examiner would want things untouched.

So they turned back toward where they had entered the canyon.

And this time they ran as fast as they could.

Born to Run begins with McDougall, its author, going to Mexico's Copper Canyons, which he calls "a kind of shorebound Bermuda Triangle known for swallowing the misfits and desperadoes who stray inside." He hopes to find the "phantom" Caballo Blanco, who seems to be "a ghost among ghosts."

For a while, some of True's friends in Boulder were particularly fond of quoting that passage. He had been a well-known fixture in the city for 25 years. Now, when he would stop in at the Trident Café or the Mountain Sun Pub and Brewery, they would genially feign surprise, shocked by the presence of the phantom.

Becoming the central character in a best-selling book is a monumental life-changer, especially if it happens unwittingly to a man who made a sacrament of living simply. A thousand conflicting feelings eddied in his head.

True told people the book contained exaggerations and inaccuracies. For one, the Tarahumara lived no such idyllic life. Then he retreated from those criticisms, praising and thanking McDougall; then he alleged more flaws.

The book was flattering, surely. But that itself was a source of unease. True did not see himself as anywhere near so eccentric and amazing. He oftentimes felt two forces were in a tug-of-war for his identity: was he the person inside his own skin or the person inside the pages of *Born to Run*?

Much of the book's significance rested in its assertion that cushioned running shoes were a hazard to the human foot. But what made *Born to Run* a superb read was the story line in Mexico. Many readers wanted to meet the celebrated Caballo Blanco, and they seemed to expect a guru or a shaman or a fleet-footed saint. "I feel like I always have to live up to the expectations of the book," True complained.

But fame was enjoyable as well. True may never have wanted the world to beat a path to his door, but now he encouraged people to follow him on Facebook. He spent hours online tending to his messages, either at the Boulder public library or in the municipal building in Urique, Mexico.

Within months of the book's publication, two Facebook friends became love interests. One was Kati Bell, a runner who worked in corporate marketing. "I told him: 'You're a celebrity now. You can make money out of this,'" Bell said.

That was an intriguing notion, though not for his own sake but for the Rarámuri. The Copper Canyon Ultra Marathon was beginning to fulfill his grand vision. The number of participants was multiplying. There were cash prizes for the winners, and every finisher received 500 pounds of corn. True was not only reviving the running culture but also feeding the hungry.

The race needed infusions of cash to sustain itself, and he agreed to a small number of personal appearances, Bell said, although he was appalled when she suggested they hold dinners and charge $100 a head.

"Let people donate whatever they want," he insisted.

True proved to be an amiable and amusing speaker. He needed no notes to tell his stories, although a few beers helped. He was shaving his head now, a look that made his face all the more striking, the large ears and lips, the protruding chin, the deep crow's feet at the corners of his eyes.

Audiences were reliably friendly, won over well before he uttered word one. True would smile at them even in mid-jeremiad. "Long after we're gone, long after greed blows everything up, the Rarámuri are still going to be subsisting," he said. "They know how to survive, they know how to endure."

A nonprofit group, Norawas de Rarámuri, was set up to handle donations. Every dollar would benefit the Rarámuri, as True demanded.

But were others willing to demonstrate the same selflessness? True was certain of his own integrity but deeply suspicious of everyone else's.

What was McDougall doing with the profits from the book, True wanted to know. And what about Ted McDonald, Barefoot Ted, another memorable character from *Born to Run?* He had started a company that made minimalist sandals modeled after the huaraches worn by the Rarámuri.

"Running is not supposed to be about getting people to buy stuff," True wrote in an email to friends. "Running should be free, man, and the Rarámuri are being used to sell lots of stuff. What do they get out of it?"

Barefoot Ted often found True irritating. "I give back every year to the Copper Canyon, but Caballo equated any business with evil," he said. "He did great things down there, but you ended up loving him and not quite liking him. I told McDougall, you've brought into being a new Frankenstein."

That is hardly a prevailing view, but True could indeed be prickly and sharp-elbowed as well as warmhearted. His mantra for running was: easy, light, and smooth. But off the trails he was an easily frazzled man living a newly frazzling life. The "whole notoriety thing," as he called it, was useful for raising funds, but he was afraid of looking like a sellout at the same time.

To him, honesty was everything. He worried: Am I pretending to be something I'm not? Am I unfairly benefiting from someone else's book?

But he continued with the public speaking gigs, usually at running stores.

Scott Leese, another of True's cyberpals, was an "executive coach" in California who "specialized in the rapid transformation of people." He, too, was smitten with the Caballo Blanco portrayed in the book and wanted him to reach a wider audience. Last year, Leese became his reticent friend's agent, "though Micah hated that word because it really screamed establishment."

Leese's new client was often a headache. He despised anything corporate. He refused to consider endorsements. But finally, last summer, he agreed to attend an event hosted by Saucony, the shoe company, going on a trail run with some of its retailers and speaking at a dinner in Utah.

Then, in the fall, True consented to a trip to Sweden, Denmark, and Britain. In England, he spoke in small theaters or halls in London, York, Chester, Bristol, and Birmingham. Admission cost £10, about $16.

All the while, the runner found reasons to bellyache. "Very high maintenance," Leese said. But when the trip ended, True regarded it as a success. The audiences appreciated him, and he wanted to do more public speaking. He was close to a multi-appearance deal with Saucony.

Micah True was making his peace with the "notoriety thing."

Not long after Ray Molina and his friends came out of Little Creek, they saw three of the Mas Locos, the so-called crazy ones, which loosely includes anybody who has traveled into the Copper Canyons to run the big race.

"We found Micah," Molina shouted.

"What?"

"We found him. He's in the creek and he's dead."

They stood together for a few moments, awash in melancholy. Two of the ultrarunners volunteered to go to the creek and watch over the body. One was Simon Donato, 35, a geologist from Calgary, Alberta. The other was Tim Puetz, 33, who had been a captain in the Army infantry in Afghanistan. *Never leave a comrade behind, dead or alive,* he was thinking. What if the body washed down the creek? This required "eyes on."

While posted in Logar Province in Afghanistan, Puetz read *Born to Run* in two sittings, and it changed his life. He used to awaken at 4:00 A.M. and jog for a few hours along a two-mile circuit around the perimeter of his outpost. He would often think of that amazing guy in the book, Caballo Blanco, who "seemed to live without limits and go wherever life led him." When it was time to leave the military, he emailed True, asking permission to run in the ultramarathon.

"You don't need permission, just come," True wrote back.

Puetz (pronounced Pits) had met Donato at the 2010 race. To them, Mas Locos felt like a brotherhood. And now there they were, scrambling up the trail to safeguard Caballo's body. They were wearing only running gear, but Molina and his friends had given them fleece jackets, a nylon cover, two flashlights, a cigarette lighter, and a couple of granola bars.

Puetz and Donato hit the water. They wanted to move quickly through the creek but were also afraid of overshooting the corpse in the waning light. Then they finally saw him, lying peacefully on his back, like a man who had stopped to relax.

They built a fire on the bank across the creek, using pine cones for kindling. Despite the flames, the chill insinuated itself through the drifting night air.

Later, they shared a granola bar and slid under the cover, sitting with their backs to True and the creek and the canyon wall behind it. They preferred to face the steep forest slope. If a bear or a mountain lion came darting out of the darkness, it would most likely come through those trees.

They figured to take turns all night, one man feeding the fire while the other slept. But then, near midnight, they heard whistles, and there was Ray Molina with several others. They had brought warm blankets and food.

In the morning, the corpse was put in a body bag, then maneuvered onto a light metal frame. It was carried through the dense, snaggy brush of the forest until the woods intersected a trail. Three pack animals were there waiting, and one of them immediately caught Puetz's eye. It was a light-shaded palomino with a cream-colored mane.

"Are you kidding me?" he said. "They sent a white horse."

The 2012 Copper Canyon Ultra Marathon, held March 4, was the biggest yet. More than 350 Rarámuri ran the tortuous course. Some were as old as 70, some barely in their teens. Many women ran in their traditional long skirts, the bright material swinging back and forth.

About 100 other Mexicans competed, as well as 80 foreigners. Three runners broke the course record. The winner was a Rarámuri. A runner from the Czech Republic came in second.

In the days before, True was on a pendulum of mood swings, happy with being the host and anxious about the responsibility. Was there enough water? What about medical support? The Rarámuri were arriving 20 and 30 at a time in cattle trucks. They needed food and places to sleep.

But not all the arrangements fell on True's shoulders anymore. In many ways, the event was outpacing him. Public officials considered the race a signature municipal event that merited their co-management. Politicians made the welcoming speeches. Goldcorp, the big mining company, had been enlisted by the municipality of Urique as a sponsor.

At times, True wished it were again just him running through the mountains with a handful of the Rarámuri. But mostly he was elated. These were tough times; a drought was in its second year, and the runners in the ultramarathon were rewarded with a voucher for 110 pounds of corn for every 10 miles they completed.

The race was the best of True's good deeds. He described himself in the third person, all at once modest and grandiose: "Caballo Blanco is no hero. Not a great anything. Just a Horse of a little different color dancing to the beat of a peaceful drum and wanting to help make a little difference in some lives."

The day after the race, he contentedly sat at a table by the municipal building handing out the valuable vouchers. The line stretched so long it took two hours to finish the paperwork. He and his charity gave away $40,000 in food.

On March 6, True left the canyons in his 25-year-old Nissan truck, driving with his dog, Guadajuko, and his girlfriend, Maria

Walton, 50. They had been a couple for about two years. She too had found him on Facebook.

A divorcée with three grown children, Walton was the general manager of a large restaurant in Phoenix. She was as reliably even-tempered as True was mercurial. The Mas Locos generally agreed: Maria was an infusion of love and serenity into Caballo's life. He called her by the spirit name La Mariposa, the butterfly.

True spent two weeks in Phoenix, then drove east with the dog to the Gila Wilderness in southwestern New Mexico, one of his favorite retreats. His friends Dean and Jane Bruemmer own a small lodge there. He sometimes stayed with them, although other times he camped out. Either way, in the mornings he used their wireless Internet connection. He remained compulsive about reading his email.

"Life was going good for Micah; actually, life was going great," Jane Bruemmer said. She had been unsure how well he was handling his sudden starburst of fame. "He didn't seek it or need it, but he was using it now to fund his favorite cause," she said. "He had an agent." She found that so astonishing she needed to repeat it with more inflection: "Micah True had an agent!"

Born to Run was being made into a movie. The business deal did not involve True, and for a while he thought: *Here it comes again. The film will bring as much upheaval into my life as the book.* Sarsgaard—the director and co-author of the script—had warned him that no one watches a two-hour movie about himself and comes away thinking, *That's me up there.*

True thought things had also taken an amusing karmic twist. McDougall, not him, was going to be the movie's main character, and after reading a draft of the script, the book's author, in an email to True, called it "ridiculous" and said his "high expectations for the movie had plummeted."

True took satisfaction in that. Now McDougall would find out how it felt to be defined by someone else. In an email sent to Sarsgaard on March 26, he wrote, "As we know, I would have much liked to at least proofread, fact-check, and/or co-write what" McDougall said about him in the book. "Soooooo . . . . It is hard to feel toooo sorry for him."

True spent much of that night writing messages, but he was up early the next day. Dean Bruemmer made him blueberry pancakes. True said he was going on a 12-mile run but leaving Guadajuko behind. The dog had sore paws from their jaunt the day before.

Caballo Blanco left the lodge at about 10:00 A.M. He was seen along State Highway 15. The sun was a hot yellow beam when he entered the wilderness.

Micah True's corpse, encased in a body bag and draped over a brown mule, was taken through the forest and out to the main trailhead in midafternoon on Sunday, April 1. Maria Walton ran up a slope to meet it, calling out, "I love you," and kissing the end of the bundle that appeared to be the feet.

Just then, a heavy wind began to blow. Dirt spun in the air. A hearse had been parked in an adjacent lot since morning, and the driver, dressed in a coat and tie, looked away to shield his eyes.

The mule was slowly led to the vehicle, and the body bag was lifted through the open door at the rear. Walton insisted that Guadajuko be permitted a farewell, cradling the dog in her arms and taking him over. "We're going to see Daddy, your best buddy," she said, sobbing.

Ray Molina, haggard and exhausted, hugged Walton and then leaned against his old Mercedes and talked about finding the corpse. "Micah was bloodied up, so I think he took a tumble and then a hypothermic night did him in," he said.

Mike Barragree, an investigator for the state medical examiner's office, had gone with the team that reclaimed the body. He speculated that "some sort of cardiac event" was the likely cause of death, and that turned out to be correct: idiopathic cardiomyopathy, a heart ailment.

The search and recovery mission was finally over. The remembrances had already begun. The evening before, Walton and Scott Leese and many of the Mas Locos hung out at a campground that also had a few small cottages. The moon was a half-circle. The stars were abundant. Someone had thought to buy beer.

For them, this was a requiem for a dead friend. They ate tortillas and eggs and canned stew, heating the food on an old white stove and subduing their sorrow with laughter. They each had a favorite Caballo Blanco story to tell, or two or three. The past flooded into the present.

Above all, their friend wanted to be authentic, they said, and no one could doubt that he had been. This was no small thing.

His death was terribly sad, and yet there was also perfection about it.

Micah True died while running through a magnificent wilderness, and then many of his closest friends came together to search for him, stepping through the same alluring canyons and forests and streams, again and again calling out his name.

MARK SINGER

Marathon Man

FROM THE NEW YORKER

IN JULY 2010, Kyle Strode, a 46-year-old chemistry professor from Helena, Montana, ran the Missoula Marathon. Completing the 26.2-mile distance in two hours and 47 minutes, he placed fourth out of 1,322 finishers, and won the masters division, for entrants 40 and older. Strode is among the most accomplished masters marathoners in Montana, with a personal best of two hours and 32 minutes. When he toes a starting line in his home state, he knows who is among the class of the field, and he's particularly aware of other masters competitors. The Missoula course, which is mostly flat, passes through rangeland and forest, crosses two rivers, and in its final miles offers a tour of the city's tree-lined neighborhoods. Early in the race, Strode broke ahead of his usual rivals, and never saw them again. The second masters runner to cross the finish line, Mike Telling, from Dillon, Montana, trailed Strode by nearly four minutes. At the awards ceremony, however, they learned that Telling had actually placed third. The official runner-up was Kip Litton, age 48, of Clarkston, Michigan. Litton, who had been at the back of the pack when the race started, began his run two minutes after the gun was fired. He had apparently made up for lost time.

Since the early nineties, technology has made it possible to clock runners with precision and to track them at measured intervals, yielding point-to-point "split" times. Runners attach to their shoe-lace or racing bib a transponder tag that marks how much time has elapsed when a checkpoint is reached. Often, sensor-equipped checkpoint mats span the running lanes. USA Track & Field, the governing body for major running competitions, mandates that "gun," rather than "chip," times determine the official results in sanctioned races. But, as a practical matter, this rule generally applies solely to elite lead runners. In a field of thousands, it might take an entrant several minutes just to reach the starting line, so it seems only fair that the diligent middle- or back-of-the-packers' order of finish is adjusted to reflect the chip time. In Missoula, the marathon's organizers made this allowance.

Strode didn't have to teach that summer, and so he had time to scrutinize the race results. Because Litton came from out of state, he hadn't been on Strode's radar, and Litton hadn't stuck around to claim his award. Strode learned from Telling that he hadn't paid Litton any mind as he passed him in the homestretch, and that he had no memory of being passed by Litton earlier in the race.

A wealth of online data about competitive running makes post-race analyses relatively easy. Several days after the marathon, Strode visited a website that displayed photographs of runners along the Missoula route. Most participants appeared in several shots, each of which indicated, down to the second, when it was snapped. Strode noticed something curious: although Litton had posted a half-marathon split time, and there were four images of him taken at or near the finish line, Strode couldn't locate him anywhere in the preceding 26 miles.

In the Missoula photographs, Litton wore sunglasses and a black baseball cap, so Strode had only a general sense of what he looked like: white, clean-shaven, and about five feet ten, with an athletic build but not the classic lean and loose-limbed runner's physique. Athlinks, a popular online database for endurance races, sharpened the picture somewhat: in 2000, shortly before turning 40, Litton ran his first race, a five-kilometer event in Flint, half an hour from his home. His average pace was seven and a half minutes per mile: a good novice result. He ran the same race a year later and improved his pace by almost 40 seconds per mile, and a year after that he whittled off 14 more seconds, to a respectable six minutes and 35 seconds per mile. In 2003, he finished 11 races, including his first marathon, in Jacksonville, Florida.

In all, during the previous decade Litton had run in more than 100 races, including 25 marathons. His time in Jacksonville,

3:19:57, qualified him for the Boston Marathon, the following April, where he covered the course in 3:25:06—a 7:50-per-mile pace. He returned to Jacksonville in 2006 and, for the first time, recorded a sub-three-hour marathon, winning in his age group. Four months later, he broke the three-hour barrier again, in Boston.

For a man or a woman of any age, a marathon performance of under three hours is considered a mark of distinction. (Typically, about 6 percent of the field at the Boston Marathon runs this fast.) In the year before Missoula, Litton had averaged a marathon a month, with sub-three-hour clockings in each. He'd traveled to New Mexico, Idaho, New Hampshire, Arizona, Florida, Virginia, Missouri, Massachusetts, Rhode Island, Delaware, Vermont, and South Dakota. Eight times, he'd come in first in his age group, and in the West Wyoming Marathon, a week before Missoula, he was the overall winner.

Exploring the websites for each of Litton's marathons occupied Strode for several days. Not every race was as well documented as Missoula's, but wherever professional race photographers had been present he hunted for shots of Litton among other runners. He found images of him at the end of a course, only twice at the beginning, and never in between. And there was the chip-gun differential: with rare exceptions, Litton started two to five minutes behind the leaders. In a crowded field, wouldn't a swift runner want to avoid weaving through clusters of slower runners?

A Google search led Strode to a website for the dental practice of Kip Litton, DDS, in Davison, Michigan. It also led to Worldrecordrun, a site, conceived and maintained by Litton, that chronicled his peripatetic habits. "World record" apparently referred to his goal of running sub-three-hour marathons in all 50 states. The quest had formally begun at a marathon in Traverse City, Michigan, in May 2009, and Montana was his 14th destination. On the site, Litton had posted his finishing times and a recap of each race. He explained that his training regimen and diet, along with nutritional supplements, had "allowed me to maintain my rigorous schedule and even improve my recent performances." His tone was alternately hortatory ("Imagine Inspire Impact!") and emotional ("I have been blessed with the greatest wife and kids a guy could ever ask for").

"Who is Kip Litton?" he asked. "I am a lifelong resident of Michigan and an alumnus of both The University of Michigan and UM Dental School. Currently I live in the town of Clarkston and have an office in Davison. I began running in the year 2000 to lose weight. I am an ordinary guy with an extraordinary desire to make a difference. At the onset of this mission I had run 11 marathons, all in the range of 3:35 down to 2:55. . . . After superficially committing to this mission, I soon discovered the devil was in the details. . . . Was I born to do this? Hardly. As a high schooler, I did play tennis, but HATED to run. My teammates and I never ran as far as the coach told us to or thought we had."

There was another, poignant motivation behind "the mission." Litton and his wife, Lisa, an attorney, were the parents of two boys and a girl. The youngest, Michael, was born, in 2001, with cystic fibrosis. A congenital illness, it most commonly clogs airways in the lungs, making breathing difficult. The average life expectancy for cystic-fibrosis patients is about 38 years. Litton wrote, "The goal is to raise a QUARTER MILLION DOLLARS for CF during the course of the mission." His site featured the logo of the Cystic Fibrosis Foundation, and people were invited to make donations by clicking on a link to the organization's website, by writing a personal check to Worldrecordrun, or by sending money to a PayPal account.

"My hope is that I can inspire others to take inventory of their talents, find their passion and pursue it relentlessly to effect a cause or impact their community," Litton wrote. "This is MY mission. It is the only thing I feel passionately about enough to ask you to PLEASE consider a donation to this worthy cause. I will also be bold enough to ask you to please alert others to this site or send a link to your e-mail list. When all is said and done, no one will care about the endless hours of training, my detailed work-out logs or fancy awards."

The compassion that Strode naturally felt upon learning of a child's illness, along with admiration for Litton's readiness to put his body on the line to raise funds for Michael's future and for medical research, was tempered, he told me, by his belief that Litton "had cheated in almost all of his 2010 marathons."

On July 24, 2010, Strode received an unexpected inquiry from Jennifer Straughan, the Missoula race director, who asked him to look at a photograph of a runner wearing bib number 759. It was Litton. "There is some question as to whether he was seen along the course," Straughan wrote. "He finished in a time similar to you so theoretically you would have noticed him."

While Strode had been immersed in what he'd assumed was his own private Kip Litton obsession, the official timer at Missoula had been contacted by his counterpart at the Deadwood Mickelson Trail Marathon, in Deadwood, South Dakota, where Litton had turned up the previous month. Photographs taken in Deadwood showed him crossing the starting line fifth from last and finishing in 2:55:50, putting him first in his age group and in third place overall. The fourth-place finisher protested: he'd been running third at the halfway mark and said that no one had passed him after that, an assertion bolstered by the fact that most of the remaining course was a trail only six feet wide. Litton had registered a half-marathon split, and the Deadwood timer was skeptical of the protest against him—"I was trying to prove Litton was legit," he told me—but he changed his mind after determining that Litton had, improbably, run the second half 11 minutes faster than the first. In addition, he found photographs of Litton only at the start and the end of the course. Deadwood disqualified Litton, and Straughan followed suit in Missoula.

Strode, who in a later web post described his mind-set as "sucked in, fascinated and pissed off," broadened his investigation. He sent an email to Richard Rodriguez, who on the website of the West Wyoming Marathon was identified as its race director; Litton had a listed winning time there of 2:56:12.

"I'm writing to ask about the winner of your marathon a few weeks ago, Kip Litton," Strode wrote. "He was recently disqualified from the Deadwood Mickelson Trail Marathon for cheating (not running the whole course) . . . I don't know the guy—I just hate cheating in running. I wonder whether he may have had a legitimate performance at your race or whether he may also have cheated in Wyoming."

Two days later, Strode received a response: "Wow, that's quite a scenario! It would have been very unlikely for the same thing to have happened at our race, as there were only 30 participants and the lead 2 runners ran almost the entire race together. I have not received any complaints. I will keep my ears open though. If there is an update, send it my way. Take care, Richard."

Strode began to wonder if his suspicions were misplaced, but he kept investigating. At the Providence Marathon, in Rhode Island, where Litton had finished first in his age group, photographs showed him wearing shoes and shorts at the end of the course that were different from those he was wearing at the beginning. (A costume change at Deadwood had involved shoes, a hat, and a T-shirt.) In the Delaware Marathon, Litton had finished first in his age group. After being prompted by Strode, the race's director, Wayne Kursh, found that, among the finishers, Litton alone had failed to register split times. On an out-and-back portion of the course, Kursh had taken photographs of the top runners at the turnaround point—but Litton was not among them. He also failed to find images of Litton elsewhere on the course.

Kursh had a blog, and on August 6, 2010, he posted a blind item about Litton titled "Another Rosie Ruiz?"—a reference to the scammer who was briefly heralded as the winner of the women's division of the 1980 Boston Marathon, before it was determined that she'd jumped onto the course less than a mile from the finish. Kursh wrote in a follow-up that he had been exchanging concerns with other race directors, adding, "I smell a rat."

In an email exchange initiated by Kursh, Litton claimed that photographs of him would be hard to find, because his shirt had covered his racing bib. He added, "Wasn't there a timing mat at the turnaround?" Kursh ultimately decided to disqualify him, explaining, "From your comment here it is pretty obvious that you have NO idea where the timing mats were on route. They definitely were not at this turn-around point."

On occasions when Litton responded to such pointed challenges, he never did so in a hostile or nakedly defensive manner. After a disqualification, he simply deleted the result and the recap from his website, as if he had never registered for the race. His default demeanor was equable mystification.

Clarkston, Michigan, is an exurban town within commuting distance of both Detroit and Flint, which ranked first and fourth, respectively, in the latest *Forbes* survey of America's most dangerous cities. Those grim statistics don't seem to impinge on Clarkston. The subdivision where Kip and Lisa Litton live with their three children—large brick and stone houses on oversized lots, with expansive lawns and SUVs parked in circular driveways—is threaded

with undeveloped woodlands and streams. In Davison, 22 miles
north, Litton's dental practice occupies a one-story brown brick
building on a commercial strip, tucked behind an auto-repair
shop, next door to a drive-through bank, and a short sprint from
the requisite conveniences (McDonald's, Jiffy Lube, Taco Bell). A
few miles south of Flint is the comfortable suburb of Grand Blanc,
where Litton grew up. In 1979, he graduated from Grand Blanc
High School. A strong tennis player—as a junior, he won a state
championship—he is remembered as bright and charismatic,
with smart-aleck tendencies. "The first party I had after I bought
a house, I invited him," a high school friend told me. "Part of his
way of getting attention at the party was to eat all the food. Kip
does odd, silly things for attention. But they're harmless."

In 1990, two years after graduating from dental school, Litton
started working in Davison with a dentist who was nearing retirement, and in 2001 he acquired the practice. Today, Litton's office
has a website, which notes that, "when the General Motors Company cut benefits for retirees, Dr. Litton devised a cost-sharing
plan that allowed patients without benefits to continue receiving
quality dental care." One day a year, Litton says, he provides free
dental care to underprivileged children; each Halloween, he offers to buy back patients' candy for a dollar a pound, then has
it "shipped overseas to the troops, along with toothbrushes." A
Google review of Litton's practice, posted earlier this year, said,
"After trying several other dentists in the area, I was so delighted
to find Dr. Litton . . . Great friendly staff, painless, lowest costs, no
interest payment plans and Dr. Litton is SO funny! I finally have
my fantastic Hollywood smile. I have already convinced several of
my friends and relatives to come to this office, despite almost an
hour drive. My search is now YOUR gain."

Litton had attracted local media attention for his running
achievements. After the 2010 Boston Marathon, the *Davison Index*
noted that Litton was "the first finisher from mid-Michigan and
the first over 40 from Michigan." Around the same time, the *Flint
Journal* ran a story with the headline "Davison Dentist Has Transformed Himself from Sedentary Middle-Ager to Successful Marathoner." The article traced a stirring trajectory: one day, about a
decade earlier, Litton, 50 pounds overweight, got on a treadmill,
hoping to run three miles. "I made it a little over a third of a mile
before I got so dizzy that I started to fall off the treadmill," he told

the reporter, Bill Khan. "I was completely out of shape. It was just ridiculous." Fast-forward: "Litton now regularly races marathons, not content to merely finish 26.2 miles but to post times that few runners his age can match." (Khan learned of Litton, he told me, when a stranger sent him an email saying that "this guy has gotten himself in shape and is trying to raise money for charity.")

Litton told Khan, "I'm starting to know every crack and pothole on that route from Hopkinton to Boston. Once you go to Boston, there's something special about it. Having all 26 miles with people lined up on both sides of the road, screaming their lungs out for six hours, is such an unusual experience and super cool."

Wayne Kursh's "I smell a rat" blog post drew the attention of Michael McGrath, a former assistant track and cross-country coach at Haverford College. McGrath had competed at Boston nine times—including the year Rosie Ruiz cheated—and his best finish was 2:49:19. Although Kursh hadn't mentioned Litton by name, McGrath soon identified him, by comparing the lists of finishers at Missoula and Delaware. Like Strode, he found Litton a more compelling impostor than Ruiz, in no small part because his methodology was so tantalizingly elusive. Somehow, he had exploited the running community's faith in the very systems—transponders, chip times—that had been adopted to prevent cheating.

"I am like a dog who cannot let go of a bone," McGrath wrote to Kursh. He spent days anatomizing Litton's races, dissecting first his 2010 showing at Boston. Litton had hit all the splits, at five-kilometer intervals. This suggested that running a sub-three-hour marathon was theoretically within his capacity. Unless, McGrath argued, the microscope was brought into tighter focus.

The Boston course has a reputation for toughness: the Newton hills, which runners encounter between miles 16 and 21, owe their notoriety to the fact that they must be climbed when the energy reserves of runners are greatly depleted. How was it, McGrath asked, that on the most leisurely stretch—just before the halfway mark, near Wellesley College—Litton's pace was a full minute slower than it was in the hills? Litton's Boston race in 2009 had the same incongruities.

McGrath learned that, in February 2009, Litton had run a 15-kilometer race in Florida. According to the split times, his pace during the second half—five minutes and 24 seconds per mile—was almost two minutes faster than during the first half. Such a divergence is called a "negative split," and a variance of that magnitude is as common as snow in Miami. Nor did Litton's past performances indicate an ability to run a five-and-a-half-minute pace. The official timer of the Deadwood Mickelson Trail Marathon, reflecting upon Litton's purported acceleration, told me, "I don't know any *Kenyans* who could do that."

Not long after McGrath began his research, he decided to go public, sort of. His medium was LetsRun, a website devoted to news about elite track and distance running. One of LetsRun's salient features is its "World Famous Message Boards," where most participants use pseudonyms, and the content quality runs the expected gamut (factual, analytical, sophomoric, inanely combative). McGrath, using the handle Anonymous.4, posted an item under the heading "Kip Litton," referred to Litton's disqualification at Missoula, and solicited feedback from anyone who might have more information.

One responder was Scott Hubbard, a former collegiate runner and high school coach who was a familiar figure on the central Michigan running scene. Hubbard measured and certified courses, often worked as a race announcer, and wrote for running publications. His awareness of Litton dated to October 2009, when Litton's five-member relay team was disqualified from winning the Detroit Free Press Marathon Relay. Litton had recruited four topnotch masters runners, only two of whom he'd known previously, paid everyone's entry fee, and assigned himself the second leg of the relay. The members of the second-place team were stunned by the race result—especially their second-leg runner, who had received his baton in first place, knew that no one had passed him, yet learned after handing off to his third-leg teammate that they no longer held the lead. With encouragement from Litton's mortified teammates, who felt potentially implicated, the second-place team protested, leading to the disqualification. Afterward, Hubbard told me, he initiated a correspondence with Litton, trying to "pin him down on how he cut the course."

Litton was initially evasive. But after about a week of questioning he offered an explanation: "Finally, he came down to 'Yeah, I must have cut it short somewhere to come in with that time.' I asked him where that might have happened. I knew the course, because I'd measured it. He named the place and said, 'I must

have followed someone.' And I said, 'No, you didn't follow anyone. You cheated.'"

A few weeks later, Hubbard came across the following item in
the online newsletter of *Michigan Runner,* a bimonthly publication:

> Reader Brian Smith passes along several great performances by
> Kip Litton:
> "I wanted to relay some info about a couple of recent perfor-
> mances that I would consider great. I see a dentist in Davison who's
> name is Dr. Kip Litton. We often talk running when I am there. Re-
> cently he had told me about a couple of marathons he was planning
> to run. When I asked about them afterwards, he just said things like,
> 'I was just glad to finish' and 'Well, I didn't injure myself!' I know
> that he is a good runner, so I looked up the race results. Now I also
> know how humble he is.
> "It turns out that he finished 3 marathons in less than 2 months,
> all under 3 hours. He placed 2nd overall & 1st master in The New
> Mexico Marathon Sept 6 in 2:57:54, 5th overall & 1st master in The
> City of Trees Marathon Oct 4 in 2:55:45 and 14th overall and 1st in
> the division in The Manchester City Marathon Nov 1 in 2:54:06.
> "I think that could be considered worthy of a mention. I didn't
> see them listed in your newsletter so I thought I would pass them
> along."

Hubbard sent another email to Litton, on the pretext that he
wanted to get in touch with Brian Smith. When Litton responded
that he couldn't recall all his patients, Hubbard pressed harder.
"The question was posed to him pointedly: 'Who's Brian Smith?'"
Hubbard later wrote on LetsRun. "He didn't say he was a patient
of his. He didn't put up much of a fight when told it was felt he
wrote the note."

During the fall of 2010, Litton entered marathons in Rochester,
New York; Portland, Maine; Huntington, West Virginia; and Charlotte, North Carolina. In Rochester, he posted a chip time under
two hours and 58 minutes, winning the masters division. Photographs at Rochester showed him wearing a gray-green sweatshirt,
a cap with a bright-yellow logo, and no visible racing bib. At the
finish, he wore a different shirt and hat. This proved too much
for Hubbard, who issued an ultimatum to Litton: take down the
Worldrecordrun site or risk an exposé in *Michigan Runner,* for
which Hubbard wrote a column.

Worldrecordrun was gone within days. (According to Litton, the site had become more trouble than it was worth, and Hubbard's threat wasn't a factor.) Cathy Zell, who at the time was the executive director of the local chapter of the Cystic Fibrosis Foundation, told me that she didn't know of any donations that had been obtained through the link on Litton's web page. "We started getting phone calls saying, 'I don't know if he's legit,'" she said. "I never had proof one way or the other." Litton, she added, "basically is the one who said, 'This isn't giving you guys a good name.'" Laurie Fink, a spokesperson for the Cystic Fibrosis Foundation, says that since 2004 the Litton household has contributed $20 to the organization.

Even after Litton dismantled the site, he continued to enter races. On December 11, 2010, at the Thunder Road Marathon, in Charlotte, his split times suggested to the race director that he had cut the course and not been overly clever about it; within 48 hours, he'd been provisionally disqualified. Just as swiftly, Litton responded with a pious defense, portraying himself as the victim of "a witch hunt" and "a smear campaign . . . ridiculous things which are ALL completely un-true." He confessed only to a failure to be remarkable: "I have legally practiced dentistry for over 20 years and have 3 kids. I have never been arrested. I have never even been sued. I have never cheated in a race. I am not perfect, but probably the worst thing I have ever done is get a parking ticket. I know, boring."

Meanwhile, the mockery on LetsRun's message boards, as Litton pointed out, was "taking on a life of its own." In late December, he wrote to Weldon Johnson, one of the founders of LetsRun, complaining about his treatment. He acknowledged his disqualifications at Detroit, Missoula, and Delaware, and floated fuzzy explanations for each. ("I inadvertently turned too soon & cut part of the course . . . I was dq'd as I should have been, but only accidentally.") He added, "I have served on my Dental Ethics Board"—in fact, he had not—"so I realize that people should take cheating seriously." But the situation had got out of control. "If these accusations held any water, it would have certainly forced me to stop racing. As you know, I have not. I have nothing to hide."

The connoisseurs of Litton's audacity were galvanized. They stared at course maps: *He could have cut it there—or there.* Rich Heller, a former collegiate runner, collated findings on an ancillary site,

Study of Kip Litton Running, including links to videos, such as one of Litton walking across the finish line at the P. F. Chang's Rock 'n' Roll Arizona Marathon, in January 2010. (Chip time: 2:51:21.) "For some races the evidence is circumstantial," Heller wrote. "For others it's [a] SLAM DUNK." For the conspiracy-minded, it was a juicy peach, and LetsRun contributors adopted handles like Lone Gunman and Zapruder. The paramount question was "How?" Did he have an accomplice? Did he drive from point to point? Ride a bicycle? Devise digital subversions?

Jennifer Straughan, the Missoula race director, was as mystified as anyone. "It's expensive," she told me. "He flies all over the country, rents cars, plans in advance, has to figure out how many chip mats there are, how you deal with those. Think about how hard you have to work to *not* run a race."

The debunkers zeroed in on the West Wyoming Marathon, the one race that Litton had supposedly won outright. One of them came across a web cache of the race's defunct home page, which included this caveat: "With a low entry fee, there will be no goodie bags, no shirts, no photographer and no finishers medals."

On January 11, 2011, a poster called Liptodakip wrote, "Still curious about the west Wyoming marathon. 29 runners total. And he won it. Anyone know anything about it? Is it a real race? The main page is down and now the results are gone. (was up last week). did he make up an entire race? That would be bold!"

Yes, it would. And, yes, he did. LetsRun exploded: West Wyoming was Litton's pièce de résistance, and even his most indignant accusers had to concede their perverse admiration. In this race, the key to winning was ingeniously uncomplicated: *Make the whole thing up!* For his fabricated marathon, Litton had assembled not only a website but also a list of finishers and their times (plus name, age, gender, and hometown), and created a phantom race director, who responded to email queries. It occurred to Kyle Strode that six months earlier, when he had raised questions about Litton to "Richard Rodriguez," the reply ("Wow, that's quite a scenario!") had omitted a crucial detail. When Richard Rodriguez looked in the mirror, Litton looked back.

In concocting the fantasy, someone had gone so far as to create a post-race testimonial for the website Marathon Guide. "Small race, with only a couple dozen runners," a post there said. "Bring your own gels; only water is available on course. Out-and-back route. No spectators to speak of. Sounds like a downer, but the view and the town are so worth it! Cross Wyoming off of your list and visit one of the most beautiful towns in the US at the same time."

This was attributed to "G.S. from Nebraska," which matched one listed entrant, Greg Sanchez, of Lincoln, age 54. "Cross Wyoming off of your list" referred to running marathons in all 50 states. More people summit Mount Everest each year than celebrate running a marathon in a 50th state. LetsRun's forensic beavers established that it made no sense for Sanchez to refer to crossing states off a list, because, according to a database at Marathon Guide, this was his one and only marathon. The same was true of the other finishers besides Litton: 28 men and women, from 12 states, with tellingly unimaginative names (Joseph Smith, Kevin Scott, Sue Johnson, Karen Nelson). This lapse notwithstanding, someone had invested considerable time and effort to create Athlinks profiles for several of the fictional runners.

The next day, two more imaginary races, in Orlando and Atlanta, were identified among Litton's Athlinks performances. Inspection of the race websites revealed that they were hosted by the same Internet server as the sites for the West Wyoming race, for Worldrecordrun, and for Litton's dental practice.

Along with outrage and stupefaction, the LetsRun community expressed gratitude: "This is the craziest thing I have ever read in my life. Ever . . . WOW . . . Better than porn . . . Is it possible that Kip Litton doesn't actually exist, and it is all an incredible ruse?"

Litton certainly existed, but his bizarre story posed a conundrum: was he just a guy with Olympic-caliber chutzpah, or did he suffer the certitude of self-delusion? After his provisional disqualification at the Charlotte marathon, in December 2010, his appeal to the race director, Tim Rhodes, brimmed with wounded resentment. He invoked the tragedy of his son's illness. ("I have a 9-year old son with terminal Cystic Fibrosis. I run to raise funds to help cure this vicious disease.") As Rhodes explained to Scott Hubbard, without definitive proof of a deception "our hands are tied." In the absence of witnesses who had seen Litton leave and reenter the course, Rhodes reversed the disqualification.

Once Litton had insinuated a few dubious times into the top

running databases, he must have convinced himself that he could celebrate his sham successes on his website without attracting hostile scrutiny. But the close call at Charlotte seemed to change his game. For the time being, it would be Litton's final race appearance. Pressed via email by Hubbard and others, he denied that he had cheated or had intended to deceive—and offered justifications that left one in awe of his gift for just making shit up. He provided this account of what happened at West Wyoming:

> The West Wyoming Marathon did actually exist. It was set up to accommodate our family trip to that area. In planning our vacation, I launched the website for the race, which was set up with race day registration. Over a dozen people indicated that they would likely come & run. I had a local resident lined up to help out. Race morning I got quite a surprise when no one showed up. I ran anyway. As the only entrant I placed both first and last. The first issue of the results contained only my name. A tech savvy friend convinced me this would look ridiculous & he could add some additional names. After thinking that this would in no way harm any other actual person, I agreed. So yes I am absolutely responsible for that. I regret making this snap decision and I realize I should not have ruined something that was meant to be legitimate.

Ben Millefoglie, a web designer in Michigan, set up Litton's various sites and entered all updates to them. He told me that Litton had misled him into thinking that the West Wyoming Marathon was legitimate, adding that the racing data had been provided to him, via email, by "Richard Rodriguez."

In January 2011, Litton was disqualified from yet another race: the 2009 City of Trees Marathon, in Idaho. The following month, Hubbard extracted from Litton a promise to disclose in advance any races he entered, so that he could be monitored.

"I look forward to being monitored," he wrote, in an email to Hubbard. "I realize that this isn't absolute vindication, but it is certainly a good first step . . . I am committed to continue my goal of running marathons in every state and raising funds for my charity. In time, I believe the questions will disappear. I welcome any and all that wish to join me."

Later that month, he said, he would run the Cowtown Marathon, in Fort Worth. When the date arrived, he was missing. The afternoon before the race, he sent race officials this email: "I was in a car accident and am unable to run the marathon. Could I please have my packet and shirt sent to me? Thanks."

Whether or not a car accident occurred was of no consequence. For a few months, at least, Litton wouldn't be going anywhere in the reality-based running community. The LetsRun message board continued to simmer with sarcasm about Litton's exploits, though the ad-hominem attacks were occasionally counterbalanced by sympathetic posts. ("He is intelligent, selfless, witty, charitable, modest, caring, generous to a fault . . . Loved by his patients and adored by his friends and family.") One poster purported to be a runner as well as a nurse "at the hospital where Dr. Litton's child has been given just a short time to live." Another described a pre-dawn encounter, in which Litton had put himself through a grueling speed workout at a high school track. "Quite a Story" was the handle of someone claiming to be a journalist. After interviewing "dozens of people," the journalist had "discovered a shocking new side to this tale"—the implication being that Litton was innocent—and welcomed information from all comers. An email address was given, I wrote immediately, and I'm still waiting for a reply.

Over a period of months, I did exchange many emails with Litton, but he refused to speak or meet in person. My questions were mainly biographical or running-related. His responses were verbose, well written, and cleverly obfuscatory in a way that left little room for doubt.

Last fall, a message, posted by someone using the handle ActuallyThisIsTheWayItIs, appeared on LetsRun:

> Some of us are runners, and we fully understand how races operate. Kip has been very open about addressing accusations with us. They have all been discussed and he has provided logical and credible explanations, in many cases backed by evidence and/or witnesses. He has shared with us email correspondences with reporters and race directors that contradict posts here that pass for gospel. We are quite satisfied. We don't want to put words in his mouth but the chances are less than zero that he will personally respond on a forum where people are anonymous.

I wrote to Litton, asking whether he'd seen the post and suggesting that we "help each other." I wanted to speak with this blogger, I said, and was eager to read excerpts from the correspondence cited in the post.

Litton replied:

> No I didn't see it. How long ago was it from? I actually don't know who it is yet, but it certainly narrows it down—I'll have to check around. I will not be able to disclose any names unless it is ok with them. I will say you have piqued my curiosity—but I will not make the mistake I made many months ago when I checked out LetsRun. Engaging in negative rhetorical sparring with anonymous strangers may be entertaining for some, but it is not where I choose to spend my time.

"I am running Boston," Litton wrote to me, on March 7, 2012. "Training has been hit & miss. I have had nearly PR"—personal record—"runs mixed with times when I was unable to run at all." I assumed that "unable to run" referred to the auto-accident injury that had been his pretext for not running the Cowtown Marathon.

His only race within the 2012 Boston qualifying calendar had been the Charlotte marathon, in 2010, and attached to that performance was a bold asterisk. Nevertheless, the Boston Athletic Association, aware of Litton's problematic history, had checked with Tim Rhodes, the Charlotte race director, and been told that the result stood.

Two weeks before Boston, I asked Litton to give his expected finishing time. "If all goes well, 2:47," he wrote. "If not, a bit slower."

I planned to be in Boston, I said—two of my sons would be running—and suggested meeting. Given Litton's prior elusiveness, I was surprised when he said, "How about after, that way I can introduce you to a few people also." The odds of that happening, I suspected, were roughly zero. Still, I appreciated his gamesmanship.

Race day was Monday, April 16. For weeks, the prevailing sentiment on LetsRun had been that Litton would not show up. Yet, at some point over the weekend, either he or someone authorized by him had picked up his racing bib at the marathon's headquarters. I gleaned this from LetsRun—a runner in Boston had volunteered the information—rather than from Litton, who for several days had ignored my emails.

As with most major marathons, the size of the Boston field—more than 22,000 runners—required a staggered start. Some 200 wheelchair and elite female runners were first out of the gate, with the rest of the participants organized in "waves" and "corrals," according to their qualifying times. There were three waves, each with nine corrals of roughly 1,000 runners, and Litton had been seeded in wave one, corral two. By coincidence, so had my son Reid and a couple of other runners I knew.

Monday morning was cloudless and unseasonably hot, heading to the upper eighties. I found a seat in a shaded section of the grandstand at the finish line, and felt open to possibilities. I might be on the brink of my first live Kip Litton sighting; a flock of green flamingos might happen by. My anticipation lasted less than an hour into the men's race. I'd signed up for a mobile-phone service that offered text-messaged 10-kilometer, half-marathon, and 30-kilometer split times. After receiving 10-K results for my sons and another runner in Litton's corral, but nothing for Litton himself, I allowed a decent interval before concluding that he was most likely in Davison, Michigan, drilling teeth. A phone call to Litton's office confirmed this.

My oldest son, Jeb, who is 30, somehow made friends with the heat and ran his best marathon: just under three hours and four minutes. Reid, the faster qualifier, finished a couple of minutes behind him. Post-race, I found them in a designated meeting area across the street from the John Hancock Tower. We hung out there for an hour or so, as runners in varying states of elation and walking-woundedness wandered past, wearing ribboned medallions. This was what Litton was missing: the bonhomie and collective uplift of one of the world's great athletic events, and the rewards that come to anyone who goes the full distance and crosses the finish line—never mind how long it takes.

Eventually, Jeb and Reid's perspiration dried sufficiently to allow for an exchange of manly hugs, and then I went to catch a plane.

Shortly before eight o'clock the next morning, Litton parked his metallic-blue GMC sport-utility vehicle (vanity license plate: DDLOVER) outside his dental office. I was standing at the building entrance, and as he turned a corner I introduced myself. "No, no!" he said, and moved past me into the building. I followed him, through a glass vestibule and past the reception desk. He went inside his office and closed the door. As I was about to knock, he opened it and said to his receptionist, "Call the police. It's a trespasser." I said that I was leaving, and retreated to the Flag City Diner, down the street, where I ordered scrambled eggs and began drafting an email to Litton.

He was in a jam of his own devising, I wrote, and I wanted him to have the opportunity to explain how it had come about. He did not reply that day, but the next evening he offered to meet with me the following day, after work.

Litton chose a Wendy's a few miles from his home. Arriving before I did, he took a seat at a corner table, with his back to the wall. Hanging above the table was a framed photograph of Dave Thomas, the departed founder of Wendy's, bearing the caption "When it comes to VALUES, I've never been one to cut corners."

Litton wore a blue windbreaker over his work uniform: a black V-neck tunic, a red T-shirt, loose-fitting gray cotton pants. Tanned and clean-shaven, he had fluffy sandy-blond hair that fell across his forehead, brown eyes, and generically handsome Nordic features. Across the table, at last, was the man at the center of one of the strangest controversies in amateur sports history. Our common aspiration, I assumed, was that this conversation would yield a counternarrative to the caricature of the heinously unscrupulous Kip Litton suggested by the less genteel posters on LetsRun. In addition to "Why?," the question I most hoped Litton would answer was "How?"

He told me that he was born in 1961, the third of four children, in Royal Oak, a Detroit suburb, and moved to Grand Blanc when he was seven. His father, an engineer, worked for General Motors, and his mother was a homemaker. They were frequent churchgoers, but not devout. Summer vacations were station-wagon excursions, typically to historic sites. His adolescent cohort had not been earnest strivers—"There were a lot of kids in my neighborhood that were delinquents, normal delinquents"—but that changed after his father introduced him to tennis. ("We went out and he said, 'Hey, why don't you try this?' And he probably let me beat him, and that got me interested, like, 'Hey, I'm good.' . . . That took me away from the crowd I was with.") Academically, he was "a decent student, but I really had no direction." When a high school guidance counselor suggested dentistry, he responded that it was "the one occupation for sure that I can eliminate."

Litton arrived at the University of Michigan in 1979, planning to major in engineering. His most enduring impression was of feeling daunted by the ambitions of his dorm neighbors. "Just hanging around those people, I felt like if I wasn't going to be a neurosurgeon I would be a complete failure," he said. "I would be the least successful person—I probably still *am* the least successful person—who lived on my hall. So that inspired me to do something more with my life." Engineering, he said, had too few women majoring in it, so at the end of his sophomore year he switched to pre-dental. (If other factors had guided this career turn, he didn't mention them.)

In 1983, he matriculated at the University of Michigan Dental School, and five years later he completed his degree. At 28, he married Lisa Hoscila, whom he'd met on a blind date nine years earlier. She had a law degree and a job at a firm not far from Davison. After commuting for a few years to a dental office in Saginaw, Michigan, he joined the practice in Davison that he eventually took over. The older dentist who had started the practice supplemented his income by working as a salesman and distributor for Amway, the multilevel marketing company, and he recruited Litton. During the next several years, Litton said, his Amway income—from direct sales to consumers or to his own "30 or 40" new recruits—at times reached into the six figures, surpassing his professional income.

Amway still generated a lot of income for him, he said: "I don't want to say exactly, but in the thousands every month. And that's way down from where it was."

Throughout its existence, the company has defended itself against allegations that its marketing program is essentially a pyramid scheme; in 2010, it agreed to a $56 million settlement in a class-action suit accusing it of exactly that, along with fraud and racketeering. When I asked Litton whether he'd ever been disillusioned with Amway, he said, "No. And I know a ton of people gave it a bad rap." His wife had joined him in Amway, he said, and it made for "a nice diversion—something we could do together. She made friends in the business, I made friends in the business."

Their first child, a son, was born in 1995, followed by a daughter in 1997. When their younger son, Michael, arrived, in 2001, he immediately received a diagnosis of cystic fibrosis and remained in the hospital for weeks.

"He knows exactly what's going on with him," Litton said. "But he can't possibly understand the scope of it . . . He has to take tons of pills every day. He won't take pills in front of other people except family members. He has a feeding tube. There's a lot of breathing apparatuses he uses. And he will not do what he is supposed to do if there are people other than our family members over at the house. He just desperately wants to fit in."

To sidestep questions about various running performances, Litton often invoked his personal tribulations. Some of the indignities that he said he'd recently suffered seemed straight out of high school, circa 1977: his tires had been deflated on several occasions, his house and his mailbox had been egged, threatening and profane messages had been left in the mailbox. His family felt unsafe.

These stories reminded me of a series of messages that had been posted anonymously on LetsRun. One said:

> My wife's friend worked at Dr. Litton's office and was recently let go. She was telling my wife about all the things that have been happening recently due to the cheating scandal . . .
> In addition to his business failing, Dr. Litton's wife was so embarrassed and it caused so much strife that they have separated. His one kid got in a fight at school in response to the other kids taunting about the cheating and was suspended.

And another:

> Perfect—we have him just where we want him.
> Personal life destroyed—check. Business destroyed—check. Family destroyed—check. Kids—check. Just think what could happen if we keep the pressure on even more.

In fact, Litton and his wife were still together. And the dental practice was doing fine.

I asked Litton, "What happened in your life to get you into this situation?"

"Can you be a little more specific?"

His credibility was being seriously questioned, and the underlying facts were troubling.

"I don't know what facts you're talking about," he replied. "But the facts I've heard and seen, most of them are inaccurate."

As Lady Gaga's "Poker Face" played on the Wendy's stereo system, he elaborated: he had never deliberately done anything wrong, never left a race course and reentered at a different point, never received money through Worldrecordrun, and never posted anything on LetsRun; had no idea who the anonymous people might be who posted in his defense, and no clue who might have posed as a nurse claiming that "Dr. Litton's child has been given just a short time to live." His delayed starts, he later added, were merely part of "a marketing gimmick," on his website, to entice potential donors, who could pledge a particular sum for every runner he passed in a race. It was "a friend" who had posed online as "Richard Rodriguez"—despite the fact that Litton had used that alias in a previous race. Regarding his midrace shoe change at Deadwood: "I was doing my warm-up, and I got too far away from the starting line. As I was running back toward the starting line . . . I still had on my trainers. I couldn't get back to where my shoes were, and then back to the start of the race, so I just started the race in those shoes. And, as I ran down the race course, when I passed my shoes I stopped and swapped them out."

Throughout our discussion, his tone remained steady and uninflected. He neither frowned nor smiled, and made no attempt to ingratiate. For a teller of tales, he was oddly unbeguiling.

He acknowledged that he had been disqualified from several races, but only for unintentional infractions. He conceded only to having "been careless, not paying attention." When it came to specific disqualifications—say, the 2009 Detroit Free Press Marathon Relay, where he had cut the course so maladroitly that he wound up in front of the pace car—he offered deflection, not explanation. In a follow-up email, he said that he had taken a wrong turn, adding, "How mentally handicapped would someone have to be to think that cartoon-like scenario would work? Did your research reveal this absurdity? It's an excellent anecdote that could be reenacted for a scene in a top Hollywood comedy film."

Usually, when you interview a fabulist, there comes a moment when you can visualize his or her mental gears churning. It took a long time with Litton, but he finally rose to the challenge, and began expanding his alternate universe on the fly. Early on, when Scott Hubbard had challenged Litton about the identity of "Brian Smith"—who had written to *Michigan Runner* to extol his dentist's achievements—Litton had claimed ignorance. But when I pressed him about it he paused, then said, "Now I remember more about that! I think that guy turned out to be someone who owed me money, and was hoping I didn't pursue him, by buttering me up."

Litton told me that he had protested several disqualifications that he felt were unjust. And at Missoula in 2010, rather than being disqualified by race officials, he had disqualified himself at the finish line, informing a race official that a leg injury had forced him to take a shortcut.

"So there's no way you would have been in contention for an award at Missoula, right?" I asked.

"Right," he said. "Okay, what about it?"

I handed him copies of two emails. The first, from him to Jennifer Straughan, the race director, was sent six days after the marathon: "Hello, Very nice race. I enjoyed it immensely. I was wondering if there was any award that I missed? I had to catch a flight right after the race. Thanks. Kip Litton, M 45-49." The second was Straughan's reply, which said, in part, "In reviewing our records for the top finishers of the 2010 Missoula Marathon, we notice that you do not appear in photos along the course . . . I regret that we had to remove you from the finishers listing."

All a misunderstanding, Litton said.

The email had been sent to the director of the Missoula Marathon—what was the misunderstanding?

"Okay," he said. "But I probably got it from an email address that—I probably clicked on the wrong one or something. I don't know. Because I disqualified myself. I told them at the race that I did not run the whole race."

"Why would someone who disqualified himself ask about an award?"

"It was probably another race."

"But this was the week after Missoula."

"There were other, smaller races that I ran."

(In subsequent emails, Litton told me that he had witnesses to his self-disqualification—but none, unfortunately, who weren't members of his family, and he couldn't provide the name of a race official who would confirm his finish-line story.)

Litton never removed his jacket. At first, this made me apprehensive, as it seemed that he might at any time stand up and bolt for the exit. As the conversation dragged on, though, I became the interlocutor eager to be on his way. Litton's story could have been a small but admirable one: an out-of-shape Midwestern dentist who, on the cusp of middle age, had transformed himself into a competitive marathoner. But he had insisted on transforming himself further, inventing a heroic avatar, "Kip Litton," that couldn't be sustained. The ruse, quite possibly, had begun with a noble intention: a father's desire to be an inspiration to his youngest child, or perhaps to his entire family. (Litton's friends told me that he was a devoted husband and father.) But whatever glory he felt was surely short-lived. Not only had he become a consuming object of contempt in one of the blogosphere's more obsessive neighborhoods; his family and neighbors had learned that the online tribunal had judged him a fraud. A scenario that once might have been explained away, with self-deprecating contrition, as a foolish prank had become something much darker: the story of a man running away from himself.

One of the LetsRun sleuths' most impressive unearthings was a photograph taken near the 30-kilometer checkpoint of the 2010 Boston Marathon. It depicted six runners wearing singlets or short-sleeved shirts, their racing bibs attached, on pace for sub-three-hour performances. At the left edge of the frame, slightly cropped, was Litton. The others were clearly in brisk midstride. Litton appeared to be walking, or slowly jogging, along the shoulder of the road, and he wore a long-sleeved black shirt, black sweatpants, a black baseball cap, and shades. He had no racing bib showing. He was credited that year with a time of 2:52:12.

At Wendy's, we did not discuss the photograph. But, a few weeks later, I attached it to an email and told him, in so many words, "Gotcha." No non-elite runner in his late forties could run a 2:52:12 marathon—an average pace of 6:34 per mile—in mild weather wearing that kind of clothing. (Before the finish line, the long-sleeved shirt and sweatpants had been swapped for a T-shirt, shorts, and a different hat.) By not showing a bib mid-race, Litton was counting on not being photographed, or at least not being recognized as a race entrant. Sticking to the shoulder allowed him to get close enough for his chip to register at the 30-kilometer checkpoint.

Based upon his own track record and my interviews with Michigan runners who had competed against him, I told him, it seemed unlikely that he'd ever run a marathon in under three hours, with the possible exception of a 2:58:08 at Jacksonville in 2006. His other probably kosher performances, I figured, were Jacksonville in 2003 (3:19:57), Richmond in 2004 (3:08:14), and Boston in 2004 (3:25:06) and 2005 (3:23:23) — all entirely creditable.

My smoking gun turned out to be no such thing. In his response, Litton directed me to photographs that I'd overlooked: images of him at the 15-kilometer split.

"The bib is still underneath but I am in the middle of the road," he wrote, triumphantly and accurately. "If I was trying to 'avoid photos' or 'not be recognized as a race entrant' why would I be in the middle of the road this time between other runners?"

The online accumulation of still photographs and video footage of Litton—walking up to starting lines when the field has already taken off, his racing bib obscured, or crossing finish lines differently attired—documented the bookends of an elaborate deception. Undocumented was what happened in between. For a year and a half, Litton's scourges on LetsRun had struggled to pinpoint the specifics of his methodology. If he traveled between checkpoints by car, he must have had an accomplice—perhaps more than one. But how did they negotiate the inevitable street closings that kept traffic far from the race course? Had Litton figured out how to hack the timing system? According to professional race timers, this was impossible. Moreover, whatever category of abnormal psychology Litton might belong to, it didn't seem to be "evil genius."

Litton's profile on Athlinks listed several completed duathlons: races that combined running and biking. While Worldrecordrun was still extant, it had a page where he reported his annual mileage totals for both running and biking. (He owned a Felt bike.) So a bicycle it surely was. But where were *those* photographs? No matter what Litton's connection might have been to the anonymous posters who defended him online, his pursuers were confounded and exasperated most by what remained unsaid. It came down to this: at the Boston Marathon, the oldest, most prestigious, and most professionally managed event on the American racing calendar, Litton had hit every split, changed his clothes along the way, and broken three hours. No one but Litton could say how he did it.

The marathon, no matter where it takes place, remains, as ever, a solitary pursuit in which every runner ultimately competes

against himself or herself. Whatever drove Kip Litton was an entirely different battle with himself, one that quite possibly escaped
his understanding. One thing, though, he grasped perfectly. Like
the most dazzling of magicians or the most artful of art forgers, by
withholding the secret of how the illusion worked he retained a
power uniquely his own: the spoils of his humiliation, perhaps, but
a knowledge that no one was about to take away.

DAN KOEPPEL

Redemption of the Running Man

THE SUN SETS on the most distant horizon I've ever seen, dropping away from what had seemed—all day—like a flat and feature-
less earth. One week ago, this dusty plain contained nothing but
promise: of triumph, adventure, even justice. If those things were
ever real, they've burned away in the desert heat, along with the
soles of my feet—scorched through my shoes by searing asphalt—
and my lips, so singed and scabbed that pressing them to a water
bottle makes me wince in pain. I've got nothing left. I can't go on.
But I have to. Even if my mind and body want to stop, I won't. This
is the run I've spent a decade waiting to do, and the wait has been
more tortuous than the run. I need to finish it, no matter what.

Australia's Nullarbor Plain is traversed by a stretch of road—the
only road, 1,663 miles long—between the southern cities of Ad-
elaide and Perth. The plain is bordered on the south by more than
a hundred miles of cliffs that tower above the Southern Ocean.
North, there's cracked and crusted desert—the Down Under
equivalent of America's Death Valley. Nullarbor means "no trees,"
but the region's dryness and distances also mean nearly no people. Physically, the Nullarbor is almost twice as big as the state of
Florida; but the vast region is so sparsely inhabited that no official
population records are kept.

However, the two-lane Eyre (pronounced "Air") Highway is
busy. Traversing the plain is the iconic Aussie road trip. Camper
vans and cars pulling trailers dart between massive, triple-loader
trucks known in this part of the world as road trains. Vehicle travelers are supported by a series of "roadhouses," spaced anywhere

from 45 to 125 miles apart, which offer gas, car repair, food, and dormitory-style accommodations. (Running a roadhouse is lonely but rewarding; the gas station at Penong is said to possess the most profitable petrol pumps in the world, and the mechanic's shop at Nundroo is Australia's most lucrative.) Completing the drive earns the traveler an I CROSSED THE NULLARBOR bumper sticker, emblazoned with images of wombats and camels (the latter now feral after being introduced to the region in the 19th century).

Those vehicles speed by me in air-conditioned bliss. Their gusting wakes are welcome, suctioning away flies and the persistent odor of roadkill kangaroo. My goal is to run the heart of the Nullarbor—the loneliest, driest, emptiest 200 miles at the plain's center. I've got two weeks.

One might think that to cross a place so formidable under one's own power would lead to acclaim, but history shows it is just as likely that you'll be ridiculed, or disbelieved, or worse. Edward John Eyre made the first east-west traverse in 1841; his partner, John Baxter, perished en route. Arthur Mason survived his 1896 journey only by eating his pet dog. That same decade, Henri Gilbert faced dehydration and injuries to his feet, according to his diaries. The truth is hard to tell, because at some point following his apparent arrival at the plain's eastern terminus, Gilbert vanished, never completing the planned global circumnavigation he'd begun several years earlier (and thus never collecting the reward—equal to about half a million current U.S. dollars—he'd been promised by wealthy backers for doing so).

I was following in a more modern—but equally infamous—set of footsteps. A century after Gilbert, a British runner named Robert Garside also attempted to circle the globe on foot. But Garside disappeared too; not physically—he returned to his starting point unharmed—but via an angry incredulity that led him to be seen not as a trailblazer but as a fraud. I was here because I'd doubted Garside, and in my journalistic expression of that had helped instigate a media lynch mob that contributed to the destruction of his reputation. And of all the places Garside ran, those who didn't find him credible argued, the Nullarbor—the impossible, wasted, torrid Nullarbor—was where some of Garside's biggest lies played out.

But Robert Garside *did* run the Nullarbor. At least that's what I'd come to believe after an encounter with the runner in London a year after he finished his journey. And I realized that in the attacks I'd joined, one of the most incredible things a runner had ever done—run around the world—was wiped out. Almost eight years on foot erased because I and other journalists had been too willing to believe somebody else's definition of what a real runner is, and decided that Robert Garside couldn't possibly be one.

So now, I want to make amends. I want to prove that running this place is possible. And when I do, I hope the remorse that has haunted me for almost a decade will burn away. I wasn't running alone. My friend Morgan Beeby had joined me. We'd trained for months in Los Angeles, developing a strategy to address the lack of water, the great heat, the vast distances. But our confidence had been shaken from the moment we'd arrived in Australia. In Sydney, we'd heard ominous talk of murdered vagabonds. We were warned, repeatedly, to bring a satellite phone (we didn't). In Ceduna, at the plain's eastern edge, we stayed in a reeking-of-cigarettes house trailer, the owner of which, after hearing our plan and collecting $10 rent, instantly pegged me: "You," he said, without a single hint from us, "must have something to atone for."

Robert George Garside was born on January 6, 1967, in Stockport, England, a suburb of Manchester, part of an industrial region that sprawls along the banks of the Mersey River. He grew up playing many sports—a self-described "all-rounder"—but especially loved soccer and was captain of his school team. Garside's parents divorced when he was a teenager, and his mother returned to her native Slovakia. He says he developed a need to travel almost as a way to follow his own mother, who—in exiting a difficult relationship with the runner's father—had finally found a sense of contentment. "I remember the day she left," Garside says. "She was so happy, leaving all that stuff behind." The joy and freedom of that escape, Garside says, is what gave birth to his own inner wanderlust. "[I wanted to see] the world because it's a way of understanding things," he says. But accomplishing that goal seemed elusive; instead, Garside says, he was haunted by a "sense of aimlessness."

As a child, he says, he ran and played in the woods near his house, in "a huge forest stretching for miles. I had some of my best times there when I was a kid." Beginning to run as a young adult, he says, brought him back to that state. "You have a good experience as a kid," he says, "and it affects the rest of your life."

Despite this, Garside felt that his future was uncertain. He was at "a crossroads," he says, and looking for a "way forward." In 1993, at that point a psychology student at the University of London's Royal Holloway College (and a volunteer with the City of London police), he found it. Garside was thumbing through a copy of *The Guinness Book of Records* (during a "rare visit to the library," he jokes) and came across the story of Dave Kunst, an American who—from 1970 through 1974—walked around the world. Garside wondered if anyone had ever tried it at a runner's pace. He contacted Guinness, which informed him that no such record existed. "That's when I knew what I was going to be," he says. Garside quit school and began training. He planned a route and lined up sponsors, dubbing himself "The Runningman."

In December 1995, Garside boarded a plane to South Africa. From Cape Town, he started running north, to Namibia. His plan was to curve up the western coast of Africa, fly north to Spain, and turn east at the Mediterranean. But the run sputtered out at around 1,000 miles. Garside says he was unprepared for the difficulties of the actual journey, especially the complications it created with his girlfriend, Joanna, whom he left behind in London. In March 1996, he returned home.

Over the next few months, Garside planned a new route that would take him from London, east through Europe—he could better stay in touch with Joanna, he says—and then into Russia. He'd veer south and work his way across Asia, then traverse Australia and the Americas lengthwise before returning to Europe. Garside departed London on December 7, 1996. This time, there was fanfare, media coverage, and a Greenpeace sponsorship. "It felt good," he says, "to be a star."

The runner's next decisions—more than anything else he'd do—would lead to the staining of his record, which would in turn foment outrage in the media and the running world. That outrage would peak over three years later as Garside, behind schedule and running a greatly modified route, crossed the United States.

Garside posted his proposed trajectory online, and was making entries in a web diary as often as he could (it was the early days of the Internet, and access was spotty). He arrived in Slovakia, where he was reunited with his mother, in January. But there Garside stalled, again preoccupied with his crumbling relationship back in London. He says he'd planned for the break to be brief—Guinness allowed pauses of up to 30 days for injury or moving from one land mass to another—but as the weeks wore on, the runner began to falsify his diaries. In early September 1997, Garside's online diaries offered a harrowing but fictional account of an attack in Pakistan: "I was robbed," he wrote, "my tent slashed with a knife." Garside says his biggest fear—driven by near-constant media coverage of his adventures—was that somebody else would set out and beat him by taking a more direct route. (The Kunst record of 14,452 miles bypassed Africa and South America.) Garside wanted to traverse every continent. "I wanted to see the world," he says, by going "the long way, not the short way. But I didn't want other people to beat me. If they knew I was having trouble, everything could go down the drain."

To himself, though, Garside had to admit that this run, like the first, had failed: he'd already stopped longer than Guinness would permit. But by the fall of 1997, Garside was ready to start a third attempt. The relationship with Joanna had ended, and it was a relief to Garside. "She wanted me to get on with my life," he says. By then, however, the run *was* Garside's life. His third version of the quest would be done with less fanfare and limited sponsorship; his plan was to start in New Delhi, India, and find local support wherever he could, keeping the effort low-key. This strategy meant less pressure on him. But there was one ticking bomb: the online diaries of his second attempt, which Garside had not taken down. The runner's made-up tales of danger and deprivation in the Hindu Kush would be repeated in most media accounts of his journey; each repetition would cement the accounts as central to the run's narrative.

There would be genuine danger and adventure ahead. But on October 20, 1997, as he left New Delhi, running toward China, Robert Garside had no idea that the biggest threat to his run would be borne of his own past actions.

What does it mean to run around the world? Give the idea a moment's thought, and you'll soon conclude that it is unimaginable, perhaps impossible. The task shares little with ultramarathoning, or even a record attempt across a great—but defined—distance or time span. One term proposed for open-ended efforts like Garside's is "journey run," and that's a good start. In such an effort, speed is unimportant; instead, there's a sort of strategic arcana. How does one define "around the world"? The criteria are a subject of debate among organizations that certify circumnavigations. Do you need to cross each continent? Is there a minimum mileage that should be required? Garside's conditions, supplied by Guinness, mandated that he travel a total distance that exceeded the length of the Tropic of Capricorn—almost 23,000 miles—cross the equator at least once, and start and finish at the same place. The record-keeping organization also set, in advance, the standards of evidence Garside would have to meet. Logbooks with official witness statements were to be the primary means of documentation, along with photographs and video—and, in a nod to the senselessness inherent in any such effort (as well as difficulty defining exactly what "running" is), Guinness noted that "the strategy employed in covering the distance is up to the participant . . . there are no minimum running distances each day."

The structural challenges involved in completing—and proving—a journey run were what initially attracted the person who would become Garside's primary nemesis, a Canadian distance-running enthusiast named David Blaikie. During the time of Garside's efforts, Blaikie wielded huge influence via his now-defunct website, Ultramarathonworld.com. At first, Blaikie viewed Garside with a sort of removed skepticism. But over time, Blaikie came to believe the runner was a fraud. He became a primary source for journalists (including me) writing about Garside. Blaikie's reporting was obsessive and meticulous; page after page dissected every element of Garside's effort, including the runner's route; his media claims; his qualifications; his physical and emotional state; even his social life. Between 1998 and 2000, Blaikie's doubts shifted toward certainty: Garside was a fake. Ultramarathonworld.com's coverage of the runner often resembled a prosecution, and one of Blaikie's key exhibits was the Nullarbor. Garside had arrived in Perth, Australia, on August 13, 1998—he'd traveled from India through China to Japan over the previous eight months—and set out from the Nullarbor's westernmost roadhouse, at Balladonia, on September 14. Less than four weeks later, Garside claimed, he arrived at Ceduna.

Blaikie believed none of this. In an article titled "Analysis of Run Across Australia—Very Long and Carefully Documented,"

Blaikie implied that nobody could accomplish a solo foot-crossing of the desert expanse: "Where did he get the 12 litres of water a day he says he required in hot conditions? Roadhouses along the Nullarbor are up to 190 km apart, and there are no rivers, lakes, streams, or puddles to drink from."

Good question, if you haven't crossed the Nullarbor, if you're reading about it or forming a thesis based on maps that depict nothing but barrenness. From an armchair, it is absolutely impossible to run the Nullarbor. Once you're out there, however, there is a way. Robert Garside discovered it. So would I.

Garside didn't detail his "method" for running the Nullarbor as he crossed the plain. Instead, his online diaries were filled with anecdotes and snapshots; he was having fun, literally hitting his stride. He was getting what he wanted out of running: "I like to be out in the wilderness—that's more in keeping with who I am." But there were also the social interactions. "I like the world," he says. "[I like] the people." Garside had found a girlfriend in Australia—a young medical student named Lucy McKinnon—and was getting ready for what he believed was the most important leg of his journey: the Americas. Garside's plan was to fly from Sydney, Australia, to Chile, and run north, all the way to the United States. The runner's planned route from there was to hug the Pacific through San Francisco, then turn east to New York, but he had a key stop to make: Hollywood. There, Garside thought, fame and riches awaited.

It wasn't going to happen. In early 2000, Garside was in Venezuela, where he met and fell in love with another woman, Endrina Perez, who then accompanied him for much of the rest of his run (and whom he would later marry). But in May, soon after he left Caracas, the simmering conflict with Blaikie became personal. In his introduction to a reposted wire-service story, Blaikie, increasingly strident, wrote: "The accounts are awash in strong prose about the dangers he faces but not much about his actual running." On May 15, Garside responded with a series of angry emails. Calling Blaikie a "mummies' boy," the Briton wrote: "Running is supposed to be a positive thing BUT the only criticism I have EVER had in the past five years is from YOU." Blaikie's reaction was to finally pronounce Garside an outright fraud: "I can't accept his claims," the Canadian retorted. "There is too much . . . to swallow at face value. And a thorough review of the diaries and press releases . . . only drives the point home."

Blaikie's tactics moved from written skepticism to near provocation; he began posting letters from his readers who sought "The Runningman" out to test him on the road. A typical challenge came from a Louisiana attorney who offered to pay Garside to compete in the Ultracentric 48-Hour Track Run, scheduled for November of that year in Dallas. The wording of the invitation, published on Blaikie's website, showed how ugly the dispute had become: "Should be a piece of cake considering your accomplishments to date," the lawyer wrote. "I'll have to warn you, though, no 'mummies' boys.' . . . only the laps you run, walk, or crawl will be counted." Garside ignored the solicitation.

On September 1, 2000, Robert Garside crossed from Mexico into southern California. TV crews recorded the event. Wearing a sombrero, the runner talked excitedly about his adventure, his plans. He had no idea that everything was about to come apart.

I met Garside by accident. I'd been assigned to write a story about another long-distance daredevil—a 19-year-old from Truckee, California, who was attempting to become the first person to skateboard across the United States. The skater had briefly traveled with Garside. A person trying to run around the world would make for a good magazine article, and when my preliminary research led me to Blaikie and Garside's likely fraudulence, the piece I was contemplating became even juicier.

The evidence against Garside seemed clear. He'd refused all chances to prove himself. And if Blaikie's reconstruction of Garside's route was correct, then The Runningman would be the fastest ultrarunner ever, faster even than runners competing on closed courses. As shaped by Blaikie, Garside's claims seemed beyond outlandish: the runner, clearly, was delusional.

Garside didn't help himself. He was the running equivalent of an NBA trash-talker, answering bluster with bluster. (In September 2000, he told the Associated Press: "I started out with $30, and I'm going to end up with $30 million. I guarantee it.")

In recounting all this, I made a classic journalistic mistake. David Blaikie seemed credible, so I didn't question either his methods or motives. Blaikie—who'd described himself as a "former journalist" and who'd earlier in his career worked as a political reporter on Parliament Hill—built a perfect campaign against Garside. When the runner left a series of angry voice-mails, Blaikie printed them verbatim. When somebody popped up to defend Garside, Blaikie's online commentary was crafted respectfully, but was ultimately dismissive.

But even all that might not have been enough to condemn Robert Garside. Then, on February 11, 2001, a bombshell dropped. Garside—by then halfway across the United States—admitted in a story written by Nic Fleming and James McDonald, printed in London's *Sunday Express* newspaper, that he'd falsified his 1997 diaries. It didn't matter that the incident occurred as part of an abortive attempt. Here it was: Robert Garside was a liar, and because he was a liar, nothing he did afterward would have credibility. My story, published in the November/December 2001 issue of the now-defunct *National Geographic Adventure,* was headlined, simply: "The Running Scam." By that time Garside says his sponsorships had dried up, and any company or media outlet that seemed to be contemplating an association got calls and emails from angry ultrarunners. *Good Morning America* canceled an announced appearance after receiving protests.

There's a philosophical question here, and like most philosophical questions, there's no clear answer: does Robert Garside's lie in 1997 disqualify him? In 2001, I thought so, and so did much of the running community. What I didn't notice (but should have) was that the dynamic between Blaikie and Garside had become so poisonous that an alternate point of view—that Garside was flawed and maddening at times, but the real deal—never even came up, and that the attacks against him simply weren't fair. Why not wait until he was finished, when he could submit his evidence? Why the attempts to destroy him? Garside was being prosecuted for not running around the world before he'd even run around the world. In March 2001, the runner, broken and almost broke, left the United States for South Africa. "I had to go on," he later told me, "but I didn't know how."

I cashed my check and congratulated myself for playing a role in guarding the purity of the sport. (I even wrote a second piece, for a media business blog, describing how the runner had fooled the press; Blaikie reprinted it on his website.) But I'd failed to ask a basic question: if Garside was faking it, what had he been doing during all the time he'd spent? Nobody—not me, not the other reporters who called Garside a fraud—had an answer for that. And as I would learn, when I finally got the chance to see the evidence, he'd clearly been to all the places he claimed to have been—and he'd moved at a runner's pace.

Robert Garside arrived in South Africa in spring 2001. He headed north, planning to skirt the shores of the Indian Ocean. His goal was to reach the Middle East. But the attacks of September 11, 2001, changed all that. Garside, still in South Africa, continued running into Mozambique, but when he got to the Malawi border, he says, he was denied entry.

The journey was at the breaking point. Around the world, national frontiers were closing. He wasn't sure how—or if—he could cross the Middle East; he was exhausted and almost out of money. Garside had always planned to run the long way across every continent. But the Guinness guidelines didn't require it. So Garside flew to Morocco. He crossed the Strait of Gibraltar, and spent most of 2002 traversing Europe along the Mediterranean. He finished this leg in Antalya on the southern coast of Turkey in the fall of 2002.

Determined to make an African traverse, though one wasn't required, Garside next flew to Cairo, Egypt. There were two false starts: first a run south along the Nile River, and a second after flying to Eritrea to run along its coast. Troubled by the dangers of crossing war-torn Sudan and frustrated at the prospect of having land gaps along his course, Garside decided to reprise his route that ended in 2001. He returned to the Mozambique-Malawi border and ran southeast to Beira, Mozambique, on the sea. He could draw a straight line, on his Africa map, from the Atlantic to the Indian Ocean, by connecting the run from Cape Town.

This terrestrial hopscotching might strike some as not entirely legitimate; but other round-the-world efforts, including Kunst's—the Guinness-certified walk that inspired Garside—skipped continents entirely. Garside *did* cross Africa by running from Cape Town, on the Atlantic, to Mozambique, on the Indian Ocean. He then flew to Mumbai and took a train to Kanyakumari, at the southern tip of India, in early April 2003. He ran north; in two months, he covered approximately 1,500 miles. He arrived at New Delhi—his revised starting point—on June 13, 2003. The finish was covered by the British press, but there was hardly a single account that didn't list the runner's effort as, at the very least, tainted, if not entirely open to question.

Even in disbelieving Robert Garside, I thought he'd done something amazing. He'd claimed to have covered about 40,000 miles. What I marveled at was not Garside's supposed achievement, but the extent—the commitment, the *years*—of his fabrication. If he was a fraud, he was the greatest fraud ever. I wondered if he might be ready to admit that. In Brazil, he let himself be photographed with Ronnie Biggs, who'd participated in the biggest train robbery in British history—1963's "Great Train Robbery," which netted the equivalent of almost $53 million current U.S. dollars. After being captured, Biggs escaped from jail and spent three decades living well and publicly in Brazil, becoming a popular anti-hero. (He even contributed vocals to a Sex Pistols album.) If he couldn't convince people he'd run the globe, I thought, maybe Garside could find a side door into fame by detailing his eight-year fabrication.

In early 2004, I contacted Robert Garside. I told him I wanted to hear his story. He refused. I persisted. "I'm going to fly to London," I told him. I named a meeting place. If the runner didn't show up, I promised, I'd never bother him again. Two weeks later, at a Starbucks in the city's Kensington district, Robert Garside appeared. He'd gained weight since the run had ended, and he looked nervous. (I was too.) We talked for 10 cautious minutes, long enough to agree to meet the next day. It wasn't really a shock, over the next week, to discover that I liked Robert Garside. (His ability to charm, his opponents said, was a talent he used to obscure his lies.) What surprised me was Garside's openness. Everything I asked for, he delivered. I became the only person, up until that point, to gain full access to his logbooks, records, photographs, and travel documents.

For the first time, I understood the misery the assault against Garside had inflicted. His struggle had been blown to bits by what he saw as an angry mob. "Of course I'm crazy," he said. "Why wouldn't I be crazy? After being harassed for years, I'm very crazy. As crazy as anyone else after being harassed, but I don't have a clinical condition."

The intensity of those attacks bordered on stalking, something I confirmed when I later contacted folks who really had accompanied Garside. David Walker, owner of a microbrewery near Santa Barbara, California, shadowed Garside as he ran the Pacific coast of the United States. Walker says he saw the runner cover 60 miles in a single day, whose primary highlights were the multiple ambushes he experienced along the way. "At one point," Walker told me, "somebody literally jumped from the bushes. He said he was a 2:30 marathoner, and kept pushing Robert to run faster and faster. Finally, Robert just sat down at the side of the road and ignored him. He just refused to say anything or even move for 15 minutes."

But I also understood the romance, the magic, that Garside must have experienced. In our conversations, Garside would sometimes trail into a stream of consciousness: "Midnight in Tibet, 4,700 meters at a peak," he mused over a beer, "the top of this mountain, with the moon shining in your eyes. It's a real journey." Then, snapping back to reality, he concluded: "Normal life? I don't like it. I don't like it." (He was also funny. When I asked him about why he decided to visit Ronnie Biggs, he laughed: "[Because] he's on the run and so am I!")

On the last day of my visit, Garside allowed me to borrow his evidence—an entire suitcase's worth—and make copies. As I stood in a FedEx Kinko's not far from Piccadilly Circus, the runner's 1996 start point, the first hints of what would bring me to the Nullarbor appeared. Maybe Robert Garside did run around the world. And if he did, I screwed him. I screwed one of the greatest runners ever.

For the next year, I stayed in constant contact with Garside. I'd persuaded this magazine to assign me a story tentatively titled "The Confessions of Robert Garside." As my deadline approached and passed, I still hadn't told my editors that what I was really doing was not detailing the lies of a fraud, but proving that Garside truly did circle the world.

I'd reconstructed Garside's run and found that Blaikie's extrapolations didn't add up. His basic technique was to combine various scraps of time-based evidence—news accounts, direct diary entries by Garside, and the file modification dates in the code underlying Garside's website—to reconstruct the runner's route using a global atlas. I didn't necessarily see Blaikie's methodology as illegitimate, but it was by no means authoritative. I had the real data: Garside's passport stamps and logbooks. I made over 100 overseas phone calls. Many witnesses didn't remember Garside, but of those who did, none said he was anything but a dedicated runner. Walker, the brewery owner, ran alongside Garside for 20 miles, then followed him in a car for another 40. The runner's average pace, Walker says, was 8.5 minutes per mile. The next day, Walker told me, Garside ran 30 miles over the steep San Marcos Pass, just north of Santa Barbara, at a similar pace. "He was the real deal," Walker says. "I can't be any more positive. He just ticks differently than other people."

I was able to confirm that Garside ran in places arguably more inhospitable than the Nullarbor. I found witnesses who saw him run up the Atlantic coast of Argentina and into Brazil; who saw him in Tingri, a Tibetan town that's often used as a staging point for Everest attempts. Garside claimed to have been arrested in China. I had copies of the police paperwork, and a friend translated them. The runner's story panned out.

Blaikie also had challenged Garside's background, noting repeatedly that there was no evidence Garside had ever completed a public run of any distance. His refusal to submit credentials was further evidence of deception. But Garside saw it differently: "How could I? He was there on his sofa at home. I was in the middle of nowhere." I was able to quickly confirm three Garside marathons in 1994. And he'd done well. In April, he finished the London Marathon in 3:01. On September 18, he placed 41st in the Brussels Marathon, pulling a 2:48. Less than 10 days later, on September 25, he clocked 3:10 in Amsterdam.

When I asked Garside why he didn't respond to the attacks by taking the high road, accepting even one challenge to prove himself, he told me that the level of vitriol had convinced him that anything he did would end up being used against him. This had turned out to be true. About two weeks after his return to London, Garside was dared by the host of a British television show to run 130 miles in 24 hours. The run took place on the 400-meter track at London's Kingsmeadow Athletics Centre. After 14 hours and 72 miles, Garside quit. In an article published on Blaikie's site, Ian Champion—a British race organizer—wrote: "If Robert Garside was no better organized during his alleged road running through isolated, barren countries than he was during his . . . 24-hour run, then I cannot believe he has run around the world."

But Garside says that the assumption that running on the track is the same as running cross-country is mistaken. "I'd never run in circles like that," Garside says. "The whole situation was demoralizing and humiliating." And nobody, he complained, gave him credit for the 72 miles he did complete. When I asked Champion about that later, he softened his opinion: "I think if he trained for it," Champion told me, "Garside could be a good runner." Was it possible that Garside's "failure," with his mind and body in a state of collapse and exhaustion, in a milieu unlike any he'd ever faced, was situational? "Yes," Champion admitted.

When I met with him in London, Garside told me he was afraid to submit his materials to *The Guinness Book of Records*. A British ultrarunning statistician named Andy Milroy had founded an organization called The Association of Road Race Statisticians. (Blaikie provided Canadian statistics to the organization.) Milroy was on Guinness's advisory committee for ultrarunning records, and already he and Blaikie had shown how powerful their influence over the records organization was. About a decade earlier, they'd brought into question an 11,134-mile run around the perimeter of the United States by a North Carolina woman named Sarah Fulcher. A Guinness editor told me that after Milroy's inquiries, which were based on an article by Blaikie, the record had been "rested," a sort of Guinness-speak version of shunning: a rested mark still stands officially, but it is not promoted or published.

When I read a story Blaikie wrote about Fulcher, I was struck by the way he compiled personal information about her, citing observers who noted her social behavior—Fulcher liked to party, the story implied—and questioning whether such behavior made her a fit runner. Blaikie had done the same thing with Robert Garside. As Garside ran across Australia, he was joined by McKinnon, the medical student who provided an eyewitness account of the runner's final weeks in her country; she rode alongside him on a bicycle for 870 kilometers. On his website, Blaikie detailed Garside's involvement with McKinnon, seeming to disapprove of the extra few weeks the runner spent in the company of a woman. "Most likely he simply wanted to enjoy himself," Blaikie wrote, "which it seems he did, because it was at about this time that he met and became involved with Lucy." In an emailed response that Blaikie also posted online, McKinnon—who has become a minor adventure celebrity in her own right; she's the on-set doctor for the television show *Survivor*—angrily vouched for her former boy-friend: "You will be hard-pressed to prove that Robert is anything but a motivated, hard-working, driven, and honest man. I have no doubts in my mind that he will [do what he claims to be doing] despite what appears to be a . . . jealous bunch of people who call themselves ultramarathon runners."

The "right" kind of ultrarunner, Blaikie told me, was someone like Al Howie, who ran across Canada in 1991 over 72 days; according to Blaikie, Howie's run was meticulously organized, with a support vehicle, constant medical attention, and a strict regimen of massage, nutrition, and fluid replenishment. But Fulcher—whom I reached in North Carolina, where she now works at an animal shelter—says she represented a different kind of long-distance runner: one who does it out of the tradition of adventure rather than competitive athletics. "The real test is personality and character," Fulcher says. "That's what drives you to do something special. What David Blaikie will never understand is that talent is important, but the answer to everything is the journey itself." After her record was rested by Guinness, Fulcher says, she became withdrawn, finding it difficult to cope with the destruction of her own life's work. "I was in tears," Fulcher says. "This man went after somebody he'd never met, never looked in my eyes." Fulcher recovered, joining the U.S. Army's 82nd Airborne Division, doing 42 combat parachute jumps; she resumed her running career and did 10-milers and triathlons for the Army. She remains, however, a nonpublished entity at Guinness.

I believe that David Blaikie thought Robert Garside was a fraud, and I believe Blaikie was defending a sport he loved. I also believe that Blaikie's expectations of ultrarunners—as much as anything Robert Garside did or said—influenced his condemnation of the Briton's entire effort, and that the acrimony between the two men so heated the atmosphere that what might have been a simple dispute turned into a protracted feud. I put this hypothesis directly to Blaikie, and he denied it; he said that his work was fair and objective, and that he was simply raising questions about Robert Garside.

I wrote my story for *Runner's World* vindicating him.

But it never got published. Reading back on it, I can see that I had gotten it right—but the piece was a mess. I sounded like a conspiracy theorist. When my editors asked me to rewrite it, I saw

the request as an effort to soften my assertions. (This wasn't the
case; I'd lost perspective.) I refused. Only by telling the story my
way—written from inside a rabbit hole—could I redeem Robert
Garside.

And so, I couldn't redeem Garside at all.

I'd failed him—I'd screwed him—again.

I lost touch with Robert Garside after that. The runner eventually
did submit his records to Guinness, and—like me, and like anyone
who'd actually seen the documentation—the book's editors concluded that the run was genuine. "I have approved many records,
and this record had an astronomical amount of evidence, and it
could be cross-checked, so we are happy and satisfied," Marco Fri-
gatti, Guinness's then head of records, told *The Telegraph* in 2007.

But when I received my copy of that year's record book, there
was no sign of Garside. Nor was there in 2008, 2009, 2010, or 2011.
The organization's database, which contains more than 40,000
records, returns a null result when the name "Garside" is searched
for. I couldn't see this being a mere oversight: circumnavigation—
if you judge by the prominence the organization gives such efforts
in its annual editions—is a very popular Guinness record category.

Had Garside's record, like Fulcher's, been blotted out by being "rested"? My contact at Guinness had moved on, and the organization's new policy, I was told, was not to comment on such
things. But I kept at it, and in late 2010—perhaps I'd worn them
down—Guinness spokesperson Sara Wilcox confirmed that Garside, despite the recognition, hadn't ever and would likely never
appear in any Guinness publication, or even on the organization's
massive web database. "This record is rested," Wilcox wrote me
in an email. "When Robert Garside completed the run, Guinness
World Records carefully checked all documentation and evidence,
and there was nothing to suggest the record wasn't true; however,
with these records it is almost impossible to be absolutely sure, and
so the category was rested."

I felt indignant. The *Guinness Book* contains other records that
can't be absolutely verified—claims of longevity, for example, are
notoriously porous. Though the organization wouldn't confirm
whether anyone had lobbied for the retirement of the Garside
category, I wondered if the runner's opponents had triumphed
again. And I wondered how Robert Garside felt. I tried to contact

him, but he'd vanished—emails to the addresses I had bounced back to me. Phone numbers were disconnected.

Garside had met with another betrayal, this time not by me, but I was the one who was going to do something about it. David Blaikie asserted that running the Nullarbor alone was virtually impossible.

So that's where I decided to go.

My strategy for the Nullarbor was based on an email I'd gotten from Garside years earlier. In it, he wrote: "I was able to play the passing traffic to my advantage. If I needed water, it was there. If I needed to stop, I could choose a road sign and log off there, and then go to another place to sleep. In this way, it wasn't hard at all. No tougher than anywhere else."

So there it was: Garside sometimes commuted between start and stop points by hitchhiking. At first, this disconcerted me—but it made sense; without doing so, the runner would have had to simply collapse at his end point every day, curl up in a ball, and sleep there.

Garside's documentation and photo diary suggest that even when this primary tactic failed, the relative frequency of traffic on the Nullarbor made the logistics of the run less pressing. Beeby and I learned that on our fourth day, after we arrived at the Nundroo Roadhouse. The longest "uninhabited" stretch of our journey— nearly 90 miles—was to follow. Earlier, we'd persuaded a couple in a caravan to forward-drop our supplies at 10-mile intervals up the road. We reached our first cache as evening fell. Beeby found a sheltered spot off the road; we pitched our tents and pried open the cans of beans and tuna the travelers stowed for us.

It wasn't a calm night. Venomous snakes are common to the region, and it isn't unknown to find one, in the morning, warming itself inside your shoe or underneath the floor of your tent. An unexpected and brief thunderstorm had turned the red dirt of our campsite to sticky clay, and we emerged from the brush filmy and soaked.

The next morning's pace was good. Beeby took a lead, and I told him to keep going; we'd meet at the next food drop. Soon I could barely see him against the horizon. After 10 brisk miles, though, his figure loomed larger. He was stopped, standing by the side of the road. Cache number two had been destroyed. The gallon-sized water jugs were empty. Even the cans of food were scattered; our gear bags were torn open. Wild dogs, most likely, we speculated.

Beeby and I quickly calculated our reserves. Beeby is a scientist—he spends all day looking into an electron microscope—and one of the reasons I asked him to come along is that I trust his rational and sober judgment. "We've got enough," he said. "Even if we're all alone for the next 20 miles."

But we weren't alone, and couldn't be. Bob Bongiorno, manager of the Balladonia Roadhouse, told me that he remembered Garside. "We looked after him for a couple of days," he said. "And we saw him run. We took him to his start point each day for a few days, then picked him up, and gave him a bed to sleep in." We were cradled in that typical Australian friendliness an hour later, when a car stopped in front of us. "I heard about you," the driver said, presenting us with two bottles of fresh orange juice—the best I've ever tasted—and an unopened can of insect repellent. Robert Garside's diary contained a similar account, and in person, he told me, "The key to running the Nullarbor turned out to be Australian hospitality."

My body was breaking down. Blisters had erupted along my heels and toes. My right pinky toe had split open, becoming infected, soaking my sock with blood. The ball of my left foot had also become swollen with fluid, feeling as if it was trying to burst out of my shoe. And an ominous blood clot seemed to be spreading beneath my heel, creating a stain that expanded with every step. I wanted to stop. What was I trying to prove? *Let it go,* I said to myself, *and you can go home right now.*

Beeby made me continue. It wasn't about proving something; it wasn't about Robert Garside. It was about, simply, choosing to run. No buses or trains are accessible from the Eyre Highway. The nearest rail line is more than 60 miles of untracked desert to the north. We'd arranged for a ride to Perth, but our pickup point was days—and miles—away. Unless we wanted to quit entirely and resort to hitching, there was nothing left to do but run, to move—slowly, if I had to, but keep moving—along the longest straight road on the planet, into a sun that seemed never to budge at all, at least until the very end of the day, when, in a heartbeat, it plunged below the horizon.

It was in that perfectly still sun, somehow, that I found my own stillness. It came after we passed the Yalata Roadhouse—abandoned at the time of my visit, but thriving when Garside visited. I'd felt a disheartening rush as we approached the ruined outpost; I'd hoped for cold drinks, but as we passed, I simply gazed forward and kept moving. What sensations I felt, over the next three days, were fleeting, almost tidal: the whoosh of a truck; the rhythm of my feet on gravel. I'd come out of my haze and realize, for a moment, that I'd been counting my footfalls, and that I'd been whispering the numbers, then fall back under the spell.

We were close to the sea now. Milky-white dunes rose at the road's southern edge. We detoured away from the highway to peer at the cliffs that tower above the Southern Ocean. I was told that a century ago, explorers attempting to cross the expanse watched helplessly—and sometimes starved or died of thirst—as vessels below signaled but were unable to effect a rescue. The palisades of the Nullarbor remain unclimbable to this day.

But the plain itself can be run. We returned to the road and decided we'd done enough for the day. We thumbed forward to the Nullarbor Roadhouse, which sits at the tail end of the plain's most barren, overheated section. At the roadhouse dorm, Beeby filled a plastic bin with ice and ordered me to plunge my feet in.

I kept them submerged as long as I could, pulled them out, waited, and did it again, and again. Finally, I wrapped everything in a towel and slept. The next morning, we woke up early. Word had spread, and at breakfast, our waiter hurried us along: "The fresh air is beautiful today," he boomed. "Boys, go stretch your legs!"

And we did. We got a ride back to the mile marker we'd finished at the day before, and began our final stretch: 15 miles by my GPS log, which we covered in just over four hours. It wasn't pretty, but it was fast enough, especially the last kilometer. One mile beyond the roadhouse is the sign marking the terminus of the Nullarbor's most intense segment, and the end of our journey: NULLARBOR PLAIN: WESTERN END OF TREELESS PLAIN.

We reached it in a sprint.

More than a year later, my feet remain injured. The blisters reappear whenever I run more than five miles. My gait has changed, probably because of the damage. I ignore it. I run.

Two questions remain.

The first is whether I vindicated Robert Garside. As I recovered, I tried again to reach him; I found a mailing address, but got no response. Then, just as this story was going to press, I got a one-line email: "Are you trying to reach me?" That resulted in a series of strained and off-the-record exchanges; even if I could publish them, there was little information revealed. (Garside did agree to be photographed for this story, however, and provided pictures from his run.)

I wondered if others had softened their opinions. After several attempts, I finally managed to reach David Blaikie on the phone. "My views on Robert Garside have not changed, but it is not a sub-ject I want to go back and revisit," he told me. "What I reported at the time remains on the record and speaks for itself. I have no comment on Guinness's decision to recognize Garside. I leave it to the running community to draw its own conclusions on the issue."

The battle over Garside went on in the pages of Wikipedia for years. Garside's opponents went through an angry back-and-forth over the content of the page; it became so ugly that the online encyclopedia's administrators have now blocked the entry from external edits.

I did make one truly new discovery, and it struck at the heart of the "smoking gun" that had inflicted the most damage. It turned out that the *Sunday Express* newspaper story—the one where Gar-side had first admitted his fabrications—had its own flaw: Flem-ing's coauthor, "James McDonald," appeared to be a pseudonym. In my earlier research, Fleming told me he'd coaxed Garside into confessing, promising a story that would vindicate him. "I stitched him up," the reporter said. "I felt bad about it, but I thought I had to." But I'd never bothered to ask about the other name attached to the scoop, and when I tried to contact McDonald, I couldn't: no reporter by that name had appeared in the paper before or since. Fleming, when asked about McDonald, said, "He was a freelance journalist. That wasn't his real name. He had reasons he didn't want his real name used." Whether or not Garside was guilty, the fact that one important accuser wasn't who he said he was made the story's hold on the moral high ground tenuous, at best.

I did manage to reach Garside's former manager, Mike Soulsby, who earlier had vouched for the runner, but then said he found himself starting to believe the flood of "evidence" against his infamous client. But time had given Soulsby more objective distance from the issue, and he supplied what may be the definitive statement on Garside, absent one from Garside himself: "I think Robert was sometimes his own worst enemy. He would boast about achievements, but couldn't back them up. I think he was talking himself up as a way to motivate himself, and sometimes it went too far."

And the run itself? "The answer is yes," Soulsby told me.

"Yes," I asked, "meaning Robert Garside ran around the world?" Soulsby then told me—just so I knew—that he had no financial stake in Garside, and that in fact, the runner still owed him money. "I was pissed off at him," Soulsby says. But that didn't make a difference, Soulsby continued: "Robert Garside ran around the world. He did it. And that's amazing."

For nearly a decade now, two cartons of Garside-related material have sat in my office, right next to my desk. During that time, I've moved, married, and become a father. All that time and obsession, the damage to my mind and body, makes me ask the second question: was it worth it? The answer to that is easier: it doesn't matter. I had no choice.

I've given myself permission to throw everything onto the fire—a hellacious, raging bonfire. It isn't that I wouldn't mind really talking to Garside. I gather, from our brief exchange, that he's happy. And I hope, and I guess, that when he reads this, he'll see that I was, perhaps, even crazier than him.

After all, my obsession with Robert Garside has lasted longer than his entire run around the world. That's long enough.

CINTHIA RITCHIE

Running

FROM SPORT LITERATE

IT'S PAST MIDNIGHT and I'm running down Flattop Mountain, the air milky gray with the Alaska twilight, the moon fat and full and hanging in the sky like something ripe. I leap over rocks, hurl myself down small ridges. All around is silence, an immense and penetrating silence that fills my chest and hums my veins until I can taste it in my mouth, linger it against my tongue.

Once I saw a wolf up here, late at night, the dog and I running in the green darkness, and we froze, all three of us. I grabbed the dog's collar, held tight. The wolf lifted its head and loped off through the brush, its stride smooth and achingly graceful. I wanted to follow, wanted to feel my own stride even out until it became lush and primal, until I lost all sense of time and logic, until wildness wept through my veins.

On the way down, I tore up the mountain, scree and mud flying as I ran, my hands clenched, tiny cries escaping my throat and lifting up in pure and terrible glory.

Growing up on a farm in northwestern Pennsylvania, I ran through the fields and pastures, down the hilly dirt roads, across the marsh and through the narrow, cold creek. Arms outstretched, eyes slit against the sun's glare. I ran in cheap Kmart sneakers, kicking them off in midstride, the grass warm and dry against my bare heels, callused tough and hard as an animal's. Sun hot, air smelling of hay and dust and sweet cow manure. I ran because I loved the feel of wind on my shoulders, loved my hair scattering my face, loved the wisdom of my knees instinctively bending to absorb the shock of rocks and hard, narrow gullies.

I ran because my father was dead, my mother was angry, and there was a new man in the house, his ugly, scarred hands pressing against me at night. But mostly I ran because the sun was wide, the corn was high, and the mud in the creek was cool and forgiving on my hot, scratched feet. Each afternoon as the shadows stretched and the poplar trees darkened and the air stiffened with pollen, I sat on the bank and offered my feet to the water. When the coolness hit my skin I arched my neck and stared up at the cruel, blank sky. I didn't yet understand how pleasure or pain could overpower and transform you before wearing you back down to your own small self. But I knew that Jesus washed the feet of beggars, that God was dead, that the words the priest spoke each Sunday cut against the round, female heat of my own body. I knew how to make myself small, how to stay quiet and look the other way, how to be a girl, yes. But mostly, I knew how to run.

I am afraid of so many things yet when I run I am fearless, gutsy; determined. I wind through trails covered in bear scat, my bear bell clinking against my water belt. I love being out in the woods and mountains, love the solitude, the birch trees glowing like milk in the twilight. Often, I see foxes and wolves, loons and eagles, moose and lynx and bears. Each time I suck in my breath, slow my pace, that childlike wonder, that thump of wildness inside my chest.

Sometimes as I'm running I thank the bears and moose for allowing me to run through their territory. I devise little songs I sing and these soothe me, keep me company, because it's easy to fall to fear. Once, I encountered a sow with two cubs and my dog took off after them as I helplessly shouted for her to return. Then a growl like I'd never heard, a fierce and wild cry as the sow charged my dog. It was a fake charge and my dog held her ground as I stood paralyzed by fright, my bladder releasing, the bear turning and heading back toward the woods with her cubs. I collapsed on the trail in the mud, sobbing, the dog whimpering, both of us scared yet strangely exhilarated. Because to see such fierceness, such wildness. To see it, feel it! To be there!

Mostly, though, I see bears as they slip off into the woods, I see the backs of their haunches or the jut of their snouts as they peer out from the trees as if wondering who I am and why I run through their trails without ever once stopping to snack on grass and berries. A few years ago, running in Kincaid Park before dark, I heard a rustle, glanced over and in the woods parallel to me a sow and a cub ran, all three of us loping along, lost in our own world, our own thoughts. I don't know if that bear saw me. Her gait never altered and for a few seconds I ran along with her, hundreds of yards separating us yet it was as if we were running together. I quickly veered off on a side trail, picked up my pace and put as much distance as possible between us. Sometimes when I can't sleep, when I'm restless and worried, I remember running in the same direction as that bear and I feel a twinge inside my chest, a thump that is as fierce and persistent as hunger.

There were years in my adolescence when I didn't run, years when I was too depressed or angry to run; years when I thought I didn't deserve to run and instead I walked, a moody, introverted girl with sun-bleached hair, cut-off denim shorts, and bare feet. I rode my horse deep into the woods, sat against an oak tree and read books about sex and dying, the only subjects that interested me. Sometimes I smoked the cigarette stubs I picked up from ashtrays around the house but most of the time I chewed on my hair, that grainy, horsey taste, and how it filled me up.

That's a lie, nothing filled me those years. I starved myself down past 80 pounds and when that didn't work, swallowed a bottle of pills, crept behind my bed, and waited to die. I sought nothingness, blackness. I wanted to escape from my body, that burdensome shell that locked me inside of my life. I don't know how many pills I swallowed before the colors began, but they came and flashed inside my eyelids until my hands felt calm and blue and real.

The next thing I remember is a cold, white light in my eyes and a doctor's breath in my face as he forced the tube down my throat to pump my stomach. Imagine the violation, the taste of rubber, the choke of it against the larynx, the sudden ugliness of consciousness returning, along with the flawed hands, the insubstantial chest. The body is puny but it wants to live, will fight to live. It is fierce and animal; it has little sympathy for the mind. I tried to kill my body and it called my bluff, called me a liar, and

I was. I never wanted to die. What I wanted, what I needed and longed and wished for was someone to show me the beauty of my own body, the wonder of my own strength.

As soon as I got out of the hospital, I started to run. It was winter and cold and dark, and I had never run seriously before. This was back before the running movement, before you saw people out jogging, before there were stores devoted solely to running shoes and gear. Still, I must have known or sensed that I needed to move, that motion would keep me safe. Each night I laced up my cheap sneakers and headed down to the basement with a portable radio and, with the Top-40 station blaring, I ran around that concrete floor, in that dusty and mildewy basement, running around the pool table and the Ping-Pong table, past the workbench, the shelves of canned goods, the old couch in front of the fireplace and then back to the pool table, over and over, 40 and 50 and 60 times, until my mind cleared and my breath burned and I felt, I thought: *Yes, now I can make it through another day.*

What I love best is distance running, 15 or 20 or 25 miles. I love the challenge and the pain, love the fight between the body and mind, love the various moods that flood my head. I can be young again, wearing a plaid dress on my first day of school. I can be old and dying. I can be fighting my way through childbirth and that helplessness that leads to giving in, to letting the body open up and show the way.

Distance flattens me out. It wears away my ego. Usually I run alone. I prefer it that way. I love the solitude, the miles stretching out ahead of me. I love the way my head locks tight within itself and how for the next two or three or five hours, there will be nothing between me and my mind. What I love most is the moment of holy terror, when things fall apart and my chest aches and my legs stiffen and my mind becomes a dark space without shadow, and I struggle and fight until I want to quit more than anything in the world.

But I don't. My pace remains even, though effort increases. And right when I'm sure that I can't go on, that I must (I must!) stop, my mind unfolds, it's like magic, my mind opens and I'm somewhere new, somewhere deep and wordless and primitive, someplace where I'm totally and purely myself, in that space before language or time. It's like sex, when it goes on and on and on. It's like the color green, the smell of rain, the way a lover's fingers curl inside your mouth. It's like licking the moon.

In high school and college, I ran competitively, training each morning over dark country roads where no cars passed and my breath rose white in the air until I understood the true meaning of loneliness. Back then, I felt no love for running. I ran because it was something I excelled at, something that came with little effort. I was fast, yes, but mostly I had endurance. I could start off a pace and hang on, no matter what. I wasn't smart or kind or particularly good-looking, but I could run. I had the body for it, and the feet. It was how I identified myself, and all my friends were runners; it was my whole world.

That came crashing down the end of my sophomore year in college, when I hurt my knee. At first the team coach shot me up with cortisone and I ran regardless of the inflammation, regardless of the pain. Each meet I gritted my teeth and raced, my knee hot and fiery so that it was as if I were on fire, and sometimes deep in a race, as I flailed and fought, I imagined flames blazing up my leg. Finally my knee gave out in the middle of a meet, and I lay on that track staring up at the sky, my eyes blurred with pain. I was sure my life was over.

There are places along the Lost Lake Trail down in Seward that are haunted by voices, places haunted by the past and the rain and the steady sound of my breath as I run through. I hear these whispers each time I run the Winter-Summer Loop, two miles straight up the mountain, followed by a mile through the valley and four glorious miles of downhill. The trail is so wet and muddy that I often lose my shoes, and as I lean down to pull them out, I smell the ground, old and pungent and alive; when I lick my hands the mud tastes slightly salty, like blood. The climb is rough and arduous, and no matter the weather, I strip down to a sports bra, the cold air soothing my hot, damp shoulders.

The voices come to me halfway up, teasing my ears like wings, like the flutter of moths. As I run higher and higher, they follow until I feel companionable and safe, as if someone is running behind me, though there is no one around but the dog. Sometimes I even imagine these people, a woman dressed in clothes from the

1920s and a man holding a hat in his hands, his forehead slick with sweat as he tries to explain something to me, but I'm too far in the future to hear. These voices or people or ghosts follow until I reach the creek before the first clearing, and as soon as I clear the water, there is only me and the dog and the mountain, and if I turn, a far-off view of the small town of Seward, the bay stretching out in silver-blue shadows. The voices never follow up the next brutal hill or through the small strand of spruce or along the final hill. I don't know where they go or why, I only know that they leave as I near the top, wind hitting my face and the sky opening up.

When I reach the forest service cabin, I stop and eat a sports gel, sip from my water pack, pet the dog, and then I'm winding through a valley so perfect and still and immense that always it stuns me, and always I feel tears in my eyes and always, I reach down and grab a leaf, a piece of bark, a small stone, and place it in my mouth, a rough and gritty communion. I lodge that bark or pebble against my cheek, where it is moist and dark and secretive, and I keep going.

For years after I had my son, I didn't run. I worked out at the gym. I swam. I biked. Sometimes, rollerblading around the inlet in the summer twilight, I'd pass a runner, watch his or her legs and think: *Why run when you can roll?* I'd feel haughty and self-important and I'd go too fast down the next hill, as if to challenge myself. Yet later that night, I'd feel loss rising up from my stomach, and after my son went to bed I'd sit in the quiet living room with the dog and cats and stare at my legs. Some mornings I'd even decide to run again, and I'd tie on my shoes and take off but I could never find a rhythm or joy because, face it, beginnings are tough and I was impatient and life was hard enough without struggling through three or five miles of pain.

That changed the Fourth of July when I was sent down to Seward to cover a news story on the Mount Marathon Race, a brutal 3,022-foot climb with sketchy handholds, slippery footing, and ankle-deep scree. The night before the race it rained and I slept in a leaky tent, and I huddled in a ball, wet and cold and depressed because a few years earlier, my sister had died of an eating disorder on the Fourth of July, and all I wanted to do was rock back and forth and weep.

Maybe it was lack of sleep or maybe I had a hint of a fever, but as

I climbed those steep cliffs to the halfway point on the mountain the next morning, I felt renewed. The rain cleared and the air was fresh, and up so high I could see out over the bay and the harbor, the boats tiny and snug. Later, as I shot photograph after photograph of women running down the mountain, muddy and bloodied and punching their fists triumphantly in the air, something opened inside to me. My head swirled and the bright light flashed behind my eyes and I heard my sister's voice, low and sardonic and husky from too many cigarettes; it was as if she were right there beside me. "What happened to you, Cin?" she asked. "You used to be so brave and fearless." And it all came back, those summer days of running through the fields with my bare and tough feet, and how when I fell down I got right back up and ran again. I felt a stab of grief so deep and pure that I cried out, not only for my sister but also for that fierce and wild girl I had once been. Why had I given her up so easily, so carelessly? Why had I left her so far behind?

After that, it was as if there were a hum inside of my chest. All winter I worked out at the gym and when spring came, I began running again, a few miles at first, each step awkward and clunky so that my knees shook and ankles ached with effort. Soon I was up to five and then eight and finally 10 miles, and the next Fourth of July I stood at the starting line of the Mount Marathon Race with 300 other fierce and gritty women, and when the gun went off I was running again, running up Fourth Avenue and Jefferson Street to the base of the mountain, where I pulled myself up over roots and fell and cried and sweated, leaving a trail of blood over those cliffs like something holy, an initiation or a communion.

I collapsed at the finish line and the woman ahead of me threw up on my shoes. I sat there, and the sky was blue and the air shimmered with heat and the blood from my knee dripped down on the pavement, and I was so happy that I couldn't stop smiling.

During a mountain race out on Knoya Ridge a few years ago, a young man collapsed and died. It was an overcast day in late spring, the air damp and moody. About 30 of us lined up at the start and ran through curved and wooded trails that slowly evened out the higher we climbed. Our pace slowed and sweat ran down our backs, and during one fierce ridge I leaned down and rubbed my fingers in the dirt and stuck them into my mouth, just to have something to taste. Up above the tree line the world opened and the breeze picked up and there was nothing but silence and mountains and a stuttered line of runners.

A small group huddled near the finish, and a woman yelled that someone was hurt, to please go around. I thought of broken bones, bruised legs, the usual running injuries, until I saw the fallen man's face, slack and blue and unmoving as a woman leaned across his chest and uselessly administered CPR.

We gathered around him, all of us. We took off our shirts and windbreakers and covered his body, and then we stood sentinel, we stood near the top of that mountain, surrounded by valleys and sky and clouds, in that place of unimaginable beauty, and nothing moved but our breaths and the flutter of windbreakers across the young man's stilled legs.

After the rescue crew arrived, after the hellish arranging of the body over the stretcher, after the liftoff and the final silence, after the run back down the mountain and the days and weeks that followed, I read in the newspaper that the man had been just 22 years old and had had a preexisting heart condition. I knew even then that I would never forget that day, not only the young man's death but everything else too: the clouds pressing close, the silence, the mist of cold air rising around us.

Often when I run I think of how it would feel to die in the mountains. Part of me rejoices, not because I want to die but because I'm running over rocks and my arms are outstretched and my breath comes hard and I am totally and completely in my body. Yet each time I run I can feel the persistent and inevitable possibility of my own death, and behind it and before it and probably even because of it, so much fucking life.

CHARLES SIEBERT

Goal to Go

FROM THE NEW YORK TIMES MAGAZINE

LAST APRIL 28, a splendid spring Saturday that fairly begged you to be outdoors, I spent all afternoon in front of my living room TV, anxiously watching the last day of the annual NFL draft, live from Radio City Music Hall. As big a football fan as I am, I had never seen any part of a draft, to say nothing of its final four rounds, which are a roughly seven-hour marathon that lasts until sundown. And yet, on that day, I sat riveted.

I had in front of me what's known as a Draft Scout Player Profile: a starkly efficient, computerized summation of every draftable player's past prowess and future prospects. I, however, was interested in only one, my nephew, my younger sister's son. His specs were, of course, familiar to me. But somehow the officious, bare-bones alignment on my computer screen—in categories befitting a prize steer at auction—rendered him a complete stranger. And a rather impressive one at that.

Name: Pat Schiller. Number: 53. Position: Outside linebacker. Height: Six-foot-one. Weight: 234. College: Northern Illinois. Under "Pro Day Results"—his audition, essentially, before several NFL scouts at the DeKalb campus of Northern Illinois University earlier in March—were 22 bench presses of 225 pounds, a 35-inch vertical leap, and, for a linebacker, a head-turning 4.65 seconds in the 40-yard dash. Under his "Draft Scout Snapshot" was a link to game-highlight footage: a rapid-fire sequence of heat-seeking-missile launches into ball carriers; the all-out, "high-motor" mode of play that garnered number 53 a team-leading 115 tackles in his senior year, along with second-team All Mid-American Conference and Northern Illinois's Linebacker of the Year honors. As for Pat's "Projected Round," there was, after the word "stock," a bright red, upward-pointing arrow, followed by the words "shot late."

Some 800 miles west, meanwhile, in a two-story modern colonial on a neatly etched cul-de-sac in the western Chicago suburb Geneva, Pat lay on the living room carpet, holding his golden retriever, Champ. Around the TV with him was his immediate family: his father, also named Pat, a longtime excavation contractor as well as an accomplished pianist and songwriter in the Billy Joel mode, with a couple CDs to his credit and a number 6 single on a 2004 adult-contemporary-music radio chart; Pat's mother, my younger sister, Cathy, a doctor's medical assistant; my niece, Stephanie, a classically trained vocalist who now works in the admissions office at Northern Illinois University, her alma mater as well; and her fiancé, Michael. My nephew, my sister had told me, wanted to keep things low-key, wanted to avoid the roomful of slack faces and well-meaning condolences should things not go as hoped.

He was, in a sense, already chosen. Of the 80,000 or so who play college football every year, no more than 1,500 are even scouted by pro teams. On average about 300 of those players will be invited to show their stuff at the weeklong NFL scouting combine held every February at Lucas Oil Stadium in Indianapolis. Hundreds more will perform at regional combines or at their college team's pro days. Among the heads Pat turned was that of Ran Carthon, son of the New York Giants fullback Maurice Carthon. Ran Carthon was also a former NFL running back before becoming a scout for the Atlanta Falcons. The Falcons called Pat four times in the previous week alone, the final call coming that Saturday morning.

"Stay by your phone for Rounds 6 and 7," he was told.

What followed was a slow-motion combo to the gut. The Falcons' sixth-round pick went to Charles Mitchell, a safety out of Mississippi State. In Round 7, they took Travian Robertson, a defensive tackle from the University of South Carolina. Four picks later, the Indianapolis Colts took as the draft's last selection Chandler Harnish, the quarterback at Northern Illinois and my nephew's close friend and college housemate.

"The room went kind of quiet," Pat told me. "There was like this skipped heartbeat. And then the waiting started all over again."

Seconds after the official NFL draft ends, a whole other netherdraft begins, one far more frenzied and dramatic than the one at

Radio City. From 1967, the year the NFL instituted a joint draft with the more recently established American Football League, until 1976, the draft went 17 rounds, with about 450 players being selected. The current seven-round format totals about 250, leaving a vast countrywide bin of talented discards that general managers, coaches, and scouts start madly ferreting through, like a group of shoppers who have been granted a limited after-hours spree for bargain-basement gems.

Not two minutes after Harnish's selection that day, Pat's phone rang. Ran Carthon was on the line. The Falcons wanted him.

"The truth is," said Dave Lee, Pat's agent, a partner of PlayersRep based in Cleveland, "when you get toward the bottom of the draft, basically from the fifth to the seventh round, the talent level isn't all that different from that of the undrafted free agents. Teams at that point are just looking for guys that fit their system, and it's anybody's guess whether you'll get drafted or not. The Falcons wanted speedy linebackers. Pat shows a lot of speed. They said, 'We think it's a great opportunity.' They went through the reasons. Obviously we said, 'We're getting other calls,' so we could play a bit with the signing bonus, but it was pretty easy to jump on their offer."

A contract was soon faxed to the Schillers' home, its terms at once bleak and beguiling. Up front, Pat would receive just a $1,000 signing bonus, along with per diem expenses of $155 during spring camp. Should he make it as far as preseason training camp beginning in late July, the payment would be the NFL Players Association's stipulated $850 a week. The big money, big for a rookie at least, was all in the offing: the standard first-year salary of $390,000 he receives only if he makes and remains on the 53-man roster for the entire season. Should he be picked for the team's eight-man practice squad instead, he would receive a salary of $5,700 a week, amounting to $96,900 over a 17-week season and more if the Falcons made the playoffs.

Pat and Dave Lee were encouraged by the fact that the Falcons hadn't picked any linebackers in the official draft. The team did, however, sign three other undrafted linebackers and a total of 23 undrafted free agents in all, the most of any team in the NFL. In the end, 623 undrafted free agents were signed in 2012 to the same basic contract that arrived at the Schillers' home that evening. It all seems wildly prodigal. But not in terms of breaking owners' bank accounts so much as players' hearts. Two, maybe three, of the undrafted free agents annually signed by each NFL team will make the 53-man roster. Of the 23 undrafted players on the Falcons roster at the start of last season's minicamp, one player made the roster.

With a signed contract in hand that Saturday evening, my nephew descended the stairs to the family's finished basement to use the fax machine in his father's music studio. The Falcons ask that their players send such contracts back before midnight. It's the undrafted free agent's peculiar inversion of the Cinderella tale: having to rush to ensure the right to arrive at the NFL's ball in a pumpkin.

Six weeks later, his sculptured frame blurring in the gridiron-warble of a Georgia June sun, Pat was standing on the Atlanta Falcons' practice field in Flowery Branch, learning the consequences of living his dream. Midway through the Falcons' six weeks of spring-training sessions—each NFL team's yearly padless orientation ritual—Pat had just got what all first-year players in the NFL most crave: a play, a "rep." Reps for a rookie are but a few precious crumbs left after the daily scrums of the first and second teams—the "Ones" and "Twos." It's one of the crueler realities of the NFL's strictly enforced hierarchy, a classic Catch-22: what you most need in order to make a team as a rookie, especially an undrafted one, are opportunities to show what you can do. You have little chance of getting those, however, precisely because you're a rookie. There are so few chances, in fact, that when a rep does come your way, the tendency is to get a bit greedy, to overplay.

Mike Nolan, a former defensive coordinator for the New York Giants, Jets, and five other NFL teams before being hired by Atlanta last winter, had just signaled for the "Threes," with Pat at middle linebacker or "Mike," to execute a "Dallas freeze," a package featuring two blitzing linebackers. As one of the scheme's designated blitzers, Pat shot toward the quarterback, then deftly swerved inside a blocking fullback to get at his target. Another head-turning display, although in this instance for entirely the wrong reasons. Coaches love speed. They love schemes even more, and in that one Pat was designated to be the "contain man." His responsibility was to go outside the blocking back to prevent the play from developing wide.

"Give me two good reasons," Nolan's voice boomed, "why you went inside."

Pat went slack beneath a bowed helmet, then shrugged.

"That's right!" Nolan replied. "Because there aren't any!"

Over dinner that evening at the nearby Legacy Lodge on Lake Lanier, where the Falcons were staying throughout spring camp, that play came up, just as it would, Pat assured me, at team meetings the following morning.

"I heard 'freeze,'" Pat said, "so I knew I was going to be one of the blitzers. I got that. But I treated it like a normal blitz, where you find any way you can to the quarterback. I didn't realize I was the contain player. Unfortunately, in this league, you don't get many chances, and that's a blitz I'd only run maybe twice in the three weeks that I've been here. So you do all these things right and then you mess up the last one, and you're getting yelled at. NFL coaches will tolerate physical mistakes but not mental ones."

Weeks earlier, when I first mentioned to Pat the possibility of my writing a story about his attempt to make the Falcons as an undrafted free agent, he was open to the idea. His time in NFL camp, however, had altered his outlook. He called me the night before I got on a plane to go down to Atlanta.

"I think you might be wasting your time," he said. "I mean you can still come down, but the story really can't be about me anymore. I'm mostly just going to meetings and trying to learn the playbook. I'm kind of nobody around here."

He paused a moment.

"Let's see . . . how do I put this? You go from being one of the top players in college. Okay, not one of the top. If I were that, I would have been drafted. But I would say one of the top three to four hundred players. And then you come to the NFL and, well, I've never felt so bad at a sport I know I'm good at."

He still looked a bit beleaguered as we sat at the dinner table at Legacy Lodge. A pained twist of his torso and head roll elicited an inner ball-bearing rumble. I noted over the years the Hulk-like morphing of my nephew's body toward the formidable adult frame that presently houses the same sensitive, soft-spoken kid. But at age 23, football's ravages had him constantly making his own chiropractic adjustments. There was no thought, he said, of seeking out a trainer. Everything a rookie does in camp is documented, and visits to the training room leave the wrong impression.

"We have an expression here," he told me. "'You don't make the club in the tub.'"

I had always followed Pat's progress from afar, heard the hopeful murmurings about him "playing on Sundays." And yet it was only now that I was getting a chance to really spend time with the guy. Watching his contortions that night, I started feeling guilty about my own delight in his achievements. I didn't know whether to give him a pep talk or the suddenly more urgent-seeming advice, given the very slim odds of his realizing his dream, to get out while he was still intact, both in body and in mind.

I thought of the conversation I recently had with his father about the constant threat of injury to his son, who had already overcome a badly shattered ankle in his freshman year of high school and a torn knee ligament at the start of his junior year at Northern Illinois.

"I don't think of the knees and hips," Pat's father told me. "They can replace those now. The thing I'm most worried about is his brain. I've been reading a lot lately about concussions."

My nephew told me that night that he had his share of concussions over the years but said he was never forced to leave a game or miss part of a season because of one.

"I've had it where I've been hit, and the lights go out," he said. "You stand up, and it's like, 'Whew,' and then you're good. I've also had it two or three times where a play will be called and you have no idea what it is or what to do, and you're just out there aimlessly wandering around the field. But it's never been to the point where I wake up the next morning really sensitive to light or I'm getting sick from it."

Another torso twist and head roll.

"You do get to this point," he told me, "where you feel your body is telling you to chill out, take a break, but your mind stays on the prize. And part of that now is the paycheck. What gets me through coaches screaming at me and the way my body feels is the thought of that $390,000. I've talked to other guys here about it, like, 'Is that okay to feel that way,' and they're like, 'Oh, man, don't even think twice about that.'"

I knew that when he was a sophomore at Northern Illinois and still living at home, he witnessed firsthand the effects of the recent financial meltdown. His father told me that late in 2007 and into the first two months of 2008, he was still receiving a number of job bids, and his bank repeatedly asked him if he needed a higher line of credit. By March, though, clients weren't able to pay him. He turned to the bank for the higher credit line, but by then the bank was drastically reducing his credit: cards with a $50,000 limit were cut to $2,000. By the fall of 2008, work had completely dried up, and Pat had no other choice but to close his business. To pay off his debts, he got whatever he could for his bulldozers, backhoes, and trucks at unrestricted auctions, $200,000 machines going for as little as $50,000. He was soon getting up at 4:00 A.M. to drive backhoes at distant work sites.

"It's tough seeing your dad break down," Pat told me when I brought up the subject at dinner that night. "His name was now coming off the building he owned. Everything he'd worked for was gone. Everything you've seen in our house, all the nice stuff. That's an illusion. He can't really afford it anymore. He keeps it going for us. I remember thinking when everything was coming apart for him, okay, I've got to help in some way. What am I good at that could also pay decent money? Well, I knew the answer to that one."

Being an undrafted free agent in the NFL is an extended exercise in ego abnegation. You're not only stripped of your college number; you're exiled from the NFL's mandated numerical bracket for your given position. Linebackers on all final team rosters must bear a number in either the 50s or 90s. Pat, for now, was given 45. As for his fellow undrafted competitors, Max Gruder, a linebacker from the University of Pittsburgh, wore 46; Rico Council, a middle linebacker from Tennessee State, 43; and Jerrell Harris, an outside linebacker for last year's champions, Alabama, 49. Some days in practice, Pat wore 40 and then was switched back to 45. Coaches and fellow players, meanwhile, were constantly confusing Pat with a third-year safety, Shann Schillinger, whose seniority naturally merited his getting dibs on the nickname "Schill," thus saddling my nephew with — for obscure reasons — "Patty Melt."

Nolan kept calling Pat "Gruder" through much of minicamp. In a practice roundup in the *Atlanta Journal-Constitution* one morning, my nephew — whom I watched the previous day grunt, sweat, and double over with the rest of the squad—was listed as absent. After he made five tackles in the Falcons' second preseason game against the Cincinnati Bengals later in August—finally turning coaches' heads for the right reasons—the team statistician, apparently confused by the presence of two number 45s on the roster that night, credited Pat with none.

"Well," Pat told me on the phone later, "at least they can't erase my film. Can they?"

After one workout that spring, all the undrafted linebackers were headed back to the locker room with an extra helmet in hand bearing numbers in the 50s.

"Yep," Gruder said, smiling. "We're also the vets' helmet lackeys."

And water boys. At team meetings each morning, before taking their seats in the very front row—the better for the coach's eviscerating explications of rookie screwups—the 40s brigade takes water and Gatorade to the veterans. The Falcons' linebacker coach, Glenn Pires, told a story one morning from his days coaching for the Arizona Cardinals. The vets sat up front at the Cardinals' team meetings, the rookies in the far back. Pires said a longtime veteran linebacker there had only to hold up a hand: one finger meant water, two Gatorade, three a cup of coffee.

Of course, getting things for vets is standard rookie boot-camp stuff. Getting any time with one of them is the real challenge. At practices each day, the Threes are forever pacing the sidelines, craning their heads to at least get mental images of the plays being run by the Ones and Twos. They sidle up to them afterward with questions. It's as though rookies are kept penned in a mental cage of the playbook schemes they've been studying from the start of camp. You can almost hear the whirring of all the Xs, Os, arrows, and bent-Ts inside their helmets, like so many gnats they would love to have swatted away with one good hit.

"They give you all this information," Jerrell Harris told me after one practice. "But without the actual reps, if you don't pick things up off the mental, then you're just out there flying around."

I always heard that rookies are overwhelmed at first by the speed of the game at the pro level. But everyone I asked about this had the same response.

"It's not the speed," the third-year linebacker Robert James told me. "It only seems like the game is a lot faster because you're always trying to figure out what you're doing and where you're supposed to be. Once I began to learn the defenses, the game slowed down for me."

Much of the learning in the NFL begins with unlearning. In college, Pat told me, coaches stressed never crossover running with your feet so that you can keep your depth and be available to make a play. In the pros they tell you to crossover run.

"It's no longer 'keep your depth.'" Pat said. "In the NFL, everything is downhill right now. Get to the ball as fast as you can. Those things you perfected to a T in college are no good here."

For Pat and the other free-agent linebackers, what made the NFL learning curve especially steep was the lack of extra time on the side with coaches.

"You don't get the patient schooling of college here," Bart Scott, a Pro Bowl linebacker now with the New York Jets, who started out as an undrafted free agent, told me by phone. "It's mostly on you to find ways to figure it out. To be mature. To be a man."

I asked Scott what advice he would give Pat.

"Get with a vet and track him," he said. "Everything he does. Learn it. Copy it. Then try to outdo it."

The one veteran Pat said he had begun to bond with was the three-time Pro Bowl linebacker Lofa Tatupu. The Falcons had just signed Tatupu, the 29-year-old former Seattle Seahawk, to a two-year, $3.6 million contract to shore up the Mike position after losing their star middle linebacker, Curtis Lofton, to free agency.

"We've been out to dinner a few times," Pat said. "A movie. He's so generous. Doesn't let me pay for anything. We were shooting pool here the other night, and somehow we got to talking about my highlight tape. We went up to my room to watch, and he's like, 'Hey, you got speed, man.' Then he told me: 'Look, you're a rookie. You can't control what you can't control. I've seen lots of guys who should have made it get cut. The only thing you can control is what you do when you go in there.'"

At the Lodge one evening a few days before the close of spring camp, Tatupu stopped by our table, dwarfing it with his mesalike shoulders. His injured hamstring, he told Pat, was going to keep him out of tomorrow's practice, and Akeem Dent, the Falcons' current starting middle linebacker, would be away as well, tending to some personal business at home.

"You're getting lots of reps with the Ones tomorrow, rook,"

Tatupu said, heading off to his room. "Better study your playbook tonight."

It had been maddeningly difficult to get any indication of how Pat was doing outside of the occasional tongue lashings in practice. I had an agreement with both Pat and the Falcons' communications coordinator, Brian Cearns, that I wouldn't tell Mike Smith, the head coach, or any of the other coaches that I was Pat's uncle or ask them specific questions about his performance. I knew my share of football coaches in the past and could well imagine the guff Pat might get if word got around camp that the no-name undrafted rookie had a reporter uncle following him.

When I asked Pat for his own assessment of his play, he just shrugged.

"It's hard to get a good measure," he said. "You don't hear anything about the good stuff. That's just the way it is here."

At the following practice, Pat got the promised reps with the Ones. It was always easy to tell when just the Threes were on the field. You couldn't hear anything. Everybody was unsure of what they were doing, and so nobody talked. Now the vets were giving Pat his checks, he was chattering back to them, and, with the doors to his mind's playbook-cage flung open, he was looking again like the guy in his own highlight reel; briefly playing in that realm of informed thoughtlessness that had turned scouts' heads in the first place.

Driving his gray pickup back home in Geneva during a break a few weeks after the close of minicamp, Pat popped in a CD. He wanted me to hear the motivational music he listens to before games or personal workout sessions like the one we were driving to that July morning at the ProForce training facility in Batavia, the adjacent town. He still had another couple of weeks off before the start of padded, preseason camp at the end of July. But on the verge of his first and perhaps only crack at the NFL, he had no intention of relaxing. He reached over and ramped up the volume, his pickup trembling now as soaring chords and tribal chants swirled above the same slow, propulsive backbeat.

"Okay, don't laugh," he said. "But when I'm listening to this, I imagine myself running through a primeval forest somewhere with just a loincloth on and a huge hunting knife in my mouth. I'm really looking to kill something."

I often found myself trying to construct some kind of half-baked genealogy of Pat Schiller's athletic prowess, his possible pigskin pedigree. His paternal grandfather, Eddie Schiller, aka the Blond Tiger, was a boxer in the late 1920s and early '30s who fought, for a time, out of Kid Howard's downtown Chicago gym. Pat's father told me he was kept from the gridiron by his mother to preserve his fingers for the keyboard. On my sister's side, there was my mother's brother, my uncle Carl Valle, a six-foot-two, 240-pound all-city lineman at James Madison High School in Brooklyn who went on to play two seasons at Boston College. Carl's equivalently proportioned nephew, my cousin Ralph, knocked about as an offensive lineman in the semipros back in the 1960s, playing for the Brooklyn Mariners and the Long Island Bulls, the New York Giants' former farm team, briefly making the Giants' taxi squad in 1968 and 1969. And then there was my older brother Bob, a linebacker and offensive guard at Archbishop Stepinac High School, in White Plains. He went on to play at Holy Cross in Worcester, Massachusetts. But the combination of an outsize will in a somewhat plodding, too-small frame led to so many concussions that he walked away before the start of his sophomore season.

Bob shaped my own football career. The summer of his sophomore year, appalled that I was still riding the bench as a wannabe fullback after my second season at Ossining High, he took matters into his own hands. Every day before dinner that summer, he put a helmet on my head, dragged me into the backyard, put me in the proper three-point guard stance, and had me charge on his count into his bare, upward-flailing forearm. We did this until my face bled. We did it until I learned to get my face mask into his chest faster than his forearm could get to my face. I never sat on the bench again. By the end of two varsity seasons with only one loss, individual all-league honors, and a late growth spurt that took me to six feet tall and 205 pounds, the college recruiters came calling. Mostly smaller schools like Bates, Colby, and Colgate. Lehigh treated me to a New York Giants game. Brown had me up to Providence one weekend to meet with coaches and party all night with some players in their dorm.

Still, I knew I wasn't going any farther with football. Even on game days, I always felt that I had one foot outside the experience. During pregame psyche drills with my friend, Mike Chernick—a standout fullback and middle linebacker who went on to play at

Yale—the two of us would be on the sidelines, pounding on each other's shoulder pads, growling. Occasionally I looked up and saw the wild whites of his eyes and thought, *He really means this.*

Pat Schiller really and wholly means it; he is all in. He flies around a football field overturning ball carriers with full-bore, joyous immersion.

"I enjoy hitting," Pat told me as we pulled into the lot of the ProForce training facility in an industrial park on Batavia's flat, barren outskirts. "Especially when you stop someone short on third or fourth down and you look up and the crowd's going nuts and you're like: 'I did that. Me. You're welcome.' That's cool. People always ask me, 'Do you change when you get on the field?' Before a game starts, I have my routine, I listen to my music, and I walk out and look up at the crowd and I . . . I'm getting goose bumps right now talking about it. It's crazy. My body is filled with emotions I can't even describe. I come out of my body, and I'm like, 'I'm going to kill somebody.' I become this lunatic. And even when I start to come back down after the first few plays, I'm still a different person. You know, a savage. But when I first come out, it's like a drug, I'm literally trembling, almost crying. I have so much emotion."

For the next three hours that morning, ProForce's founder and head trainer, Chris Browning, a defensive end and linebacker who starred at Batavia High School and Western Michigan University, had my nephew and his workout partner, Pat Brown, an undrafted free agent from the University of Central Florida who played offensive tackle for the Minnesota Vikings in 2011, gasping for breath in the 90-degree, midsummer heat. This was their daily, self-imposed "off-weeks" regimen, designed with Browning, to get them in the best shape possible for the start of preseason camp now only a few weeks away.

Pulling thick steamship lines, they each took turns dragging a half-ton weighted sled atop which sat a screaming Browning, back and forth across ProForce's hollowed-out industrial warehouse space. They repeatedly flipped an enormous tractor tire. They did position-specific agility drills tethered to wall-mounted resistance bands. Pat occasionally slipped out a side door to be sick and then bounded back inside to start anew.

Sitting afterward with the two Pats and Browning in his office, I realized I had before me the entire spectrum of the undrafted free-agent experience. Browning got eight phone calls from NFL teams on the last Saturday morning of the 2002 draft. Four days later the Bears invited him to rookie camp, but he failed to make the team. The following season he was invited to try out with the New Orleans Saints and again failed to make the squad. He ended up playing Arena Football for the Chicago Rush, New Orleans Voodoo, and Columbus Destroyers.

"Arena was very big then," he said. "Guys could get a shot at the pros. For a lineman like me, you could make $60,000 to $80,000 a year. You didn't have to mess with all the ups and downs of the NFL."

No one knows those up and downs better than Pat Brown. Signed by the Carolina Panthers after the close of the 2009 draft, he was released, picked up, and released again five times from 2009 to 2010.

"I lived in hotels the first two seasons," he recalled. "It can be a bit of a shot to your ego. Getting told multiple times on multiple teams that you're not good enough. Some guys can handle it. Some guys can't. You just have to love it, because it's mostly out of your hands."

Brown just completed his first full season with the Vikings, and had playing time in 16 games. I asked him if he was finally feeling a sense of security.

"Never," he said. "Never. I'm always looking over my shoulder. You don't relax until you get that five-year, $25 million deal and so much money guaranteed. Then you know you're an investment."

Undrafted free agents are forever asking themselves how long they'll stick it out; how long they'll continue to work out and wait by the phone, forestalling a real job. When I asked Rico Council, he didn't hesitate: "As long as it takes, man. Football is what I know. I'm going to be in it one way or another. I'd rather it be as a player." Max Gruder told me that he would figure it out as he went, that he had a lot of other interests to pursue when he was done with football. Pat said he would probably give himself a full year of not getting anywhere and not hearing from anybody and then move on.

"I'd finish my degree in education," he said. "I still have to do a semester of student teaching. But I'll also not commit to anything serious for a while. I could end up playing in Canada. I'd do that."

All of those in the tribe of the undrafted can cite the inspiring precedents for persistence; the well-known NFL Cinderella-man tales they repeat to themselves like soothing bedtime stories. Kurt Warner quarterbacked for the Iowa Barnstormers in the Arena Football League and stocked groceries before his meteoric rise. James Harrison of the Pittsburgh Steelers was cut four times and did a stint with the Rhein Fire of NFL Europe before becoming a four-time Pro Bowl linebacker and, according to a poll last year of his fellow NFL players, the most feared man in football. Chase Blackburn was back home in Marysville, Ohio, at week 12 of last season, about to take a job as a middle-school math teacher, when he got the call from the New York Giants. He ended up making the key interception of a fourth-quarter Tom Brady pass that set up the Giants' game-winning drive in last year's Super Bowl victory over the New England Patriots.

"I've been telling your nephew, he may bounce around three or four times before he finds a home," Browning told me. "That's tough, but, hey, he's young. Have fun. So few people get this experience. And don't get too logical about it. He could get cut because of salary considerations. Some other guy's agent might have a better relationship with the team. But then what if someone like Lofa goes down. Pat beats out the other undrafted free-agent linebackers and guess what, that boy is dressing."

Later that evening, my last night in Geneva, Pat and I stopped into a few of the local haunts along his hometown's historic main street (a location for the period film *Road to Perdition*). Wherever I went with "Mayor Schiller," as one friend called him, drinks materialized and tabs disappeared. Owners, managers, friends, and friends of friends all stopped by to ask how Pat was doing and to wish him well.

"It's weird," he said to me during a rare lull. "For some reason I'm cool because I'm able to play a game. And they don't realize how hard and cutthroat it is now. They'll say things like, 'Hey, worst-case scenario, you'll be on the practice squad.' And I'm thinking, *Are you kidding? That would be unbelievable.* But these people are really counting on me, and I feel a lot of pressure to not let them down. That's a big part of what drives me. And I like being the interesting guy, you know? I want to be talked about and turn heads when I walk into a place. Who doesn't? It sounds so egotistic, but it's what it is. And to think this is all going to be done one day, probably sooner than later, and I'll have to face reality.

Have a nine-to-five job, not be Mr. Interesting anymore, and never have the rush that I get before games. That's scary to me."

A week before Pat was scheduled to return to Flowery Branch for the five weeks of preseason camp, he received a text message from Lofa. He had torn a pectoral muscle while lifting weights. Less than a week later, the Falcons released Tatupu and signed Mike Peterson, 36, a 13-year veteran who wasn't re-signed by the Falcons at the end of last season after three years at linebacker. My nephew's stock as a middle linebacker, Lofa's intended role, had suddenly soared even as his heart sank.

"People keep texting or talking to me about what a big break Lofa's injury is," Pat told me. "But they don't get it. This was the one guy I could really talk to about stuff. Plus, you just hate seeing anybody go down, especially someone that you were getting to know and feel closer to. But that's the NFL. Injury is the number-one thing on a player's mind."

Two weeks later, in early August, I was watching Pat from the sidelines at the Flowery Branch facility as Keith Armstrong, the special-teams coordinator, closed a practice with a kickoff-coverage drill. Special teams, it is constantly stressed at NFL camp, are about the only place for rookies to get reps in preseason games and "make good film." One or two eye-catching plays can be enough to prompt a phone call from a team looking to fill roster holes constantly being opened by injury.

On Armstrong's signal, one waterfall of would-be tacklers after another was unleashed—the Ones, followed by the Twos: swift, downfield flows soon met at staggered, eerily soundless intervals by pad-wielding blockers. A consequence of the heightened concern about concussions in the NFL is that even fully padded practices have become largely clashless choreography, like ballet without the music: that singular symphony of crashing bodies we cringingly thrill to on game days.

All through camp, Nolan stressed being offensive on defense. The simple 11-on-11 math of football inherently favors the offense. It has a "12th man" in the form of a play only its players know. What Nolan wants from his defensive unit is to find ways to "change the math." Players, especially linebackers, are expected to "shock and shed": engage their respective blockers and then throw them off on the way to the ball. To stay within their defensive scheme and yet be fast and supple enough to invent ways to be offensive and make a play.

Pat seemed to be ever balanced on that edge between his natural speed and the confines of the scheme. When the Threes' rotation came up in the kickoff-coverage drill that day, he was repeatedly the first one down the field. His swiftness, however, would soon send him flying past his scheme's scripted pas de deux with a notably tardy counterpart. Seeing that his man wasn't there, Pat just blew by and got directly to the ball carrier.

"Schiller?" Armstrong fumed in his deep, drill-sergeantese. "Schiller, you're killing me!"

The only time I could get with Pat now was quick snatches of conversation along the sidelines after practice. Preseason camp days started at dawn and didn't wind up until 10:00 P.M.: days of meetings, meals, practices, more meetings, and then bed, all confined to the Flowery Branch facility. But as a sweat-drenched number 45 headed toward the team locker room after kickoff-coverage drills that day, he gave me a knowing wink and smile as he passed.

Two days later, just hours before the Falcons' first preseason game against the Baltimore Ravens, Pat exuded the same sense of inner assuredness, one that he, too, seemed surprised by. "It's crazy," he told me in the lobby of the team's downtown Atlanta hotel. "We play tonight, but I'm not worried. I feel calm. The key thing the coaches are looking for is how fast we play with the right technique. If they see that your footwork is wrong or that you're at all hesitant, that sends up red flags. That's trouble. When you do things fast, it means you're confident."

From the Georgia Dome press box that night, I watched the Blond Tiger II pace the sidelines, still looking for some way out of his mind's playbook cage. It wasn't until midway into the third quarter that he took the field. Not on special teams, but as the Atlanta Falcons' middle linebacker. On his first play in an NFL game, a run off-tackle, he flew through the offense and brought the runner down at the line of scrimmage: speed and scheme melding at last.

He tallied four tackles for the night. In the postgame locker room, he and his fellow undrafted linebackers, Max Gruder, Rico

Council, and Jerrell Harris, were all wide-eyed from the adrenaline rush of finally having their first taste of NFL action. As he dressed, Pat handed me his cell phone to read the pregame text he received from Lofa: "Tear it up tonight!"

The last three weeks of preseason whirled by in a maddening vortex of Sphinx-like silence from the coaching staff about the makeup of the final roster and increasingly rampant speculation by everyone else. My younger brother, Joe, was sending me so many emails with the latest blog predictions that I finally had to repeat to him Pat's admonition to me way back in minicamp, when I kept citing blog posts picking him as the most likely to make team.

"Ignore that stuff," he said. "It's not really based on anything."

By the night of the Falcons' final preseason game against the Jacksonville Jaguars on August 30, the original 90-man roster had been cut to 75. Gruder was the only linebacker released. The final cuts down to the 53-man roster would be made by noon the next day.

The math of making an NFL roster seems straightforward. There are 40 or so players who are Ones and Twos on offense and defense. Then there is a punter, at least one kicker, a long snapper, and often a third-string quarterback. This leaves just a handful of positions available. The Falcons' starting linebackers were set: Akeem Dent would be the starting middle linebacker with Mike Peterson as his backup. Sean Weatherspoon and Stephen Nicholas would play on either side. For the other two backup linebacker spots (if the Falcons decided to go with six), Spencer Adkins, a three-year veteran from the University of Miami, and Robert James, an undrafted free agent from Arizona State who spent the last two seasons on the practice squad, seemed favorites. It would be up to the three remaining undrafted free-agent linebackers to find some way to change that math.

I watched that final preseason game on TV. Pat didn't get a single rep on special teams, but he played the better part of the second half at middle linebacker in an inspired trance, calling checks, conducting the defense, and taking down ball carriers like a seasoned pro. On one sweep, he shocked and shed two blockers, did a full 360-degree turn, and somehow found the running back again, taking him down for a loss.

He ended up tying Akeem Dent for the team lead in tackles

with eight. In the postgame locker room, thoroughly drained by the Florida heat, he had to hydrate intravenously.

"I was dead," he told me later. "Played something like 60 reps. My sweat was sweating. I went into that game thinking, *This is the last time you're ever going to put on a helmet.* I did everything like I did in college. Wore my face paint. Got into a zone. Didn't give a damn what anybody thought or said. I was out there just flying around. I was a savage. Whether I got cut or not was out of my hands, but I never felt more at peace. I had no regrets."

Coach Pires made a point of stopping by Pat's locker. "He said: 'You played your tail off tonight. No matter what happens tomorrow, you've got to be proud,'" Pat told me.

At just past 9:30 the following morning, Pat was back at the Flowery Branch facility getting a long-craved training-room massage when he got a phone call. It was from the Falcons' football operations office. They wanted to see him in the team meeting room.

"I knew right then," Pat told me. "I'm thinking, *You have got to be kidding.*"

Followers of HBO's NFL training-camp series *Hard Knocks* know this moment well: the solemn handing over of the team playbook, the heart-to-heart send-off by the coach. The Falcons, however, have players turn in their playbooks at the end of each week. Pat entered the meeting room empty-handed to see 16 other teammates with the same empty expressions. Among them were the other undrafted free-agent linebackers, Rico Council and Jerrell Harris, and also Spencer Adkins. The team was going with only five linebackers. Robert James got the fifth spot.

They all sat there together, quietly talking about how lousy it felt, as one by one each player was escorted up to Smith's office. Pat was among the last three guys to be called. After waiting well over an hour, he now found himself sitting before Smith and the general manager, Thomas Dimitroff.

"They shook my hand," Pat said. "Coach Smith did all the talking. I can't remember his exact words. I was half-listening. I was so bummed. I'm getting cut. The thrust of it was that of all the players in camp, I was one of the guys who'd improved the most from week to week. He said: 'You played your heart out last night. We really feel you're going to be playing in this league somewhere.

Unfortunately, we're releasing you. We just don't have a spot available for you now, but if anything changes, we'll call you.' I thanked them for the opportunity, and that was about it."

Downstairs, he noticed a group of five players sitting off to one side.

"I went over and asked them what's up," Pat told me. "They said they were being kept around for the practice squad. That's when it all really hit me that I was finished."

At 11:56 that morning I received an email from Pat's father.

"C, Patrick was released. He's not in the mood to talk to anyone at this time. FYI Pat."

On the hour-drive south that afternoon from Flowery Branch to Hartsfield-Jackson Airport in Atlanta, my typically text-happy nephew numbly watched as one message after the next came in. The veteran linebackers Stephen Nicholas and Sean Weatherspoon both texted to say how great he played against the Jaguars and that he shouldn't be surprised if he got picked up by someone right away. Pires, the linebacker coach, phoned as well. None of it was helping.

Back home that night, his parents wanted to take him to dinner. They purposefully chose a place in Elgin, a couple of towns over. "Mayor Schiller" couldn't bear the thought of coming face to face with any of his eager hometown followers. His reputation, however, clearly extended beyond one suburb's borders.

"We're just sitting down," Pat told me, "and sure enough, this waiter comes over. 'Hey, you're Pat Schiller. You play for the Falcons, right?' And I'm like: 'Well, not anymore, dude. Just got cut.'"

In his old bed that night, beneath the framed photo of the Blond Tiger that he keeps above a pair of bronzed boxing gloves, Pat felt deeply conflicted about being back home. He said he hated himself for liking it so much, right down to the warm heft of his dog Champ and the chance to just hang low for a while and heal.

He slept well into the following morning, got up around 11:00 A.M., and shortly after noon headed out the front door with his father to shop for a new laptop. By then, Pat told me, he was beginning to take some stock in what Smith, his teammates, and his agent all told him: he had made good film.

"But, dude," Pat told me, "I've got to admit, I was thinking, *If*

someone is going to call, I hope it's two or three weeks from now. I was really looking forward to some time off."

Pat and his dad had just climbed into the cab of his pickup
when his phone rang. It was the Falcons. They wanted to know if
Pat would consider coming back to be on their practice squad.

"Consider?" Pat told me. "I mean a couple of weeks off would
have been nice. But to play for the team whose guys and system I
know?"

He was back in Flowery Branch by nine that night, having never
unpacked his bag.

Six weeks later, I flew down to Atlanta to watch the Falcons' away-
game matchup, against the Washington Redskins, on TV with
Pat. There's a certain ghostly quality to being on an NFL practice
squad. You work all week with the team, attend all the same meetings, eat the same meals, accrue all the same weekly bumps, aches,
and bruises, and yet walk the sidelines in the team's official civilian
clothes for home matchups and don't travel for away games. An
injury to one of the Falcons' five active-roster linebackers could
have Pat dressing for the next game. He could also be dropped at
a moment's notice for a needed backup at another position. Or
he could be picked up by any of the league's other teams for their
active roster, forcing Pat to pack his things and break the lease
he signed on the two-bedroom town house in Atlanta's northern
suburbs.

The farthest Pat had previously lived from home was the place
that he and Chandler Harnish shared near the DeKalb campus of
Northern Illinois University, just 25 miles from Geneva. His parents took care of most of his bills, including car and gas and his
auto and health insurance. His mother did his laundry at home.
He never balanced a checkbook. Now, before a small whiteboard
in his narrow kitchen, the two of us stood reviewing the monthly
cost of living his dream.

> Rent: $975
> Furniture rental: $400
> Gas/power: $55
> Car: $310
> Fitness: $30
> Cable: $40

He knew he could save more of his weekly $3,500 paycheck (after taxes) if he bought furniture. But to stay as mobile as possible in case of a sudden call to another team, he chose to rent: the headboard and clothes dresser in the bedroom; a spare wood table with four metal chairs in the dining room; and the L-shaped leather living-room sofa with a coffee table/ottoman. All the pieces seemed to barely touch the carpeting, as if they, too, were somehow keenly aware of just how provisional the life is that they're furnishing. The air mattress in his guest bedroom was a last-minute donation from his former practice-squad mate Bryce Harris. Harris was signed by the New Orleans Saints to fill a hole in their roster during the first week of the season, just days after he moved into a condo a few doors down from my nephew's.

"It's not easy," Pat said, "having to pick up everything just like that, break your lease, go to a new town, and learn a whole new system. But, hey, for $390,000 a year, you break your lease."

He told me he feels much more relaxed now with his teammates, more like one of the guys, but is still very aware of where he stands in the NFL's strict hierarchy.

"You have to know your place," he told me. "And believe me, I know. I'm always the first guy at meetings, and I'm the first guy back in the room after breaks. I still get the vets water and Gatorade. I dropped over $100 at Costco the other day on bulk candy, fruit roll-ups, Starbursts, beef jerky, sunflower seeds. We're in there watching film for hours, so that's my contribution."

He occasionally goes out with some of the other guys on the practice squad, but not much with the veteran linebackers.

"I talk more now about the game with them," he said, "and they're all cool guys, but I don't want to say, 'Hey, you want to hang out?' You don't want to be that guy. Everybody does their own thing. They're living their lives. But it's not like I sit at home and say: 'Oh, this is so sad. I don't have any friends.' It gets lonely at times. But I just kind of chill, and I find things to do."

That afternoon, Pat and I sat in front of his new flat-screen TV—the only thing in his place other than a coffee maker that he bought—watching his teammates' come-from-behind victory over the Redskins, the Falcons' fifth win against no losses. Pat watched like any modern-day, tech-savvy youth: a MacBook Air propped on his belly, an iPhone beside him, deftly surfing the Internet, fielding and sending texts between plays and during commercials, eyes darting between multiple screens until a play propelled him off the sofa with a thunderous roar.

"That's it!" he yelled at the tight end Tony Gonzalez. "Give me more of that YAC" (yards after contact).

Somehow it wasn't until we were watching postgame highlights that either of us noticed the backup linebacker, Robert James, whose former place on the practice squad Pat now held, had come into the game sometime during the fourth quarter. Pat sat bolt upright, grabbed the remote, and scrolled back through the game to determine the precise moment James entered. He then went to the Falcons' game thread on his computer, eyes narrowing, lips slightly parted in anticipation.

"Stephen Nicholas," he muttered. "Ankle."

For the next two days of my visit, we were on the Stephen Nicholas ankle watch. Texts and calls came from all directions. Everyone Pat knew, it seemed, was aware of Nicholas's ankle. Gruder, with whom Pat had only exchanged a couple of text messages since Gruder was released in August, wrote, "You getting called up this week?" Chris Browning of ProForce phoned to ask the same thing. Over dinner the following night, the number of Dave Lee, Pat's agent, flashed up on Pat's cell phone. Pat held the phone to his ear. A protracted silence.

"No, dude," he finally interrupted. "That's a funny story. I just thought you were calling about something else."

He hung up. A moment later he looked down with a quizzical head tilt at another call coming in.

"Crazy," he said. "You see a number pop up you don't know, and you think: *This is it. A team calling to pick me up.*"

Nicholas's ankle injury turned out to be less serious than originally thought. But in the Falcons' seventh game of the season, the linebacker Sean Weatherspoon was carted off the field with his own ankle troubles. He was out of the lineup for the next two games. When I checked with Pat a few days before the Falcons' game against the Arizona Cardinals, Weatherspoon's status was being listed as questionable, and the Weatherspoon ankle watch was still on.

"Who knows?" Pat told me. "But if the call comes, I'm ready."

My last night with him in Atlanta, we went back to his town house after dinner to watch a little Monday Night Football. During a break in the action, he led me into his clothes-and-sneaker-strewn bedroom to show me the huge walk-in closet he felt would allow him to send back his rented dresser. I noticed that the dresser was topped with all manner of balms, unguents, and painkilling medications: a 23-year-old with the medicine cabinet of a septuagenarian.

Somehow, it was only then that I felt the full weight of what my nephew had managed to pull off: the ridiculous odds he overcame; all the excellent players he beat out. I suddenly felt more like one of his hometown acolytes than an uncle to a kid who grew up a thousand miles and, in terms of life experiences and career pursuits, a world away from me. A kid I only came to know at this juncture because he is so good at a game that I, like millions of others, so love to watch.

"Dude," he said, as I stood staring at his dresser. "I swear to God, if someone tells me right now there's some miracle body cream out there that would make me feel 100 percent and prevent me from getting hurt but that could also cause cancer or liver damage down the line, I'd use it in a heartbeat. I would."

He picked up an empty bottle of anti-inflammatory pills and tossed it in the trash.

"Even if I make it," he said, "the average career is what, three or four years tops. But if I get hurt now, I'm gone. It's nothing personal. If I'm injured, I'm deadweight. I'm stealing their money. Do you know how many linebackers there are sitting home right now that want my job? Hundreds. I mean, let's get real. As much as Coach Smith or Coach Pires might like me, it would be: 'Hey, it's been a fun ride. You're a good kid. But see ya, Schiller!'"

DAVID SIMON

Fear the Bird

FROM SPORTS ILLUSTRATED

THEY DRIFT ON YOU. They do.

One minute, they're belt high and shading their eyes with a Rawlings mitt, brows furrowed at the green of the field, listening intently as you explain how the infield fly rule gathers the shards of an otherwise broken universe. Next minute, they realize that girls have a fundamental purpose, and they've parsed their last box score for a decade or so. Next moment after that, their minds are racing down deeper, wooded paths of their own choosing, and the batting splits for Wieters or the merits of trading for another corner outfielder cannot possibly matter when, say, the fearful symmetry of Monk's chord voicings are to be admired, or the macroeconomic to-and-fro of Keynes-Hayek waits to be argued.

My son was born in 1994. Three years later, long before he could buy me a Natty Boh and bring it back to my bleacher seat, the Orioles went to the playoffs for the last time. I'm not sure I remember what happened with that. Something about some kid in the stands, Maynor or Maier or whatever. I don't want to talk about it.

For a decade or so, he waited for our turn, and—as kids still do—he planned for the moment when it would be his turn as well. A southpaw, he'd heard me joke often that if he could get some movement on the ball, I wouldn't have to pay for college. So he was out in the yard all the damn time, making his mother catch him when I wasn't around. Once, when she told him not to throw so hard, to try to control his pitches, he shook his eight-year-old head in fierce disgust.

"Mom, don't patronize me. I'm trying to do this for a living."

Life was Ripken and a cast of thousands, and a wait-till-next-year mantra that began to rival anything ever heard in Brooklyn. But then, at 15, he had a cell phone and Facebook and, finally, a girl-friend. It was over. He had grown up in a losing town, with a losing team, and there were other passions in this world.

A month ago, as the Orioles were still strangely late for their summer swoon, I drove him to college in Boston. August slipped to September, and two weeks ago, finding myself pumped and alert at two in the morning, I pulled out my cell and fired him a text:

O's win again on a run in bottom of ninth. Still tied for first.

The Apple phone made that hopeful airfoil noise as it sent the news north. Day after, nothing came back on it. Next game, I tried again:

Ok I need you to focus. O's win today in the 14th. Thirteen extra in-ning games in a row they've won.

I waited an hour or so. No response. Then I walked down to the harbor and the nearest jersey shop, where, still, Ravens gear was selling better than O's swag. I bought one of the cartoon-bird caps—glad they're back; the ornithologically correct Oriole takes some of the blame for our long years in Babylon—and an Adam Jones jersey. I shipped them both with a note: "If you come home a Sox fan, you're out of the will."

It was pathetic and cloying, I know.

As a matter of rank expectation, this is supposed to be the man-in-the-street piece, the return-of-the-pride ramble in which the long-suffering, bone-weary common folk of a second-tier, rust-belt American city are brought to life again by the winning antics of their no-name baseball franchise.

The grime and pain of losers and also-rans are washed away with each magical success at the ballyard. The metropolis begins to believe in itself again, to greet the new daylight with small glances upward toward the heavens, with laughter and newfound kinship among rowhouse neighbors, who regale each other with last night's on-field heroics as the children tumble into the street and head for school in a seaflow of orange-and-black ball caps and jerseys. Fathers come home from work, drop briefcases, and grab mitts for a catch with sons, then adjourn to the den for a Talmudic reading of the latest box scores. Fresh graffiti is scrawled atop the

RIPs and gang tags in the heart of the toughest Westside neighborhoods: ORIOLES MAGIC. FEAR DA BIRD. And come the night of the big game, the mayor leads the rally on the steps of City Hall, flicks a switch, and lights the ornate dome orange. A city rises as one.

Well, it's been sort of like a montage from *Major League IV,* only not so much. For one thing, we weren't entirely ready when they cued the song and the cameras caught us. The Orioles have been so bad for so long that our eyes weren't exactly fixed on Camden Yards from the outset, and as the one-run and extra-inning wins began to accrue we were still nurturing past resentments—over Angelos, over the Jon Miller banishment, over the Albert Belle contract and the Schilling-Finley-Davis trade and a dozen other miscues. We were wise to these charlatans, and our hearts were held in reserve as they are every year, waiting not for a pennant race but for the opening kickoff and the arrival of purple jerseys and real possibility.

Three weeks to go in the regular season and the Orioles pull near-even with the hated Yankees and are actual favorites for a wild-card slot. And yet, good seats can be had at the Yard. With a rare Thursday day game on the television set in a South Baltimore diner, my cell phone rings and I find myself harangued by New York cousins, uncharmed by any Cinderella story. They're watching the game as well, and they're looking at empty seats along the baselines.

"Pennant race. September. And you can't fill the box seats? Don't even talk about Baltimore being a great baseball town."

Through the phone, I can smell the arrogance, the entitlement. These are the people who used to outnumber us in our own ballpark, who could, on a bad day, drown out the locals with "let's go Yankees" in the late innings. Once, writing for a television show, I conjured a story line in which a man was murdered at Camden Yards during a ball game. Stadium authority officials and Orioles execs shook their heads. Why would we let you show a murder at the stadium?

"A Yankees fan is the victim."

They were intrigued enough to venture a second question: "Who kills him?"

"Another Yankees fan."

Sold.

Still, this is a blood relative. I try to reason with the sonofabitch.
Eschewing the usual small-market inequities and hypocrisies, I
don't even bother bringing up elephantine cable television contracts or those $1,500-a-night box seats in the Bronx that are just as
noticeably empty on the baseline camera pans. I go instead to the
practicalities of a postindustrial blue-collar town:

"This isn't New York. People here work. They can't get off for a
day game."

"You guys are a half game out! The seats are f— empty!"

"You're drawing from what, 19 million? You know how many
people are in the Baltimore metro area? Maybe a sixth or seventh
of that . . ."

"Sad, cuz. Pathetic."

"Bite me, O pinstriped whore."

I hang up, turning to the television in time to see the Orioles'
bullpen hold the line for yet another inning. I look around at the
diner. Eight or nine people, a couple of waitresses, the cashier. All
of them watching the television, quiet, pensive. No cheers, nothing demonstrable, but not a word of conversation either.

Fact is, you asked the wrong guy for this little essay.

For one thing, I'm not generally known as a glass-half-full kind
of guy. I'm the fellow who writes all these dystopian sociopolitical
dramas from whatever dark corner of the American experience
offers the best chance for grievous tragedy. I'm not even a glass-
half-empty kind of guy. I'm more the glass-broken-over-the-end-of-
the-bar-and-used-to-splay-the-jugular-of-whichever-character-stood-
up-and-dared-assert-for-human-dignity-two-scenes-earlier guy. I'm
that kind of guy.

So when Nick Markakis breaks his thumb in the season's last
month, I'm supposed to see that as foreshadowing. And when the
O's drop two of three to Oakland, I'm supposed to run with that
as my leitmotif. As it ever was, as it ever shall be. Somewhere a
17-year-old urchin with bright eyes is sticking a needle in his arm.
Somewhere, a misinformed Marine officer is calling an air strike
on a civilian ville. Somewhere, a wry, humanist street musician is
getting shot in the face.

For *Sports Illustrated* to call the bullpen of Baltimore writers and
ask for Simon to get loose is a twisted little joke. What about John
Waters? I mean, *Hairspray*, that opening number? Good morning,

Baltimore! Or Taylor Branch, an O's fan who chronicled the entire civil rights movement in prose. Talk about uplift. Talk about eyes on the prize. Or Barry Levinson, for chrissake. Levinson would be perfect for this. I mean, never mind that last, saintly home run in *The Natural*—did you see his short flick on the Colts' marching band? Dude had people crying real tears *over the halftime band.*

My wife, a first-rate novelist, grew up here. She's the one with Brooks Robinson memorabilia scattered across her office. She's the one who knows all the words to the "World of Orioles Baseball" song. She's the one who met Ron Swoboda and actually told the man she was still aggrieved by 1969 and The Catch.

"It's been 35 years," he said. "You need to get over it."

"No," she replied calmly. "I don't."

This could have been done right and proper. Instead, the plan is to squeeze warm blood and nostalgia and little-engine-that-could optimism from *The Wire* guy.

And it's worse than you know because, honestly, I'm not from here. And I grew up hating the Orioles. Hating them more than a tetanus shot. Hating them way more than the Yankees. In my childhood the big bad birds from Baltimore were forever coming to town and stomping the very humanity out of the team that I truly loved. The Robinsons. Boog. Belanger. Palmer. McNally. Cuellar. What those guys did to my youth is harden me for a lifetime of writing unhappy endings.

I am from Washington. And I was born a Senators fan.

Does the darkness make sense now? Does it? You sick bastards.

It is April 1988, and I am pretty much living inside the Baltimore Homicide Unit, a newspaperman who has finagled his way into a year with the murder police in a town ripe with bloodletting, hoping to write himself a book.

In one interrogation room, Bunk Requer is writing up a witness statement on a Morrell Park cutting, and in the larger Box, I can hear Kincaid yelling at some 17-year-old prodigy who shot and killed a man over a three-piece chicken combo outside the Kentucky Fried on Fayette Street.

I'm in the main squad room, trying to watch the ball game on the office black-and-white. Constantine plays with the rabbit ears, working to solve the insubordinate vertical hold. And the O's are losing. Again. It is wondrous, actually. Amazing.

The dominant baseball franchise of my youth is on its way to
ending the whole season in April, losing its first 21 games. The rest
of the detectives are abject and disgusted, cursing the owner, the
coaching, the players, the fates. One of the guys has a share in a
season-ticket package and looks as if he's ready to pull his .38 and
fire five into the television, saving the last one for himself.

A uniform walks in with a transport, another witness sent downtown from Kincaid's crime scene. He hands off paperwork, waits a
moment, watches Larry Sheets ground into a double play.

"Christ. Losing again? What's the score?"

He's told.

"This is worse than getting the clap from your sister."

Constantine grunts a laugh. Good one, kid.

An inning more and the TV is shut down. The detectives drift
away. Me, I say nothing to anyone, of course, but from deep within,
I can feel the shrunken Grinch-heart of a Senators fan growing. In
fact, I can feel love everlasting. The O's are really awful this year.
They're so bad, so desperate in fact, that I can once again devote
myself to a baseball team.

I got to Baltimore in '83. Even went to the first game of the
World Series when someone laid a ticket on me. Watched im-
passively as the O's beat the Phillies for their last title. Ripken,
Murray, the Demper. But they weren't mine. They were still the
Visigoths who had raped and plundered their way through old
RFK Stadium. But now, this exquisite misery, this Homeric run of
failure that reminds me of Howard and Epstein, McMullen and
Brinkman and Casanova, that gently fingers the broken part of my
baseball soul.

I came aboard in '88. Six years later, when my son was born, I
was still waiting for what we all assumed would be a return to the
power and the glory, to The Oriole Way. It never occurred to me
that Ethan might grow up as I grew up, and that he might go away
without the two of us sharing so much as a winning season.

A week ago, I sat up late watching that 18-inning epic in Seattle.
The game ended magnificently, and of course, I wanted to be
around other people. Baltimoreans. Fans. It was four in the damn
morning.

Still, I was wired. I walked down to the 7-Eleven for I don't know
what, hoping against hope. The aisles were empty, but a 20-some-

thing kid was stumbling, half lit, around the register, trying to pay for a Big Gulp. He'd come from a house party, he told me. They'd been playing poker, but then the ball game got good, and instead of dealing cards, they sat around drinking, hearts in their hands, waiting for the Orioles to sneak away with another one.

"Even the guys who aren't from here were into it. You gotta love it. I mean, a different hero every night. Taylor f— Teagarden!"

"You from here?"

"All my life. I never seen a season like this. Have you?"

Not for a long while, I allowed. I wandered home, thought about texting my son, but no, this all comes too late. Too many years late.

Except the next night at 7:08 P.M., my phone throws out its little tone, and I see a text from an 18-year-old university freshman, who is with a childhood friend also in school in Beantown.

Sitting atop the Green Monster with Thomas Bottomley. Yelled "0" in the anthem. Now fearing for my life.

I thought of my son at Fenway, draped in that Adam Jones jersey, bird cap crowning him at the jauntiest of angles, surrounded by rows and rows of embittered Sox fans for whom this September is dry, empty death.

You go, brah, I texted him. *Die like a commando.*

The Kid stays in the will. If he makes it back to the dorm, I mean.

GARY SMITH

Why Don't More
Athletes Take a Stand?

FROM SPORTS ILLUSTRATED

PARDON ME, I'D like to interrupt your regularly scheduled programming and introduce you to America's rarest athlete: Wonman
Joseph Williams. His first name's a Korean word that means *full
harmony,* but you don't need to check his papers. He's a defensive
back on a Division I football team. You know, a student-ATHLETE.

He's a 19-year-old who stands up during team meetings at Virginia so that he won't fall asleep, but not because he's sluggish or
disengaged. You see, he's attempting to do something that's nearly
impossible at a college in the United States today. He's trying to be
a student, an athlete, *and* a human being. He's trying to live in full
harmony.

Lotsa luck, kid! See you around!

Wait. That's him again, darting through a frigid rain and dripping into UVA's Alderman Library. His eyes fix on a student whose
head has sagged onto a table amid the laptops, books, and coffee
cups. "That's one of the hunger strikers," murmurs a classmate.
"He's two days in. They're doing it for the Living Wage Campaign."

Full Harmony stares in puzzlement. He has attended Living
Wage rallies on campus, has friends in the crusade. He knows
what's at stake for the thousands of campus workers barely scrap-
ing by, many on incomes at or near minimum wage. He knows
the scrapers too: the old black dudes who scrape the snow and
dog crap off this gorgeous green playground for the mind that
Thomas Jefferson wrought nearly two centuries ago, the women
who scrape the gravy and mayo off the plates in the dining-hall
kitchens. Full Harmony's not another one of those students who

cross campus with their eyes locked on their smartphones. He sings out greetings to total strangers, popping the bubble wrap around his school's elite matriculants, slicing at the distance between the students and the townies who serve them, perplexing all who've yet to perceive what he and they share. So how—besides the fact that he's a student-ATHLETE, one of 444,000 young American men and women who annually turn over their lives because they wish to play a college sport—has he missed hearing about this hunger strike?

He flashes a text to one of the Living Wage campaigners, a classmate named Hallie Clark: *I didn't know y'all were hunger striking.*

We sure are, she replies.

A thought and a nervous tickle run through him: he needs to join them. He needs to stop eating and watch the muscles on his five-ten, 207-pound body begin melting away so that Mama Kathy, the woman he hugs when she swipes his ID card at the dining hall, and Miss Mary, the lady he always chats with at the convenience-store cash register in the basement of Newcomb Hall, and all of their coworkers can . . . But, *c'mon.* He's busy rehabbing the surgically repaired ligament in his left ankle, the one that wiped out most of his second season, so he'll be ready when spring ball starts in a few weeks . . . and besides, imagine what his coaches would say . . . and *really,* sports and social justice, they just don't mix anymore. Who in the last 40 years, in the wave after wave of American student-ATHLETES—not to mention the 4,100 young men on the rosters of the four mainstream professional sports each year—has made a stand like this?

Good. He can't hear that bitter cackle in the distance. It's one of the old, gray warriors from the front lines of the 1960s and early '70s who'd be willing to bet what this kid's going to decide. It's John Carlos, the bronze medalist in the '68 Olympic 200 meters, who raised his black-gloved fist on the medal stand to bring attention to racism in the United States and brought all hell down upon his head. "Athletes today?" he cries. "They don't know history! They don't want to come out of their box and risk people taking away their lollipops!"

Full Harmony whips out his cell phone again. Coach can't say no if Coach doesn't know. *Count me in,* he types.

Eat your last meal, Hallie replies.

*

Full Harmony's last meal: a double burger, chicken nuggets, french fries, and a chocolate chip cookie, to the din of a pounding rain in his girlfriend's car in a McDonald's parking lot at 10:30 P.M. on a Sunday in February. Gone in four and a half minutes—he's never been one for ceremony. He balls up the wrappers, his excitement rising as the grease settles. He's your crème-de-la-crème college student, carrying a 3.43 GPA in one of his university's most selective and challenging majors, Political and Social Thought, while doing volunteer work at a Charlottesville Boys & Girls Club, mentoring Charlottesville teenagers in the Collegiate 100 Society, teaching English as a second language to a refugee from Burundi in UVA's Visas program, raising funds for the homeless as part of his fraternity's untiring community service, and, oh yeah, playing on an ACC football team. Doing *this*, though—true activism for a greater cause—is what he dreamed college would be back when he signed up for it, but he has barely seen a trace of it in his three years on campus.

At 9:00 A.M. the next morning he enters the anthropology building, Brooks Hall, and joins the gaunt gang of protesters. Perhaps he's naive. Perhaps they are too. Nobody, especially Full Harmony, regards him as anything more than Hunger Striker Number 13 . . . except for one woman. Emily Filler's a UVA grad student and an adjunct instructor at nearby University of Mary Washington who's serving as the Living Wage Campaign's publicist during the strike, and when Hallie casually mentions Full Harmony's extracurricular activity to her, she *knows* at once: a handsome, high-cheekboned, square-jawed, ever-smiling, *humble football player* hunger-striking against his university administration's wage policy for thousands of mostly African American campus workers. *Yahtzee!*

She calls Frankie Jupiter, reporter for CBS affiliate WCAV, and by the time the hunger strikers have gathered on the steps of the Rotunda for their daily noon rally, Jupiter's got a camera rolling and a microphone under Full Harmony's jaw. Capturing his vow that he won't eat until UVA, the biggest employer in town, does what 17 of the other 22 elite universities considered to be its peers have done and agrees to pay its service-sector workers a "living wage." That's a sum that the nonpartisan Economic Policy Institute, calculating the cost of living on a city-by-city basis, has determined for Charlottesville to be $13 an hour, which is anywhere from $2.35 to $5.75 more than the starting wage for UVA service workers.

Full Harmony finishes the interview, hoists a sign—WORKERS ARE PEOPLE TOO!—and becomes the loudest chanter of all: *One! Two! Three! Four! No one should be working poor! Five! Six! Seven! Eight! UVA! Living wage!*

A hundred students, a handful of them his friends, stop and gawk, then hurry away. Damn. Full Harmony, empty stomach, watches them all head off to lunch.

He awakens on day two to a discovery: nothing's harder to ignore than a hollow belly. Get up, he tells himself. Get moving. He crosses campus and slips into the football trainer's room, bracing for the tap on the shoulder and the nod toward the coaches' offices. He begins banging out his hour and a half of rehab work: underwater treadmill, calf raises, balancing exercises, stretches, crunching towels and picking up marbles with his toes, cold and hot whirlpools. It hits him halfway through: he's operating a Maserati on an empty tank. He drags himself into the locker room, pouring his last few volts into that high-beam smile, the everything's-hunky-dory look, just in case. The football facility's crawling with assistant coaches and athletic department staffers. Either they still don't know . . .

. . . or just don't care. Yeah, maybe he can get away with this because of the scarlet *W* he wears. *Walk-on.* He's accustomed to feeling like a penny in a gold mine, dressing over here in Walk-On Corner, aka the Hood. Because in the Hood you don't get your own locker, sharing one with another walk-on, and you're not even just a number—you share that with someone far above you on the depth chart—and you're not allowed to take out your frustration on the starters or the second-stringers in practice because *We gotta get them to the game, son! Just wrap 'em up and keep 'em vertical!* And still Full Harmony loves it, approaching every practice as if it's the ACC championship game in front of 73,675 screamers, bent on being a weekday superstar.

He has found himself on the field for only a handful of kickoffs in the second halves of games that the Cavaliers have salted away . . . but his teammates, they know Joe-Joe. That's what they call him, because no one named Wonman or even Joseph—that's the name his nonfootball friends call him—could possibly be as hy-

per and happy, as earsplitting and ever-ready as Joe-Joe. Quickest
on the scout team to suss out the first-stringers' offense and call
out the appropriate defense, to call aside Cavaliers wide receivers
and warn them about what they're tipping off, to clap and bellow,
"Give that boy a scholarship!" when one of his fellow scout-teamers
makes a play.

He exits the locker room and surveys the facilities where football players pump their iron, do their cardio, eat their meals, and
attend their study halls, all far from the rest of the student body.
He gazes at the two state-of-the-art synthetic practice fields, with a
third one, a $13 million indoor facility, about to get green-lighted
by the school's trustees, the Board of Visitors, because, well, what
if it rains? Green-lighted at a budget meeting during this very hunger strike, even as administrators are insisting to the strikers that
budget constraints prevent them from paying a living wage! That's
like food to Joseph. It fills his empty tank with fury.

How has all this happened in the blink of the evolutionary
eye? Twenty-five hundred years ago, the earliest of such athletic
fields—gymnasia—were being built by the Greeks. Centers where
philosophers strolled and teachers instructed young men in ethics, morals, science, math, and poetry, where the playing field was
a grand courtyard surrounded by libraries and lecture halls and
classrooms with the intent of fully harmonizing the development
of body and mind. A lad couldn't run, jump, or hurl anything
without learning how to question, how to think, how to see *connections.*

Somehow it has all become about separation, the promising
athlete culled from the pack as early as nine or 10, placed with his
select peers on travel teams, enthroned on an ever-rising pedestal
through high school, isolated from the student body in college,
fattened on the myth of his onliness by well-meaning coaches,
parents, and fans, then pricked and prodded weekly for psycho-
logical advantage by those same coaches: *THEY don't think you're
good enough! They don't respect you!* Us against them, you against the
world, the cult of self-anointing the athlete as its Ultra Self . . . Is it
any wonder in 2012 how many players, rather than join their teammates to hug and celebrate after catching a touchdown pass or
nailing a game-winning three-pointer, strut *away* from them and
glare? *Showed you I'm special! Showed you I'm better than all of them
(and even all of "us")!* Is it any wonder that from such soil, no such

thing as a sportsman social activist has sprung since the days of Jim Brown, Bill Russell, John Carlos, Tommie Smith, Arthur Ashe, Billie Jean King, Bill Walton?

Tiger Woods took one step down that path, early in his career, in a Nike ad in which his words rolled on the screen — *There are still courses in the United States I am not allowed to play because of the color of my skin. I've heard I'm not ready for you. Are you ready for me?* — and, in the wake of a backlash, stopped there. Labor activists who requested Michael Jordan's support in their quest to improve sweatshop conditions and reduce child-labor abuse in the production of Air Jordans in Southeast Asia got none. "Moral jellyfish," Dave Meggyesy, a linebacker and antiwar activist with the St. Louis Cardinals in the '60s, labeled these athletes.

But scores of modern athletes, led by Woods and Jordan, create remarkable charity foundations, raise funds, and donate millions. Taken one step further — watered with an investment of time and heart nearly equal to the money — a miracle such as Andre Agassi's academy for at-risk children in Las Vegas has bloomed in the desert. But when it comes to social action that might step on toes, that might send a shiver down the spine of their publicists or their corporate sponsors, what have American athletes done? "The scared generation," former Yankees pitcher Jim Bouton calls them.

"They've put the dollar bill in front of the human race," grouses Carlos. "That's why they stopped standing up."

"They *have* to speak up," insists Harry Edwards, a track and field and basketball star at San Jose State in the early '60s who went on to become a sociology professor there and at Cal. "They're the most visible expression of achievement and financial success in this country. Actors in Hollywood have always been very outspoken. Athletes have surpassed them as the number-one entertainers; they should be at least as outspoken. Those who set the table that today's athletes are dining at, they exercised that responsibility. Now you have to get past an athlete's corporate and personal advisers, and so he's got to think what's in the best interest of Buick and Nike and Starbucks and General Electric."

Fascinating how many of the recent sportsmen who've taken stands didn't spring from our system or our soil: Canada's Steve Nash, flayed by players, coaches, and media for wearing a NO WAR, SHOOT FOR PEACE T-shirt on media day at the NBA's All-Star weekend in 2003, as the United States was girding to invade Iraq;

Adonal Foyle of St. Vincent and the Grenadines, who founded Democracy Matters during his 12-year NBA career to educate young people on how money was strangling U.S. politics and to pressure politicians to change campaign-finance laws. The modern athlete who sacrificed by far the most for his cause—first his fortune, then his life—died here on Joseph's campus, and he, of course, was foreign-born too. Retired NBA center Manute Bol gave away virtually his entire $6 million in savings to build schools and hospitals in his native southern Sudan, then extended his stay there for a week in 2010 at the request of the president to oversee South Sudan's first independent elections even as a potentially deadly disease he'd contracted there, Stevens-Johnson syndrome, began devouring his flesh. He finally headed back to his family's home in Kansas, got off the transatlantic flight at Dulles Airport, and was rushed to UVA Medical Center, where he died in searing pain virtually next door to the building where Joseph took Early African History as a freshman. "That," Joseph says, "blows my mind."

The only emergency he's facing now is the ever-shrinking time until Virginia's next football game, ticking away like frantic heartbeats on a scoreboard clock beside the locker-room door: *193 days, 2 hours, 14 minutes, 37 . . . 36 . . . 35 seconds* until the 2012 opener against Richmond. He heads back onto campus, relieved that his coaches haven't cornered him.

He digs up some phone numbers and calls NBC News, ABC, *The Today Show*, BET, and NPR, leaving word of the UVA hunger strike in hopes of drumming up coverage. He fails to mention one thing: he's a football player. No one calls him back.

The strikers, most on their fourth day without food, are reeling when he joins them for their noon rally: an epidemic of headaches, dizziness, racing hearts, fatigue, and irritability. One has strep throat. Some can chant only for a few minutes, then have to lie down. "I feel fine," Joseph assures Greg Gelburd, the family physician who's monitoring them.

Two hours later he raises his hand as his Political and Social Thought class discusses a renowned letter that Martin Luther King Jr. wrote from a Birmingham jail to his fellow clergymen. "Yes, Joseph?" says professor Michael Smith. Joseph opens his mouth to speak . . . but hasn't the faintest clue *what*, and falls silent.

But he knows exactly what he wants to say at a student council meeting that evening, after the strikers ask the council to issue a resolution to the trustees in support of a living wage for the workers. One opponent of the resolution insists that it's un-American to pay workers "more than they're worth on the free market," that it's an assault on the "sanctity" of the market, one of the country's founding institutions. "Slavery was one of the founding institutions of America!" Joseph cries. How many rules and regulations have human beings, over time, understood more deeply and altered? The resolution gets tabled and dies.

He discovers three messages on his cell phone and an email from the football staff, all saying the same thing: *Report to the office. Now.*

Two massive black gladiators in football regalia rise over the right flank of coach Mike London's desk. One mannequin wears the Cavaliers' blue home jersey, the other visiting orange. They possess everything that an athlete in 2012 could desire: pectorals sculpted by years in a weight room, arms that hang at their sides like chiseled clubs, red biceps bands, white gloves, Nike swooshes. Everything . . . except heads.

They're the easy metaphor for the athlete that the U.S. system produces today. Too easy. The separated-out, year-round, one-sport jock we're creating is often steeped in discipline, fighting spirit, leadership, and time management skills. If he's, say, a UVA player such as Joseph, he's up at 5:30 A.M.; getting taped at 6:00; practicing, pumping iron, and doing agility drills till 10:30; dragging his weary legs and sore shoulders to class; returning at 3:15 for another hour and a half of meetings and film study; then squeezing in his homework after dinner and collapsing into sleep. The 20-hour limit on weekly practice mandated by the NCAA? Every university skirts that by establishing all manner of "voluntary" activities and preparation for games that any *non*volunteer, of course, will never play. If he's a baseball player, he's reporting three hours before a game that lasts another three hours, taking a knee in the outfield grass afterward while his coach recounts his version of the whole affair, cleaning up the dugout and regrooming the field, wolfing down a meal and straggling back to his books or his pillow eight and a half hours after pulling on his jock . . . 56 times in the regular season and up to 13 more in the postseason! Off-season? No off-season exists for college athletes anymore. Minor sports? Virtually no minor sports exist either, even at Division

II and III levels. Lacrosse, volleyball, and field hockey programs have morphed into one *more* opportunity for an institution to market itself and a coach to burnish his résumé and climb his career ladder as university presidents turn a blind eye to the absurd number of hours required of student-ATHLETES . . . because . . . well, aren't sports the glue that binds the college, that lures alums and their checkbooks back onto campus, that creates TV revenues and free media advertising? In a society in which coaches are left to play the role of tribal elders, too many tribal elders have lost their way. Louisville coach Bobby Petrino thought fullback D. J. Kamer's priorities were all wrong when he requested to miss a practice—a *practice*—in 2003 so he could serve as a pallbearer at a dear friend's funeral, a mind-set that, along with his 41-9 record with Louisville, reaped Petrino big leaps to the NFL's Falcons and Arkansas until a blonde and a Harley-Davidson undid him.

Yes, the system allows an athlete to pursue his dream . . . but what if his head or heart is large enough for *two* dreams? What of the athlete wise enough to know that this dream has, oh, perhaps a one-in-100 chance of panning out beyond the next few years, and even if it does, another half century or more of life awaits him— rich decades for those who've begun pursuing other passions and curiosities, more likely fallow for those herded into this tunnel?

Could Tommie Smith and John Carlos have become bronze statues on San Jose State's campus had they come of age today? Would Smith, in 2012, have attended the provocative sociology classes taught by Harry Edwards that helped inspire the sprinter to shut his eyes, bow his head, and raise his right fist during the national anthem in Mexico City in 1968 after breaking the world record in the 200 meters, provoking a national debate and one more advance in our long crawl to humanity? Not if those sociology classes couldn't have been crammed into today's ever-narrowing windows of time between practice and conditioning and meetings, and not if—as has become commonplace—Smith's coaches had persuaded him to take a less challenging major so he could commit fully to his sport.

"It's like a job," says Joseph. "We're only students to a certain extent. Sports have become such a big moneymaker that it's all about the bottom line, like so much else in our society. It not only limits your potential to pursue academics but *punishes* you when your dedication to academics interferes with your sport. Most football and basketball players can't take any of the difficult classes. You're not able to take advantage of what these great schools have to offer. It's not even amateur athletics anymore. It's professional."

"It's a horrific schedule," says Edwards, who over the last three decades has watched athletes stop taking classes that start after 1:00 P.M., classes with labs, classes that require their time on Fridays, Saturdays, or Sundays. Study abroad in the off-season, even if you're a Division III relief pitcher? Don't be silly.

"Joseph is the first football player who's ever entered our program," says professor Smith, the director of UVA's Political and Social Thought Department. "He soaks up learning. He's got intellectual curiosity. He's refreshingly open. I have enormous respect for the kids in our sports programs—plenty are smart and have enormous discipline. It suggests to me the potential of these athletes if we challenge them intellectually the way we do athletically. But we're selling these kids a bad deal. They're doing a job here— full-time athletics. To pretend otherwise is to engage in denial. They're on an island within the university. A subset of the staff is paid highly to get them through, but it's not about engaging their minds with the outside world. They lead a regimented life, no time to loaf, to think, to read a book. It's a precious four years of a human life when you acquire the habit of inquiry, when you acquire your intellectual capital. We have to ask ourselves, Why do we do this? To fill the endless demand for cable TV programming? Are athletes really in college or in some quasi-factory? We've *shrunk* them."

Joseph refuses to be shrunk. That's why he has gotten in trouble in the past for dozing during defensive meetings and twice sleeping through the 6:00 A.M. alarm he'd set for his seven o'clock weight workouts. That's why he's stood during meetings and devoured bananas, having heard that they're a more effective energy booster than coffee. He's written essays at 3:00 A.M. because he wouldn't allow the six hours a day of football commitments to annihilate the rest of his student life and volunteer work. But now, on day three of his hunger strike, it's time to face the consequences. Right or wrong, he has violated one of sports' bedrock values, submission to authority—the one that's *not* pounded into actors as they grow up, making it so much easier for them to turn and stand against the tide. Heart thumping, he trudges upstairs to the football offices.

But not to Coach London's office. This hunger strike's a moral
swamp that London has no wish to wade into. He's not a tunnel
coach, he's a big-lens guy, an African American who has felt the
same hot breath on his neck as these campus workers; who had
a child when he was in college, divorced soon after, and drove a
Boys & Girls Club bus to get by; who as an undercover detective in
Richmond had a gun pointed at his head by a thug and heard the
trigger click, the weapon malfunctioning; who beat 10,000-to-one
odds when his bone marrow matched that of a daughter afflicted
by a blood disorder that often leads to leukemia and death; and
who has his players plugged into a multitude of volunteering activities. What muddies it all even more is that London is Joseph's
frat brother, a product of community-activist, predominantly African American Phi Beta Sigma, whose motto is "culture for service and service for humanity," a group fiercely proud of its members' leadership in the famous civil rights March on Washington
in 1963, the Selma protest march two years later, and the Million
Man March in 1995. But now London's receiving $2.1 million a
year from the same employer that the hunger strikers are howling
at over precisely such vast wage disparities, and he's passed word
to his media relations man that he has no comment for reporters
who've begun to inquire about Joseph's hunger strike.

So Joseph's sent to Jim Reid, the associate head coach and defensive coordinator. What will he do, Joseph wonders, if Reid lays
down an ultimatum: give up the hunger strike or give up your
football jersey. Will he have the strength of one of his heroes, Muhammad Ali, who walked away from his world heavyweight crown
and boxing career for three years rather than accept induction
into the U.S. Army during the Vietnam War? Joseph loves Reid,
considers him genuine, fair, and interested in his players as more
than athletes. Didn't Reid invite Joseph to sleep in his office during team meetings in the fall of 2010 when the kid's father was
dying in Washington, D.C., and all the traveling back and forth
to the hospital, piled on top of his other commitments, pushed
Joseph past the brink of exhaustion? Didn't Reid once tell Joseph
that he could envision him becoming the president of the United
States or a Supreme Court justice? But now . . .

"You can be in sympathy with a cause, but some people shouldn't
be doing this," Reid tells him. "You have to be responsible to your
rehabbing and to your health. I'm a little disappointed that the

people you're with, they're not aware you're at greater risk than they are."

Joseph's mind spins. Greater risk? He's an athlete, for crying out loud—he's the only hunger striker whose blood pressure isn't plummeting! What should he do? Turn and lock his coach's office door, the way Edwards did 51 years ago when his moment of truth came with San Jose State track coach Bud Winter? Glaring *down* at Winter—Edwards was a six-foot-eight, 225-pound nationally ranked discus thrower—he demanded humane treatment of black athletes who were being flown in from as far as Philadelphia for track tryouts and given no money for lodging or transportation home if they were cut, leaving some to sleep in the team's equipment shed.

Coach Reid's not finished. "There's a way to precipitate change," he continues. "It happens through political solutions, and you work within a certain set of rules. You prepare and convince people, you prepare hard, you work hard, you win—just like football!" And one more thing. Reid doesn't want this hunger strike being linked on the news with the Virginia football program.

Joseph blinks. Should he come right back at his coach the way Bill Walton did 40 years ago on the car ride home from jail when John Wooden—furious that he had to bail out Walton after his center had been arrested for helping take over a campus building during an anti–Vietnam War protest—reprimanded the redhead for working "outside the rules" instead of expressing his beliefs in a letter? "But, Coach, my friends are coming home in body bags and wheelchairs!" Walton fired back, then called Wooden's bluff by marching into his office and using stationery with Wooden's photo on the top to write a letter to President Richard Nixon demanding that he resign and getting all his teammates to sign it.

But Walton had just been named NCAA Player of the Year and led UCLA to a 30-0 record and a national title, and Edwards was so dominant an athlete that the San Jose State basketball coach simply picked up his full athletic scholarship and made him his starting center when Winter threw him off the track team. Joseph has *one* career tackle . . . if you count the Orange-Blue spring game.

He swallows his anger, says little, and nods farewell to his coach.

Joseph has learned the hard way—in cop cars, in handcuffs, in courtrooms, in a fluorescent jumpsuit, in a juvenile detention cen-

ter—to follow his mother's advice: *Watch that hole beneath your nose!*
But he feels as if his loyalty to the football program and UVA are
being questioned, and, wait a minute, are those loyalties supposed
to be larger than his loyalty to the human race? No, he *can't* wait
a minute, can't wait till he gets home to respond to his coach. He
flips open his laptop on a stool in front of his locker, takes a deep
breath, and summons every bit of his UVA education to compose
his reply.

> Dear Coach Reid and the UVA Coaching Staff:
> . . . This morning I met with you to discuss my involvement in the
> hunger strike and you expressed your disappointment that I and my
> fellow strikers are not seeking to resolve this grave issue in a more
> "political" manner. You told me that you had thought higher of me
> before you learned of my involvement in this campaign and stated
> that you were dismayed by my perceived unwillingness to "follow the
> rules."
> . . . I would firstly like to point out that this campaign has ex-
> isted at UVA for 14 years and has thoroughly exhausted all manner
> of negotiations "within the rules" without any tangible results . . .
> Secondly, no great injustice has ever been overturned by following
> the rules. Our great country was founded on the wholly evil institu-
> tion of slavery, which was only overturned when the nation split in
> two and engaged in civil war. The Jim Crow reign of segregation
> and fierce race hatred in the south, though challenged repeatedly
> through purely political and judicial actions, was eventually over-
> turned only as a result of the nonviolent protest tactics of the Civil
> Rights Movement.
> . . . I believe it is my responsibility as a member of the University
> community, and even moreso as a member of the human race, to
> stand up for those whose voices have been silenced and whose liveli-
> hoods are being marginalized by the policies of the current Univer-
> sity administration. In fact, I firmly believe that the workers that the
> Living Wage Campaign represents are just as important to this com-
> munity, if not moreso, than any football coaches, players, or fans.
> Thus, it disheartens myself and my fellow campaigners that while
> these workers, the majority of whom are women and African Ameri-
> cans, are being systematically discriminated against and exploited,
> there are plans to spend millions of dollars on a domed practice
> field and other accommodations for the athletics department . . .
> I refuse to comply with rules, regulations, or restrictions that rein-
> force the discrimination, persecution, and exploitation of human
> beings.

... I happily sacrifice my bodily needs for the greater cause of economic and social justice and I would, without hesitation, sacrifice my membership on the football team and my enrollment at the University if it would result in the University administration recognizing and meeting the demands of the Living Wage Campaign . . . I wish you, the rest of the coaches, and all of my teammates nothing but the best and I sincerely love you all as my family.

—Best, Joseph

A few hours later, he ups the ante. His letter to his coaches becomes the heart of a "Why I'm Hunger Striking" post that he writes for Michaelmoore.com. In no time the Huffington Post and *The Nation,* upon discovering that he's an athlete, publish it too.

He decides to ignore his coach's reservations and keep starving. Stairways grow daunting. His body grows colder. His sense of smell intensifies, a primal response to food deprivation: he can scent a ham sandwich a first down away. Over and over, the gut flashes the mind a message—*I'm hungry*—and the legs begin walking automatically toward the dining hall, and over and over the mind flashes back the same reply, *Stop! You can't eat,* until finally the loop exhausts itself and the body says, *To hell with it all, then, just let me sleep . . .*

Hunger's fourth day dawns. The campus workers send word to the strikers—*We can't show up at the noontime rallies; we're afraid of getting fired.* But Miss Mary can't be fired for riding by on her bike and smiling and waving her gratitude to Joseph. "Every time I see him," she says, "it's a joy to my eyes." Mama Kathy can't be fired for shaking a finger at him and crying, "Eat, gorgeous! Just eat when nobody's looking and act like you're hungry! Pretend you're in the drama department and you're going for the Academy Award!"

"Aw, I can't do that, Mama," Joseph replies.

He has lost a half-dozen pounds. His mind's mush. He raises his hand three times in Martin Luther King's Political Thought class and forgets each time what he meant to say. Fellow striker Breezy Pitts blacks out in economics class. The doctor orders her to eat.

A dozen teammates keep tabs on Joe-Joe with texts or calls. "Some appreciate his hunger strike," says wide receiver Miles Gooch, "and some think it's a bit extreme." *All* are stunned by the swelling media attention.

Suddenly, a fourth-string cornerback's being featured in the

Washington Post, the *Chicago Sun-Times,* SI.com, Yahoo! Sports, *Ebony,* msn.com, AOL News—in *45* Google pages' worth of websites! Suddenly the hunger strikers have a national bullhorn and UVA has a major publicity problem, all because of a walk-on football player of whom the school's media relations department doesn't even have a photograph in its files. All because sports is our obsession.

But *do* our athletes have any more obligation to rush to the ramparts in the struggle for social justice than our bank tellers or mailmen or stockbrokers? No, probably not, Joseph says, but omigod, the platform and the wattage at athletes' disposal if they do. The tidal waves of attention paid to sports are an energy stream that can be diverted anywhere, even to the plight of a janitor or a dishwasher, even by the most insignificant of athletes. Joseph emails his fellow strikers, expressing his worry that the media focus on him might rub them wrong. Rub them wrong? They're thrilled. They're reaching audiences they never dreamed they could. Joseph's email account is about to explode, messages pouring in from professors and students and pastors and football fans across the country.

"A rose will bloom even through the crack of a concrete sidewalk," says Edwards. "That's what has happened at the University of Virginia."

Day five for Joseph. Day eight for more than half of the 21 others now going hungry. They're hoarse, frayed, frantic, marching to the doorstep of the university president's house, screaming, *You're not meeting! We're not eating! You're not meeting! We're not eating!* Marching on the Board of Visitors meeting in the Rotunda and shrieking, *The people, united, will never be defeated! The people, united, will never be defeated!* Marching on the administrative offices, howling, *When workers' rights are under attack, what do we do? Stand up! Fight back!*

The administration won't budge, sending emails to tens of thousands of students and faculty explaining its financial predicament, pointing out that its minimum starting pay of $10.65 plus benefits to its direct employees is the second-highest in Virginia regardless of the fact that the university is hiring ever-growing numbers of contract workers from outside agencies that pay them as little as $7.25 an hour with little or no benefits. Outsourcing on the cheap, no different from many U.S. corporations. At their noon rally the strikers take turns on the bullhorn pleading their case and sharing their personal stories, then sag to the ground in exhaustion, a few dissolving into tears.

It's Joseph's turn to tell his tale. So how *did* this kid slip through the cracks of the U.S. sports system — or bloom through one? Oh, it's clear right away, he's not been washed here by the mainstream. This is what it takes for a Division I athlete in 2012 to end up starving and chanting for human rights: a childhood lived in homeless shelters, transitional housing, a church basement, a friend's attic, a tiny camper, fleabag motels, grandparents' houses, cramped apartments . . . *30* homes in his 19 years. Got off easy: his older sister, Joy, tallied 50. Moving because the joint was infested or the landlord a creep or the plumbing pitiful or a job in some other town might actually pay just enough for them to survive. Four children and a parent sleeping in one bed at one shelter, piled in with families whose adults had addictions or physical handicaps, piled in with people wondering what was odd about *this* family, besides the obvious: it's an interracial family in Virginia. Again and again, someone somehow materializing and offering them a hand, saving them from the streets and starvation.

How did Joseph's mom, Rhonda — raised Jewish and middle-class and suburban in Blue Bell, Pennsylvania — end up a gypsy trying to keep four children out of oblivion's clutches? Married to Bruce Williams, a burly, good-natured black man, a reformed drug addict from the hard half of Norfolk. Both had joined Reverend Sun Myung Moon's Unification Church, done years of volunteer and mission work, and, still strangers to each other, committed to wedding in 1982 as part of the church's plan to erase the barriers between races and nations through intermarriage. Bruce ricocheted from job to job, a security guard one day; a counselor at a home for troubled kids the next; a taxi, truck, and bus driver who kept crashing taxis, trucks, and buses . . . and then seemed to give up. There was never, because of all of his and Rhonda's mission and volunteer work, a cash reserve to tide them over. And so Mom kept bursting through the door to announce, We're moving again! Right *now!* Scavenge the dumpsters behind the grocery and liquor stores for cardboard boxes! Jam the sheets and towels in those plastic bins! Dismantle the cinder-block bookshelf! Heave everything else into those crates! Don't forget the mousetraps! Leave the place cleaner than when we arrived! You know the drill!

Truth was, they didn't—it was usually helter-skelter, a ransacked
army on the run, one eye out for the roaches and rodents that
kept moving with them. Between the moves and job changes,
Rhonda would round up the kids on weekends and summer mornings, dress them in donated clothes, funnel them into a clunker,
drive past all the ball fields where all those kids in crisp unis were
playing weekend tournaments, and find someone, somewhere, in
worse shape than they were to help out. Or *better* off; didn't matter. The Williams Crew cleaned up streets, parks, schools, hell,
even rivers, wading into the Anacostia River in waist-high boots to
have at the 20,000 tons of trash entering it each year. They planted
trees, organized a summer school for underprivileged kids, made
sandwiches for poor people, baked cookies for old people, sang
"Take Me Out to the Ball Game" and "O Little Town of Bethle-
hem" in nursing homes.

Somebody in that flock of saints had to rebel, so Joseph, in ninth
grade, volunteered. Puberty had come, Dad had gone—Bruce and
Rhonda had split six years earlier—his two older siblings had just
moved out, and the feeling that everything was falling apart was
confirmed when his mother couldn't scrape together the $200
to get Joseph's heart murmur checked out, so his big love was
lost too: no high school football. He started getting in fights and
disrupting classes, then skipping them altogether, drinking and
smoking pot at a pal's aunt's apartment, once even funding his
mutiny by pocketing cash he collected for Hurricane Katrina victims. He landed in a youth shelter, slugged a kid there who blew
on his neck, and was charged with assault and battery and hauled
off in shackles to a juvenile detention center.

Rhonda stared at her 13-year-old delinquent in disbelief. Sure,
the kid had been hyper right out of the chute, had been class
cutup and funkiest dressed, wearing a big green clock on a string
as a necklace to school or picking his hair out into a puffy 'fro,
then having his younger brother shave a bald stripe down the center and one down each side: Reverse Triple Mohawk, Ma! But he'd
always been the Williams's prodigy, spewing five-syllable words
at age three, bypassing first grade altogether, and reading at an
eighth-grade level at—*What? He can't be six!* When he cursed his
mother one day in the summer after his to-hell-in-a-purple-hand-
basket ninth-grade year, Victor, his best buddy as well as his older
brother, beat him to a pulp and left him sobbing in a bush in

the front yard of a town house they'd just moved into on government vouchers . . . and Joseph's fever finally began to lift. Domin-
ion High principal John Brewer, rather than expel him, gave him
an *eighth* chance, the assault charges were dropped, Victor moved
back home, Joseph passed his sophomore football physical, and
the two brothers went on to become stars and leaders of their football team in Sterling, Virginia.

Something else happened too. *How,* Joseph asked a man in the
100 Black Men society who mentored him on weekends, *can we ever
pay back all the people who've helped us?* And the reply struck him in
the heart: *You pay them back by helping someone else.* He began staying
after school to tutor struggling classmates and signing up—even
before his mother could—to help those hurting. When his college
application landed at UVA, admissions officers panting over his
volunteer-work list had no air left when they got to his 1420 SAT
score, and they fell over themselves to help cover tuition, board,
and books of an incoming 16-year-old.

That's how Joseph made it through high school still holding on
to the strange notion that he's not separate from other human
beings, not different from custodians and dormitory maids. That's
why he's the one in 444,000 U.S. student-ATHLETES standing at
the hub of his campus imploring his peers and professors and administrators to care. He had to be incubated in a way that neither
money nor poverty incubates in America, grow up differently from
other fledgling white, brown, and black athletes. Grow up without
the buckling weight of his extended family's expectations, without
his consciousness narrowed to the needs of kin and posse, chained
to the lifetime role of Clan Messiah—the poor African American
athlete's fate ever since the 1980s, when the money got crazy—and
without ever climbing aboard the middle- and upper-class striv-
er's conveyor belt of camps, clinics, private coaches, travel teams,
weightlifting programs, and every-weekend tournaments. All of
them, from both backgrounds, kept anxiously aware of their place
in the pecking order by Internet scouting and ranking services re-
minding them what their height, weight, bench press, and time in
the 40 needed to be, tunnel vision hardwired by their Sweet 16th.

Developmental compression: that's what the caretakers of psyche
and spirit call a phenomenon that became normalized over the last
few decades. Truth is, Agassi, perhaps the most developmentally
compressed athlete of modern times, could never have wrought

his groundbreaking educational initiative—which includes plans for more than 75 charter schools serving up to 50,000 students nationwide—if he hadn't leaped off the compression track in his twenties for long stretches that outraged and bewildered sports fans. Truth is, any athlete of this era, unless he attended a tiny high school that had to scrounge up enough kids to field a team, probably *had* to be developmentally compressed for at least a few years if only to experience the simple joy of starting on the varsity.

Joseph's speech is slowing down, it's growing difficult for him to form sentences. And still the story he tells on the steps of UVA's Rotunda brings tears to the eyes of an English professor at the rally. He never even mentions to his listeners that he plays for UVA. He doesn't want them to stereotype him as a football player.

Hope surges through Joseph and the hunger strikers: UVA president Teresa Sullivan has agreed to meet with them. At an odd hour, 7:00 A.M., and two more days of hunger hence, but they're desperate now, fearful that their sacrifice will evaporate in the dry air of apathy, praying that the national attention Joseph has attracted has finally begun to make the administration flinch.

On his sixth foodless day he and a roommate who has joined the hunger strike, Peter Finn, can't stop obsessing about food: sushi . . . pizza . . . chicken . . . steak, sushi, pizza, chicken, steak, *sushipizzachickensteak*. They go out to dinner just to watch their girlfriends eat. "Can we sniff your food?" Joseph begs his girlfriend, Kathy Storm. She hands him a french fry and he holds it beneath his nose, closing his eyes, swooning. "Can you eat one with your mouth open?" he begs. She complies. He's getting lightheaded, goofy. He leans in to inhale another french fry and knocks over a glass, splashing water all over the table.

He falls silent on his seventh day. Opening his mouth only now and then to say to Peter, "God, I'm hungry."

"Please," their other roommate, Toye Falaiye, keeps pleading with them, "just eat."

LoVanté Battle, Virginia's junior safety, comes by to check on Joseph. "You look pathetic," he tells him.

Joseph feels the pressure growing. He's entering the final week before spring break, has papers due and exams to take for which he can't possibly focus, and he has a flight to Belize in five days to co-lead a group of a dozen UVA students in renovating an orphanage, a commitment made weeks ago.

He feels doubt arising. He knows that doubt always arises in movements like this one, and that here is where his heroes dug in . . . but their battles were so much more personal than his. Ali was getting drafted into an army during wartime. Walton's friends were getting shot at in Vietnam. Jim Brown, Tommie Smith, and John Carlos had to go to the other side of town to eat and sleep. Billie Jean King was playing for prize money that was sometimes one-sixth of what men received and breaking the law to get an abortion in 1971. Their success as activists four decades ago is one more reason that today's athlete doesn't feel he *must* stand up. If he's black, he can eat or sleep anywhere his wallet allows, make just as much money as any white icon, and, like everyone else, leave wars to men and women who choose to fight them. It doesn't seem necessary to risk his playing time, reputation, or commercial popularity . . . unless . . . unless he fully understands the hero's quest and wishes to fulfill it.

It's not enough, in that quest, to overcome all the obstacles and enemies in the forest and seize the Holy Grail. "The mystique of the hero is that he goes into a realm that the rest of us can't go to, but he's got to come back with something that's important for everyone," says Edwards. "If he comes back with the Grail and doesn't use it to support the people and place he came from, there's a huge chunk missing from his halo. Jackie Robinson isn't a hero because he was a great baseball player or Ali because he was a great boxer. Joe Frazier and Larry Holmes were great boxers too. It takes something more than that. Heroism has been downgraded into a pursuit of celebrity, and celebrity doesn't carry any obligation to anything except to fame and money."

Pssst. Here's the secret that Jackie Robinson and Muhammad Ali discovered, the one that no agent or handler whispers into the modern athlete's ear: when you play your sport for something much larger than yourself, than your wallet, than your ego or even your team, when you tap into *that* power, son . . . look out.

Crunch time. Summit meeting with the university president. Eighth day of Joseph's hunger strike. He crawls out of bed at 6:30, slogs across campus to stand vigil with 30 others outside Sullivan's office. In the rain. For nearly two hours. Does she know that ESPN's next, that Joseph and the hunger strike are about to be featured on *Outside the Lines* and ESPN.com?

The meeting finally ends. Six Living Wage supporters walk outside, nearly empty-handed. The administration agrees to little more than to meet again. At the second meeting, two days later, it agrees to form a student advisory committee to look further at the issue.

Joseph walks his hollow gut through the drizzle, feeling a little bit of everything. Hollowness spreading into his chest because the clock's running out on him. Disappointment that there'll be no fourth-quarter game-winning drive. Excitement about ESPN. Worried that "success," even if it comes, might amount to little more than what previous Living Wage Campaigns have achieved: a small raise for the workers that's not tied to the living wage, that doesn't cover the growing legions of contract workers, and that can get swallowed in no time by inflation . . . which is, in fact, exactly what will happen two months later.

He has lost 12 pounds. He has to start eating, the campaign's doctor has told him, to give his body a chance against the new bacteria he'll be encountering in Belize in just four days. He twitches back and forth for hours over his decision, and finally, at 9:30 P.M., he gives in. He and his roommate order takeout.

A half hour later, in silence, Peter tears into a slice of pizza and Joseph lifts a spoonful of miso soup and a sushi roll to his mouth. Sushi tastes great. Sushi feels lousy. He tells his fellow strikers the next morning that eating just doesn't feel right, and how much he appreciates their carrying on, then wonders what the consequences of his act will be.

Carlos and Smith, acting on a far larger stage, were immediately suspended from the U.S. team and banished from the Olympic Village, then received death threats at home and watched one door after another close when they applied for jobs. Carlos took a claw hammer to his furniture in the middle of the night to use as fuel to keep his family warm. "It was like I had cancer," he says. The FBI worked up a 3,500-page dossier on Edwards, some of it coming from informants placed in his sociology classes. Joseph? He just takes a cyber-beating.

SCBIGTIME: What an idiot. If this cause is so important to him, he should organize charity events to contribute to those he feels are in need rather than attack job creators.

TOBY21155: Excuse me while [I] throw up . . . another brain-washed progressive.

MATTHEW055062: Sounds like he needs to fast for playing time, this fool sucks b— and he knows it!

CVILLEPSUFAN: Who cares? There will still be a college game on Thursday.

BRONCO-FORCE: doesn't take this lying down: Honestly . . . how can some of you people sleep at night. He's a young, obviously socially conscious athlete, who is doing something to stand up for what he believes in. Why do so many wish to see the me-me-me athletes of today, while scorning young men of purpose like this one . . .

Plenty of other fans and media members jump to Joseph's defense. His roommate shakes his head. "If a walk-on player gets this coverage," concludes Peter, "just imagine what a star could do!"

Joseph's girlfriend, Kathy—half Norwegian, half German—can't explain this to her countrymen. "It's *amazing* in this country how much power sports gives you," she says. "*A football player!* I didn't think that would be of any importance. *A football player!*"

And Joseph? He's still a little dazed by it all, astonished by the media storm and the admiring emails that came in, one from NFL Players Association president DeMaurice Smith, another from the leader of the Service Employees International Union expressing interest in helping the UVA workers form a union, and yes, even a response from Coach Reid saying that he hoped this wouldn't drive a wedge between them and that he still had great respect for Joseph. "I feel more empowered," Joseph says. "It inspired me. I want to commit deeper. This is how it goes with every major change in society. It requires activism. People don't change without pressure. Athletes are so magnified and have such an opportunity to use that, but they don't, and so the focus on them often gets put on the negative. It really works against them in the end. Sports are the main arena that black males are seen in, and there are so many intelligent ones, but they're not heard from on these issues, so all you hear is *dumb jocks* or *violent black men*.

"Maybe I'm an idealist, but in a world where people are starv-

ing while others are making millions of dollars a year, it's about
the *will* to change it. It's about people who don't care. At the core
of all great injustice is greed. It's not an American problem. It's
a human problem. If my mother hadn't gotten housing vouchers after my father left and moved us into a neighborhood with
a high school that really cared about its students, it likely would
have turned out very bad for me. The teachers in my previous
school system were unqualified and unhappy people. How are you
going to go to college attending schools like that? That's not a
merit system. That's *chance*."

What battles loom for the next Wonman Joseph Williams . . . and
will we have to wait another 30 or 40 years for him to arise? Two
issues fester right on sports' doorstep, ripe and ready to burst.
The first is the emergence and acceptance of the first openly gay
athlete in a mainstream team sport. The second is the systemic
corruption of college athletics, from the tens of millions of dollars being made by TV networks, conferences, and the NCAA on
the sweat and toil of the college athlete to the absurdity that me-
dian spending on athletics by universities in major conferences is
four to 11 times higher per athlete than that spent on education-
related expenses per student and growing at double to triple the
rate of academic expenditures, resulting in a net *loss* for all but
seven athletic programs nationwide, even with all those TV revenues, according to the Knight Commission—a deficit that must
be made up by increases in tuition or increased allotments drawn
from state taxes or general university funds.

Who knows? *This* Wonman Joseph Williams, after all, has two
years of eligibility left at UVA and plenty of time after that to consider his next stand. "There needs to be a radical revolution of the
way we view sports, especially on the amateur level, in America,"
he says. "I'd love to be a part of it if it ever happens. But it's hard
for an athlete to say he's going to protest for the sake of athletes at
large, because most of us have just four years, and we want to win
now and to get playing time *now*."

But the biggest looming battlefront, the one that cries for athletes at the ramparts yet transcends sports, the one that will require the most heroic investment from athletes because they're
the ones reaping the status quo's richest rewards, is the very cause,
says Edwards, for which Joseph just laid his stomach on the line.

"*The* problem of the 21st century is going to be the deepening economic disparity, about the have-mores and the have-nones. What this young man in Virginia did spoke *exactly* to that."

The old, gray warriors from the 1960s and '70s, they're watching, they're waiting. "Sure," says Walton, "there are people just retreating to their mansions on the hill and pulling the ladder up behind them, but the great thing about any group dynamic is that it always comes down to *one guy*. And we all have the chance to be that guy. The one with the willingness to stand tall for those who can't. It still comes down to: do you care, and does it really matter? *I* do, and *it* does. And I salute this young man for standing tall."

Carlos isn't holding his breath. "The people who do these things start building the courage of others to think about taking a stand too," he says. "What this kid did might bring a light to other athletes. But it won't start a stampede."

It's the morning after the end of Full Harmony's hunger strike. He and athletes all across America are pulling on their sweats and hurrying to weight rooms, to conditioning and agility drills, to classes. Don't peer at them, these determined young men and women on college and professional teams, and ask where their social conscience and voice have gone. Look at us. We're the soil from which they grow. If we don't change, they can't, and so the first revolution that would have to occur is the one that no one's talking about.

Our next Wonman Joseph Williams, the ground-changing one, would have to be so bold and so radical even to *consider* attempting that revolt. Then he'd have to pray that enough other athletes, among the 99 percent who aren't going pro, understand deep inside. They'd stop pumping iron, refuse to run sprints, quit reporting to gymnasiums and practice fields, stop being *entertainment*, demand to be reunited with the student body, insist that the runaway developmental-compression train slow down long enough for them to find out who they are *besides* athletes. Long enough for them to expand. They'd sit down not for money—a real concern as well—but for time and for space. To be human-being-student-athletes.

Yes, that's hard to imagine. The whole edifice is likelier to collapse first, from forces outside of sports: excesses of all kinds have a way, eventually, of being leveled.

There's no whiff of that this morning in the world of sports. Joseph's blinking the sleep out of his eyes, wolfing down a bowl of cereal, heading to a rehab workout. Everything's back to normal, nothing unusual to report. We return you to your regularly scheduled programming. There's still a college game on Thursday night.

PATRICK HRUBY

Did Football Kill Austin Trenum?

FROM WASHINGTONIAN

ON THE DAY he took his own life, Austin Trenum ate cheese-cake. He was 17. He loved cheesecake. He loved the Beastie Boys too, and SpongeBob Squarepants and the silly faux-hawk haircut he spent months cultivating and two minutes shaving off because, well, that's what teenagers do. He loved his little Geo Metro convertible, neon yellow and as macho as a golf cart, a gift from his grandfather, the two driving all the way from Texas to Austin's home in Nokesville, Virginia, a close-knit community of 1,354 in Prince William County.

Austin loved his parents, Gil and Michelle, and his younger brothers, Cody and Walker. He loved his girlfriend, Lauren. He loved cheering for the girls' volleyball team at Brentsville District High School, smearing his chest with paint and screaming his lungs out alongside his lacrosse teammates; loved sneaking out of his chemistry class to sing "Bohemian Rhapsody" with his friend Carmen in the band room; loved fishing and paintball, roller coasters and blasting "Sweet Caroline" with the top down.

He especially loved football. Loved watching the Dallas Cowboys. Loved playing for the Brentsville varsity team—fullback and linebacker—taking hits and delivering them, seldom leaving the field, eating two Hostess cherry pies before every game. He was a handsome kid, green-eyed like his mother, six feet tall and 190 pounds, growing stronger and more confident all the time. Under the Friday-night lights, in his beat-up helmet and shoulder pads,

you could see the man Gilbert Allen Austin Trenum III was becoming.

It was Sunday, September 26, 2010. Michelle Trenum woke up
around 8:00 A.M. Gil was out of town, returning that afternoon
from a weekend drill with his Navy Reserve unit in New Jersey.
Walker, 10, their youngest, was on the living room couch, hiding
under a blanket. He jumped up when Michelle walked in. Boo!

"Austin's awake," Walker said. "He's in the basement playing a
video game."

That's odd, Michelle thought. Austin never got up early on Sundays. Not voluntarily.

Michelle made her sons breakfast. Austin drove his other
brother, Cody, 15, to a lacrosse game and cheered from the sidelines. He took more pride in his siblings than himself; he was
that kind of brother. On the way home, he teased Cody. "You did
good," Austin said, before delivering the punch line. "You surprised me!"

Back at the house, Austin ate lunch. And cheesecake. While
Austin surfed the Internet, he and Michelle talked about Adam
James, a Texas Tech football player who had allegedly been locked
in a dark electrical closet by the school's head coach, Mike Leach,
after suffering a concussion. The story, which ultimately ignited a
media firestorm and led to Leach's firing, began when the injured
James showed up to practice in sunglasses and street clothes; Austin joked with his mother that he should do the same, just to see
how his high school coach, Dean Reedy, would react.

Austin then turned serious, balancing on one foot to mimic a
neurological test.

"Am I going to be out all week?" he said. "I don't want to be out
all week. Do you think I'll be out two weeks?"

"You'll just have to see," Michelle said.

During a football game the previous Friday night, Austin had
sustained a concussion. Brain trauma had been in the news. There
were reports of retired NFL players suffering from depression and
dementia linked to their hard-hitting careers. There were congressional hearings, some of them dealing with high school football.
In the coming months, the sport would be engulfed in a full-blown
health crisis. Austin's parents were mostly unaware of the contro-

versy. They had both grown up in Texas, where football was king, where getting your bell rung was just a part of the game. Almost a badge of honor.

Gil and Michelle had been in the Brentsville High bleachers on Friday night, chatting with friends, a full moon overhead. Neither of them saw the hit, but Gil spotted their son standing with his helmet off, touching his index finger to his nose at the direction of team trainer Richard Scavongelli. Just like last season. Good grief.

On the sideline, Austin was dazed, slurring his words. During the drive to the emergency room, he was alert enough to call Lauren, his girlfriend. By the time he was standing in line at Prince William Hospital, shirtless and sweaty, he seemed fine. He cracked jokes, flirted with the nurses who brought him a sandwich and a soda. He begged a doctor to let him leave, asked if Lauren could come back to the examination room.

A nurse asked if he wanted Tylenol.

"The last time you got a concussion, you got a headache," Michelle said. "Are you sure you don't want it?"

"Mom, I'm fine," Austin said. "I don't have a headache. Except for my normal football headache. I get them after every game."

The medical staff gave Gil and Michelle a sheet of instructions: Watch for vomiting and clear fluid coming out of Austin's nose, signs of a more severe brain injury. Limit their son to "quiet activities" for the next 24 hours. Wake him from sleep every few hours to check for evidence of intracranial bleeding, such as confusion and extreme drowsiness.

Heading home, the Trenums stopped at the Chuck Wagon, a restaurant around the corner from their house, where the Brentsville High players gathered after games. Austin's teammates recounted his sideline exchange with Scavongelli.

SCAVONGELLI: Do you know where you are?
AUSTIN: Yeah. This is my field!
SCAVONGELLI: No. Do you know what school you are at?
AUSTIN: Yeah. My school!
SCAVONGELLI: Do you know who you're playing against?
AUSTIN: No.

*

This is my field! Everyone laughed. They laughed at the way Austin had gotten emotional on the field too, cussing out one of his buddies, something he never, ever did.

On Saturday morning, Austin attended football film study; that afternoon, he went fishing; in the evening, he took Lauren to a Sugarland concert, a belated celebration of her birthday. They sat on the Jiffy Lube Live lawn, taking pictures under the stars. When Austin got home, he texted Lauren good-night. The next day, he was sitting in his family's dining room doing homework, texting her again about meeting up two hours later to watch a Redskins game.

Austin was a good student, ranking in the top 6 percent of his class. He planned to study chemical engineering in college and was deciding between Virginia Tech and James Madison. The former had a better football team; the latter, he deduced during a campus visit, had better-looking girls. As Austin studied for his Cold War history class, Michelle went online to check his academic progress. There was a problem. He hadn't turned in two papers. Michelle was upset and lectured him about slacking off.

Gil came home around 2:30 P.M. Michelle gave her husband a kiss and cut him a slice of cheesecake. She told him about Austin's schoolwork. Austin looked irritated—almost angry. That was out of character. Michelle saw his jaw clench. His mouth moved. She was stunned. *Did he just call me a name?* Austin stared straight ahead.

"If you don't finish your work," she said, "you can't see Lauren tonight."

Gil and Michelle went outside. Cody and Walker were on the living room couch, watching a football game. At some point, Austin went upstairs.

"I don't know what's wrong with Austin," Michelle said. "He shouldn't disrespect me like that."

"He's a teenager," Gil said. "I'll go talk to him."

Gil went inside. He passed the kitchen table, where his cheesecake sat untouched. He walked up the stairs, the same stairs where Austin would ambush Walker when he came home from school, peppering him with foam darts from a toy gun. The door to Austin's room was open.

Michelle Trenum heard her husband scream.

*

On her way to the hospital, Patti McKay made a deal with God. *Not Austin. Please. Take me instead.* The boy was like a second son. Every summer, the McKay and Trenum families vacationed together at a lake in Maine, where the kids would play King of the Dock—wrestling for control of a wooden swimming platform, tossing one another in the water, Austin always making sure the younger children won their share.

When her cell phone rang, Patti was in her sister's garden, kneeling in the dirt. It was Cody, panicked. Austin wasn't breathing. Gil was trying to resuscitate him. An ambulance was on the way. What should they do?

Keep performing CPR, Patti said.

A cardiology nurse, Patti suspected a subdural hematoma. A brain bleed. Which was odd. She had just seen Austin, about 90 minutes earlier, pulling up in her driveway—the top down on his little yellow convertible, Cody in the passenger seat.

Austin had been grinning. He had a gift with him, a Snickers cheesecake.

"Here, Ms. McKay," he said. "Look what we brought for you."

"How are you feeling?"

"Okay."

"No, really—how are you feeling?"

"I'm *fine.* My headache is almost gone."

Patti had been at the game on Friday night, standing with Austin in the Brentsville High parking lot, holding his arm to help him balance. But today his gait was normal, his hands weren't shaking. She called the emergency room, professional instincts taking over. *You're getting a boy who had a concussion two days ago. You need a neurosurgeon. If you don't have one, have a helicopter ready to evacuate.* Arriving at Prince William Hospital, she didn't see a helicopter. She saw Rob Place, the Trenums' next-door neighbor.

Austin hanged himself, Place said.

Nothing made sense. Not suicide. Not Austin. Not the boy who went deer hunting in West Virginia with his father and crafted elaborate zombie-apocalypse defense plans with Walker. Not the young man who always said "Yes, sir" and "No, ma'am" and was adored by his friends' parents. Not the charmed kid who never got mad on the lacrosse field, who'd scored a goal six seconds into his first high school game.

"If someone came to me and asked me to rank, one to 25, the kids on the team most likely to have problems and the kids who were the most stable, Austin was number one on the stable end of the list," says Carl Kielbasa, Austin and Cody's former high school lacrosse coach. "His maturity level was extremely high. Never experimenting with drugs and alcohol. Almost fatherly to his brothers. Had a wonderful sense of humor. He was a great teammate, very attentive and aware, very patient and kind. A big-time leader on the team and in school—he could hang out with the kids who were partyers and be in an honor society meeting the next day. Everyone loved him."

Austin was taken to Inova Fairfax Hospital, where he died at 2:00 A.M. on Monday. The entire community was stunned. The boy was beloved. Football was beloved. In the Nokesville area, plans were under way to build a new $850,000 youth football complex; elementary school students were let out early on Friday afternoons, the better to high-five Brentsville High players as they made their march down the town's main road.

How could this have happened?

The Trenums went home. Later that day, their phone rang. Laura O'Neal answered. She was Austin's godmother, one of Michelle's best friends. She'd been there for Austin's first birthday, eating cowboy-themed cake; there when he got his first lacrosse stick, which he carried everywhere, like a scepter. Now she would plan his funeral.

There was a man on the line, Chris Nowinski, a former Harvard football player, calling on behalf of scientists at Boston University. They wanted Austin's brain.

The human brain is a wondrous thing. It enables us to throw a football, allows us to breathe, think, and love. In its neurons and glial cells, synapses and neurotransmitters, it is essentially who we are.

And who we are is fragile.

Gerard Gioia opens his laptop. On the screen is a video depicting a brain inside a skull. The brain, he explains, is a spongy mass of tissue. Surrounded by fluid, it moves independent of the skull, just slightly, the arrangement providing a protective measure of shock absorption.

"And this," he says, "is why the helmet will never be the simple answer to this injury."

Helmets prevent skull fractures but not concussions. Gioia clicks a button. The head rocks back and forth. The brain smashes against the inside of the skull. The screen flashes like a strobe light, a comic-book *pow!* Such is the basic dynamic of a concussion, an injury that occurs in football with alarming regularity: according to the American Association of Neurological Surgeons, 4 percent to 20 percent of high school and college players will suffer one during a single season. That's likely a low estimate—some experts believe as many as eight of 10 concussions go undiagnosed.

"When the head or the body takes force, the brain moves," explains Gioia, head of Pediatric Neuropsychology at Children's National Medical Center and an expert on youth and adolescent sports concussions. "It has a certain threshold, beyond which it stretches and strains."

Gioia loves football—played it himself in high school and college. He wants to make the sport safer. Three weeks after Austin's death, he met with Gil and Michelle in his Rockville office, where a New York Giants–themed street sign hangs on the wall. Michelle brought a picture frame containing three photos of Austin, including one of him joyfully painting his face before a volleyball game the week before his death.

"Look at this boy," she said, fighting tears. "Look at these pictures. He wasn't depressed."

Shock giving way to despair, the Trenums wracked their brains. *Was there something we missed?* They talked to Austin's friends, checked his text messages, read the journal he kept for English class: *I heard my favorite Sublime song. Today was good. I forgot to wear my Hawaiian shirt. Bummer.*

No angst. No suicide note. No sign that anything was wrong. Nothing. The concussion, they figured—it had to be the concussion. But how? Didn't they go to the ER, keep Austin from strenuous activity, do everything right? Scavongelli, the Brentsville High trainer, had immediately pulled Austin from the game, protecting him from second-impact syndrome, a rare but horrific condition in which athletes suffer a second concussion while recovering from a previous one, causing rapid, catastrophic brain swelling that ends in severe disability or death.

After a concussion during his junior year, Austin was held out of football practice for a week. A medical-hotline operator advised Michelle to watch for signs of depression. She told Austin. He laughed.

Oh, please, Mom.

"Why?" says Michelle. "Why did he do this? We must have said that seven million times."

A concussion is not a bruise. It's a disruption of the intricate system of electrochemical signals that constitute normal brain function. Contrary to widespread belief, concussions don't always coincide with loss of consciousness. Symptoms include headaches, sensitivity to light, confusion, lack of focus, irritability, and loss of interest in favorite activities.

With rest and a gradual return to regular activity, most athletes who suffer a single concussion experience no permanent ill effects. Some, however, suffer post-concussion syndrome, in which symptoms persist for months or years, in rare cases permanently. Having one concussion may increase the risk of another. Multiple concussions are associated with an increased risk of post-concussion syndrome as well as depression and memory loss.

Think of your brain as a computer, Gioia says. The tissue is the hardware, and the electrochemical signals are the software. Concussions can scramble both, disrupting healthy equilibrium. Moreover, they leave the brain drained of energy, like a cell phone with a bad battery.

The best treatment? Rest—lots of it. Waking a sleeping concussion patient every few hours to check for brain bleeding has long been conventional medical wisdom, Gioia says, but actually is not a good idea: you should check on them, but not disrupt their sleep. "The essential aspect is allowing the cells to rebalance themselves. Overworking the brain interferes with that recovery. And it's not just avoiding additional blows to the head. You can't be out running. You need good sleep. You have to manage school, any activity that involves a lot of thinking."

For two and a half hours, Gioia and the Trenums talked, going over Austin's final weekend. As they connected the dots, two things became clear: football had injured his brain, which sub-

sequently was overworked. Texting. Video games. Driving. Studying. Staying up late. Normal teenage activities. All of them too
much.

Looking back over the weekend, they saw warning signs, subtle
indicators that something was amiss. Austin had trouble sleeping
on Sunday morning. He got lost on the way to Cody's lacrosse
game, even though the directions consisted of a single right turn.
He forgot what month it was while fishing with his friend Carmen.
He had "football headaches."

When Austin was concussed a few plays before halftime during
a football game his junior year, his teammates were the first to
notice. In the locker room, he couldn't figure out how to work his
chin strap and began to bawl. Similarly, his final concussion left
him cursing out his best friend, Ryan Hall, for an on-field prank
meant to make Austin laugh.

Gioia showed the Trenums a diagram of the brain. He pointed
out the frontal lobes, about one-third of the total brain mass, the
portion just behind the forehead, where so much football contact
takes place. These gelatinous hunks of meat, he told them, are our
executive control centers. They allow us to reason, to choose right
from wrong, to override impulses, to connect current actions to
future consequences.

In teenagers, the frontal lobes are still developing; in everyone,
they require a great amount of energy to function properly. Damage or disrupt them, stretch them like Silly Putty, and concentration suffers. Memory gets spotty. The systems governing emotion
and reason are thrown out of whack. You might forget how to work
a chin strap; you might consider that unbearably tragic. Nothing
makes sense.

Austin's parents believe that their son may have suffered as
many as four concussions during three years of playing football.
Did those injuries lead him to take his life? Gioia can't say. There's
no direct causation. The brain remains mysterious.

"My thought to the Trenums was that Austin's brain wasn't functioning properly," he says. "It was drained in terms of overall energy, unusual emotional response was one of his manifestations,
and the argument about academics hit at that time. Bam! Those
emotions go off, and now the decision-making is not working
properly either."

Meeting with the Trenums, Gioia was more succinct. He told them Austin's case was a perfect storm.

On the first snap of Brentsville's first football game without Austin, the school's quarterback mimed a handoff to his absent fullback, then took a knee. He pointed to the night sky, where cheerleaders with the number 43 painted on their cheeks had released the same number of balloons. The whole school wore white. Cody and Walker wore jerseys bearing their brother's number, 43, and watched from the sideline. At the end of the game, a Brentsville player carried Walker off the field on his shoulders.

Football went on. The Trenums understood. Gil, 46, had grown up in Ohio and Texas, states where the sport is practically a religion; Michelle, 48, was raised an hour and a half from Odessa, Texas, the real-life setting of *Friday Night Lights*. She remembers pep rallies and rabid boosters, caravans of cars with shoe-polish-painted windows, what seemed like entire towns turning out for high school games. Gil and Michelle attended Texas Tech, where Austin went to summer football camp. They loved the sport. So did Cody, a member of the Brentsville High JV squad, and Walker, who played on a youth team.

As the Trenums grieved, friends and neighbors brought them food, mowed and reseeded their lawn, even repainted their front door. The family watched football. Tuesday nights. Thursday nights. All weekend long. College and pro. Tackle after tackle, hit after hit. "I don't know why," Gil says. "We just did. It was a distraction, something you had to focus on."

Gil and Michelle kept in touch with Gioia. They had donated Austin's brain to the Boston University scientists, who were studying the effects of concussions and head trauma. The Trenums came to a frightening realization: like so many others around the country, the Prince William County school system wasn't doing enough to address athletic concussions. What happened to Austin could have happened to anyone.

Six months before Austin's death, Virginia had passed a law requiring schools to educate students and parents about concussions and to remove students suspected of sustaining the injury from the field of play until cleared by a medical professional. In Fairfax County, education meant watching a 10-minute online video; in Loudoun County, it meant signing a two-page form. Prince William's policy was still being written, not scheduled to take effect until 2012.

A member of the Prince William County school board, Gil wanted something quicker and better. A policy with teeth. He lobbied administrators. He had Gioia make a presentation to the board, got input from Nowinski, the former Harvard football player now with the Boston University program. Spurred by his son's death, Gil was relentless.

Prince William's new concussion policy went into effect in the summer of 2011, mandating stricter return-to-play guidelines and more thorough education for school athletic trainers. Students trying out for sports are now required to attend an hour-long concussion seminar with at least one parent.

"I have families contacting me all the time, telling me they can't thank Gil enough," says Kendra Kielbasa, an advocate for youth concussion care and the wife of Austin's former lacrosse coach. Working with Gil to draw up a policy that stresses post-concussion cognitive rest—the kind Austin didn't know enough to get—Kendra had drawn on her own experience. Her son, Connor, was concussed after being dropped on his head during a seventh-grade wrestling match. Emergency room doctors checked Connor for a brain bleed and cleared him to return to school the next day. Three weeks later, with his grades plummeting and his emotions off kilter, he asked his mother if he could lie down.

"Sure," Kendra said. "Why don't you go to your room?"

Connor looked around the living room. "I don't know where it is," he said. "Can you take me?"

"The hardest part is that people don't understand—your child looks like he is fine, but he's not," Kendra says. "People have to understand that it's not just a bad headache for a day or two. And it's not enough to do [concussion education] in the high schools. We have to bring it to the middle and elementary schools."

Would more education have saved Austin's life? The Trenums think so.

Last fall, Cody played in a lacrosse tournament in Williamsburg. Michelle was in the stands. A boy from another team was hit hard and concussed. As his parents pulled him off the field, a woman approached. She said she was a nurse. Michelle could overhear their conversation. The boy was dazed, struggling to remember things.

"Well, he's not passed out," said the nurse. "That's a good sign."

Actually, Michelle thought, episodic amnesia is more of an indicator of serious problems than passing out is.

The nurse continued to offer medical advice, much of it dated. Michelle began to panic. As soon as the nurse left, she ran over to the parents. "Take your son to a doctor," she implored. "A neurologist. Get him some rest. Keep a close eye on him."

The parents asked, "Are you a doctor?"

"No," Michelle said. "But my son died last year after a concussion."

"That scared them," she says. "And all I could think was, *At least your son will live.*"

The brains come here, to a red-brick building in suburban Boston. Each is weighed, photographed, and examined for signs of trauma and disease, then carefully sliced in half. One half goes to the upstairs laboratory, where scientists create tissue samples 10 microns thin, chemically stained and mounted on slides for microscopic inspection. The other half is placed in a closet-size, stainless-steel freezer, preserved for future study.

"There are more freezers," says Victor Alvarez, a researcher at the lab. "We're always looking for more space."

Football has a problem. The sport kills too many players. Some slowly, some all at once. The evidence is in the freezers and in the stacks of slides cluttering the office of Ann McKee, a neuropathologist and codirector of the Boston University Center for the Study of Traumatic Encephalopathy.

Each brain tells a story: former Pittsburgh Steelers lineman Justin Strzelczyk, dead at age 36 after leading police on a high-speed chase that began with hallucinations and ended in a fireball; former college football player Mike Borich, dead at 42 from a drug overdose; former Philadelphia Eagles safety Andre Waters, dead at 44 from shooting himself; former NFL safety Dave Duerson, dead at 50 from shooting himself in the chest—*specifically* in the chest—after scrawling a note to his family asking that his brain be donated to science.

Austin Trenum, dead at 17.

Last summer, Gil and Michelle came to McKee's office. They looked at slides of Austin's brain. Through the microscope, they saw axons, the long, slender fibers that connect nerve cells and conduct electricity in the brain. In a healthy person, axons run together like fiber-optic cable, straight and smooth. Austin's were twisted, bulbous, broken. In scientific language, it was a multifocal axonal injury; in layman's terms, the equivalent of frayed automobile wiring. Turn on the radio and the windshield wipers might move; turn off the lights and the whole car might shut down.

Michelle choked up. *This,* she thought, *is my baby. This is what ended his life.*

Austin's case isn't unique, McKee says. There have been other sudden, inexplicable suicides following concussions—some in the military, some among high school football players. Scientists are struggling to understand the connection. But something is happening. Something terrible.

"It's the same pattern," McKee says. "They have disordered thinking and electrical impulses in the brain. They have a minor irritation. And they just want to end it. It's like having a fly in your room and deciding to blow up your house."

A decade ago, McKee wasn't studying dead football players. Nobody was. That changed when Bennet Omalu, a forensic pathologist and neuropathologist, examined the brains of former Steelers linemen Mike Webster in 2002 and Terry Long in 2005. Both had suffered slow, puzzling descents into erratic behavior and madness, with Long ultimately killing himself by drinking antifreeze and Webster dying of heart failure after an extended period of living in his truck in which he sometimes shot himself with a Taser gun in order to sleep and other times sniffed ammonia to stay awake.

Omalu found that each had suffered from chronic traumatic encephalopathy (CTE), a progressive neurodegenerative disease similar to Alzheimer's and linked to the absorption of repeated blows to the head, a condition previously associated with prizefighters—in layman's terms, "punch drunkenness."

Evidence suggests that CTE is caused not only by concussions but also by subconcussive trauma. Little hits—the ones inherent in football that occur on every snap, like the 1,000 to 1,500 hits to the head that Boston University researchers estimate the average high school lineman takes each season, some at forces equivalent to or greater than a 25-mile-an-hour car crash.

CTE has been found in a number of deceased football players, including Strzelczyk, Creekmur, Borich, Waters, Duerson, and Chris Henry, a former NFL receiver never diagnosed with a concussion. Early stages of the disease also were discovered in the brain of Owen Thomas, a 21-year-old University of Pennsylvania football captain who hanged himself, and in Nathan Stiles, a 17-year-old high school player from Kansas who collapsed during a game and died of a rebleed of a brain injury suffered in a previous game.

Because their brains are still developing, children and adolescents are particularly vulnerable to brain trauma. A recent Virginia Tech study measuring head impacts among seven- and eight-year-old football players found that some hits generated more than 80 g's of force, equal to the blows delivered in college football.

"I think that in 10 years we're going to look back at this and say, 'Whoa,'" says McKee, who has examined thousands of brains over 26 years. "The public only knows some of the evidence. It's overwhelming. And as it accumulates, it's impossible to deny."

Austin Trenum showed no signs of CTE, none of the telltale clusters of dark brown spots on slides of stained pinkish brain tissue.

The sport damaged his brain nonetheless.

At a 2009 congressional hearing, Ann McKee presented a summary of her work, acknowledging that hundreds of thousands of former football players seem perfectly healthy. She then asked: Do we expect that 100 percent of cigarette smokers will develop lung cancer? Do we expect 100 percent of children who play with matches or even chainsaws will get hurt?

Representative Ted Poe, a Texas Republican, said that parents and players already know football is dangerous. He said government involvement would mean "the end of football as we know it" because the sport would end up becoming "touch football."

Such are the terms of an ongoing national debate over football's safety and long-term viability, an argument that has intensified since the May suicide of popular former NFL linebacker Junior Seau. Mismanaged concussions can cause permanent harm and death. But even players who never have a concussion are at risk of developing CTE. How much is too much?

McKee is no abolitionist. She grew up in Wisconsin rooting for the Green Bay Packers. Her favorite player was Willie Wood, a D.C. native now suffering from dementia. Her two older brothers played the game. She doesn't want to end football; she wants to save the sport from itself. Three years ago, she ran into a group of players from her daughter's high school at a doughnut shop outside Boston.

"So," McKee asked, "you guys know anything about concussions?"

"Oh, yeah," said one of the boys. "I've had five."

"I've had seven," said another.

"It was a badge of honor," McKee recalls.

For years, McKee loved attending prep football games. Not anymore, she says. You just don't know what will happen.

The room remains as it was. A lacrosse helmet. An SAT prep book. A half-empty pack of gum. All on a desk. Austin and his friends mugging in a photo booth, young and happy and full of life, the snapshots tacked to a mirror. Clothes are piled on the closet floor, the bed unmade. Sometimes Michelle will come upstairs and lie down, just to feel her son's blanket.

Downstairs is a bathroom. When Austin was in the hospital, doctors working to save his life, Michelle tried to make a deal with God: *I'll rip out the bathroom, make it bigger. Austin can be a vegetable and we'll take care of him. Just let him live.*

"But I knew," she says, her voice trailing off.

The first months were the hardest. Gil, a senior engineer at SAIC, went back to work. The boys were in school. Michelle, a stay-at-home mom, would lie on the living room couch—the family's golden retriever, Biscuit, at her feet—and sob. Before Austin's death, she had been outgoing, involved in the community, digging up local land-use records and political campaign contributions to lead a successful fight against a planned rock quarry. Not anymore.

She withdrew, felt vulnerable, couldn't be around people who didn't know Austin. She threw herself into spy novels, then science fiction, sometimes reading for seven hours a day. She had once favored Anne Tyler and Pat Conroy, selections from Oprah's book club. "But I couldn't read those," Michelle says. "Nothing with mothers and kids and emotions."

When children take their lives, parents blame themselves. Michelle wondered why she'd gotten on Austin about his homework; Gil wondered why he'd let him do homework in the first place. A grief counselor told Michelle it would take a year for the guilt to pass. "Even I have trouble sleeping sometimes," says Patti McKay, the Trenums' close friend. "I think about what Gil and Michelle saw. I don't know how they sleep. I can't imagine living with that."

Michelle still watched football, but not in the same way. She winced at every big hit, noticed that concussed players almost always fell with their forearms extended away from their bodies, a reflex scientists call "the fencing response." She began investigating sports concussions and teen suicide, spending hours online, reaching out to military and academic experts.

Researchers at the Centers for Disease Control and Prevention tracked suicides, but they didn't correlate those deaths with recent brain trauma, never mind athletic participation. Nor did anyone else.

Michelle befriended Dustin Fink, an Illinois-based athletic trainer who runs a concussion blog. Fink's anecdotal evidence suggested that boys who played both linebacker and running back were at greater brain-trauma risk. Michelle made a spreadsheet, one she still maintains, logging every instance she could find of high school and college football players killing themselves: name, age, position played. She saw a pattern. *Linebacker. Running back. Linebacker. Running back.* Just like Austin.

Two football helmets rest on a table. One is black, matte and battered, with an orange mouthpiece wedged in the facemask. The other is reddish and gleaming, decorated with a skull and crossbones and a breast-cancer-awareness sticker. Two gashes run down the front.

The first helmet belonged to Austin. The second belongs to Walker.

Michelle pushes them together. "This," she says, "is how it happens."

It's a Saturday, exactly one year after the weekend of Austin's death.

Cody finished the previous Brentsville High football season, then quit. He didn't say why. Walker continued to play for a youth squad, fullback and linebacker, same as Austin. Gil and Michelle didn't want to overreact, give in to emotion, cocoon their son in bubble wrap. Besides, Austin always took such pride in Walker.

The boy loved to hit, so much so that he bragged about it: *Mommy, that kid is a baby. He cried, and I didn't even hit him that hard.*

Walker wore a special chin strap, rigged with accelerometers that measured the force of every blow he absorbed. If built-in software deemed any hit powerful enough to cause a head injury, three green LED lights on the chin strap would flash red. While Walker was making a routine block, his head whipped sideways. Red lights. His coach pulled him off the field. Two sideline nurses checked him out. Dizzy and frightened, he cried.

"My head," he said. "My head."

The Trenums followed Gioia's instructions. They made Walker rest. They took him to a Sunday-night bonfire—a memorial for Austin—but didn't let him run around with his friends. On Monday morning, a neurologist diagnosed Walker with a concussion. Sensitive to light and sound, he was held out of football practice and gym class for a week. One week after that, he was back on the field, Michelle looking on.

"You're so calm," one of the other mothers said.

Michelle wasn't. Watching football on TV was bad enough. This was worse. Also, the chin strap. It was supposed to make things easier, safer. But the lights kept turning red, once when Walker hadn't even been hit. Michelle made him sit out the entire game. Walker fumed, said he wouldn't wear the device again. Michelle sent the faulty chin strap back to the manufacturer, got a replacement, then sent that one back too. More red lights. Was the problem a bad battery? Water leaking into the electronics? Was the problem football?

Michelle wasn't watching her son. She was watching the lights, waiting for green to go red. She worried about punch-drunk football players, the blows adding up over time—wondered if Walker's concussion was God's version of a yellow flag. It was all too much.

Michelle Trenum kept coming back to the same question.

"If you're that worked up," she says, "then what are you doing letting your kid out there in the first place?"

Losing a child, Michelle says, is like jumping from one train onto another headed in the opposite direction. In an instant, you're barreling away from everything you once knew, farther and farther with each second.

Brentsville High has a scholarship in Austin's name. In their living room, the Trenums keep a large photo of Austin, sweaty and beaming, coming off a football field. On the ceiling above the kitchen table is a spot with his fingerprints, smudged and faded, where he and his brothers once liked to test how high they could jump. "I sometimes think we can never repaint that," Michelle says. There's sadness in her eyes—green like Austin's—and pain.

"I love football," Gil says. "I loved watching the kids play. But it's not the same anymore."

Twelve years ago, Dallas Cowboys quarterback Troy Aikman retired after suffering the 10th concussion of his Hall of Fame career, the result of a vicious hit from Washington Redskins linebacker LaVar Arrington. Aikman since has become a successful broadcaster, a man who owes much to football. After the Super Bowl in February, however, he said that the sport was "at a real crossroads . . . If I had a 10-year-old boy, I don't know that I'd be real inclined to encourage him to go play football in light of what we're learning from head injuries."

Michelle showed Walker the comment.

"I don't think I want you to play football," she said.

He was upset—for a moment.

"Can I play another sport?"

Gil and Michelle are not against football. They don't judge others. But they've made their decision.

"As a mother," Michelle says, "I'm a lot more relaxed watching basketball."

WRIGHT THOMPSON

Urban Meyer Will Be Home for Dinner

FROM ESPN: THE MAGAZINE

Part One

BEFORE YOU JOIN Urban Meyer, who is walking toward the exit of the Ohio State football office, there's a scar you need to see. A few years ago in Gainesville, his middle child, Gigi, planned a celebration to formally accept a college volleyball scholarship to Florida Gulf Coast University. It was football season, so she checked her dad's calendar, scheduling her big day around his job. As the hour approached, she waited at her high school, wanting much, expecting little. Some now-forgotten problem consumed Meyer, and he told his secretary he didn't have time. He wasn't going. His beautiful, athletic, earnest daughter would have to sign her letter of intent without him. Meyer's secretary, a mother of four, insisted: "You're going."

Eighty or so people filed into the school cafeteria. Urban and his wife, Shelley, joined their daughter at the front table, watching as Gigi stood and spoke. She'd been nervous all day, and with a room of eyes on her, she thanked her mother for being there season after season, year after year.

Then she turned to her father.

He'd missed almost everything. *You weren't there,* she told him.

Shelley Meyer winced. Her heart broke for Urban, who sat with a thin smile, crushed. Moments later, Gigi high-fived her dad without making eye contact, then hugged her coach. Urban dragged himself back to the car. Then—and this arrives at the guts of his conflict—Urban Meyer went back to work, pulled by some biological imperative. His daughter's words ran through his mind, troubling him, and yet he returned to the shifting pixels on his television, studying for a game he'd either win or lose. The conflict slipped away. Nothing mattered but winning. Both of these people are in him—are him: the guilty father who feels regret, the obsessed coach who ignores it. He doesn't like either one. He doesn't like himself, which is why he wants to change.

Meyer strolls through the Ohio State football parking lot with his 13-year-old son, Nate. Years from now, when Urban either succeeds or fails in remaking himself, he will look back on these two days in June as a dividing line. On one side, the past 18 months of searching, and on the other, the test of that search. In the car, he turns right out of his new office, heading some two hours north. There's vital business at hand, which requires him to leave the football bunker on a summer afternoon.

Road trip!

"All right, fun time today," he says, amped and smiling at his son.

Fun? Smiling? Urban? There's gray in his brush cut, weight back on his hips. The radio in the car, as always, is tuned to 93.3, the oldies station. "I Got Sunshine." Tomorrow he will meet with the 2012 Buckeyes for the first time, beginning the countdown to the first practice, the first game, the first loss. Today he's driving to Cleveland to take Nate to an Indians game.

In front of him is a second chance. Behind, there's his old dream job in Florida, which he quit twice in a year, and the $20 million he left on the table, unable to answer the simplest of questions: *Why am I doing this?* During the break, he studied himself for the first time in his life, looking for a new him or maybe trying to get the old him back—the person he was before a need for perfection nearly killed him. At least he can laugh about it now. During one of his many recent visits to a children's hospital in Columbus, he told a group of nurses on an elevator, "My wife's a nurse."

They turned and he said, "A psych nurse," which is true.

He paused.

"I'm her patient," he said.

Like any man who destroys himself running for a finish line that doesn't exist, Meyer often longed for the time and place where that race began: Columbus, 1986. As a 22-year-old graduate assistant for the Buckeyes, right up the road from his hometown of Ashtabula, Ohio, each day brought something new. He romanticized the experience; in later years, when the SEC's recruiting wars got too dirty, he waxed about the Big Ten, where it was always 1986, which was just another way of hoping he could look in the mirror and see his younger, more idealistic self. After Jim Tressel resigned in shame a year ago, a joke passed among SEC insiders: "Who's gonna tell Urban there's no Santa Claus?"

It might have been genetic. His father, Bud, idolized Woody Hayes, who died a year after Meyer arrived in Columbus. Bud Meyer thought Woody offered the perfect template for a man: Hard work solves every problem. Never accept defeat. Stay focused on the future; reflection is weakness wrapped in nostalgia. Urban grew up in a house free of contradiction. Bud Meyer believed in black and white.

"No gray," Urban says.

Bud studied three years to be a priest before he met Gisela, who escaped Nazi Germany as a child. They raised three children and never missed a game or a recital. A chemical engineer, Bud enjoyed Latin and advanced mathematics, but when his son struck out looking in high school, he made him run home from the game. The Braves drafted Urban after his senior year, and when he tried to quit minor league baseball, realizing he wasn't good enough, Bud told him he no longer would be welcome in their home. Just call your mom on Christmas, he advised. Not only did Urban finish the season, he told that story to every freshman class he recruited. His whole life had been unintentionally preparing him to coach; after baseball, he played college football at Cincinnati, and the stern men in whistles seemed familiar. Some boys rebel against demanding fathers. Urban embraced his dad's unforgiving expectations, finding a profession that allowed him to re-create the world of Bud Meyer: the joy of teaching, the lens of competition, the mentoring, the pushing—the black and white.

He discovered more than a calling in college. He met a beautiful woman named Shelley, and after he got his first job in Columbus, she moved to town. Once, a possum peeked its head over the television, and Urban and his roommates screamed and stood on the couch, yelling for Shelley, the Ohio farm girl, to do something. Urban made less than his rent. He lived on happy-hour egg rolls.

Staying up all night during the season, he cut 16-millimeter tape, nursing a six-pack of beer through the tedious job. He loved it. To make ends meet, he picked up shifts at Consolidated Freightways, driving a forklift. Shelley calls it his "Archie Bunker job." He bought steel-toe boots, and three or so nights a week during the off-season, he pulled the graveyard, getting off at 6:00 A.M., showering and heading to the football office. At the warehouse, they got a breather about 2:00 A.M., those callow faces yellowed in break-room light, eating peanut butter sandwiches, maybe a bag of chips. He looked around and saw the same question on every face, one he knew they could see on his: *Why am I doing this?*

In 1986, he knew the answer.

Often he lets in only what he wants; you can watch him listen to a story and pick certain details, turning the facts into an allegory that either confirms some deeply held belief or offers a road map to one he'd like to hold. For instance, there's a book he loves, written for business executives, called *Change or Die,* which shaped his ideas about altering the behavior of athletes. He has talked about the book in speeches, invited the author to Gainesville, handed out copies, and never, not once, did he realize the book almost perfectly described him.

"I know," Shelley says, laughing. "He didn't have any self-awareness at all."

In the car on the way to Cleveland, he is read a paragraph from page 150:

"Why do people persist in their self-destructive behavior, ignoring the blatant fact that what they've been doing for many years hasn't solved their problems? They think that they need to do it even more fervently or frequently, as if they were doing the right thing but simply had to try even harder."

Meyer's voice changes, grows firmer, louder. "Blatant fact," he says.

He pauses. A fragmented idea orders itself in his mind. "Wow," he says.

He asks to hear it again. "Blatant fact," he says. "It should have my picture. I need to read that to my wife. I'm gonna reread that now. Self-destructive behavior?"

The car is quiet. Those close to Meyer say he lives in his head, with a constant interior monologue, which is why he'll zone out at dinner with his kids or start calling people he knows by the wrong name.

"Wow," he says. "This is profound stuff. Profound. Now as I sit here talking about it, I know exactly what happened."

Part Two

He lost things one at a time.

He lost 15 pounds during every season as the head coach at Bowling Green and at Utah, unable to eat or shave, rethinking things as fundamental as the punt. Purging the weak, he locked teams inside a gym with nothing but bleating whistles and trash cans for their puke, forcing the unworthy to quit. The survivors, and their coaches, were underdogs, united. His children often asked why they kept moving. Shelley always said, "Daddy's climbing a mountain."

His desire to mentor battled with the rage that often consumed him, a by-product of his need for success and his constantly narrowing definition of it. He threw a remote control through a television. Players whispered about Black Wednesday, about Full Metal Jacket Friday, about a drill named Vietnam. His own body rebelled against the intensity: during his time as an assistant, a cyst on his brain often sent crushing waves of pain through his head when he was stressed. He kept coaching, moving up, each rung of success pulling him further away from his young wife and kids. A voice of warning whispered even then. "I was always fearful I would become That Guy," he says. "The guy who had regret. 'Yeah, we won a couple of championships, but I never saw my kids grow up. Yeah, we beat Georgia a couple of times, but I ruined my marriage.'"

At Bowling Green, at Utah, and finally at Florida, the teams celebrated with something he called Victory Meal. They'd gather after a win, eating steak and shrimp, watching a replay of the game. They'd hang out, enjoying the accomplishment. Players and coaches loved Victory Meal, and Meyer often sat at the front of the room, glowing inside.

Then he won the 2006 national title.

Bud Meyer joined him in the locker room. They hugged, cried, and before Urban left, he took his nameplate from his locker as a souvenir. Back at the office, he gave his secretary his credit card and told her to buy everything she could find from the game. She spent around $5,000 on blown-up photographs. Urban essentially scrapbooked, collecting mementos of the success he couldn't really enjoy. There was something melancholy about it. Truth is, he loved reflecting—his favorite song, Jimmy Buffett's "One Particular Harbor," is about someone who imagines an escape, dreaming of being an old man able to look back—but he'd learned that reflection is weakness, so he didn't indulge beyond the pictures on the wall and those moments in the locker room with his dad.

He lost even that.

Success didn't bring relief. It only magnified his obsession, made the margins thinner, left him with chest pains. After the 2007 season, he confided to a friend that anxiety was taking over his life and he wanted to walk away.

Two years after he cried with his father, Urban Meyer stood on the field with his second national championship team, the 2008 Gators, singing the fight song. After the last line, he rushed into the tunnel and locked himself in the coaches' locker room. He began calling recruits as his assistants pounded on the door, asking if everything was okay. Back in Gainesville, his chronic chest pain got worse, and he did test after test, treadmills and heart scans, sure he was dying. Doctors found nothing, and the pain became another thing to ignore. "Building takes passion and energy," Meyer says. "Maintenance is awful. It's nothing but fatigue. Once you reach the top, maintaining that beast is awful."

A few months later, during the 2009 SEC media days, a reporter asked what it felt like knowing anything but perfection would be a failure. Meyer tried to laugh it off, but he walked away from the podium knowing the undeniable truth of the question.

Success meant perfection.

The drive for it changed something inside him. For the first time, Meyer needed an alarm clock. Shelley called his secretary to ask whether he was eating. Unopened boxes of food sat on his desk. He lost even when they won, raging at his coaches and players for mistakes, demanding emergency staff meetings in the middle of the night. He stopped smiling. Days ended later and later. He texted recruits in church. He ignored his children, his fears realized: he'd become That Guy.

The tighter he gripped, the more things slipped away. *The bla-tant fact.* The Gators beat Georgia, another step closer to perfec-tion. He'd been skipping Victory Meal, heading straight to his of-fice to watch film, but after that win he stopped in. The room was almost empty.

"Where the hell is everybody?" he asked.

His strength coach and friend Mickey Marotti didn't want to answer.

"Where the hell is everybody?" he repeated.

"Coach," Mickey said, "they don't come."

The unbeaten streak reached 22 games.

Four days before the SEC title game against Alabama, Meyer got an early-morning phone call: star defensive end Carlos Dunlap had been arrested and charged with drunken driving, threatening the perfection, triggering the rage, which had always been con-nected for Meyer. He wanted order, and this desire had turned him in a circle, or, more accurately, a spiral: losing filled him with loathing, for himself and everyone connected to the loss, and over time his personality came to define losing as anything short of perfection. His rage was the exhaust of whatever hidden motor turned inside him. After the campus police officer delivered the news about Dunlap, Meyer went to the office, overcome, driving in the dark. That week, everything came apart.

He popped Ambien but couldn't sleep.

The morning of the game, early in a quiet hotel, Meyer waited to do an interview, and when his public relations guy, Steve McClain, saw Meyer gaunt in the television lights, he felt panic. Meyer's pants sagged off thin hips. McClain called Shelley Meyer and asked her to come down: they needed to talk. An intervention loomed. That afternoon, Florida lost to Alabama, and afterward, the cheers from the Crimson Tide echoed in the concrete halls of the Georgia Dome. Meyer limped to the bus, ghost white, settling next to Shel-ley in the front right seat. His head slumped. An unopened box of chicken sat on his lap.

He'd lost 35 pounds that season.

Six or seven hours later in Gainesville, around 4:00 A.M., Meyer said his chest hurt, and he fell on the floor. Shelley dialed 911. She tried to sound calm, but a few shaky words gave her away.

"My husband's having chest pains," she said. "He's on the floor."

"Is he awake?" the operator asked.

"Urban, Urban," Shelley pleaded, "talk to me, Urb. Urban, talk to me, please."

Meyer lay on his stomach, on the floor of his mansion, his eyes closed, unable to speak. Soon he'd resign, come back for a year and resign again, but the journey that began with hope in Columbus in 1986 ended with that 911 call and the back of an ambulance.

Urban Meyer won 104 games but lost himself.

Meyer didn't just give up a job. He admitted that the world he'd constructed had been fatally flawed, which called into question more than a football career. Follow the dots, from quitting to asking why he'd lost control to trying to understand himself. *Who am I? Why am I that way?* When the facade fell down, the foundation crumbled too, so he needed more than a relaxing break. If he came back and allowed the rage to consume him again, his quitting would have been meaningless. He didn't need a piña colada. He needed to rebuild himself. His dad sneered at the weakness when he quit, leveling his stark opinion: "You can't change your essence."

Five months after retiring, Meyer woke up early in a hotel near Stanford University, there for his new job as an ESPN analyst. His chest didn't hurt; a doctor finally thought to suggest Nexium. Turns out esophageal spasms mimic the symptoms of a heart attack. That morning, he went for a run, on a whim grabbing a book he'd started the night before: *LEAD . . . for God's Sake!*

He ran with the book in his hand, stopping on campus to sit and read. He ran an hour, read an hour, back and forth. The sun climbed, and he couldn't turn the pages fast enough. He finished that day and emailed the author from his phone, saying, "That is the most profound book I've ever read."

The novel tells of the winningest high school basketball coach in Kentucky, a man consumed by success. When players make a mistake, he punishes their weakness, destroys watercoolers, but he doesn't understand why his star breaks his hand punching a wall. *They skipped Victory Meal because I did.* Finally, his family fades away. The character's son begs him to shoot baskets, and the coach can't make time. When things collapse and his team can't win, the man is forced to ask, "Why do I coach?"

"That hit home," Meyer says. "That was in my backyard. Even closer, that was in my living room. It brought me back to 1986 and why I made a decision to get into coaching, as opposed to what was going on in 2009—chasing perfection. Never one time did I say, 'To go undefeated at Florida.' All of a sudden, every step, every time I had a cup of coffee, every time I woke up in the morning and shaved, it was all about somehow getting a team to go undefeated at Florida."

The coach in the book forms a relationship with the school janitor, a mystical Christ figure, who becomes a spiritual guide in his search for himself. Meyer left Stanford looking for his own guides. "Without anyone really knowing it," he says, "I went on a yearlong research project. How can you do both? How does Bob Stoops be a good dad and husband and still have success?"

Meyer traveled to Norman, Oklahoma, and met with Stoops, who said, "Live your life. When you go home, go home."

He flew several times to Texas to sit with Mack Brown, who told him to remember when he loved the game. Before you wanted a perfect season, before million-dollar homes and recruiting wars, once upon a time you loved a game.

Meyer visited West Point, stayed with Nate in coach Red Blaik's old house. He sat with Army coach Rich Ellerson in the little café behind the cemetery, in the shadow of General Custer's grave. Holding hot cups of coffee, they talked about the essential truths often hidden by the contradictions, the things obscured by money and success. Ellerson told Urban that football itself helped nurture and protect its values. The snippets of life lived between the snap and the whistle could purify everything bad that people did to the game. "It clarifies," he said. Meyer, who'd seen the lines blurred in the SEC and within himself, said he wasn't sure. Ellerson offered his sermon on MacArthur and the Corps and the West Point mission: "To educate, train, and inspire . . ." Urban stared at him. "Wait a minute," Meyer said, "you really believe this." They talked about why they loved a game, following the question: *Why do I coach?* At Bowling Green, he'd loved tutoring his players in math. Could he have that back again? The game was the problem, but maybe it could be the solution too.

West Point came in the middle of a 13-day road trip with Nate, maybe the best 13 days of Urban's life. The two helicoptered to Yankee Stadium, hung out for almost a week in Cooperstown, where they held Babe Ruth's bat. "I was seven years old again," he says.

Back home, Urban slept in. Shelley couldn't believe it, getting up around 7:30 to work out, leaving Urban in bed. When he finally dressed, he'd walk a mile to a breakfast place he loved, lounge around and watch television with the owner, then walk a mile back.

"His mind shut off," Shelley says.

Shelley begged him to do this forever. She'd never seen Urban so happy. He coached Nate's baseball and football teams. He played paintball. The family went out for dinners, and Urban was *present,* cracking Seinfeld jokes and smiling.

But he still felt empty. He'd ask, *Is this it?* He missed the ability to make an impact; he'd gotten into coaching to be a teacher. A challenge grew from his trip to West Point: What if he could have the feeling of Bowling Green on the scale of Florida? What if he could answer the question posed in the novel: Why?

Yet beyond the intellectual journey, he missed football on an almost biological level, deep down in the place where his ambition—where his love, and his rage—hibernated. In early November, he stood on the sideline at Bryant-Denny Stadium in Tuscaloosa. The crowd roared. God, he loved the crowd. Sometimes, when it felt as if they'd never lose again at the Swamp, he'd slip his headset off just for a moment and let the noise cover him like a hot rain. In Tuscaloosa, with LSU and Alabama waiting to take the field, the stadium lights bright on the green grass, something awoke. The person standing next to him looked over to find the old Urban Meyer, eyes dark and squinted, arms crossed, muttering, "I miss this."

In late November, Meyer wanted to accept the Ohio State job. Shelley demanded a family meeting. They had all gathered around Thanksgiving in the Atlanta apartment of their oldest daughter, Nicki, who played volleyball at Georgia Tech. Shelley told the kids to ask anything. He heard the fear in their voices: how could he be sure he was ready to go back?

"We wanted him to make promises," Shelley says.

*

During the fall that Urban spent searching, as the rumors circled about his return to the game, Bud Meyer was slipping away. Lung disease had left him frail and weak. Urban used his freedom to visit whenever he wanted. Around the LSU-Alabama game, Urban and Bud watched a television news report about the open Ohio State job. Urban's picture appeared on the screen.

"Hey, you gonna do that?" Bud asked.

"I don't know," Urban said. "What do you think?"

Bud turned to face him, gaunt in the light. An oxygen tube ran to his nose. Twenty seconds passed, the silence uncomfortable. Thirty seconds.

"Nah," Bud said. "I like this s— the way it is. I don't care who wins or loses."

His response couldn't have been more out of character. Never before had Urban asked his dad for his opinion and not gotten direct, blunt advice: "I think you should . . ." In his father's answer, there was a measure of absolution—maybe for both of them. Sometimes walking away isn't quitting. Sometimes, when the fire burns too hot, walking away is the bravest thing a man can do. Bud offered the best mea culpa he could, in his own way. Maybe he knew this would be one of their last conversations. Ambivalence was his final gift. Whatever Urban chose to do with his future, he could walk through the world knowing he had his father's blessing. They never discussed coaching again.

Two weeks later, Bud Meyer died in his son's arms.

Three days after his father's funeral, five days after his family demanded promises, Meyer accepted the Ohio State job. During his first news conference, he reached into his suit jacket and pulled out a contract written by Nicki, which he'd signed in exchange for his family's blessing. These rules were supposed to govern his attempt at a new life, as his father's example had governed his old one. So much was happening at once, and as he said good-bye to the man who molded him, he began undoing part of that molding.

He went to work.

Meyer unpacked his boxes, setting up little shrines on the blond wood shelves of his Ohio State office. To the right, positioned in his most common line of sight, he placed a blue rock with a word etched into it: BALANCE. Behind the rock went a collage of photographs, the orange of a sunset from his lake house—his particular harbor—and of his old church in Gainesville. The shrine was a gift from his pastor in Florida, a prayer from people who love him that he won't lose himself again.

Framed above his desk hung the contract he signed with his kids, written on pink notebook paper.

1. MY FAMILY WILL ALWAYS COME FIRST.
2. I WILL TAKE CARE OF MYSELF AND MAINTAIN GOOD HEALTH.
3. I WILL GO ON A TRIP ONCE A YEAR WITH NICKI — MINIMUM.
4. I WILL NOT GO MORE THAN NINE HOURS A DAY AT THE OFFICE.
5. I WILL SLEEP WITH MY CELL PHONE ON SILENT.
6. I WILL CONTINUE TO COMMUNICATE DAILY WITH MY KIDS.
7. I WILL TRUST GOD'S PLAN AND NOT BE OVERANXIOUS.
8. I WILL KEEP THE LAKE HOUSE.
9. I WILL FIND A WAY TO WATCH NICKI AND GIGI PLAY VOLLEY-BALL.
10. I WILL EAT THREE MEALS A DAY.

Part Three

Seven months later, Meyer drives through the outskirts of Cleveland, 60 miles from Ashtabula, past the refineries and smokestacks, his son Nate in the backseat. They're almost at the Indians' stadium, where Urban is scheduled to throw out the first pitch in a few hours. Meyer's living his life, keeping the promises he made.

"I've really been working on that," he says. "I'm gonna do that in the fall. I'm gonna go home. I'm not gonna bring my work home with me and not be able to sleep at night. I'm not . . .

". . . that's easy to say now."

The season is still a few months away. He hasn't lost a game yet. That's what pushed him into the darkest corners of his own personality. He squeezes the steering wheel.

"Can I change?" he asks.

The question hangs in the air. In public he talks a good game, but he knows how hard the next year will be. Maybe, deep inside, he already knows the answer. The skies darken. Rain will soon land on the windshield with heavy thumps.

"TBD," he says. "To be determined."

*

Father and son play catch in the rain, standing in shallow left at Progressive Field, the bowl of seats empty around them. Urban smiles when Nate backhands a grounder, a schoolboy grin, the one that believed what the girls whispered in the hall back in the day. Meyer's enthusiasm is as powerful as his rage. Halfway is for other people. When he took his girls to Rome and Israel for nine days, they begged to sleep in just once. Nope. "We attacked Rome as hard as you possibly can," he says and then mimics his own stern voice: "'We are gonna have fun on this vacation!'"

Urban throws one high into the air, watching as Nate settles underneath it, the scoreboard right on top of them, thunder clapping in the air, the drizzle coming and going.

"I can't believe they're letting us do this," he says.

These are the things he lost in Florida, and the things he's found in Ohio. He's missed only one or two of Nate's baseball games since taking the job, an astonishing change. Nicki is entering her final year at Georgia Tech, and her coach scheduled Senior Night on the Saturday of the Buckeyes' bye week. Urban will walk onto the court with Nicki, a walk he's made with other people's children but never with his own. He's eating, working out, sleeping well, waking early without an alarm clock. On the night before the 2012 Buckeyes gather for the first time, he's playing catch with his son in Cleveland.

"Bucket list," Urban says.

The Indians arrange for Nate to throw out the first pitch with Urban, and in the dugout, the team gives Nate a full uniform, number 15, with MEYER on the back. Urban pulls out his phone and takes a picture, sending it to Shelley. He follows his son into the clubhouse, calling out in his best announcer voice, "Leading off for the Cleveland Indians, Nate Meyer."

Two hours fly past, and they're led back onto the field. Now the bleachers are full. The speakers echo their names. Urban loops it a bit, but Nate throws a bullet for a strike.

"What a night, Nate!" Urban says, turning to the Indians guy following them with a camera. "Get me those pictures. I'm gonna blow them up. My man brought it!"

They find their seats. Nate holds a slice of pizza. Urban pours a cold Labatt's and digs into a bowl of popcorn. The sun sets over the Cleveland skyline, and the lights shine on the grass. Urban's mind and body are in the same place. Urban and Nate recite fa-

vorite movie lines and list the ballparks they've visited. "I'm melting inside," Meyer says finally. "You can't get this back. Remember
That Guy? I'm not That Guy right now."

The next morning begins back in Columbus with heavy metal music grinding out of the weight room. Shouts and whistles filter in
from the practice field. No other place in the world sounds like a
football facility, and the effect is seductive, pulling anyone who's
ever loved it back in, like a whiff of an ex-girlfriend's perfume.
Outside, hundreds of youth football campers run around like wild
men. This week, Meyer's constant nervous pacing—"I'm so ADD,"
he says—includes laps around the camp, taking pictures with parents, urging moms to make their meanest faces for the camera. He
spots Godfrey Lewis, one of his former running backs at Bowling
Green, who's now a high school coach.

"What's up?" Meyer asks, beaming.

"You," Lewis says. "That's what's up, Coach."

"You look good," Meyer says. "You got kids?"

"My son is over there," Lewis says.

"Make sure I meet your son. Where's he at?"

"Alex!" Lewis yells.

A boy at the water station turns his head, finding his dad standing with Urban Meyer.

"Alex!" Meyer yells. "Hurry up. Let's go. Let's go."

Alex Lewis runs over.

"Your dad played for me," Meyer says. "He was a great player.
Good father, good guy, right? How old are you?"

"Twelve."

"Can you run?"

"Yes," Alex says.

A cocky, curious kid comes over too, poking his head into the
conversation, popping off about how he's faster than Alex. A look
flashes across Meyer's face, his eyes bright. He cannot help himself.

"Right now!" he barks.

Meyer calls to Lewis. "Godfrey," he yells, "this guy says he's faster
than your boy. We're gonna find out right now."

Godfrey is wired too.

"Right now!" he says.

"Right now!" Urban yells. "Right now! You ready?"

He calls go, and the kids break, Alex Lewis smoking the opposition. Urban and Godfrey stand together, elated, a messy world shrunk to a 10-yard race. Someone wins and someone loses, and there's no ambiguity, no gray. The heat makes the air smokehouse thick. The morning smells like sweat and rings with whistles and coach chatter, the game always the same no matter how much the men who love it change, a simplicity that waits day after day, beautiful and addictive.

Meyer grimaces and wipes a streak of sweat off his face with his shirt. Lunchtime racquetball is war. The football ops guys know to ask Meyer any difficult questions before the game, because losses blacken his mood and rewire a day. It's a running joke: did Coach win or lose? Today Meyer's playing Marotti, his friend and strength coach. Best of three, tied at one game apiece. Meyer works the angles, lofting brutal kill shots that just die off the wall. Marotti smacks the bejesus out of the ball. Muffled curses echo through the glass door. Meyer chases after a ball and doesn't get there. He cocks back his racket, about to smash it into the wall, but he pulls back. *Be calm.* The end is close, a few points away. Shoes squeak, and the ball pops off the strings, laid over the backbeat of Marotti bellowing, "F—!" Meyer loses another point, then another. About to lose the match, he grimaces, flexing his racket to slam the ball off the floor in disgust, then checks his rage. *Be calm.*

The football facility pulses with the rush of building, and through a series of decisions and coincidences, Meyer has somehow managed to go back in time. He feels like he felt in the beginning: unproven, energized by the challenge. Beneath the surface is the idea that maybe this time, with his father's absolution and the lessons he's learned about himself, he could return to 1986 and not make the mistakes that led him to 2009. There's joy in starting a climb, for a 48-year-old coach and for the newly arrived freshmen sitting in the team meeting room, waiting for Meyer to welcome them to Ohio State. The recruiting class, Meyer's first, is nervous, unsure what to expect. He senses their fear and stands at the podium relaxed and calm. All their dreams are right there, waiting to be grabbed.

"I've seen life-changing stuff happen," he tells them.

He describes walking across a graduation stage, your family in the crowd crying, and when you reach out to shake the president's hand, there's a fist of diamonds: championship rings. Meyer bangs his fist on the podium, asking if they've ever heard how much noise five rings make when they hit something.

"I'll do it for you sometime," he says. "It's loud as s—. Some guys get to do that. I've seen it."

Eager faces stare back. He does not tell the story about his dad threatening to disown him for quitting. Reflect, he says. Look around this room.

"These guys will be in your wedding," he says.

They will come back to Columbus as grown men, bringing their sons and daughters to this building, walking the halls. They will point at old photographs, smile at out-of-style haircuts, telling stories about 2012.

But even in his new world, nostalgia must be earned. Contentment must be bought with work, with sacrifice, and, since competition is still black and white, with wins.

"That team that goes 4-7, how many reunions do they have?" Meyer says. "How many times does that senior class come back? You never see 'em."

This is the difficult calculus of Meyer's future, of any Type A extremist who longs for balance. They want the old results, without paying the old costs, and while they'll feel guilty about not changing, they'll feel empty without the success. He wants peace *and* wins, which is a short walk from thinking they are the same.

"How about that 2002 national championship team?" Meyer says, his voice rising, the players leaning in. "All the time. When they hit their hands on the table, what happens? It makes a lot of noise. It makes a lot of noise. Let's go make some noise."

Another coach is on the phone, asking for advice about a player who got into trouble. Meyer gives his honest answer, a window into the murky, shifting world of big-time athletics, into how nobody emerges from the highest level of anything with every part of himself intact.

The first year at Bowling Green, Meyer tells him, he'd have cut his losses. His fifth year at Florida, when he needed to win every game, he'd have kept him on the team.

The caller asks about the Buckeyes. "I like it," Meyer says. "I don't know how good we're gonna be, but I like it. We've got one more week, and then we get on the ship to the beaches of Normandy."

On the northwest side of town, Shelley Meyer sits in their new house, praying, literally, that this time will be different.

He's made promises before.

She believed his first news conference at Florida in 2004 when he said his priorities were his children, his wife, and football—in that order. She believed in 2007 when she told a reporter, "Absolutely there's a change in him. There's definitely an exhale."

She wants to believe today. His willingness to admit the possibility of failure is oddly comforting. He knows he could end up back in 2009, which is worth the chance to reclaim 1986. "There's a risk," he says. "What's the reward? The reward is going back to the real reason I wanted to coach."

There's confidence in his voice. She's heard it, seen how calmly he handled the arrest of two players or his starting running back getting a freak cut on his foot.

"Man, I just feel great," he'll say.

"But you haven't played a game yet," she'll remind him.

Shelley moves to the bright sunroom overlooking the golf course, with pictures of the girls when they were little, grinning with Cam the Ram, the Colorado State mascot. There's a Gator on the table and Ohio State pictures on the walls. Another room contains a helmet from every school where Urban has coached and all the memories, good and bad, evoked by each. Once they sat in a gross apartment with a possum over the television, young and in love, wondering where their journey would lead. It's led here, to this dividing line. All the things they want are in front of them. So are all the things they fear.

"I've seen enough change already," Shelley says. "I'm convinced. We still have to play a game, though."

She bites her fingernail and sighs.

"The work he's done," she says, "the books he's read, people he's talked to. He's gonna be different."

She stops between sentences, little gulfs of anxiety.

"He's gonna be different. I totally believe it . . ."

". . . I'll just kick his butt if he's not."

One more hopeful pause.

"But he will be."

The door shuts, and his last meeting of the day begins. For the first time, the freshmen and veterans gather, the 2012 Buckeyes in full. Meyer sits calmly at the front of the room, as composed as the crisp lines on his shirt. A quote on the wall is from Matthew, 16th chapter: "What good is a man that gains the world yet loses his soul?" Behind him in his office, there's a blue rock and a pink piece of paper. He's been at the facility almost 12 hours. Breaking number 4—working no more than nine hours a day—couldn't be helped. Meyer lived up to all but one of his promises today.

His calm lasts until a player giggles.

From the back of the room, it's not clear who laughed, or why exactly, only that the players were making fun of a teammate while an assistant coach gave a speech. Meyer listens, waiting for the coach to finish, stewing, simmering, slowly beginning to burn. If he were transparent, like one of those med school teaching dummies, maybe you could see exactly where his rage lives and how it spreads. In imagination, it's a tiny, burning dot, surrounded by his humor and love for teaching, by the warm memories of 1986, by his desire to grow old and gray with Shelley, and the dot spreads and spreads until there's nothing but fire.

Meyer rises and interrupts the flow of the meeting, looking out at his team. His voice holds steady, but he says he's struggling not to climb into the seats and find the offending giggler. The fire is growing. He paces, back and forth, back and forth, waving his finger toward the center of the room. The air feels tense. Nobody makes a sound. There is one voice.

"Giggle-f—s," he says.

He slips, his language rough and mean, giving himself over to his rage: f-bombs, a flurry of curses, pounding on the soft and the weak, the unworthy who'd rather giggle than chase something bigger than themselves.

In 43 days, he says, Marotti will hand him a piece of paper with a list of names. "Grown-ass men," he says. That's who belongs on his team. No "giggle-f—s," he promises, pointing toward the big pictures of Ohio Stadium to his right.

"We're talking about our season," he roars. "We're going to that place."

His mind is there already.

The players will gather in the tunnel, walking out in scarlet, sunlight blinking off their silver helmets. He'll raise his fist and call the first-team defense. He can see it, a personification of his hopes and fears, of his contradictions: first the grown-ass men moving as one, then the giggle-f—s who can destroy what he spent months building. The sun will shine on silver helmets. The crowd will roar. The band will play. Maybe he'll slip off his headset for a moment, feeling the hot rain. Nothing else will matter. The helmets will sparkle, and the Buckeyes will advance, an army of gray. Standing before his players in the meeting room, he can smell it, hear it—feel it even, in places he doesn't understand and can't control. Nobody makes a sound. Meyer's shirt is wrinkled, untucked a bit. Thick veins rise on both sides of his neck. He squints out at the team, his eyes dark, hiding everything and nothing at all.

PAUL SOLOTAROFF

The NFL's Secret Drug Problem

FROM MEN'S JOURNAL

HERE COMES THE PAIN AGAIN, extra-strength, a loud, blue blade down the shank of his left arm, carving from spine to wrist. Sitting in a clamorous Midtown steak house a block from his studio at SportsNet New York, Ray Lucas goes into pneumatic shakes, like a kid who's stuck his pinkie in a light socket. The 40-year-old ex-quarterback of the New York Jets—six-foot-three, 240 pounds, and still built like a mine shaft nine years after retirement—puts his head down on the table for several moments, waiting for the sizzle to stop. Seated beside him in the booth, Jennifer Smith, the player-program director of PAST (Pain Alternatives Solutions and Treatments), a consortium of surgeons and specialists who repair the bodies of NFL veterans free of charge, lays her hand on his shoulder and says nothing. There's little to do but wait with Lucas and count off the days till his next surgery.

Time was, Lucas could feel it before the nerves at the base of his neck went into spasm. He suffers from, among other ailments, stenosis of the spine—a compression of the open spaces in the canal causing pressure on the spinal cord—the result of blindside shots and face-plant tackles. But now, 18 months after a drug rehab during which he torturously withdrew from the pain pills he was taking just to get out of bed—six or eight Vicodins with his morning coffee, half a dozen Percocets to wash down lunch, double that to make it to bedtime—Lucas has lost his early-warning system and lives at the mercy of these flashes. Off all meds now except for monthly epidurals to dull his pain till surgery, he's facing his seventh operation in less than seven years and is walking around with steel plates and screws in his neck that will have to be replaced at some point.

Still, all in all, this is a *good* day for Lucas, who, when he retired in 2003 after being waived by the Baltimore Ravens, hurt wherever you could hurt and still draw breath. There's relief in the offing— once the surgeons go in and saw down the bones that pierce his discs. More, he's still loved by his wife and three daughters, who've flourished since he weaned himself off narcotics in 2011, shucking the 800-pill-a-month prescription-drug habit that had turned him into a red-eyed monster. And while, yes, he's lost his dream house, his NFL savings, and the small air-conditioning business he built after football, the great, improbable fact is he's still here to tell his story. For that, he can thank Smith, who took his last-chance call when he was in danger of becoming the next ex-NFL player to kill himself.

"I had it all planned: I was going to do it that Sunday, when my wife and kids went to church," says Lucas. "I was gonna drive straight off the George Washington Bridge, and if I didn't clear the barrier—I got a big truck—I was gonna get out and jump. I was on 17 different drugs: narcotics, psych meds, sleep aids, muscle relaxers, and nothing, man—none of them worked."

Lucas's intake was extreme, but his story is not. Pain-pill dependence is the NFL's dirty secret, and the next wave of trouble to breach its shore. In a months-long investigation involving dozens of former players, as well as their attorneys, physicians, and addiction counselors, what emerges is a picture of a professional league so swamped by narcotics that it closes its eyes to medical malpractice by many of its doctors and trainers. It does so not because it lacks the will to police its staff and players, but because the game itself could not survive without these powerful drugs. "The wear and tear on our spines and knees—we all had to take that to play," says Richard Dent, the Hall of Fame terror of those great Chicago Bears defenses of the 1980s and 1990s, who is now hobbled by back pain and headaches. "We got pills from a trainer, and where he got them, I don't know. But we were all involved with that."

"Your body ain't made to go through a wall 50, 60 times a game," says Fred McCrary, a Super Bowl fullback with the New England Patriots in 2003, now belabored by daily migraines and bum shoulders. "By week three, they'd give you whatever you wanted—and, still, guys smoked weed for the pain."

"Our doctors, who've seen everything, were shocked when they saw these guys; their prescription-pill addictions were literally deadly," says Smith over her seafood salad. Formerly the director of Gridiron Greats, the first nonprofit to come to the aid of disabled retirees from the NFL, she's helped build PAST from a charitable notion into a medical oasis for broken-down vets, offering full surgical care, drug-rehab stints, and long-term pain relief. Funded entirely by one doctor, a wealthy New Jersey internist named William Focazio, it has stepped into the void and saved the lives of men who've been ditched by the richest league on earth. "We've taken guys in their forties who were weeks or days from dying on a 1,000-Vikes-a-month-and-tequila diet."

"And trust me: we don't quit without a fight," says Lucas. "I drove this woman crazy with my addict bullshit, stunts she doesn't even know about till this day."

"Like what?" says Smith, a pale, pretty blonde, checking a Black-Berry that never stops buzzing.

"Like copping a gang of Percs at the Super Bowl and gulping 'em before the plane ride down to rehab."

Smith closes her eyes, letting this information settle. In February 2011, she'd flown him to Dallas to come clean before the national football media, telling hundreds of reporters during Super Bowl week about the pain-pill epidemic beneath their noses. Lucas did face the writers (who largely ignored him), then hit the streets of iced-in Dallas for one last brain-freeze binge. "That's just friggin' wrong, Ray. If you'd gotten arrested trying to score, or . . . or something worse had happened—"

"I know," says Lucas, "but there it is. An addict's gonna do what he's gonna do."

When it comes to pro football, the news is no longer new: we all know the wages of this sport. Brain death. Bountygate. Concussions. Crippled ex-players living in penury, unable to support themselves and their children. "This is a game with a 100 percent injury rate, according to the league's own stats," says DeMaurice Smith, the executive director of the NFL Players Association. "The average career for players is three and a half years, then the league fights in court to deny them lifetime insurance for the injuries that forced them out. That's the state of play: they're fungible assets."

But for decades, the sport's most transparent scandal has gone untold, if not unseen. Since the advent, in the 1980s, of modern narcotics like Vicodin and Percocet, and then later OxyContin, team doctors and trainers have dispensed pills in the millions to keep hurt players practicing and playing. That fact has long been an open secret among writers who cover the game, an unspoken pact between league and press to protect what's left of the sport's mythos. In the wake, however, of the concussion pandemic and the cluster of ex-player suicides, the football media has begun to stir. Articles have appeared in regional papers (the *New York Daily News*, the *Minneapolis Star Tribune*) that delve, for the first time, into opioid abuse, though only on the part of the players, not the teams that fed them the drugs. Last year, ESPN filed a report on the plight of ex-players with toxic narcotics habits, releasing the results of a survey of pain-pill abuse it had commissioned with a team of researchers at Washington University School of Medicine in St. Louis. The survey found that more than half the league's veterans had taken narcotics during their playing days; that almost three-quarters of that cohort had misused the drugs, taking them longer, and in greater amounts, than suggested; that the majority (63 percent) received their drugs from a nonmedical source like a trainer instead of the team doctor; and that a third were using them habitually in retirement. Given the population of 18,000 current NFL retirees, that means at least 5,000 are taking narcotics, and at least 2,000 suffer from pain-pill dependence that compounds their chronic conditions. "They addict these guys to drugs to keep a product on the field, then cut them when they're too hurt to play," says Mel Owens, a former outside linebacker with the Los Angeles Rams who's now a disability lawyer in Southern California with hundreds of ex-players as clients. "The guys file for workmen's comp, and the teams say, 'Why should we pay you? You're nothing but low-life addicts!' It's the next big front in our battle with the league: a class-action suit for drug malpractice."

When you talk to retired players, the thing you're always struck by isn't their size or what's left of their physical pride. Instead, it's the love they still bear for the game that took years, or decades, off their lives. They reverence the coach who made them play hurt, give thanks to the trainer who shot them up at halftime, and praise the opponent who hit them head-high for the top plays on *SportsCenter.*

But even for a true believer like Lucas, who entered the league in 1996 as a special-teams gunner and backup QB, loyalty has its limits. "If I ever see Dave Wannstedt on the street, there's gonna be a bad misunderstanding," he snarls as we drive to an appointment with Dr. Arash Emami, the PAST surgeon who will repair his neck. Wannstedt was his coach with the Miami Dolphins in 2002 when Lucas was hurt running a double-reverse just before the half against the Buffalo Bills. "I got blindsided on the toss and driven into the turf; my [throwing] shoulder popped out and was hanging down." Taken off the field for X-rays, Lucas put the shoulder back in himself, and, he says, the team doctor barred him from returning to the game. "For once, a doctor did what he's supposed to," says Lucas. But, he claims, the doctor then left and Wannstedt and the trainer came in and said, "'We need you—[backup QB Sage] Rosenfels isn't ready.' So the trainer shoots me up with lidocaine or something and gives me a bunch of pain pills and I go back out there. But I couldn't feel my arm and threw four picks because I wasn't man enough to say no." (Both Wannstedt, who is now the defensive coordinator for the Bills, and the trainer deny that Lucas was given any medication during this game, and say they have never pressured a player back into a game against doctor's orders.)

It wasn't the worst injury Lucas had weathered in eight hard years spent mostly on the margins of four teams—just the hit that pushed him out the door. Lucas played the next month in electric pain, then was waived by Wannstedt at season's end. He carried a clipboard for the Ravens the following year, but his spine was so ravaged that when he sneezed during practice, he couldn't move his legs for several hours. Again, though: no grudges, Wannstedt excepted. "Bill Parcells, the greatest man next to my dad, told me Rule One my rookie year. He said, 'If you want to stay here, shut your mouth and open your eyes: watch what the vets do and follow suit.'" What he saw that first summer was a roomful of grinders palming fistfuls of pills from the trainer and forming long lines for Toradol shots just to make it to practice. Toradol, an anti-inflammatory with stiff side effects if abused—kidney damage, ulcers, bleeding in the brain—should never be given more than several days running, except for post-op pain. Lucas took Toradol for months at a time and was scarcely alone in that. "Toradol was my friend: I'd take pills to practice and big old needles on game day," says McCrary, the Super Bowl fullback who now, at 40, lives in head-to-toe pain. "I'd get IVs of Toradol mixed with painkillers, but other guys just took shots," says Leander Jordan, an offensive lineman with the San Diego Chargers and Jacksonville Jaguars before back woes forced him into retirement in 2006. "You'd see 10 needles laid in a row, and the trainer would go right down the line."

When it wasn't Toradol, it was Indocin, another anti-inflammatory. "They'd give us those in plastic bags: anti-inflammatories in one bag, painkillers in another, and stuff to help you sleep in the third," says Harvey Armstrong, a nose tackle who played for the Philadelphia Eagles and Indianapolis Colts and had seven knee surgeries in eight years. "And if you said you lost 'em, the trainers gave you more. Whatever you wanted, no questions asked." None of the teams cited in this article made their trainers available to confirm or deny this.

In his four years with the Jets, Lucas ripped a tendon in his patella, severely herniated two lumbar discs, frayed ligaments in his elbow, and tore his rotator cuff. Each of these called for reconstructive surgery that would have cost him a full year out of football. But Lucas, who earned the league minimum most seasons and always sweated the final round of cuts, couldn't afford that luxury. He had minor procedures done by surgeons over the winters—arthroscopic stitch-ups and bone-chip removals—and bought in fully to the rehab process with yoga, Pilates, and plyometrics. That, and took Vicodin year-round to dampen the pain, and Ambien, scotch, and Xanax to get some rest. "People don't understand: you can't sleep when everything hurts. Legit pain needs legit medication."

He also leaned on his football rabbi: then–Jets trainer Dave Price. Lucas calls Price, now with the Kansas City Chiefs, the "best fucking trainer I had in eight years. The only one who really gave a shit. I broke a bone in my leg against the Colts, for instance, and he got a room next to mine at the Marriott so he could run and change the ice every hour." That was in 1999, Lucas's breakthrough season, when he started nine games and won six of them, though his back was so gnarled he could barely crouch under center for the sciatica singeing both legs. "Wednesdays were bad for me, Fridays too. I'd need extra, and he saw that I got 'em. And the plane home from games—forget it, man. No one knows what happens on team planes." (Price declined to comment on these allegations.)

As described by Lucas, those New York–bound jets were booze cruises minus the sea: players plying themselves with top-shelf liquor and beer, with the team providing all the Vikes and Xanax they could eat. That combination of toxins can "play havoc with lung function, depressing it or stopping it altogether," warns Dr. Amrish Patel, PAST's director of pain management, adding that it can also cause strokes and seizures. The Jets, of course, weren't alone in this: "Liquor and pills on planes go back decades," says Owens, the lawyer and ex-Ram who played in the 1980s. "One of my clients says the team brought beer kegs onto flights; guys would be drunk and doped up every Sunday."

To be clear: no trainer can legally give narcotics or Toradol injections to players; only team doctors are licensed to do that. But physicians are generally available just three days a week: on game days, Mondays, and Tuesdays, to tend to the injured. The other four days, it falls to trainers to keep players on the field. For decades, they did so, according to these veterans, by doling meds out, by hand or in packets, from bucket-size bottles of tablets. Those bottles, containing 250 or 500 pills, were ordered from medical-supply houses using the team doctor's DEA number. The bottles were kept in safes or in padlocked cabinets to which the doctor was supposed to have sole access. In fact, they were freely available to trainers, who dispensed from them as needed.

NFL commissioner Roger Goodell was among those who declined to comment on this or any of the allegations in this article. Instead, the league put forth Adolpho Birch, an NFL vice president who handles substance abuse policy; Birch denies that such things happen, then or now. "Every pill is accounted for, to the dose, and noted in players' records," he said by phone. "We have an intricate system to regulate inventories and auditing conducted by outside experts that cross-reference against prescriptions written." When told of players' insistence that they got pills by hand, instead of via prescription, Birch scoffed: "This isn't something we've heard anecdotally." Furthermore, he added, the league has drug-tested players for narcotics since 1989, "and the levels don't have to be excessive."

The players I spoke to burst out laughing at Birch's comments, particularly in response to being tested. "Test for narcotics! There would be no one to play—they'd have to suit the ball boys up," says Lucas. "Do we know that our players are seeking meds, both before and after games?" says DeMaurice Smith, the union chief. "Yes, we've done our own internal surveys. But when we spoke to the league about the bucket-of-pills problem, its response to us was nothing, no new proposal. In fact, when we demanded that they get informed consent before injecting guys with Toradol, they said they'd only do so if players signed a waiver holding them harmless in future lawsuits."

"In college, you heard about needles and pills and said, 'Those NFL dudes are crazy. I'm not doing that to my body,'" says Lucas. "But then you get here, and it's not even a conversation. No one talks about it, you just do it." Like many players, he stopped pilling before games for fear that the drugs slowed response times, relying instead on the Toradol shot to block his pain for four hours. By age 31, though, the jig was up: he'd been waived by the Ravens, gone to fat on Devil Dogs, and was sleeping on a recliner in the family room because he couldn't lie flat without screaming. He had a modest nest egg, three daughters, and four years of health care paid by the league to get his surgeries done. He also had a ravening morphine habit that he angrily denied for six years. That nest egg, and those girls, never stood a chance.

Dr. William Focazio does nothing by half-measures. He lives in a mansion bought from Russell Simmons, summers in a compound on the Jersey Shore, and owns three outpatient surgical centers that churn from morning till night. An Italian American whose bull-chested gruffness masks an all-access heart for hard-luck stories, he thought he had a sense of what he'd let himself in for when he created PAST in 2008. "I'd seen a TV thing about NFL vets who were busted up and needed a little help," he says, referring to an HBO *Real Sports* piece focusing on Brian DeMarco, the 30-something, back-broken former Jags lineman whose story was first told in these pages in September 2007. Recruiting from his circle of distinguished peers—surgeons, neurologists, presidents of medical boards—Focazio assembled a tier-one crew of volunteers to patch up vets, retool their medications, and send them back to productive midlife work.

What showed up, however, was a series of men with what Focazio is calling Pan-Athletic Traumatic Syndrome: crippling in-

juries to spines and soft tissue, front-brain damage coupled with
mood disorders, and—a condition new to him—"polypharmacy,"
meaning mass consumption of many drugs at once, all or most
of them prescribed. "Ten, 12 scrips written by different doctors,
none of whom knew what they were treating," says Focazio. "Sleep
stuff, benzos, antipsychotics for mood—half this stuff was blocking other drugs. Some guys were so toxic, we couldn't operate on
them. They'd have stroked out on the table during surgery."

Focazio, a gastroenterologist with 30 years' experience but not
a whit of social work training, knew he was overmatched. He called
Jennifer Smith, who'd run the day-to-day affairs of Gridiron Greats.
But "I was burned out and told him no," says Smith, who had spent
five years helping men so damaged that she barely got home to
Dallas and her aging parents. In the end, she relented, saying
she'd come east for a year to scale PAST up to a full-serve clinic.
That was three years and 200 veterans ago, and mission creep has
long since set in. Her two phones never stop ringing, and each
month brings a new crop of patients to northern New Jersey for
salvage. Smith flies them in, usually six at a time, boards them
at the Marriott near MetLife Stadium, and puts them through a
two-day diagnostic blitz of MRIs, blood draws, and workups. Then,
before their surgeries and neurology appointments, she shuttles
them five miles north to Paterson, New Jersey, where Dr. Manuel
Guantez, director of the Turning Point drug treatment center,
pushes a group of vets to own their addictions. "What's different
about these guys from the people we usually treat is, they didn't
know they were addicts," says Guantez. "They've abused pills for
years, their wives and kids are gone, and they barely leave the
house except to cop. But because they've been using for their 'injuries,' it just now hits them that they're junkies."

At one of those group sessions, I ran into Ben Smith, a handsome ex-safety with the Eagles who couldn't look less like a dope
fiend. Clear-eyed and robust after nine months with PAST, he presents as a man who's sailed a smooth line since his seven-year career
ended in 1996. Instead, he's emerging from a long stretch in hell
and is just now tallying up his losses: a third of his life given to a
narcotics addiction that pushed him to the brink of suicide, plus
the $600,000 he'd set aside for retirement but had already long
since burned through.

Smith, now 45, and clean since last Christmas, was Philly's first-round pick in 1990, a warhead of a safety with tailback speed and the smarts to start for Buddy Ryan as a rookie. One of four children bred in small-town Georgia by teetotaling Baptist parents, Smith was a rarity in that wild-child clubhouse: a quiet man of God who lived his faith. "My daddy raised us up on church-structure-church, and if we didn't do it his way, he'd beat us blind," says Smith. "Extension cords, fan belts, branches, what-have-you. It was abuse, but he had high expectations."

So did Smith, who played a Pro Bowl–worthy corner, shutting down the likes of Jerry Rice, Michael Irvin, and Art Monk. Then, on a bitter cold day in his second season, he picked off Cleveland Browns quarterback Bernie Kosar and was flying to the end zone when someone clipped him sideways at the knee. The knee was destroyed, all three ligaments torn, a rare and by no means simple reconstruction. "The team doctor said it was the worst he'd seen, and that's coming from a surgeon with 20 years."

The doctor operated that winter, harvesting the cruciate ligament from a cadaver to remake Smith's anterior, posterior, and medial collateral ligaments. Well before minicamp, though, it was clear the surgery wasn't a success. Smith's swelling persisted, the pain was relentless, and the joint felt squishy when he tried to pivot. To expedite his progress, Smith says, team trainer Otho Davis (now deceased) fed him the diet of oral narcotics—Percocets, Lortabs, oxycodone—that was standard in that clubhouse. "Otho'd come by your locker with his bags of pills, give you a four-day supply," says Armstrong, the nose tackle who played three years in Philly before a trade to Indianapolis in 1985. "On the bus to play the Giants, he'd have his black bag out and go down the aisle with pills."

After months of failed rehab, Smith went to specialists in L.A.—sure enough, his MCL hadn't been fixed. "In hindsight, I should've wrapped it up right there and sued the doctor for millions," he says. Instead, he got the knee rebuilt again and sat out the 1992 season. He came back in 1993, but even that was too soon: the knee swelled and throbbed after every practice. There was no thought of taking a second year off, though; he had children to feed and clothe. "One of my sisters had got hooked on crack and couldn't look after her five kids. I'd bought my mom a house, but now she had to raise them, and put it on me to provide."

Two things typically happen to injured vets who try to prolong careers. One, they hurt themselves in different places favoring joint(s) that haven't healed. Two, they end up playing year to year for the veteran minimum salary. So it went with Smith, who signed in 1995 for $200,000 to hang on, in Phoenix. But he damaged his back and shoulder trying to tackle one-legged, and by 1996 found it difficult simply to dress for games. When the Cardinals waived him in the middle of that season, he was in too much pain to give a damn—and on too many meds to feel it if he did. His usage had nearly tripled since he first started pilling in the winter of 1991, from 90 Percs to 250, and he'd learned to supplement what trainers gave him with scrips from outside doctors. "I had a doc in Atlantic City that I'd cop from when I was with the Eagles," he says. "Everyone wants to help out NFL players—till they cut you and your ass is out on the street."

Like Lucas, and many others who leave the game in pain, Smith didn't promptly file retirement papers or call a union rep to discuss his rights. Had he done so, he'd have learned he had a league retirement check waiting and a three-year window of paid health care. (The term was bumped to five years in the 2011 agreement between the league and union.) This last, in particular, was vital to know. It's prohibitively expensive for vets to buy insurance once their league-paid coverage expires—the premiums can blow past $50,000 a year, and the list of prior conditions not covered by HMOs can render the policy moot. Again, though, Smith, like Lucas, wasn't thinking straight. Depressed and addicted, he holed up back in Georgia, planning only as far as his next prescription. The doctors he bought pills from stopped taking his calls, though he did manage to sweet-talk two cancer-ridden seniors into selling him their pain meds. But at $10 a pill, that added up fast, and Smith, reduced to unskilled jobs paying $8 to $12 an hour, wasn't earning enough to feed his habit. "I tried so many times to stop," he says, "or space it to a couple pills a day. But the pain would get on me where I couldn't work. I lost a lot of jobs behind that mess."

By 1998, he had to sell the house he'd bought his mother, moving her and her five grandkids into a rented Colonial in a drug-ridden section of Macon. "It killed me to do it, but I was going through my savings, 10, 20 thousand at a time," he says. Worried for their safety, he bought his mom a pistol and devised a place to hide it for safekeeping. But one of the kids saw where he'd stashed the gun and took it to school to show off. The boy, then 10, was caught and suspended and the gun returned to Smith's mother. Beset by cares herself—she'd had heart surgery twice and was recovering from a bout of lung cancer—she slipped it under her pillow till she could think of someplace better. One morning shortly after, her five-year-old granddaughter, Connis, stayed home with an upset stomach. Taking to Grandma's bed, the girl found the .45 and held it up close for a look. The gun discharged, as guns will do when left around children, safety off. Somehow, Connis was still breathing when medics got there, though the bullet tore a tunnel through her brain before taking a chunk of her skull off.

Two hours north, Smith got the call. "That child was my heart," he says, his voice still catching more than a decade after her death. "She was brain-dead when I got there, breathing off machines. I had to tell my mom to let her go." Connis's passing sent her siblings into deadfall: two of her three brothers wound up in jail, and the third boy, once the star of the family, had drug dealers banging on his grandma's door, looking for money they said he owed them. Smith, the gun's owner, took it harder still. He stopped seeking work or the company of his friends, dropping more or less completely out of sight. Unable to sleep, he limped the streets till dawn, trying to find the grit to shoot himself (he kept a Glock .40 in his dresser) or hoping that some basehead would do it for him. That he's still alive today owes, at least in part, to the pusher who was selling him Percs: "He told me about a methadone program downtown, where they'd fix me up for nothing, or next to it," he says.

Methadone, the nondeliriant cousin of morphine, seemed like a boon when Smith started in 2002. Even at low doses, it blocked his pain and cost him $3 a day at the walk-in clinic, not the $70 he'd been spending on Percs. But it also began rotting his teeth and bones and made it impossible to work for any firm that drug-tested hires for opiates. By 2009, when an old flame found Smith on Facebook and invited him to visit her in Philly, he was dead broke and weeks from eviction, begging the players' union for assistance. "They turned me down flat, but she kept on me—she said there'd be a way if I kept searching," says Smith of his now-fiancée, Marti Stewart, a social worker pregnant with their first child. One night last winter, he was searching the web when a link to PAST popped up. He wrote Jennifer Smith an email, pouring out his heart to her. She called the next day to book an intake. "They did my MRIs and X-rays, my stress test, you name it, plus drained my knee of fluid," he says. "I called up Marti and said I can't believe it—someone finally gets it this time."

Boosted by their care, Smith bit down hard and enrolled in detox. The two weeks of treatment at Eagleville Hospital, a state-run facility near Philadelphia, were his worst since the phone call about his niece. "The pain was so bad, I wanted to give up and die, not once but every damn day. I was calling Dr. B. and hollering at him. I'm sure he thought I was crazy," says Smith of Dr. Joseph Battaglia, a soft-spoken, boyish-faced neuropsychiatrist who is PAST's director of behavioral health. "We talked a lot on the phone, trying to get Ben comfortable," says Battaglia. "The biggest problem was just getting him some rest." Twenty years of dousing his brain with morphine had frogged Smith's circadian clock. Like Lucas, he'd go days without sleeping, then collapse in a twitchy stupor. It took months of tinkering with diet and medicine to reset his neural rhythm. Since May, though, Smith has slept through the night and gotten sturdier by the month. He'll get his knee fixed this fall by Dr. Vincent McInerney, PAST's director of orthopedics, and have the herniated disc in his back repaired by Dr. Arash Emami, the organization's director of spine services. And then, he hopes, he'll land a job as a football scout and be able to help support the woman who took him in, as well as the son they are about to have. "I've been given these gifts—by Marti, by [PAST's] people—and all I want is to pass it on. The best way I know is to share my story; my own father doesn't know, after all these years. But there's thousands of guys like me and only these few doctors, and here's the league sitting on billions. Why's it these guys' job to fix us up?"

When you talk to an official like Adolpho Birch, who refutes the pain-pill crisis in sweeping terms and touts the league's enforcement as "world-class," you're tempted to think the league will treat this as it did concussions—a thing to be denied until the lawsuits come. Certainly, the players' union deems that so: "We would welcome Congress's involvement on health and safety issues," says a senior executive who asked not to be named. In truth, though, NFL officials have quietly taken steps to begin to address the problem. In the past several years, say recent retirees like McCrary, Lucas, and others, teams have cracked down on dispensing pills by hand to players in chronic pain. Doctors are writing scrips now that players get filled outside of team facilities, and a few teams no longer stock narcotics, using outside pharmacies to deliver. "When I played, we got what we wanted," says McCrary, who retired in 2008 after being cut by the Seattle Seahawks. "Now, from what I'm hearing, they've tightened up some. Guys gotta see the doctor to get their pills."

But pain is pain; it doesn't honor new rules or stop when the doctor is out. Has the clampdown altered player behavior?

"Nothing has changed. Not a single thing. If anything, it's worse than ever." The speaker is Dr. Alex Stalcup, the founder and director of the New Leaf Treatment Center near San Francisco. Stalcup knows as much about opioid abuse as anyone connected with the league; he's treated hundreds of players over more than two decades and has a dozen or so currently under his care. "I've gotten the call so often, I can recite it by heart," he says. "'Doc, I'm sick but I gotta play Sunday—can I swing by your house in the morning?'"

Stalcup has quietly helped players keep their jobs while weaning off Oxy and Vikes. "They get to where they can't find enough pills, or their liver has started bleeding, and they're scared. So they come to me because I'm known around the league as the guy who'll treat off-site and keep a secret."

He describes the current clubhouse as a pharmaceutical swap meet, in which players trade drugs and links to "star-fucking" doctors who are happy to write scrips for famous clients. "Team doctors have gotten cautious about the amounts they dispense, so guys who were getting X now get X-minus-10 and have to go elsewhere to make it up. They either cop from the guy next to them or road-trip to Florida and load up at the legal pill mills."

Florida has the softest opioid laws of any state on the Eastern Seaboard, and is overrun with walk-in, cash-only clinics that hand out prescriptions to all comers. Despite a recent push to shut down huckster physicians, the state accounted two years ago for almost 90 percent of the OxyContin sold in the country. "Florida's a sewer: you can see three doctors in one day," says Stalcup. "Each of them will do a bogus MRI to make the visit look legitimate, then give you a scrip to treat whatever they 'found'—and they'll always find something on a player's scan."

Dubbing himself the "anti-Florida doctor," Stalcup switches players to Suboxone and maintains them on the drug for several years. Suboxone, a semisynthetic variant of morphine, is the treatment of choice now for opiate addiction and chronic pain. As Suboxone is a safe but potent painkiller that lasts longer than its cousin methadone, I asked Stalcup about its potential use as game-day analgesic. "No one should ever play in pain, or load up on drugs to try and mask it," he said. "But if you're asking me if guys are taking Suboxone or methadone on game day, the answer, unequivocally, is yes. I know, because I prescribed them myself."

He does so knowing that if he doesn't prescribe, the players will find someone, or something, worse. "A lot of these guys are three game checks from broke, so they're going to go out there regardless. But the news flash here isn't that football players are junkies: I've been cleaning them up since 1986, and it was going on before I showed up. No, the real news here is that there's treatment that works, no matter how bad your addiction. If we pull you into care once you do stop playing, we'll get you well, with dignity and on an outpatient basis, while you go about the next phase of your life. You don't have to be another guy who loses it all and breaks your loved ones' hearts."

Ray Lucas wishes he'd gotten that message while he still had something to lose. "If I could take back anything, it's not the money or the house—it's the shit show I dragged her through." He nods across the table at his wife, Cecy, a fine-boned woman whose liquid eyes seem parked on the shoulder of tears. We're sitting in the kitchen of their house in Harrison, New Jersey, once a working-poor town of Irish pubs now engulfed by bodegas and taquerias. "No one tells the story of our women and kids. Their dudes became some full-time fucking monsters."

Cecy huffs a sigh and eyes her nails, content to let him tell the story. She cuts in only to correct his memory, which after a dozen or more concussions, can stand the help. "You took more pills than that," she says when he talks about the period after his first back surgery, post-retirement. In 2005, he had a lumbar laminectomy to fix three vertebrae in his back, and got healthy enough to hold an executive position with an office-cleaning outfit in New York. He also cut back on his pill consumption—though not quite as much as he recalls. "It wasn't just a couple a day," she says. "The co-pays for your pills—the sleep stuff, the Vicodins, plus the muscle relaxers—that was in the thousands, babe."

Lucas seems stunned. "You sure that wasn't later, when my neck got bad?"

"Baby, we were broke, even with your TV gig. Every last dollar went to drugs."

By 2008, Lucas's NFL coverage had ended, and his cervical nightmare began: short, sharp spasms that had Cecy fearing he'd developed Tourette's. Dropped by his doctors because he had no insurance and couldn't pay cash for visits, he hit the street and found dealers happy to help a TV star. "I'm talking professionals in Manhattan, not some kid on a corner; for a while, they wouldn't take my money. They'd just say, 'Bring me to the club when you go out.' I'd get them past the ropes, introduce them around, and be on my way to the tunnel with my stash."

But addiction is a beast whose belly can't be filled. Lucas's intake doubled, then quadrupled. In a year, he'd lost his start-up business because he was so doped he couldn't make meetings; lost the big, suburban house downstate that Cecy spent years remodeling; pulled his daughters off dance teams and cheerleading squads because he needed their travel money for his jones; and moved the family, Christmas week, to a saltbox in Harrison, where they were awakened by drunks banging on their door. "All I did then was break their hearts; why they didn't leave me, I'll never know."

"Because you wanted to die, and we wouldn't let you. Tell about the time Rayven stopped you."

Rayven, his oldest, walked into Lucas's bedroom on a morning he'd set aside to shoot himself. "I was at my worst, just filled with fuckin' poison," he says. "She's standing two feet from where I'm hiding the gun and says, 'Daddy, I know you're sick and having a bad time, but I just really, really love you and want you better.' I mean, what do you say to that but I love you too, baby, and I promise I'll keep trying?"

He made a series of calls to the league and players' union, seeking cash and medical help. What came back, says Cecy, was a disability application "the size of a frickin' phone book. We filled it out the best we could, and six months later: denied." Ultimately, they managed to get him partial disability, borrowed against his NFL pension; meanwhile, his checks from SNY went "directly to drugs—I never saw them," she says. Then came the break that saved his life: a back-channels call from a former league physician, passing on Smith's private number. "He said, 'You can't use my name, but she'll take care of you. Please call her before you do something crazy.'"

Three days later, Lucas was on an examining table at PAST's surgical center in Clifton. "The nurse who took my pressure ran out to get the doc. I'm thinking, Hmm, this probably ain't good," he says. After 12 years of pilling, his heart had doubled in size, and his blood pressure readings ran so high that any strain could have triggered a stroke. He was rushed to see Dr. Bart De Gregorio, PAST's pulmonary director, and put on a crash course of diuretics and beta blockers. Through diet and medicine, doctors reduced his triglycerides while weaning him from a dozen toxic drugs. That October, PAST's Emami performed a spinal fusion, resolving at least some of the pain in his neck and allowing him to enter rehab.

For three full days, Lucas writhed on the floor, shitting and barfing and hearing voices. When he managed to get upright, the joint pain was savage: "He walked," says Smith, who flew him to Florida and stayed through the worst of it, "like an 80-year-old guy with gout." As the Suboxone built up, though, the pain receded; in a fortnight, he was stretching and taking long walks, things he hadn't done in nearly a decade. After 42 days, he went home to his family, who'd moved to their current house across town. "I came through the door, and it was just tears, hugs, and more tears: the real me was back, not the zombie," says Lucas. He looks over at Cecy, who stands to clear the dishes in order to keep from crying. "All the wrong I did her, the times I broke her heart: for her to still love me . . . man, you don't know."

It's about to get seriously moist in that kitchen when Lucas's daughters burst in: two tall, lissome teens and a 10-year-old colt with their mother's heartfulness. They kiss Mom hello, then hover over Dad, sensing something amiss. "You okay?" they ask him. "Does your neck hurt? Your knee?" "I'm fine," he says. "Stop mothering me." "Then, good," says Rayven, grabbing his hand. "You can drive us to Wendy's: we're starved!"

JEFF MacGREGOR

Waiting for Goodell

FROM ESPN.COM

IN WHICH WE RETURN yet again to the work of Samuel Beckett in the interest of clarifying American football.

A country road. A tree.
Evening.
ESTRAGON: Nothing to be done.
VLADIMIR: I'm beginning to come around to that. All my life
    I've believed, but not now.
They sit a long time in silence.
ESTRAGON: Believed in what?
VLADIMIR: Which what?
ESTRAGON: In what did you once believe?
VLADIMIR: The NFL.
ESTRAGON: In football?
VLADIMIR: Not just football. *NFL* football. The Shield. It was
    a symbol.
ESTRAGON: A cymbal?
VLADIMIR: A symbol of quality. It was unquestionable.
ESTRAGON: Incontrovertible.
VLADIMIR: Ineluctable.
ESTRAGON: Indisputable.
VLADIMIR: Undeniable.
ESTRAGON: And now?
VLADIMIR: I question. I dispute. I eluct.
ESTRAGON: What was once indubitable is now dubitable.
VLADIMIR: The whole apparatus is in doubt.

ESTRAGON: Replacement officials?

VLADIMIR: Scabs.

ESTRAGON: The very same! Like a skinned knee!

VLADIMIR: It's tragedy masquerading as comedy.

ESTRAGON: Comedy rebranded as tragedy.

VLADIMIR: It's a leaguewide lockout.

ESTRAGON: Union-busting cahoots! The league is in league with The League.

VLADIMIR: The league isn't the players. The league is the owners.

ESTRAGON: Maybe the league left its wallet in its other pants, because the league needs to scrounge a few dollars.

VLADIMIR: Very few.

ESTRAGON: So the league is using bargain officials from other leagues.

VLADIMIR: From the Lingerie League.

ESTRAGON: Safety first! Who would know better the risks and rules governing high-speed helmet-to-helmet contact and potential brain injury than a back judge from the Lingerie Football League?

VLADIMIR: And at an attractive discount.

ESTRAGON: So except for the absurd incompetence, it's been a win-win-win right down the line.

VLADIMIR: He'll have to explain it all to us when he gets here.

ESTRAGON: Who will?

VLADIMIR: Goodell.

ESTRAGON: We're waiting for Goodell?

VLADIMIR: Yes. He can explain it.

ESTRAGON: Of course he can. Maybe. But can he make good on it?

They wait.

VLADIMIR: In his defense, you can't be half a gangster.

ESTRAGON: Or even half a Gangnam.

VLADIMIR: Those nickels and dimes add up.

ESTRAGON: Too true.

VLADIMIR: Especially in Las Vegas.

ESTRAGON: Where they gamble on football?

VLADIMIR: Professional American football is the most beloved and lucrative random numbers generator in human history.

Both rise, look up into the lights, and hold their hats over their hearts for a very long time. Their eyes well with tears. They sit again, exhausted.

ESTRAGON: But it has to be on the up-and-up.

VLADIMIR: On the level.

ESTRAGON: On the square.

VLADIMIR: Or it might as well not be football at all.

ESTRAGON: Like operetta, or the New York Jets.

VLADIMIR: Or anything else you can't reliably bet upon.

ESTRAGON: Because the league sells physical marvels and unbelievable feats of nonfiction.

VLADIMIR: And if people can't believe them . . .

ESTRAGON: Real trouble.

VLADIMIR: It's a question of epistemology . . .

ESTRAGON: And the betting lines.

VLADIMIR: Exactly. Goodell has to fix it because all of a sudden it looks fixed.

The sky darkens.

ESTRAGON: Will he never get here?

VLADIMIR: I'm not entirely convinced he ever left.

ESTRAGON: True. He's everywhere.

VLADIMIR: And nowhere.

ESTRAGON: He'd want us to remember.

VLADIMIR: Remember that it's slow-motion violence set to music?

ESTRAGON: The very thing. Sentimentalized carnage. The Shield is a cymbal of integrity, after all. And your assurance of highest-quality action.

They sit a long time in silence.

VLADIMIR: Still. It's not a strike.

ESTRAGON: It's a lockout.

VLADIMIR: Time to shake off the dust. Shall we go?

ESTRAGON: Yes, let's go.

They do not move.

Curtain

Contributors' Notes

Notable Sports Writing of 2012

Contributors' Notes

KENT BABB is a sports enterprise writer for the *Washington Post*, which he joined in October 2012 after spending the previous five years covering the NFL and writing columns and longform pieces for the *Kansas City Star*. He also has worked for *The* (Columbia, South Carolina) *State*. A graduate of the University of South Carolina, he lives in northern Virginia with his wife, Whitney.

CHRIS BALLARD is a senior writer at *Sports Illustrated*. He is the author of three books, including *The Art of a Beautiful Game* and *One Shot at Forever*, about the 1971 Macon Ironmen baseball team. A graduate of Pomona College and the Columbia University Graduate School of Journalism, he lives in Berkeley, California, with his wife and two daughters. This is his third appearance in *The Best American Sports Writing*.

BARRY BEARAK joined the *New York Times* sports staff in late 2011 after many years as a foreign correspondent for the newspaper. He won the Pulitzer Prize for international reporting in 2002 for stories from Afghanistan and Pakistan. He has twice received the George Polk Award, once for his coverage from Afghanistan and then, along with his wife Celia Dugger, for work from Zimbabwe. Bearak, a Pulitzer finalist in feature writing, has also been a staff writer for the *New York Times Sunday Magazine* and a visiting professor at the Columbia University Graduate School of Journalism. He was raised in the Chicago area and attended Knox College and the University of Illinois.

BURKHARD BILGER has been a staff writer at *The New Yorker* since 2001. Bilger's work has also appeared in *The Atlantic, Harper's Magazine*, the *New York Times*, the *New York Times Book Review*, and numerous other publications and has been anthologized in *The Best American Sports Writing, The Best Food Writing*, and *The Best American Science and Nature Writing*. Bilger's book

Noodling for Flatheads: Moonshine, Monster Catfish, and Other Southern Comforts
was a finalist for the PEN/Martha Albrand Award for First Nonfiction.

BILL GIFFORD has been an editor at *Philadelphia* and *Men's Journal,* and
his work has appeared in numerous magazines, including *Outside, Wired,
Men's Health,* and *Bicycling.* He is at work on a book about the future of
medicine.

ALLISON GLOCK is an award-winning journalist whose work has appeared
in the *New York Times,* the *New York Times Magazine, Esquire, GQ, Rolling
Stone,* and *The New Yorker,* among many others. She is a senior staff writer
for *ESPN,* a columnist at *Southern Living,* and a contributing editor at *Garden & Gun.* Her memoir of her grandmother won the Whiting Writers'
Award for nonfiction and was a *New York Times* Notable Book of the Year.

PATRICK HRUBY is a writer for *Sports on Earth* and a contributor to *Washingtonian* magazine and *The Atlantic* online. He has worked for ESPN.com
and the *Washington Times* and taught journalism at Georgetown University.
He holds degrees from Georgetown and Northwestern and lives in Washington, D.C., with his wife, Saphira. This is his fourth appearance in *The
Best American Sports Writing.*

DAN KOEPPEL lives in Los Angeles, California, with his wife and son. His
most recent book is *Banana: The Fate of the Fruit That Changed the World.* In
his spare time, he organizes marathon walking events. His website is www
.dankoeppel.com.

THOMAS LAKE is a senior writer for *Sports Illustrated* and a graduate of
Gordon College. This is his fourth appearance in *The Best American Sports
Writing.*

From WBUR in Boston, BILL LITTLEFIELD hosts National Public Radio's
weekly sports magazine program, *Only A Game.* He was the guest editor
of *The Best American Sports Writing* in 1998 and is the author of six books,
including the novels *Prospect* and *The Circus in the Woods.* He is writer-in-
residence at Curry College in Milton, Massachusetts.

JEFF MACGREGOR is a senior writer for ESPN and the author of *Sunday
Money.*

ERIK MALINOWSKI is a senior writer for BuzzFeed Sports. He has previously been the night editor of Deadspin.com and the sports editor of
Wired.com. A graduate of Boston University with a degree in journalism,
he lives with his wife, Rebecca, in San Mateo, California.

MICHAEL J. MOONEY is a staff writer at *D Magazine.* He also writes for *GQ,
Outside,* SBNation.com/Longform, and Grantland.com. He is a graduate

of the Mayborn School of Journalism and is on the advisory committee of the Mayborn Literary Nonfiction Conference. His stories have appeared in *The Best American Crime Reporting* and multiple editions of *The Best American Sports Writing*. He lives in Dallas with his fiancée, Tara, and their retired racing greyhound.

NICOLE PASULKA is a writer living in Brooklyn, New York. Her work has been published in *The Believer*, Salon.com, *Mother Jones*, and the *Globe and Mail*. You can find her online at www.nicolepasulka.com.

BRIDGET QUINN has written a memoir, *Home Team*, about growing up in a big Montana family and becoming a new kind of woman in the American West. Three excerpts from the book have appeared in *Narrative* magazine, including the piece here, "At Swim, Two Girls," and "One-on-One," which was noted in *The Best American Sports Writing 2010*. Her essay "Back in the Pool" was a finalist for the 2006 Annie Dillard Prize in Creative Nonfiction. A grateful denizen of the San Francisco Writers' Grotto, where she works, she lives in San Francisco with her husband Rick, a cyclist; her son Lukas, an avid surfer; and her daughter Zuzu, a goal-scoring soccer machine.

RICK REILLY is a columnist for ESPN.com and an essayist for *ESPN SportsCenter*. From 1985 until 2007, he was a writer for *Sports Illustrated*. He is the author of 10 books, including *Sports from Hell: My Search for the World's Dumbest Competition*. He served as guest editor for *The Best American Sports Writing 2002* and lives in Denver.

CINTHIA RITCHIE writes and runs mountains in Anchorage, Alaska. She is the recipient of two Rasmuson Individual Artist Awards, a Connie Boochever fellowship, residencies at Hedgebrook, Hidden River Arts, and Kimmel Nelson Harding Center for the Arts, and the Brenda Ueland Prose Prize, the Memoir Grand Prize, and a Sport Literate Essay Award. Readers can find her work in the *New York Times Magazine*, *Under the Sun*, *Water-Stone Review*, *Memoir*, *Sport Literate*, the *Boiler Journal*, *damselfly press*, *Third Wednesday*, *Foliate Oak Literary Review*, *MARY: A Journal of New Writing*, *The Quivering Pen*, *42opus*, *Sugar Mule*, *Cactus Heart Press*, *Evening Street Review*, and others. She is also the author of a novel, *Dolls Behaving Badly*.

KAREN RUSSELL is the author of the story collection *St. Lucy's Home for Girls Raised by Wolves* and *Swamplandia!*, which was a Pulitzer Prize finalist and one of the *New York Times's* Top Five Fiction Books of 2011. Her new story collection, *Vampires in the Lemon Grove*, was released in February 2013.

JASON SCHWARTZ is a senior editor at *Boston* magazine, where he has covered sports, politics, business, and education since 2007. His writing has also appeared in *ESPN: The Magazine*, *Slate*, the *Boston Globe*, and other places.

JONATHAN SEGURA is the author of *Occupational Hazards* and has written for *GQ* and National Public Radio.

CHARLES SIEBERT, a contributing writer to the *New York Times Magazine*, is the author of *Rough Beasts: The Zanesville Zoo Massacre, One Year Later.*

DAVID SIMON is an author, a journalist, and a writer/producer of the HBO television series *The Wire.* He formerly worked for the *Baltimore Sun* and is the author of *Homicide: A Year on the Killing Streets* and, with Ed Burns, of *The Corner: A Year in the Life of an Inner-City Neighborhood.*

MARK SINGER has been a staff writer at *The New Yorker* since 1974 and is author of the books *Funny Money, Mr. Personality*, a collection of his reporting from *The New Yorker, Citizen K: The Deeply Weird American Journey of Brett Kimberlin*, and two more collections, *Somewhere in America* and *Character Studies.* He lives in New York.

GARY SMITH is a senior writer for *Sports Illustrated.* His stories have appeared in *The Best American Sports Writing* more often than those of any other writer. A graduate of La Salle University, he wrote for the *Wilmington News-Journal*, the *Philadelphia Daily News*, the *New York Daily News*, and *Inside Sports* before coming to *Sports Illustrated.* His writing has also appeared in *Time, Rolling Stone*, and *Esquire.* A collection of his work, *Beyond the Game*, was published in 2001.

PAUL SOLOTAROFF is the author of *The Body Shop, Group*, and *House of Purple Hearts.* A contributing editor at *Men's Journal* and *Rolling Stone*, he has written features for *Vanity Fair, GQ, Vogue*, and the *New York Times Magazine.* This is his eighth appearance in *The Best American Sports Writing.* He lives in New York.

WRIGHT THOMPSON is a senior writer for ESPN.com and *ESPN: The Magazine.* He lives with his wife, Sonia, in Oxford, Mississippi. This is his eighth appearance in *The Best American Sports Writing.*

Notable Sports Writing of 2012

SELECTED BY GLENN STOUT

JOHN AKERS
Who Is Rick Ray? *Basketball Times,* Scptcmbcr 2012

CHRIS FELICIANO ARNOLD
Asleep at the Roger Clemens Trial. Salon.com, June 10, 2012

BEN AUSTEN
The Glorious Plight of the Buffalo Bills. Grantland.com, November 7, 2012

JIM BAUMBACH
Falling Star. *Newsday,* December 2, 2012

ADEMOLA BELLO
Crossed Countries. *Anchorage Press,* March 15, 2012

ALEX BELTH
The Two Rogers. SBNation.com/ Longform, October 24, 2012

GREG BISHOP
In Next Scene. *The New York Times,* December 30, 2012

SAM BORDEN
A Soccer Prodigy, at Home in Brazil. *The New York Times,* July 9, 2012

FLINDER BOYD
The Ricky Rubio Experience. TheClassical.org, November 28, 2012

JOHN BRANCH
Snow Fall. *The New York Times,* December 20, 2012

WILLIAM BROWNING
Coach. SBNation.com /Longform, October 9, 2012

MATT CALKINS
Suicide Story Hits Close to Home. *The Columbian,* May 4, 2012

MATT COKER
The Lost Boys of Summer. *OC Weekly,* March 30, 2012

JORDAN CONN
Let It Fly. Grantland.com, August 20, 2012

MATT CROSSMAN
A Time to Heal. *The Sporting News,* December 2012

BRYAN CURTIS
No Chattering in the Press Box. Grantland.com, May 2, 2012
On the Trail of the Piggyback Bandit. Grantland.com, July 11, 2012

DAVID DAVIS
Still Richard. SBNation.com /Longform, November 29, 2012

MARK DENT
Everybody's Doing the Tweener.
TheClassical.org, May 10, 2012
TOM DINARD
Sunlight for a Moonlight Man.
ThePostGame.com, January 17,
2012

DAN ENGLAND
Getting Back into the Stroke
of Things. *The Greeley Tribune,*
November 25, 2012

KATE FAGAN
Dream Role. ESPNW.com,
October 18, 2012
BRUCE FELDMAN
The Middle Man. CBSSports
.com, September 21, 2012
NATHAN FENNO
A Trip Back in Time. *The
Washington Times,* October 5,
2012
PETER FRICK-WRIGHT
Their Vision Is Sound. *Bike,*
July 2012
STEVE FRIEDMAN
Meteor. *Runner's World,*
December 2012

DAVE GESSNER
Ultimate Glory.
BillandDavesCocktailHour.com,
January 26, 2012

BRETT HABER
In the Name of the Father.
Washingtonian, March 2012
ERIC HANSEN
Quoosiers. *Outside,* June 2012
JUSTIN HECKERT
The Loneliest Number. *Sports
Illustrated,* December 31, 2012
MIKE HEMBREE
A Tree Grows in Stuart. Speed
.com, September 18, 2012

JUSTICE B. HILL
Saving His Own Soul First.
SBNation.com/Longform,
December 19, 2012
EVA HOLLAND
Three Kites on the Ice. VelaMag
.com, August 28, 2012
PATRICK HRUBY
Let's Eliminate Sports Welfare.
SportsonEarth.com, December
12, 2012
The Truth Out There. ThePost
Game.com, May 30, 2012

PAT JORDAN
In Uncle Ted's Head. Roopstigo
.com, October 2012

JENNIFER KAHN
Born to Run Back. *Runner's
World,* January 2012
ZAK KEEFER
One in a Million Shot. *The
Indianapolis Star,* December 9,
2012
KIBBY KLEIMAN
Moneyball 2.0. *The East Bay
Express,* September 12, 2012
MICHAEL KRUSE
The Fabulous Sports Babe.
Grantland.com, September 11,
2012

THOMAS LAKE
The Boy They Couldn't Kill.
Sports Illustrated, September 17,
2012
JEANNE MARIE LASKAS
Guns 'R Us. *GQ,* September
2012
ARIEL LEVY
A Ring of One's Own. *The New
Yorker,* May 7, 2012
TOM LEY
Boom or Bust. Deadspin.com,
December 10, 2012

GUY MARTIN
Horse Power. *Garden & Gun,*
December 2012
J. BRADY MCCOLLOUGH
The Pride of Clairton. *The
Pittsburgh Post-Gazette,* November
21, 2012
JOHN MCLAUGHLIN
In Chariots, They Ran. *Runner's
World,* February 2012
ELIZABETH MERRILL
Where Did It All Go Wrong?
ESPN.com, December 12,
2012
MEGAN MICHELSON
Tunnel Vision. *Outside,*
November 2012
DOUG MILLER
The Mudville Line. MLB.com,
December 12, 2012

JASON NARK
Deer Dad. *The Philadelphia Daily
News,* December 23, 2012

DANNY O'NEIL
Ryan David Leaf, Defendant.
Seattle Times, April 8, 2012

JOSH PARROT
The Upset. *Basketball Times,*
December 2012
JEFF PASSAN
Long, Maddening Fall for
Former No. 1. Yahoo.com,
March 26, 2012
From Prospect to Priest. Yahoo
.com, September 27, 2012
JOE NICK PATOSKI
Turnover! *Texas Monthly,*
October 2012
RICK PAULAS
The Cup of Coffee Club.
TheAwl.com, May 30, 2012
BEN PAYNTER
Perfectly Suited. *Wired,* August
2012

BARRY PETCHESKY
Where Would the NHL Be
If Bain Capital Had Bought
the Whole League in 2005?
Deadspin.com, October 15,
2012
ALAN PRENDERGAST
Going to Extremes. *Westword,*
August 2–8, 2012
ERIC PRISBELL
Transsexual Gabrielle Ludwig
Returns to College Court. *USA
Today,* December 5, 2012
SHANNON PROUDFOOT
Hell Frozen Over. *Sportsnet,*
March 26, 2012

JON RONSON
Clear Eyes, Full Plate,
Can't Puke. *GQ,* November
2012
KRISTINA RUTHERFORD
"I've Got Nothing Left."
Sportsnet, June 4, 2012
ALBERT SAMAHA
Familiar Ring. *Riverfront Times,*
February 23, 2012
Swoosh Dreams, *SF Weekly,*
June 20, 2012
ROBERT SANCHEZ
Golden Girl. *5280,* June 2012
ELI SASLOW
A Trip to the Threshing Floor.
ESPN: The Magazine, December
11, 2012
LEANDER SCHAERLAEKENS
Out of Bounds. SBNation
.com/Longform, September
28, 2012
WHIT SHEPPARD
He Paid the Price. *Richmond,*
September 2012
JESSE SIDLAUSKAS
Putting on My Old Cockfight-
ing Shoes. *Mayborn,* July
2012

FRANK SOOS
Who's on First. *Sport Literate,* Winter 2012

EVELYN SPENCE
Extremely Long and Incredibly Close. *Bicycling,* June 2012

SEBASTIAN STOCKMAN
The Problem with Sportswriting. TheMillions.com, August 6, 2012

JOHN JEREMIAH SULLIVAN
Venus and Serena Against the World. *The New York Times Magazine,* August 23, 2012

PATRICK SYMMES
The Beautiful Game. *Outside,* October 2012

MIKE TANIER
Faith and Football. Sportson Earth.com, November 1, 2012

RACHEL TOOR
Falling. Athleta.net, June 3, 2012

MATT TULLIS
Feet of Clay, Heart of Iron. SBNation.com/Longform, October 17, 2012

KEVIN VAN VALKENBERG
Games of Chance. ESPN.com, December 19, 2012

GRANT WAHL
The World's Team. *Sports Illustrated,* October 6, 2012

MICHAEL WEINREB
A Failed Experiment. Grantland.com, July 12, 2012

DAN WETZEL
Tom Brady in Postgame Daze . . . Yahoo.com, February 6, 2012

SETH WICKERSHAM
Into the Wild. *ESPN: The Magazine,* May 28, 2012

MARK WINEGARDNER
One in a Million. *ESPN: The Magazine,* January 9, 2012
The Last Time They Met. *ESPN: The Magazine,* November 2012

MIKE WISE
Washington Wizards: An Embarrassment by Design. *The Washington Post,* January 9, 2012